The C...itics

CONTEMPORARY POLITICS

Series editors

David Held (general editor)
David Beetham
Bob Jessop
John Keane
Anne Sassoon

Already published

The Context of British Politics
David Coates

Contradictions of the Welfare State
Claus Offe
Edited by John Keane

Women and the Public Sphere
A critique of sociology and politics
Edited by Janet Siltanen and Michelle Stanworth

In preparation

On Freedom and Power
Vaclav Havel et al.

Class and State in Britain and America
Joel Krieger

The Rule of Law and the British Constitution
Norman Lewis and Ian Harden

The Myth of the Plan
Peter Rutland

The Context of British Politics

David Coates
Senior Lecturer in Politics, University of Leeds

Hutchinson

London   Melbourne   Sydney   Auckland   Johannesburg

Hutchinson & Co. (Publishers) Ltd

An imprint of the Hutchinson Publishing Group

17–21 Conway Street, London W1P 6JD
and 51 Washington Street, Dover, New Hampshire 03820, USA

Hutchinson Publishing Group (Australia) Pty Ltd
PO Box 496, 16–22 Church Street, Hawthorne, Melbourne, Victoria 3122

Hutchinson Group (NZ) Ltd
32–34 View Road, PO Box 40–086, Glenfield, Auckland 10

Hutchinson Group (SA) (Pty) Ltd
PO Box 337, Bergvlei 2012, South Africa

First published 1984

© David Coates 1984

Phototypeset by Wyvern Typesetting Limited, Bristol

Printed and bound in Great Britain by
Anchor Brendon Ltd,
Tiptree, Essex

British Library Cataloguing in Publication Data

Coates, David
　　The context of British politics.—
　　(Contemporary politics; 3)
　　1. Great Britain—Politics and government
　　—1979-
　　I. Title　　II. Series
　　320.941　　JN231

Library of Congress Cataloging in Publication Data

Coates, David.
　　The context of British politics.

　　(Contemporary politics)
　　Bibliography: p.
　　Includes index.
　　1. Great Britain—Politics and government—1979-
　2. Great Britain—Economic conditions—1945-
　3. Great Britain—Social conditions—1945-
　I. Title　　II. Series.
　JN231.C575　　1984　　941.085　　84-12931

ISBN 0 09 159151 1

Contents

Figures

Tables

Abbreviations

ACAS	Advisory Conciliation and Arbitration Service
AES	Alternative Economic Strategy (of the Labour Party)
ASTMS	Association of Scientific, Technical and Managerial Staffs
CBI	Confederation of British Industry
CND	Campaign for Nuclear Disarmament
COHSE	Confederation of Health Service Employees
COPPSO	Conference of Professional and Public Service Organizations
CPSU	Communist Party of the Soviet Union
DEA	Department of Economic Affairs
EEC	European Economic Community
EFTA	European Free Trade Area
GATT	General Agreement on Tariffs and Trade
GDP	Gross Domestic Product
GNP	Gross National Product
IMF	International Monetary Fund
IRC	Industrial Reorganization Corporation
MSC	Manpower Services Commission
NALGO	The National Association of Local Government Officers
NATO	North Atlantic Treaty Organization
NBPI	National Board for Prices and Incomes
NEB	National Enterprise Board
NUPE	National Union of Public Employees
OECD	The Organization for Economic Co-operation and Development
OPEC	Organization of Petroleum-Exporting Countries
QUANGO	Quasi Non-Governmental Organizations
TUC	Trades Union Congress

Acknowledgements

The author and publishers would like to thank the copyright holders below for their kind permission to reproduce the following material:

Tables

Basil Blackwell, Anna Coote and Beatrix Campbell for p. 167; Batsford and T. Noble for pp. 114, 115; *British Journal of Industrial Relations*, R. Price and G. S. Bain for pp. 133, 138; Cambridge University Press, P. Stansworth and A. Giddens for p. 112; Croom Helm Ltd and M. Campbell for p. 233; Croom Helm Ltd and C. Crouch for p. 239; Croom Helm Ltd and M. Currell for p. 169 *above*; Fontana Paperbacks and T. R. Coogan for p. 186; Fontana Paperbacks, James Curran and Jean Seaton for p. 209; George Allen and Unwin and S. Delamont for p. 169 *below*; Heinemann Educational Books, The OECD, S. Hughes and J. R. Davies for p. 49; the Controller of Her Majesty's Stationery Office for pp. 160, 161, 172 (Crown copyright 1981), 173; *Industrial and Labour Relations Review* and A. W. Thomson for p. 245; *Lloyds Bank Review*, S. Aaronovitch and M. Sawyer for p. 68; Longman, R. King and J. Reynor for p. 120; Macmillan, London and Basingstoke and Ian Gough for p. 220; Macmillan, London and Basingstoke and J. Scott for p. 237; The Merlin Press Ltd, M. Sawyer and K. Schott for p. 47; New Left Books and E. Mandel for pp. 35, 36; *New Left Review* and E. O. Wright for p. 125; *New Socialist* and John Westergaard for p. 105 *above*; Penguin Books Ltd and David J. Smith (Copyright © PEP 1977) for p. 175 (2 tables); *Political Studies* and P. Dunleavy for p. 148; The Runnymede Trust for p. 175 *below*; Spokesman and M. Barrett Brown for p. 27; Spokesman, K. Coates and T. Topham for p. 84; Spokesman and J. Hughes for p. 69; Wiedenfeld and Nicolson Ltd and P. Abrams for pp. 103, 105, 139, 161.

Figures

MacGibbon and Kee and W. L. Guttsman for p. 241; *Political Studies* and P. Dunleavy for p. 149.

Preface

What follows is offered as an introduction to British politics, but one that is different in many ways from the vast majority of the introductions which you will find in libraries and bookshops around the country. Both its focus and its underlying theoretical framework are different from those given in introductory texts of a more conventional kind. Unlike so many, this book focuses on the context of political life rather than on the detail of decision-making; and in doing so, it draws on a body of Marxist theoretical perspectives which rarely surface in public discussions of national political events. This book also has a very distinctive political anchorage of its own. Key sections of the text, and particularly its closing pages, are concerned to assess the consequences of its analysis for left-wing politics in contemporary Britain. Since such a set of preoccupations, theoretical frameworks and political sympathies are not usually found in introductory texts, I would like to explain why they are here and how they will shape what is to come.

The relationship between political commitment and academic scholarship is a contentious one, and has long been so. There are those who think that the two must be kept apart, and that they can be. Max Weber's writings on methodology in social science remain one important source of such a view, and one that has influenced many contemporary scholars. However, this is not a Weberian text, but a Marxist one. Indeed, I had thought of calling the book a 'committed text', but now realize that it ought more properly to be labelled an 'alternative' one. For all textbooks in political science are shaped by the political commitments of their authors. Choices about the information to gather, about the kinds of explanation to offer for that information, and about the prescriptions for political action which are to be derived from those explanations – choices of those kinds structure every introductory text available to us. Because that is necessarily so, the rigours of proper scholarship require not that we search out some specious neutrality from which to write, but rather that we are open and clear from the outset about what our commitments and politics actually are, and about how they inevitably colour and shape the analysis that we will make.

I write as a socialist, and offer one socialist's interpretation of the context of contemporary politics in Britain. Readers whose political sympathies already lie with the Left should therefore find what follows of particular interest and relevance to them. At least I hope that they do. But I hope too that readers with more moderate politics, and readers with none, will also find this book of interest. I particularly hope that they will not be alienated by the kind of material they are asked to consider, or by the theoretical framework within which that material is so obviously situated. For what is striking about the context of political life in Britain is that it is a matter of academic as well as of practical political contention. Academics just disagree on how best to explain economic performance, social class, cultural processes, state policy and the like. I have a view on all those things, as will become clear; and I hope that my view will come over as coherent and convincing. But it may not. Even if it seems coherent, it may not convince; and if it does not, then I hope you will find it easy, from the discussions in the text and the Notes and references section at the end of the book, to turn to alternative sources for other views – sources which will be equally committed but normally less radical in their anchorage. Moreover, even if, in the end, the drift of argument here fails to persuade, I do hope that at least the importance of its subject matter will be established in the pages which follow. For that is what an alternative text of this kind exists to do: not simply to demonstrate another view on British politics, but also to indicate the range of alternative views available to students, and to demonstrate how important it is to set British politics in its economic and social context if it is ever to be understood in the full.

You will find that the last chapter of the book will talk again to the Left, exploring the consequences of the analysis for contemporary socialist strategy and tactics. I hope that by then many readers will have found sufficient of interest in what follows to want to read that section too, if only to see the difficulties faced by a form of politics for which they still feel no sympathy. For in the end, as in the beginning, politics will turn on a question of choice; and no textbook can free itself of that. What it can do is to help its readers to make (or to deepen, to re-examine) their own choice on the basis of a fuller understanding of the range of explanations available, and of the nature of the context with which those explanations have to cope. Competing theoretical perspectives have to be judged eventually on their ability to make that explanation – and to make it with the utmost coherence, comprehensiveness, sensitivity to detail and complexity, and due regard to the strengths of the perspectives foregone. As will become clear in the pages which follow, I believe that a Marxist perspective, properly handled, meets these requirements in a way which no other can; and it is for this reason that I approach British politics in the way that I do. Certainly I have tried, to the best of my ability and with all the care which I can muster, to present as coherent and comprehensive a Marxist explanation of the context of politics in Britain as my capacities can manage and as the state of contemporary academic knowledge will permit. Yet whether in the end you come to agree with me on the adequacy of such an approach will turn, I realize, on the quality of the argument that follows, and on its strength when compared with introductory texts of a more traditional kind. The proof of the pudding, as it were, will be in the eating. All I can do is to hope that the book will convince; or that if it does not, that even in its deficiencies it will prove to be sufficiently serious, honest and careful to invite your attention and to shape your reactions. That at least is what I have set out to achieve.

The intellectual debts accumulated in the writing of a book of this kind are truly enormous. To write it at all is possible only because of the prior existence of left-wing scholarship of the very highest quality; and the scale and range of the Notes and references should be taken as one index of the magnitude of the debts accumulated here, and of just how high that quality is. For this is not a work of original scholarship. It is a work of synthesis, a putting together of the insights of others, and an introduction to the richness of contemporary intellectual life on the Left to which it is but a preliminary pointer. The faults within it are doubtless many, and are entirely mine. What strengths it has derive in large measure from the comments of the many friends who have been kind enough, and sufficiently generous with their time, to comment on earlier drafts. These include Roger Ballard, David Beetham, Ray Bush, Andrew Cox, David Held, Ann James, Bob Jessop, Gordon Johnston, Arthur Lipow, Bob Looker, Keith

Nield, Dick Taylor, Sue Thomson, Tessa ten Tusscher and Nicola Tobias. Sections of the manuscript were also discussed with two groups of graduate and undergraduate students: with Peter Cafferty, Mick Cunningham, Peter Dorey, Annette Fitzsimons, Chris Guest, Paul Norris, Len Rawling, Paul Wetherley, John Williamson, Mike Sakalis and John Charlton; and Mick Shaw, Stephen Nolan, Howard Oddy, John Wallace, Wendy Wilson, Tony Blick, Peter Walker, Paul Thompson, Melvyn Ruff and Bibi Martial. I am very grateful to all of them for the time and effort which they put into my education; and I am also grateful to Ernie Jacques for material on the training policy of the Thatcher government that is discussed briefly in Chapter 11.

Let me add too that Lionel Cliffe has had, and continues to have, a considerable influence on my understanding of politics and society, so that working with him on the MA in Political Sociology at Leeds has shaped much of what follows. Lionel is a great friend and a fine teacher, and it is a pleasure to be able to record that in so public a place. But there is no pleasure at all in reporting the death of someone else who was at various times a comrade, colleague and friend. Peter Sedgwick died as this manuscript was being completed. He would have been one of the first to whom I would have turned for comments and guidance; and all those who are familiar with his scholarship on Victor Serge, his political writings for the International Socialists, his work on the politics of mental health, or his many fine essays and book reviews, will know just what a tragic loss his death has been. I mention him here both to record his memory and to remind us all of the value of his many writings. I would like to dedicate this book to his memory. It was a privilege to know Peter Sedgwick, and the Left is significantly poorer for his passing.

David Coates
Leeds
January 1984

1 Introduction

Traditionally, most textbooks on British politics have focused on a particular and quite distinctive set of institutions and governmental processes. They have looked at the Commons and the Lords, the Cabinet and the parties, the civil servants and the pressure groups, the electoral process and the relationship between national and local government. They have done so because they have emerged from a tradition of political science which saw its job in those terms – as preoccupied with studying *how* decisions were made in national and local government, what the procedures were that governed parliamentary institutions, and how the relationships within the formal machinery of democratic government actually operated in practice. The level of sophistication of scholarship in that tradition has been and remains high; and increasingly of late has shown a willingness to move out from that narrow governmental focus, to watch the emergence of political demands and interests in the constituencies that governments service. But the centre of gravity of scholarly interest has, in the main, remained with government itself, on the widespread but often unexamined assumption that it is both meaningful and useful to treat the institutions of the modern democratic state in isolation and in detail, as though a full understanding of the political process could be grasped primarily through an examination of those institutions alone.[1]*

The approach and the premise of this text are quite different. The argument here will start from the view that this traditional approach is inherently limited, and in need of supplementation, because of its failure to situate systematically the modern state in the context of the wider society from which it derives its authority and over which it presides. As a result, the chapters that follow will focus, not on the actual decision-making procedures of the modern state as such, but on the *relationship* between the state in Britain and the social and economic structures and processes dominant in contemporary British society. For once it is recognized that the modern state faces a highly structured universe, from which it has to recruit its own personnel, from which it takes its own agenda of problems, over which it has to preside, to whose imperatives it is subject, and by which in the end it will be judged, so it becomes both legitimate and essential – if the full complexity of modern politics is to be understood – to ask a much wider range of questions, of the following kind:

What kind of society do politicians in Britain face? What have been, and are, the main groups, institutions and processes in that society, and what determines the character of the political demands, resources and alliances that those groups and institutions deploy?

---

* Superior figures refer to Notes and references beginning on p. 264.

How have those social groups, institutions and processes shaped the agenda of politics in Britain in recent times? What impact have they had on the content of political problems, and the outcome and consequences of political decisions?

How does the state relate to that society at the level of its personnel, linking institutions, major policy areas, and pattern of dependence and influence on the main social, economic and cultural processes at work there?

How does the state emerge from, and how is it shaped by, the society it would govern? What autonomy does the state enjoy from the centres of power which it faces? What impact does it have on the society which surrounds it?

The chapters that follow will explore the relationship between the national political process in Britain and the main features of contemporary British society, by focusing on the origins of political issues, the limits within which issues are resolved and the social consequences of particular governmental policies. At times, of course, that exploration will involve us in looking at the detail of government decision-making, but only in the context of asking a series of wider questions about the character of the society faced by politicians, about the role played by the state, and about the mutual relationship between social structure and political decision.

By doing this, we should eventually be in a better position to understand our situation here in Britain in all its complexity. We should be able to explain the origin and character of the political issues central to our day, and to say why those issues have arisen and come to dominate political debate, why they have come to dominate now and in this particular form, and why they are likely to be resolved (or to fail to be resolved) in one of a restricted and recognizable number of ways. Moreover, we should be in a better position to handle the

bigger questions that confront contemporary political activity: the freedom of manoeuvre of the democratic state, the nature of power in modern societies, the balance of authority and coercion in contemporary politics, and the possibilities of political change through reform and revolution. Because the answers to all these questions turn also on the relative strengths and weaknesses of competing theories of modern politics, we will be in a position to situate our analysis in the wider dispute within and between Marxists and non-Marxists on the nature of contemporary capitalism.

In pursuit of this aim, the argument that follows will be characterized by a particular approach and by a particular set of themes. It is important to make both of those clear before going any further.

The approach

Let me begin by differentiating the concept of 'government' from that of 'state'. The government of the day will be understood here in its colloquial sense, as a collection of politicians who hold ministerial office, and who are sustained by a set of parliamentarians of the same or related parties in the Commons and the Lords. But the government is not the state. The state ought to be understood, and will be here, as a wider set of institutions over which any particular government at any particular time has a limited degree of both formal and actual control. The precise width of the state is itself a matter of controversy.[2] At the very least it contains the agencies who implement government policy (particularly permanent civil servants) and those who enforce it (the police, the judiciary and the military). It may also – depending on your definition – stretch out to include the agencies of cultural dissemination (schools, churches, the media – even, on some accounts, trade unions)[3] and semi-autonomous administrative bodies (a whole range, from the managerial strata of the nationalized industries through QUANGOs to the permanent bureaucracies of the major pressure groups). But whether the state is understood in its narrow or its wide sense, two things are clear. The first is that a full understanding of the character of modern politics must take the state and not just the government as its focus. The second is that, wide or narrow, the state is no passive or automatically subservient tool of government, but has itself to be governed.

Politicians in office necessarily find themselves locked into relationships of power with the various agencies of the state, patterns of mutual dependence and authority which dominate the daily life of even senior ministers.[4] It is easy to be misled by the appearance of things, and to see political parties as powerful bodies in their own right. In reality they are not. A government and its immediate parliamentary supporters are normally less than 450 people, a mixture of former professionals, businessmen, white-collar workers and union officials who draft legislation, talk about it in public, and vote on it. That legislation is in no sense self-enforcing, although of course it enjoys an immense legitimacy and authority (because of the way in which it was made) that helps to make it so, and is buttressed by the administrative and co-ercive apparatus of the state, which also helps to give it force. But governments have found on many occasions that they cannot rely on the automatic and full co-operation of even the civil service and the judiciary. They have found too that, even where public servants have been entirely loyal and pliant, the complexity and resources of the private centres of power that they face mean that no government is in a position to coerce all its citizens into submission to its will on all issues. This is particularly true in liberal democracies such as ours, where governments do not enjoy the freedom to use coercion on the scale and in the character of more authoritarian regimes. The governments to which we are directly

subject are obliged instead to canvass support, and to mobilize coalitions of self-interested parties, if they wish to see their policies implemented. To help them do this, such governments have at their disposal many resources but they are never extensive enough to remove entirely the need to negotiate and to cajole.

Moreover, the problem of power faced by politicians encompasses more than the character of the state institutions and private élites that they face.[5] There are, in addition, broad processes at work in the wider society that are not in the direct control of any élite, public or private. There are market forces to face, popular sentiments to which to react, the relative strength of class forces to operate within and to shape, and an international order with which to contend – processes, institutions and private concentrations of power that are all manifestations of the cumulative legacy of past generations, that remain to shape the options available to the politicians of the present. As Marx said, 'men make their own history, but not of their own free will, not under circumstances they themselves have chosen but under the given and inherited circumstances with which they are directly confronted'.[6] When this is recognized, what stands out above all is the *constraints* on politicians in a modern democracy, and the *intractability* of both the power structure and the social context which surround them. A study of politics, then, requires more than an immediate examination of the procedures of government and the resources of the state. It requires too a mechanism for grasping the origin, character and complexity of the relationship between those politicians and that intractable social, economic and cultural environment.

Strange as it may seem, one such mechanism can be forged simply by thinking of the government first as a pebble and then as a tree. Consider it first as a pebble, dropped into a still pool of water. The ripples that spill out from the central point can be thought of as an ever widening ring of power constraints, each occupied by a set of particular institutions and élites. As Figure 1 suggests, and as later chapters will try to substantiate, it seems valid to see the first constraint on ministerial freedom of action as lying in Parliament, then in the civil service, then in the unions, in the forces of industrial capital, and finally in those of international finance. The precise map of ever-widening constraints will vary according to the issue, of course. Not all those institutions impinge *directly* on the freedom of action of one government department on one small technical issue. The Department of Education and Science only rarely, if ever, comes up directly against the dictates of an international bank.[7] And again, the relative strengths of financial and industrial interests, or those of labour and capital in general, and the degree to which their concerns converge or clash, vary over time and between issues, giving a volatility to the actual position of specific élites on each ring of the figure, and to the distance to be drawn between each ring. But as a first approximation, and on the central issues of

economic and social policy that set the parameters for detailed legislation or long-term foreign affairs, this book will argue that the range of key institutions and their positions will be broadly as in Figure 1; and that therefore one of our jobs will be to map out and characterize each of those power relationships in turn (in Chapters 4 and 5 for capital and labour, for example, and in Part 3 for the internal nature of state bureaucracy).

However, such a figure is rather static, and emphasizes the *position* of élites at the expense of the social and historical *processes* that created and now sustain them. Nor does the figure, as it stands, give any clue to the origins of interests that the élites will pursue, or any way of beginning to explore the connections between those interests. To do that it is worth recasting the figure, to think of our rings now not as those of a sinking pebble but rather as those of a tree cut down to give a cross-section of its trunk. If, as in Figure 2, we cut that trunk at various points we can locate broad social and economic phenomena whose character will provide us with insights into élite interests, and whose history will explain the origin of élite structures. The tree can be most productively cut in three places: to show an underlying social structure, a national economy and a world order. Each lower cut throws up institutions, interests and issues to be handled by the levels above, shaping the content and preoccupations of each higher level while setting the ultimate limits to that level's freedom of political action. At the same time, the precise impact on the top political level of forces released at the base is determined by a process of filtration through the levels that intervene. Some institutions arrive at the top level directly from the bottom – the IMF is one. Others, such as multinational corporations, filter their way into British national politics in part through the place occupied by their local affiliates in the local economy and class structure. But it is clear none the less that their political preoccupa-

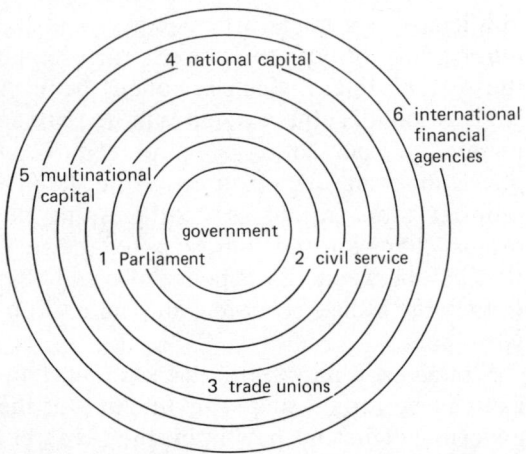

Figure 1   *Constraints on ministerial freedom*

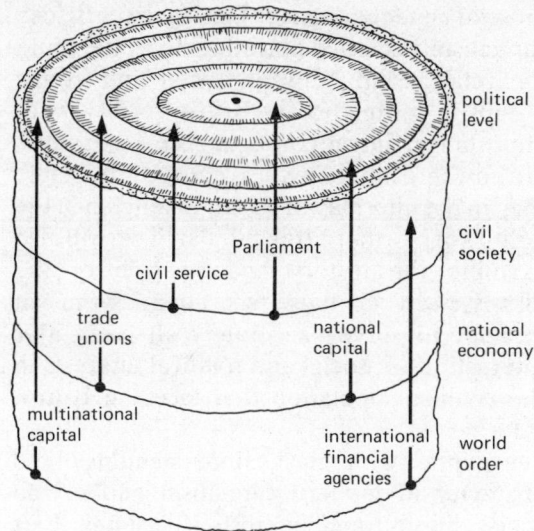

Figure 2 *The origin of élite interests*

tions here arise only as part of their global strategy as multinationals, which means, among other things, that to understand their role in British politics requires that we first fix the character of the world order and the national economy in which they are themselves situated. And as we do that, we will locate the origins, and the interests, of more locally-based actors – national capital, labour unions, whole social classes – whose influence in British politics we also need to identify and explain.

It is Figure 2 that holds the key to the structure of all that follows. It suggests that to understand the full complexity of British politics it is necessary to begin far from the British state or from any particular British government, in an examination of the institutions and processes of the world order that are so important a source of that government's political agenda and constraints. It suggests too that a necessary second task is the systematic examination of the national economy as a part of that world order, as a source indeed of many of the key institutions, interests and issues which dominate daily

political life in Britain. And it sets as a third necessity the examination of how all this is filtered into the contemporary crisis of the modern British state by the character of the social structure that that economy sustains. Only then, having examined each level in all its historical complexity and social interrelatedness, will we be in a position to look at the modern state itself, its role and its problems, and at the options historically available to us to facilitate its control and our emancipation.

Themes

The advocacy of such an approach is itself an argument, but it is an argument that is more procedural than substantive; and it is as well to be clear now that an argument of substance will also emerge in the chapters that follow, an argument that will move through four main stages.

1 The text will argue first that British politics is best understood when the world order that surrounds it is seen as a divided one, with a capitalist centre that is subject to processes of accumulation and class struggle of the kind first isolated by Marx, ones that have since been most accurately monitored (and at crucial moments even shaped) by the political theory and practice of certain later Marxists. It will be argued that many of the issues and institutions now dominant in British politics originate in the economic processes, class struggles and internal contradictions of that capitalist world order in its monopoly stage – in late capitalism as it is often called – and have to be located there before their true place in British politics can be properly understood. To establish that will be the task of the chapter that follows.

2 Later chapters will argue that it is impossible to grasp the full range of issues, groups and institutions faced by successive British governments, or indeed even to locate the

precise impact of the general trends of late capitalism, without also seeing that the British economy occupies a particular place in, and has a particular history as part of, that capitalist world order. The growing competitive weakness of British industrial capital – the inability of British firms to compete or to attract investment on a sufficient scale, and their associated loss of jobs – is itself a (even *the*) major political issue in Britain today – one that attracts state action, one that sets the ultimate limit on the freedom of manoeuvre of governments in fields far from the immediately economic, and one that therefore is itself in need of explanation. Chapter 3 will do that, tracing the character of the British ruling class, the divisions between different sections of capital within it, and the defensive strength of the labour movement, before, in Chapters 4 and 5, assessing the contemporary political strengths and role in Britain of capital and labour.

3 Politics in Britain are also intimately shaped by the social divisions that have emerged as British capitalism has developed, and which have themselves been shaped recently by changes in work processes, labour migration and state activity general to late capitalism. Part Two will trace the origins and character of key social classes, locate the determinants and content of their interests and attitudes, and examine the impact of the institutions they sustain. It will also examine the relationship between class divisions in British society and those of gender and race. The legacy of British capitalism's colonial period remains to mould the relationship between social and ethnic groups in contemporary British society, with important political consequences – and these are nowhere more obvious or more intractable than in the interplay of class and religion in the politics of Northern Ireland. Part Two will also examine the history and struggle of the dispossessed in those six counties, in an attempt to survey accurately all the major interactions of social and political interests in the civilian population that face the British state.

4 Equipped with such an understanding of the character of modern capitalism and of the social division and interests it sustains, Part Three will turn to the state itself, to examine the relationship between its parts, its changing role in late capitalism, the relative strengths and weaknesses of its coercive and ideological apparatuses, and the characteristic responses of successive governments to the range of issues, interests and institutions generated for them by the complex character of the capitalist order that they face. Then, and only then, it should be possible to draw together the strands of the argument, to characterize the crisis faced by the contemporary British state in all its major detail, and to probe for ways forward of both an intellectual and a political kind, that might take us beyond the politics of a weak capitalism to those of a revitalized democratic and socialist Britain.

Part One: The Economic Context of British Politics

2 The character of the world order

The overriding characteristic – politically, economically and militarily – of the world order surrounding the British state is that that world order is a profoundly divided one. It is divided by the differing levels of economic development in the various nation states that compose it, into a First and Second World that contain highly industrialized economic systems and a Third World that, except in parts, does not. The industrialized part is itself divided into competing and mutually antagonistic blocs, each with its satellite states in the underdeveloped world, each bloc resting on quite different economic and social systems, and each containing massive military structures directed primarily at the other. I will explain the origin of those divisions, and their significance, in a moment, but first we have to grasp the obvious: namely that the British state is firmly established in the industrialized and capitalist parts of those divisions. We must therefore establish the character of capitalism and industrialization before we can proceed further.

The political and social structures of all societies are intimately shaped, as they have always been, by the way in which their economic activity is organized and controlled. Capitalism must be understood as merely one way of organizing that economic activity – a way that has special characteristics which both distinguish it from other modes of production (such as the feudal mode in the past, or the state-socialist mode now) and which give to its economic life, its social system and its political agenda a quite distinctive tonality. Capitalism is best understood as a system of commodity production based, in its metropolitan centres at least, on a system of free wage labour.[1] In contrast, medieval Europe was not capitalist. It was not, in the main, underpinned by an economy geared to trade, nor by one in which wage labour was a significant component. Instead the predominantly subsistence economies of Western Europe and Japan were only slowly transformed into capitalist ones in a long historical process that involved a number of qualitative economic and social changes: including the development of trade, first regionally and then globally; the commercialization of agriculture; the accumulation of capital in part through processes of unequal exchange ('buying cheap and selling dear');[2] the consolidation of a new class of owners of that capital (first merchants, then industrialists and later financiers) who depended for their survival on its perpetual expansion; and the associated creation of another social class – a proletariat, peasants no longer in possession of their land and artisans no longer owning their own tools and output – who were left with only their labour power to sell in return for money wages. It was these capitalist economies, in which trade was initially in agricultural goods and artisan-produced commodities, that spawned the industrialization process in the eighteenth and nineteenth centuries. The 'industrial revolution' in Britain marked the arrival of industrial capitalism on the world scene after 1760, and was followed by similar (though differently initiated and differently paced) industrializations in the United States after 1830, in Germany and Japan after 1870, and in France, Italy, Scandinavia and Russia prior to 1914. British politics today is still intimately shaped by that pattern of industrialization, just as it is shaped too (as we shall see) by the fact that it was British industrial capital that consolidated itself first, only subsequently to be overtaken by others.

This is not the place to examine all the intricasies of that industrialization process,[3] nor to probe into all the complexities of economic life in a fully industrialized capitalist economy.[4] What we need to note instead are several of the broad processes at work in that industrialization, processes which continue to set the parameters of British politics.

The first of these is the way in which capitalism emerged, and came to dominate economic activity on a world scale, only in the form of competing nation states. The history of the last century has been one of the rise and clash of national economies – economies that were capitalist (with industrial plant owned in the main by private individuals and companies seeking to profit by the production and sale of commodities) and national (in that increasingly the pursuit of profit both required a stable national framework for internal trade, property dealing and money transactions, *and* the support of national governments for the overseas opening and exploration of markets, sources of raw material and outlets for capital). The ruling groups that controlled the machinery of the nation state had, of course, fought and competed with one another long before capitalism arrived. But the rulers of the modern capitalist state quickly found that capitalist industrialization offered an enhanced military capacity in that struggle, and made the relative economic strength of their own national economy a crucial preoccupation of the state élite itself.

Those élites also found that they, as ruling groups based initially on precapitalist sources of wealth and power (normally land and religion), had both to adapt their own power base and to accommodate in some degree to the rising social force of this new mercantile and industrial bourgeoisie. Different precapitalist ruling groups did that more or less successfully in different national contexts, and quite how they settled this nineteenth-century struggle for power had a profound influence on whether their societies industrialized into liberal states (often where feudal aristocracies gave way or fused with bourgeoisies) or into fascist/authoritarian militarisms (where aristocracies played the dominant role) or fell in revolution (where neither aristocracy nor bourgeoisie was strong enough to withstand the pressure of radicalized peasantries and proletariats). Even liberal states experienced that pressure to a considerable degree, so that the dominant social classes within them were obliged eventually to extend both voting rights and welfare provision in order to accommodate capitalism's subordinate classes. Indeed liberal democracies emerged after 1945 as *the* characteristic state form of advanced capitalism; but the 'naturalness' of the relationship between capitalism and democracy in our epoch should not obscure the extent to which the *form* taken by the state in both the First and Second Worlds has been (and continues to be) intimately shaped by patterns of class struggle and accommodation produced by the tensions and upheavals of capitalist industrialization.[5]

Which brings me to the second broad feature of capitalism as a mode of production which is of central political importance – and that is its inherent instability caused by the conflict within it. Because capital can be accumulated only through both the organization of production and the sale of the commodities produced, the arrival of capitalism introduced a new volatility into the whole of social and political life. The pursuit of profit, and the protection of existing market strength, imposed on each capitalist the necessity perennially to innovate: to seek new sources of raw materials, new ways of organizing production, new technologies, new products, new sources of cheap labour and new markets. All of this culminated in a rate of economic growth unknown before in human history, and made possible 'the construction of a world economy that is based not just on trade but upon a world division and specialization of labour'.[6] That economic growth offered to politicians a new source of legitimacy in the eyes of their subjects, to replace the waning force of religion and habit. But the competitive struggle from which that growth emerged also brought new sources of economic instability, new social tensions, and new demands on the state; and as capitalist relations of production spread to include more and more people, any downturn in the accumulation process was capable of creating generalized crises – both nationally and later internationally – that were bound to have powerful negative political consequences and bound at times to put the legitimacy of the whole system in question. Indeed 'capitalism as a world system has suffered twenty such general crises of overproduction since 1825', each 'progressively more severe, because the scale of production and degree of interdependence has grown during every period of expansion'.[7]

Moreover, these crises had of necessity long-lasting political consequences. The struggle between capitalists even in one national economy exposed the state to a differentiated set of pressures from different types of capital (financial against industrial, manufacturing sector against manufacturing sector, international against national, and so on) and left the state able to throw its weight behind one or the other in the pursuit of policies which those in charge of the state felt to be in the interests of capital as a whole, while at the same time leaving the state vulnerable to disproportionate pressure from whichever section of capital was then in the ascendancy. Again, each crisis in economic activity sent small firms to the wall, and left behind an ever greater degree of industrial concentration and control, and so

shifted the balance of political resources in favour of this emerging monopoly sector. The perennial search for markets and cheap sources of labour and raw materials sent the stronger capitalist concerns out on to the world stage, and pulled national governments behind them to give them political and military backing. So it was that early liberal small-scale capitalism quickly gave way by the end of the nineteenth century to a world order of imperialism and monopolies – one in which national governments in the advanced capitalist world competed with one another to divide the rest of the globe into areas of special privilege for their particular capitalist firms.

This is an important point to grasp, not least because politicians of the Right hark back so often to a golden age of small-scale business and free trade. That world has gone, destroyed not by the political strength of the Left but by propensities to the concentration and centralization of capital, and to expansion on a world scale, endemic to the capitalist system the Right would defend. Capitalism has gone through stages: a stage of liberal capitalism, where production was organized through large numbers of small firms; a stage characterized by the emergence of large firms and powerful banks, often intimately connected to one another; and a more recent stage – what I will call 'late capitalism' – in which production in virtually all industrial sectors is dominated by a few *very* large firms, and in which the state has come to play a major role in economic and social life. In the second of those three stages, which began towards the end of the nineteenth century, one major area of state activity for the governments of the emerging capitalist powers was the straightforward military creation of colonies and the destruction of the natural economies there. This expansion served the interests of certain sections of capital, and perhaps more important, it provided a new source of stability and legitimation for the capitalist system as a whole. For a prime motivation in that colonial expansion, for the ruling élites of late nineteenth-century Europe, came from their belief that imperial glory offered both an ideological and a material alternative to socialism, a way of offsetting the rising opposition of the working class that capitalism had called into existence to the instabilities and hardships that capitalism released upon them.

Not every ruling class played that card successfully. Where capitalism was weakest, and the pressure of the peasantry and proletariat greatest, the military conflict between competing imperialist powers produced not social stability but revolution, most noticeably in Russia in 1917, and took the Soviet Union (and later the Soviet bloc) out of the capitalist world market altogether.[8] But elsewhere, not least in Britain itself, imperialism proved extraordinarily successful in cementing class loyalty to the new industrial order. So the fact that the British state now faces a world divided between blocs, a world of uneven economic development and colonial legacies, a social structure profoundly divided by the interests of capital and labour and still coloured by the legacy of precapitalist social classes, and an economy driven by processes of competition and private capital accumulation that no one controls and to which states have to respond as best they can – all this was put in place through the emergence of the world capitalist system in the two centuries that divide us from the beginning of the industrial revolution. If we wish to locate the origins of much of the modern world, it is to the detail of these historical processes that we need to turn.[9]

The system of nation states and the great power rivalries that surround the British state continue to be vital elements shaping internal politics, as we shall see in a moment. But before we turn to look at the cold war context of contemporary politics in Britain, there is one other feature of the pattern of capitalist industrialization on a world scale that is of importance here; and that is the propensity of the processes of accumulation to settle into broadly fifty-year cycles of expansion and decline. Why this should be so, and whether it is so with any exactitude, remain matters of controversy. The Belgian Marxist, Ernest Mandel, for one, has described the rhythm of the emerging capitalist world order as settling into these fifty year *waves*, 'each characterised by the generalised application of a new technology that precipitates leaps in labour productivity, each triggered by accumulations of profits in preceding periods of working class defeat, and each brought to an end by the way in which the new technology, once generally applied, ceases to be a source of further dramatic productivity gains, and hence of profits'.[10] Certainly it is possible to discern a broad sweep of expansion and contraction that fits Mandel's picture – a long wave of capitalist economic activity on the world scale between 1848 and the 1890s, between 1894 and 1940/8, and since 1940/8. In each, twenty-five years of broad expansion, coloured of course by shorter trade cycles of seven to eight years duration, were followed by twenty-five years of relative stagnation and decline, in which the accompanying trade cycle produced deeper recessions and briefer booms to embroider the long term trend. It is with this in mind that it seems fruitful to suggest that British politics now must be seen as situated in the downturn of one such 'long wave' – dominated, that is, by the end of the twenty-five year post-war boom, and obliged to operate in the restricted space of a downturn in the world economy. It is to the character of that post-war boom and slump that I would like now to draw your attention.

The post-war boom

For twenty-five years after 1948 the capitalist section of the world economy experienced a quite unprecedented and unbroken period of economic growth. Indeed, so extensive and persistent did that prosperity seem that a whole generation of people in Britain came to

Table 1 *Economic growth, 1950–70 (annual percentage rate)*

	1950–5	1955–60	1960–5	1965–70
OECD	5.7	3.9	5.9	6.0
USA	5.0	2.4	5.8	4.8
EEC	8.2	6.7	5.6	6.5
Japan	18.0	16.0	11.6	16.5
UK	3.5	2.3	3.2	2.0

Source: M. Barrett Brown, *From Labourism to Socialism* (Spokesman 1972), p. 101.

take it for granted that jobs here would be available for everyone and that living standards would persistently rise. For more than two decades this prosperity acted to remove the experience of inter-war depression from the expectations people brought to politics, so that even in Left-intellectual circles it became commonplace to feel that politics now were situated in a *post-capitalist* society – one freed from the contradictions and crises of the inter-war type by the success of Keynesian policies[11] and the stability of the mixed economy. Yet in fact that boom, long as it was, was built on foundations that in the end only reproduced those contradictions and crises at a new and higher level. To understand the character of (and the shock produced by) the return of unemployment and stagnation to the vast majority of the advanced capitalist economies in the 1970s, we need therefore to grasp the scale of the boom and the nature of its causes.

The figures of economic success in the OECD[12] area as a whole after 1948 are dramatic enough, and are brought together in Table 1.

The new technology

Why then did this boom happen? It was certainly underpinned by the emergence of a particular pattern of *technological innovation and industrial restructuring.* Just as capitalism's first 'long wave' after 1848 had been constructed on the generalized application of machine-built steam engines, and the second after 1893 on the generalized application of electrical and petrol driven machinery,[13] so this third 'long wave' had as its base the generalized application of machines controlled by electronic power. It was this 'third technological revolution',[14] the *spread* of these automated and semi-automated production processes first developed in the United States, and their dissemination through the economies of Western Europe and Japan, that fuelled the boom. The growth industries of the second 'wave' – shipbuilding, coal and textiles – went into secular decline, to be replaced by new growth industries deploying the new technology: cars, electronics and chemicals in particular.

The economic results and political consequences of that were many and varied. The application of the new techniques in ever-wider fields brought an unprecedented leap in the productivity of labour. Labour productivity in manufacturing industry in the 1950s and 1960s doubled every ten years in Japan, every fifteen in the EEC, and every thirty in Great Britain and the United States. 'During 1964–73 the annual increase in labour productivity (in the OECD as a whole) averaged 5.2% and in employment 0.8%, the former accounting for 87% of the total increase in industrial production.'[15] That productivity provided the base for sustained growth without inflation, the surpluses on which massive service and welfare bureaucracies could be created and sustained, and generated a level of mass consumer affluence in the West which legitimated the system in general and the ruling politicians in particular. But it also released new sets of political actors and problems. The sheer scale of investment required by companies in these new industries, and their dependence on ever more active processes of research and development in their competitive struggle with one another, was a powerful encouragement to industrial concentration, leaving politicians facing ever fewer and more influential centres of private industrial power. The amounts of money tied up in industrial plant, and the length of time that had to elapse between that money being committed and the resulting commodities being sold, encouraged many of these private monopolies to turn to the state, seeking the planning of future levels of demand through wages policy, requesting state aid and protection in the sharing of risks, and requiring emergency state funding if those risks proved so great as to overwhelm them. States found that the rise of this new technology altered the relative competitive strengths of their various national economies, eroding that of countries too tied to the industries of the second long wave, and favouring those capable of a rapid redeployment of investment into the new growth areas. States found too that the boom could last only so long as the generalized application of the new technology was not complete in the world system as a whole; for when it was, the capacity to achieve rapid leaps in labour productivity by its use would begin to falter, with severe consequences, as we shall see, for the interaction of profits and employment, productivity and inflation.

American dominance

The other overriding feature of the long post-war boom was the way in which it was associated with the *political, military and economic domination of the United States*, and the associated availability of the dollar as a unit of international exchange. The United States emerged from the war as the leading capitalist power, locked in a struggle for world domination with the USSR. The strength of communist parties in war-torn Western Europe, and the discredited nature of many ruling groups there, was perceived in Washington as a potential source of Russian

expansion; and the American solution to the problem they perceived (namely giving United States military and economic aid to 'defend' and reconstitute capitalist economies in Western Europe) went hand-in-hand with an internal American need to find overseas outlets for its own commodities and capital.

As a result the post-war years were dominated by the steady and horrendous build up of both Soviet and American war machines, and by the associated outflow into Europe and Japan of US dollars in the form of military expenditure, economic aid and capital export.[16] The USA ran a balance of payments deficit[17] annually after 1952, and that flow of dollars lubricated world trade by increasing the money supply in the capitalist part of the now divided world system. The acceptance of the dollar (and in a secondary role, sterling) as reserve currencies reflected the higher productivity of the United States economy in comparison with the rest (just as the strength of sterling had reflected the United Kingdom's industrial superiority in the nineteenth century); and it enabled Western European countries to buy American (and to a lesser extent, British) goods with which to reconstitute their war-shattered industries. It also allowed both the United States and (for a while) Britain to exploit the relative superiority of their economies in the immediate post-war period by running payments deficits on their overseas accounts which lesser economies would have had to deflate to avoid. There was literally no limit to the amount of money that United States governments could print and spend so long as governments abroad were prepared to hold dollars (rather than gold) as payment for United States debts.

British politicians too initially enjoyed that freedom, particularly in the so-called 'sterling area', but that did not last. Instead, as Britain's relative economic position deteriorated rapidly from the mid 1950s, British governments (and their electorates) had to endure a painful process of readjustment to the lower status of a non-reserve currency. As we shall see, the pain of that process was made worse by the prolonged refusal of the British governing élite to accept their new and restricted status until they were in the end forced to do so by a series of balance of payments crises, IMF loans and devaluations which left governments here, as elsewhere outside the USA, obliged to fix their domestic policy within limits set by the health of their overseas trade. But the loss of sterling as a reserve currency was a local problem. It did not seriously affect the system as a whole; so that for as long as governments, central banks and private companies in Western economies were prepared to accept the dollar in payment of goods, for as long as the dollar appeared to be 'as good as gold', the general boom held – and it was to end only when the dollar followed sterling down the route to devaluation in 1971.

Prior to that, United States dominance in Western economic circles had been reinforced by the international monetary arrangements laid down at Bretton Woods in 1944. From these originated the IMF, charged with the supervision of a system of fixed exchange rates tied to the dollar, and through the dollar indirectly to gold, participation in which required the opening of one's home market to the free flow of (predominantly American, of course) Western commodities and capital. The IMF and GATT were, to Western capitalism, what the Berlin Wall was to the Eastern bloc – a critical mechanism for holding your side together and keeping the others out. Trade *between* the blocs was on a bilateral basis with unconvertible currencies, but trade within the Western bloc (in principle from as early as 1944 and in practice after 1958) rested on currency convertibility at fixed rates of exchange with the dollar. With this security of fixed exchange rates and the plentiful supply of dollars, world trade inside the capitalist bloc grew as never before, as first West Germany and Japan, and later France and briefly Italy, enjoyed 'economic miracles' that transformed

them from supplicants for American aid and defence into major competitors even in American home markets. Indeed, as we shall see, it was their re-emergence as major economic powers, and the growing financial burdens involved in United States military activity overseas (particularly in Vietnam) which in the end eroded the financial stability of Bretton Woods and the economic dominance of the USA, to force dollar devaluation in 1971 and to release massive inflationary forces into the world capitalist system. But for as long as United States economic and political dominance held, so did the boom, and so did the 'space for reform' enjoyed by all Western governments, including those of even a relatively weak national capitalism such as Britain.

The American empire

American dominance was underpinned too by quite enormous military spending and the creation of the most extensive and potentially destructive military machine in human history. Politically and militarily, the boom years were dominated by a cold war and arms race of gigantic proportions, with the level of armaments in one bloc geared to, and responding to, increases in the level of armament in the other. In the Western bloc, the ferocious anti-communism of the cold war years served a number of vital political purposes. It constituted the central defining strand of the official belief system of the West – one central axis on which the political and social systems of the West were legitimated by their rulers, and by which, as a result, popular compliance was guaranteed. Inter-war Europe had lacked such an axis, and class struggle had been rife. In the post-war years the extensive orchestration of anti-communism by state agencies of every kind legitimated the suppression of any manifestation of class conflict and popular radicalism – whether from liberals in McCarthyite America, communist-led trade unions in France and Italy, or radicals in West Germany. Moreover, anti-communism as official ideology legitimated the establishment of United States military installations not just across Western Europe but also in Asian countries bordering the Soviet bloc, and was used to justify United States (and British) economic aid of military support for a whole host of repressive political regimes in the Third World whose governmental élites professed opposition to Soviet, Chinese or (after 1959) Cuban influence. Anti-communist attitudes among Third World governmental élites were enough to win Western toleration (and indeed encouragement) of their internal repression of dissidents or replacement of civilian democratic régimes by military rule. In addition, anti-communism as official ideology underpinned heavy government spending on military equipment and personnel.

It would be quite wrong to see arms production in the West as simply derivative on that of the USSR. In fact it is more likely that it is Russian arms production that sustains its own thrust inside the Soviet political system because of the strength and growth of NATO and other forces around Russia's borders. But even in the Russian case, and certainly in the American, arms production has its own logic and its own place in the heart of the economic and political system, where (to use E. P. Thompson's phrase) it is deeply 'enstructured', and where it is sustained by very powerful internal interests that are less and less open to easy political control.[18] In both blocs powerful military–industrial complexes emerged in the post-war years – each in command of enormous political resources, including jobs, access to the media, proximity to leading politicians, and the capacity to shape dominant definitions of international relations. Indeed, in the West, it has been just these war industries that have functioned in the United States economy 'just as cotton did in the industrial revolution in Britain, as the "leading sector"', not 'as a single or multiple

industrial sector . . . but rather as a cluster of industries joined by a common objective and a common customer. Given an expanded market and an assured, high, rate of profit, this leading sector has in turn stimulated the boom in electronics, civil aerospace etc. as well as in secure enclaves of civilian research and development'.[19] And like growth industries before, military expenditure in the boom years had its own internal contradictions to rob it in the end of its positive impact on economic activity, generating in this case 'both inflationary pressures and unemployment, since the manufacture of advanced weaponry is capital-intensive' and subject to 'its own form of technological obsolescence, as innovation becomes harder to achieve'.[20]

The military industrial complex in the United States economy has now moved through three periods of rapid expansion: in the early days of the cold war, in Vietnam and from the mid 1970s, to bring the United States defence budget to US $69 billion in 1979[21] and to encourage Third World military spending to rise from 10 per cent of the global total in 1960 to 24 per cent in 1978. The USA is, of course, not alone in selling arms there. France currently has 11 per cent of that market to the USA's 47 per cent, with Italy and Britain having 4 per cent each – and significantly, the Soviet Union having 11 per cent. For the arms race is just that, a race between two sides, 'a situation both of antagonism and reciprocity' with 'the increment of weaponry on both sides' taking 'place in part according to a reciprocal logic . . . and regulated by elaborate agreed rules' so that 'what is being produced by the USA and the USSR is the means of war, just as, increasingly, what is being exported, with competitive rivalry, by both powers to the Third World are war materials and attendant militarist systems, infrastructures and technologies'.[22]

This arms race has 'an internal dynamic and reciprocal logic' of its own, but 'this logic, while reciprocal, is not identical'.[23] For the

USSR, as the weaker of the two imperialist powers, an effective case can be made that its military–industrial complex is basically defensive and reactive, driven by a genuine fear of US attack, sustained by bureaucratic infighting within the CPSU, and buttressed by the CPSU's own internal needs as a power élite periodically threatened by dissent *inside* its own empire (Poland and Afghanistan for instance). The motive force in the West is a more obviously capitalist one: the desire for profits by the big corporations coinciding with the world ambitions of the United States ruling class and the powerful ideological currents created in the early cold war years which now possess a logic and an autonomy beyond the control of the class that initiated them. Those capitalist imperatives have combined in the post-war years to guarantee that the boom in Western capitalism under American dominance would be bought at the price of the steady expansion of American military power and the prolific sale of weapons to the governments of the Third World, and the consolidation of a nuclear capacity whose use would destroy not simply capitalism but human existence as we know it. Likewise the decline of American power (and with it the boom) was heralded in the late 1960s by United States military defeat in Vietnam and in the late 1970s by the growing resistance to the deployment of a new generation of United States nuclear weapons in Europe. Capitalist prosperity and arms production were intimately linked in the boom years, and localized wars and internal repression were important Third World consequences of the way in which Western capitalist prosperity was underpinned by American attempts to reduce the appeal there of Soviet politics and development programmes that would close Third World markets to easy penetration by United States capital and commodities.

That facility of capital movement was just one requirement demanded by United States corporations of successive American govern-ments in the post-war years. For it is clear in retrospect that the consolidation of the American empire was a vital prerequisite of generalized economic growth in the West after 1948. By then, if trade across national boundaries was to grow unhindered, a number of state functions had to be performed internationally. Those functions included 'those of a world central bank, organising and controlling the international credit system and acting as a lender of last resort; the guarantee of adequate and appropriate supplies of labour and raw materials; and the maintenance of the necessary international stability and legal system to enable contracts, trade and production to proceed with security'.[24] To a degree since the war, supra-governmental institutions have existed to provide these functions – particularly the IMF and the World Bank, and militarily NATO. But 'the problem with such institutions is that they rarely have any independent power of their own . . . their ability to organise then depends primarily on their status as a representative for a hegemonic power, or on their success in obtaining the support of a powerful group of nation states'.[25] It was America's overwhelming economic and military strength which provided that hegemonic status through the years of the long boom, and allowed the IMF to function as the 'policeman' of an American-directed system,[26] just as it has been the loss of American dominance in the 1970s which has transformed the IMF into the role of 'honest broker' between competing national capitalisms, and seen the boom replaced with more 1930s type conditions of protectionism, recession and unemployment. But for twenty-five years after 1948 American dominance held, and in that period

the US was the king-pin of the world capitalist and imperialist economy, providing the latter with a vehicle (or trading) currency and with much of the capital for economic reconstruction and the internationalisation of production. It was also a key source of the technological innovations necessary for large scale industry in Western Europe and Japan. An international commercial regime of relatively open markets and free trade was created with a supporting system of convertible currencies and fixed exchange rates. This constituted the post-war economic system under US hegemony, to which was added a network of security arrangements to consolidate the balance of power resulting from the war.[27]

The labour force

Three other features of the boom are also important to our understanding of contemporary British politics. The first of these is the *character and situation of the labour force* that it brought into existence. As the boom progressed, a generation of workers emerged used to full employment, workers who – at least in the new growth industries of the boom – were well used by the 1960s to improving their working conditions and pay by localized bargaining through their shop stewards. The boom produced a limited but novel kind of working-class industrial strength that was to have important political consequences, as we shall see, both for state policy and for the way workers viewed the political process and the parties of the Left. Moreover, the growing scarcity of labour drew forward new supplies of less well organized and less experienced workers; and different national capitalisms grew more or less quickly in part because of their differential access to these labour reserves. *Peasants* moved into the cities to fuel the economic growth of France, Japan and Italy. *Women* entered the labour force in increasing numbers, particularly to occupy the lower levels of the new public and private bureaucracies. *Migrants* came from the underdeveloped world literally in their millions to do the 'dirty jobs' that indigenous workers were keen to leave behind. Between 1950 and 1965 seven million people left the Japanese countryside;[28] and prior to 1961 the West

German economy absorbed ten million refugees and foreign workers. Between 1951 and 1971 the percentage of women employed in Great Britain rose from 27 to 42; and in Japan the number of women similarly engaged in wage labour rose from three million to a staggering twelve million in the twenty years after 1950. Women and young people generally were vital new sources of labour for advanced capitalism everywhere in the boom. 'Thus in the United States, for example, the number of adult women employed rose by 71% between 1950 and 1970, and that of employable teenagers by 65%, while the increase in employment of adult males was only 16 per cent in the same two decades.'[29] 'The period 1945–75 (also) witnessed one of the most remarkable peacetime shifts of population in history – comparable in magnitude only to the European migrations to North America in the nineteenth and turn of the twentieth century. Approximately 37 million immigrants arrived in the United States between 1945 and 1975 (and) some 15 million immigrants and their families have settled in Northern Europe.'[30] Each former colonial power drew most heavily for its 'guestworkers' on the under-employed of its former colonies (Algerians and Tunisians went to France, West Indians, Pakistanis and Indians to Britain, and the poor of Mediterranean Europe and Asia Minor to a West Germany unable to draw on any such colonial links).

Moreover, the percentage of that labour force occupied in service industries grew dramatically in the boom years, a shift made possible by the increase in productivity in the manufacturing sector, the growth of state activities and the expansion of private credit and banking functions. Between 1950 and 1973 the percentage of the labour force employed in manufacturing in Great Britain fell from 39.3 per cent to 32.3 per cent, and this was matched by similar expansions of service sectors elsewhere in the economies of the OECD.[31] So many of the social processes which we will discuss in detail later have their origins here – not least the industrial relations practices that await us in Chapter 5 and the social divisions of Part Two (the new white collar salariat, and the patterns of gender and racial discrimination dominant in contemporary Britain). All these will have to be explained in part by referring back to the labour conditions of the long boom. Indeed, as we shall see, that boom ended only when there was a significant alteration in the balance of class forces as a result of just these changes in the labour force, and when the potentially inflationary consequences of a high level of service employment was made evident by a downturn in the rate of growth of productivity in the manufacturing sector. We shall see too that when this happened it was the marginal categories of workers (women and migrants in particular), whose arrival had fuelled the economic expansion, who were to bear (in the company of young male workers) the highest burden of unemployment and social displacement when that expansion ended. In this way, the boom and its demise constitute an important explanatory variable for all that will follow, a key not just to the existence and experience of major social groups whose political demands we will have to chart, but also one source for so much of the social unrest that has characterized Western political life at times since the late 1960s.

State spending

One other casualty of economic stagnation in the 1970s has been state spending on welfare provision; and this fact serves to remind us of a further feature of the long boom – namely the role played in it by high levels of state spending. Throughout the boom, governments in advanced capitalist countries kept their spending at abnormally high peace-time levels, sustaining economic prosperity as they did so by the deliberate use of government funds to alter levels of total demand, socialize costs and maintain political and social stability. Variations in the level of public spending were used – Keynesian style – as a counter-cyclical force, in effect avoiding economic crises by expanding or contracting the basis for private credit, and so easing the full impact of an otherwise unregulated trade cycle by artificially controlling levels of demand for commodities, and hence the ability of firms to realize profits. Public money was also used to purchase directly the products of private industry. For example, 10 per cent of the output of United Kingdom manufacturing industry (and a much higher proportion of output in certain sectors such as aerospace) was, and still is, purchased by central government in Great Britain alone.[32] Public money was used to provide a growing number of public sector jobs and services, and to aid and restructure industry, as electorates looked increasingly to governments to maintain full employment, guarantee rising living standards, and protect the international standing of the home economy in a competitive world order.

The pressure for this level of public expenditure, and this expanded set of government roles, has come from many sources, including both capital and labour, as we shall see in Chapter 3. Large private firms with heavy fixed costs and large research and development budgets increasingly looked to the state for a viable infrastructure of transport networks and credit facilities, assistance in restructuring production processes and finding risk capital, and for guarantees on future levels of wage costs and home demand. That is, they wanted state spending to improve their productivity, stimulate their markets and lower their costs, and they were big enough by the 1950s to let politicians see just how vital that assistance was if the politicians themselves were to retain their popularity. For those politicians also faced pressure from their electorates to expand the range of their spending and responsibilities. In Britain in particular, the labour movement they faced, made more confident initially by their wartime resistance to fascism and then by full employment, looked to governments to guarantee that full employment and to sustain and improve levels of welfare provision, not least for the working class poor, old and sick. 'Public spending (of this kind) both underpinned the boom and permitted the construction of a welfare consensus which created a political context for instrumental bargaining and the integration of the working class into the political system.'[33]

In addition, the governments of certain national capitalisms came under heavy pressure from sections of the state bureaucracy and the growing military–industrial lobby to spend large sums of money on military equipment at home and abroad. They did this partly to keep open markets in the Third World for capital exports and the sale of commodities, partly to allow themselves to play a world role congruent with their imperial traditions and expectations, and partly to lock the West into a terrifying and escalating nuclear arms race with the Warsaw Pact countries. Not all capitalist governments were so militaristic, of course. West Germany and Japan, in particular, were initially subservient and demilitarized through military defeat, and as a result escaped from the full burden of this wasteful military spending.[34] Moreover, Japan shifted a significant proportion of its social provision on to large private companies. By so doing it increased the dependence of Japanese workers on the goodwill of these *zaibatsu*, weakened the Japanese labour movement by leaving that portion of it outside the *zaibatsu* without adequate social provision, and kept the level of government spending significantly below the level elsewhere. Yet overall the trend was clear. Government expenditure grew faster than GDP during the boom in all OECD countries: 23 per cent faster on average overall between 1955 and 1972.[35] Government spending shifted increasingly from war spending to the provision of industrial aid and social welfare; and in the 1960s larger and larger percentages of GDP passed through the hands of state agencies as governments across the capitalist world regulated their own economies to maintain demand and buy electoral popularity and social peace by policies of full employment and a growing social wage. Here too the boom gave way only as the contradictions endemic to this level of spending became evident: as United States military expenditure in Vietnam fuelled inflation, and as low productivity in the public sector combined with high demand for social services and strong public sector trade unionism to produce a generalized 'fiscal crisis' of the state in the 1970s.

Credit and banking

One final feature of the boom is of political importance: that is the enhanced role of credit in, and therefore the centrality of the banking system to, post-war capitalist economic growth. The Western economies literally 'sailed to prosperity on a sea of debt'[36] as credit expansion through the banking system was encouraged and supervised by governments as *the* post-war method of avoiding crises of the inter-war kind. As Mandel put it, 'from the standpoint of the functioning of the international capitalist economy as a whole, the major characteristic of the long phase of post-war expansion was the emergence of a credit cycle partially independent of the industrial cycle, the former attempting to compensate for the latter'.[37] That is, banks lent systematically and on an increasing scale through the post-war years, particularly to individuals and companies but also to governments, and their lending constituted one vital source of investment funds and consumer demand for the products that investment eventually helped to produce. The growth of private debt as a percentage of GDP was quite striking, as Mandel's figures in Table 2 for the United States and West Germany show. Such bank lending within monetary limits set by national governments enabled politicians in the boom years to lubricate production and trade, sustain employment and win votes. But it also set in chain economic processes that would eventually erode the conditions on which the boom was based. It released inflationary pressures sustainable only so long as production continued to grow. It consolidated large industrial monopolies with dangerously low liquidity schedules (or what is the same thing, with enormous fixed costs needing ever greater levels of outputs and sales to keep profit rates intact). And it called into existence ever larger and increasingly internationally-linked banking networks that were less and less subject to control by any one national government, and which were instead more and more prone to link one national capitalist economy to another, so reducing the freedom of manoeuvre of individual national governments in the face of broad trends in the world capitalist economy as a whole. Like the other factors we have mentioned, the expansion of credit both provided the basis for twenty-five years of

sustained economic expansion in the West, and helped to create the conditions in which that economic expansion would in the end falter. But while the boom lasted, governments found that credit control was one of their prime responsibilities, and the banking system one of the most powerful and most internationally co-ordinated centres of private power with which they had to deal.

The end of the long boom

For at least one generation after the war, politicians and their electorates in the Western capitalist democracies came to believe that such Keynesian credit management by the state could guarantee steady and prolonged economic growth, rising living standards and full employment. Yet it is now clear that was not so; such state policies were only one feature of a whole complex of conditions underpinning post-war economic expansion, each one of which contained within itself contradictions that would eventually bring the boom to an end. Indeed, as the 1970s progressed, it became more obvious that Keynesianism was not so much a solution to the crises of capitalism as one key element in

Table 2 *Public and private debt in the United States and West Germany (in thousands of millions of dollars (US) and deutschmarks (WG))*

| | United States | | | | West Germany | | |
	GNP	Public debt	Private debt		GNP	Public debt	Private debt
1946	208.5	269.4	153.4				
1950	284.8	239.4	276.8		98.1	1.2	20.6
1955	398.0	269.8	392.2		181.4	7.0	63.6
1960	503.7	301.0	566.1		284.7	17.6	116.2
1965	684.9	367.6	870.4		460.4	49.5	259.3
1969	932.1	484.7	1383.8				
1970					685.6	95.4	416.7
1973	1294.9	598.4	1947.8				
1974	1397.4	642.9	2134.4				
1975					1043.6	220.6	656.4

Source: E. Mandel, *The Second Slump* (New Left Books 1978), pp. 29, 30.

one phase of capitalist development, a phase that would itself be transcended by the return of crises on a new and higher level.

That is not to say, of course, that the trade cycle vanished entirely between 1948 and 1973. On the contrary, individual economies had their localized booms and slumps even then, as individual governments organized their own anti-cyclical policies. The British economy, for example, was in mild recession between 1961 and 1963, and between 1966 and 1970, and managed a brief but spectacular 5 per cent rate of growth in the speculative boom of 1972–3. But in the boom years, recession in one economy was more than matched by growth in another, so that the output and trade of the capitalist system as a whole never significantly faltered until 1966–7. Instead, 'between 1953 and 1963 the volume of industrial production in the capitalist countries rose 62% while exports rose 82% (and) between 1963 and 1972 industrial production rose 65%, exports 111%'.[38] Then in 1974 and 1975 all the advanced capitalist countries went into recession together. The volume of world trade fell, for the first time since 1948, by at least 7 per cent, and industrial production in all the capitalist powers tumbled with it. An average annual growth rate in the 1960s of 5.1 per cent and a 1973 rate of 6.2 per cent gave way in 1974 to one of 0.1 per cent, and the average growth rate in 1975 actually fell to −1 per cent.[39] The scale of the fall in 1975 is made clear in Table 3.

Thereafter, recovery was limited everywhere, was unevenly distributed, and was characterized by economic recoveries that 'turned out to be not only of limited duration but also of a diminishing size. Evidently, a more basic movement of decline had come to superimpose itself on the cyclical swings in production and employment in the 1970s'.[40] So world trade, which had grown at an annual average of 8.5 per cent per annum between 1963 and 1972, fell back to only a 5.3 per cent growth rate between 1973 and 1982; and once more failed to grow at all in 1981.[41] Moreover, both the recession and the limited recovery were characterized by two phenomena which had been missing from the post-war Western world: high rates of inflation and large-scale unemployment. The incidence of each varied

Table 3   *Differences between maximum industrial production before the recession and minimum industrial production during the recession in the major imperialist countries*

Country	Quarter of maximum production	Quarter of minimum production	Fall in production (per cent)
USA	4th,73	2nd,75	14.4
Canada	1st,74	3rd,75	6.9
Japan	4th,73	1st,75	19.8
West Germany	4th,73	3rd,75	11.8
France	3rd,74	3rd,75	13.6
Britain	4th,73	4th,74	10.1
Italy	2nd,74	3rd,75	15.5
Netherlands	1st,74	3rd,75	11.7
Belgium	1st,74	3rd,75	17.1
Sweden	3rd,74	2nd,75	4.1
Switzerland	2nd,74	1st,75	20.3
Spain	April 74	April 75	10.0

Source: E. Mandel, *The Second Slump* (New Left Books 1978), p. 14.

between different national economies, but each was higher everywhere. Inflation rates in the OECD area had averaged 3.7 per cent in the ten years to 1971. They reached 13.4 per cent in 1974 and 12 per cent in 1975, and 'with an even higher level of unemployment (were still) running at 12–15% on average'[42] in 1980. Officially recorded levels of unemployment in the same economies reached fifteen million by 1975 and twenty million by 1980, and the actual job loss was still greater, augmented by the million migrant labourers 'sent home' from the EEC, and by the massive number of women driven from the labour force (and from official statistics) altogether.[43]

Thereafter, and to the present, politics in the OECD area have been dominated by this industrial stagnation, inflation and unemployment, and by the intensified competition, profits crisis and cutbacks in government spending with which the generalized recession has been associated. Politics have been dominated too, of course, by the differential impact of all these in different countries. As we shall see in the next chapter, the particular weakness of British industrial capital has made the impact, and political consequences, of these trends more severe here than say in West Germany and Japan. But we should not let our pressing local difficulties obscure the fact that 'stagflation' has been a problem even there, and that its origins are not just domestic and local, but lie in the disintegration of the conditions that sustained the long post-war boom across the capitalist world as a whole. Britain's economic problems have at least two – and not just one – sources: not just a weakness of local capital but also a generalized recession across capitalism as a whole. Therefore to understand the limits within which British politicians now operate, and to find the origins of many of the problems and group interests with which they struggle, we need to understand why that recession occurred, and why its coming took the historically unprecedented form of stagnation and inflation together.

Signs of demise

Even before 1973 the signs of impending decline were already evident. As Mandel was later to put it, the whole Western capitalist world was moving from 'a long wave with a basically expansionary tone' to a 'long wave with a basically stagnant'[44] one. As the boom progressed, the advanced capitalist economies traded increasingly with each other, and grew ever more interconnected and interdependent.[45] Their banking networks in particular, as we have already seen, linked the health of one capitalist economy to that of another, as did the ever more multinational scale of operations of the leading private industrial firms in each. 'This internationalisation of production . . . in the form of ever more advanced international concentration and centralisation of capital' ran 'increasingly counter to the attempt of the national . . . states successfully to apply anti-cyclical policies, the impact of which remain[ed] essentially limited to national frontiers'.[46] As a result, politicians found that the 'space' for their own industrial-credit cycle was increasingly restricted by the resulting re-emergence of a world trade cycle, and that it was less and less possible for 'a decline in production and domestic demand in the countries hit by recession (for example, the United States in 1960 or West Germany in 1966–7) . . . to be compensated by an expansion in exports to countries that had escaped the crisis'.[47] Politicians were already finding, that is, that after 1966 booms were, when they came, shorter and more speculative in character than had been the norm between 1948 and 1966, and that 'a synchronisation of the international industrial cycle'[48] was beginning to emerge again for the first time since the 1930s. As a result, all the advanced capitalist economies expanded together between 1971 and 1973, and by demanding raw materials in increasing quantities at exactly the same moment, fuelled a primary commodities boom that quickened the rate of domestic inflation even before the Yom Kippur war and the emergence of a more powerful OPEC.[49] As we know, all the advanced capitalist economies did not simply expand together. They also slumped together in 1974 in the economic crisis triggered by OPEC's action.

Technology

That the Western capitalist economies should have been so vulnerable to that oil crisis reflected more than a heavy dependence on Middle Eastern fuel sources. *It reflected too the erosion of those five processes that had underpinned the boom: the third technological revolution, United States hegemony, the reserve army of labour, state spending and expanded credit.* To take technology first: the vulnerability of the Western economies in the early 1970s reflected in part the way in which productivity was no longer growing so quickly and so extensively through the application of automated production processes in the boom industries. As we have seen, 'the more or less general increase in the application of labour saving fixed capital provided the main source for the otherwise impressive increase in labour productivity and national income growth'[50] between 1948 and 1973, by reducing the real cost of raw materials, foods and manufactured goods; and 'the virtual collapse' of this growth in labour productivity in capitalist industry in the 1970s was itself one important cause of the quickening inflation rate of the decade. Currently, 'in the United States the growth of productivity may now be negative. Elsewhere productivity growth has more than halved, with the exception of West Germany'.[51] Why this should have been so is less obvious, but it seems to have involved two things. It is not simply that 'the technological backlog accumulated during the war was [now] used up' as Europe and Japan 'copied and adopted the more advanced US production techniques'. It was also that 'as each of

these countries accumulated large capital stocks specific to particular types of process and technology, the costs of changing (in particular, the need to scrap large amounts of existing plant and equipment) grew larger, inhibiting productivity growth'.[52]

The decline of the United States

The vulnerability of the Western capitalist economies to OPEC in 1974 also reflected the weakening economic and military position of the United States. The twenty-five years in which United States governments had 'fought socialism' on a world scale by military adventures and the support of anti-communist ruling classes was bought at a high price in the United States itself. Manufacturing investment there remained sluggish, with too much industrial plant protected from the full rigours of international competition by guaranteed 'cost-plus' arms sales to the United States government, and with too much American capital flowing abroad.[53] By the late 1960s the military might of the United States faced defeat in Vietnam, and the USA's post-war economic lead had already been eroded by the rise of strong competitor economies in West Germany and Japan. One striking indicator of that is the level of manufacturing production. 'Through 1966, the total value of North American manufacturing production was higher than that of Western Europe and Japan combined. Since 1975, however, it has been lower than that of Western Europe alone.'[54] In 1971, for the first time this century, America's trade balance went into deficit, 'imports exceeding exports by $2.7 billion',[55] as the greater productivity of these new economies cut American exports and left the American internal market open to West German and Japanese commodities. 'The US share of industrial exports went down from 28.7% in 1957 to 18.9% in 1970, when it was surpassed (at least briefly) by that of West Germany.'[56] The overall American balance of trade was weakened further by massive military spending in Vietnam, and by the export of capital by United States companies seeking increasingly profitable outlets, particularly in Europe.[57]

This flow of dollars occasioned by trade deficits, capital export and the Vietnam war increased the money supply in the capitalist world economy as a whole, and as productivity rates slackened, fuelled inflation. Moreover, because Western economies no longer needed dollars to buy United States goods on anything like the scale of the 1950s, these dollars stockpiled in Western European banks. There were less than US $7 billion such dollars in the vaults of foreign central banks in 1952, but over US $150 billion in 1980, US $140 billion of which were held in Europe, and by 1979 the major commercial banks of Western Europe held a further US $427 billion – dollars that they had not surrendered to their own central authorities and which they retained instead to augment their own assets.[58] These accumulated and unwanted dollars constituted the base of a new credit source – Eurodollars – lent in large units by those banks to increasingly hard-pressed multinationals struggling to maintain sales and profits in ever more sluggish markets and in the face of ever-greater competition. This Eurodollar credit system expanded at 'dizzy speed' in the 1960s and 1970s, largely from London and effectively outside the control of any national government, and came to constitute an important source of extra money in the international capitalist system, and, as such, an extra source of inflation as production stagnated.[59] In the end, the decline of United States capitalism's competitiveness became so advanced that the European banking system's growing resistance to the holding of dollars (first in France in 1964, and generally by 1971) forced dollar devaluation in 1971 – and in so doing destroyed the system of fixed exchange rates tied to the dollar on which post-war growth had depended.

Labour force

That growth, in any case, was being increasingly jeopardized by difficulties of two other kinds: by an alteration in the balance of class forces produced by twenty-five years of economic growth and full employment; and by a generalized crisis of profits in the big multinational corporate sector that had dominated that growth and employment process. By the late 1960s labour was in short supply in many OECD countries, and groups of workers in many manufacturing industries had already established a significant degree of control over their own working conditions and take-home pay. 'Several decades of sustained accumulation had virtually exhausted the huge post-war reserves of unemployed and cheap rural labour. Although employers imported foreign workers, they were never able to do so on a sufficient scale to eliminate the shortages',[60] and the social impediments blocking the easy entry of female workers into the wage labour force also helped to bolster male working class industrial strength. Skilled workers in particular had consolidated a uniquely strong bargaining position for themselves in the growth industries of the boom by the late 1960s; and this new-found industrial power and confidence of workers in late capitalism was reflected both in the political importance attached to adequate social welfare provision by governments, and in the wave of industrial unrest that swept France in 1968, Italy in 1969–70, and Britain between 1970 and 1973. The share of wages in national income rose significantly in the 1960s, as the rate of surplus value extraction managed by the growth sectors of late capitalism began to falter: 'between 1965 and 1972 real wage earnings in manufacturing industry rose by 1.8% p.a. in the US, 7.3% in Japan, 5.7% in West Germany and 2.8% in Britain. This growth in real earnings coupled with the improvements in the social wage undermined the previously high rate of earnings on capital and emerged as a major barrier to the future accumulation of capital'.[61]

In terms of traditional Marxist political economy, this rise in working class strength prevented the capitalist class from offsetting the adverse impact on profits of a rising organic composition of capital[62] by any easy increase in the rate of extraction of surplus value. For it is clear that, quite independently of this working class militancy, the big corporate giants responsible for up to half of the industrial production of the advanced capitalist economies by the late 1960s were themselves experiencing problems of profit realization and capital accumulation, problems created by the sheer volume of investment associated with the long boom. The technological changes that lay beneath the boom had required massive capital outlays, leaving the companies making those outlays with enormous fixed costs that were coverable only if sales were of an equally large scale, and in any case had drawn the companies into ever larger research and development programmes as the only reliable way of maintaining their competitive edge. In such a context, size was of the essence, and as the boom reached its peak companies in the growth sectors of late capitalism reacted to the first signs of faltering demand by participating in a merger boom of 1920s proportions. Then, using their new-found size to penetrate not simply the export but also the home markets of their competitors, they participated in an ever more intense and desperate competitive battle which further reduced profit levels and brought even giant companies to the edge of bankruptcy and beyond. Thus by 1973 the rate of profit accruing to these enormous and vulnerable economic dinosaurs had fallen to levels that were no longer capable of easily sustaining the rate of accumulation and growth common in the twenty-five years before. It is significant here just how early that crisis of profits in the corporate sector had begun. 'There were clear signs *generally* of a decline in profitability in the late 60s and early 70s, *prior* to the slump of 1974 onwards. Since the early 1970s was a period of general boom when profitability would usually be expected to rise, this is clear evidence of growing strains in the international capitalist economy well before the slump developed.'[63] Therefore, it should never be forgotten that, even before the oil crisis of 1973–4, politicians in the advanced capitalist world had already begun to face not only militant labour movements, but also monopoly firms in desperate financial straits and economies subject to ever more intense foreign competition and import penetration.

Inflationary forces

So even before the oil crisis broke, the basis of the post-war boom was already under attack: as the growth rate of technologically-induced productivity waned, as American dominance eased, as Bretton Woods collapsed and as the multinational companies of the boom began again to experience problems of labour shortages and declining profit levels. What the oil crisis then did was to spark off a generalized recession that released strong inflationary forces into depressed economies. The oil crisis did not produce either stagnation or inflation. It simply enhanced both. Even before it broke, the last 'rush to growth' of 1971–3 was already releasing massive inflationary pressures. Inflation was already present in the system from 1945, manifesting itself first as a slow but steady fall in the value of money caused by the 'repeated application of a policy of monetary expansion every five or six years',[64] and one kept in check in the boom years only by the dramatic rise in labour productivity in the manufacturing sectors of the OECD that we have already discussed. By 1973, the rate of inflation was quickening everywhere for a number of important reasons. Labour productivity was no longer rising fast enough to keep pace with the wage levels of the massive state and private sector bureaucracies it had hitherto sustained, bureaucracies whose members were too well-entrenched to be cut down in size quickly and easily. Inflation was growing too because years of full employment and relatively easy market conditions had softened management, and left key groups of workers well placed to block any rapid changes in, and intensification of, work routines. Inflation was quickening too because the large companies created in the boom responded to any fall in demand not by reducing prices, but by increasing them. As oligopolies in their own home markets, they had that option. With heavy fixed costs, they had that need; and governments allowed them to do that (that is, governments responded to signs of recession in the early 1970s by increasing levels of credit) because politicians feared the domestic consequences of allowing big companies to go into liquidation.[65] That the politicians had that option by the early 1970s was itself a consequence of the fall of Bretton Woods. All Western governments (not just the American government) were able in 1972 and 1973 to increase their own money supplies, because they were no longer constrained by fixed exchange rates. Instead they were able to sustain home demand, bear extra import bills and see domestic inflation quicken, by allowing their exchange rates to float downwards with no external control. The result was an enormous increase in the money supply in the international capitalist system as a whole. In all these ways the break up of the conditions underpinning the post-war boom was already producing inflationary waves through the Western economies prior to 1973. OPEC's reaction to the Yom Kippur war then simply made things worse.

When OPEC put up its oil prices four times in 1974 it did a number of things. By adding to fuel costs, OPEC's price rises at least temporarily shifted the terms of trade away from the Western capitalist powers, and reduced the ability of profit rates there to be sustained by unequal exchange between the First World and the Third. More immediately, by creating massive balance of payments problems for all Western governments, OPEC's price rises forced them to deflate (and hence bring the boom of 1971–3 to an abrupt end) earlier and more severely than they might otherwise have done; and by inducing 'a diminution both in world income and in export possibilities for all countries'[66] made it more difficult for even the big multinational companies to realize their profits. In that way OPEC intensified the profits crisis of the corporate sector. Moreover, by concentrating large quantities of money capital in the hands of oil-producing governments, they added an extra speculative dimension to the workings of international money markets and to the volatility of exchange rates, as those governments recycled their petro-dollars into the Western banking system, and then moved their capital about there in an attempt to sustain its real value amid the inflationary spiral and weak currencies they were helping to create. By adding to the energy costs of capitalist production, OPEC fuelled Western inflation, and altered the balance of competitive forces within the system as a whole. National capitalisms highly dependent on imported oil were relatively weakened, particularly 'Europe, Japan and those non oil-producing developing countries that are excluded from the channels of private international credit'.[67] But technologies inefficient in the use of energy (the American and the British rather than the Japanese and the West German) also suffered a competitive loss. Japan, in particular, was able to offset the extra import bills for fuel by quickly replacing inefficient capital stock and rapidly increasing its exports, whereas 'elsewhere much fixed capital could no longer be operated profitably at existing prices given the increase in fuel costs'.[68] As a result, from 1974 onwards, the ruling classes of each national capitalism vied with the others for advantage in a world system beset by expensive fuel, and characterized by uneven and generally lower rates of growth of trade and production; and faced a Third World divided into the oil rich (who began a rapid process of internal industrialization) and a Fourth World of the poor and the oil-less, whose experience of the world recession was of truly horrendous proportions.

Inter-imperialist rivalry

In the depressed conditions that the oil crisis left behind, national policies had to operate, not simply within the limits set by the struggle internally between capital and labour, but also within limits fixed by a world-wide struggle for relative economic advantage waged between the ruling classes of the two big power blocs, and within the capitalist bloc, between advanced and less developed capitalisms and between advanced capitalisms themselves. Behind the regularly reported figures on the changing exchange rate of the dollar against the pound, the mark and the yen, and behind the wrangles of ministers at one EEC or OECD summit after another, lay a bitter battle for relative position waged by politicians on behalf of the national economies on whose health their own political survival so intimately depended. In that battle, as the 1970s progressed, advantage shifted away from the weak to the strong (from Britain and Italy among the advanced capitalisms to West Germany, Japan and the USA; from an oil-less Fourth World to OPEC in the less advanced) – from those, that is, who were already insufficiently competitive to be unable to offset extra oil bills by rapidly increasing their exports, to those who were competitive, and to those to whom extra oil bills meant extra revenue. Advantage shifted even within the strong, back from OPEC to the advanced West as recycled petro-dollars, low levels of oil demand, a weakening dollar, inflated prices for manufactured goods and ambitious development programmes eroded OPEC's initial leverage; and in the West itself, away from West Germany and Japan as the United States' unique ability to pay for its oil in its own currency gave it a margin for internally-generated economic growth still denied to the rest.

International economic life in the capitalist bloc since 1974 has been dominated by the struggle for economic advantage between these three big capitalist powers: West Germany, Japan and the United States. Their exports have competed with one another at home and abroad. Their governments have sought to protect their own markets, and open those of others, in a series of unilateral trade restrictions and tough bilateral trade negotiations.[69] Each has striven to mould the pattern of international credit and military alliances to facilitate its exports alone; and each has at times sought to depress the exchange rate of its currency in the pursuit of market advantage. The United States has been particularly active in all these fields, seeking to reconstitute its own dominant position by deliberate government policy, but never able quite to succeed because of the sheer competitive power of highly efficient German and Japanese manufacturing capital.[70] All three economies pulled steadily out of the 1974 recession: the United States by internal expansion, West Germany and Japan by a spectacular growth in the volume of their exports. As they grew the weaker capitalist powers slipped back still further, locked into an increasingly subordinate position not just by oil bills but by the penetration of their home markets (and the erosion of their balance of payments) by West German and Japanese manufactured imports. Britain and Italy in particular were left behind in recession in 1976 and 1977, and were back there by 1980, in spite of the resurgence of the three big economies, because their governments were obliged to deflate levels of home demand for balance of payments reasons – reasons intimately connected (in Italy's case) with oil bills and (in Britain's) with heavy imports of foreign manufactured goods.

Politicians in those weaker economies lived in hope of a rapid return to a generalized expansion in world trade that never came – one, in fact, that was blocked by fierce inter-imperialist rivalries within the capitalist bloc. The United States in particular had no interest in the emergence of a new internationally acceptable currency that could lubricate world trade, if that currency was not dollar-based, for that would only reduce the USA's own ability to expand internally while running balance of payments deficits, and would only strengthen still further the position of its West German and Japanese competitors. They for their part were insufficiently strong economically or militarily to superimpose their own alternative world currency or their own hegemonic role, but they were strong enough to challenge the United States at every stage; and the resulting plethora of economic summits between capitalist powers after 1974 was one testament to just how much 'brokerage' of interests between strong competitor economies had to go on to maintain the stability of the system as a whole. The ruling classes of the United States, West Germany and Japan were able to ease the pressure of their own class struggles by exploiting their relative advantage in a capitalist world no longer characterized by rapid economic growth, and in so doing denied to the ruling classes of the weaker capitalisms a similar route to easy politics through a more generalized and higher level of economic expansion. It is in this very important sense that politics in Britain in the last quarter of the century was, and is, constrained by the barriers to world economic growth created by the struggle between the ruling classes of stronger capitalist powers in the wake of the 1974 recession.

State spending and credit expansion

In such depressed and inflation-ridden production and trading conditions, politicians here in Britain quickly found that 'they could no longer spend their way out of recession'. Keynesian policies could no longer cope with the simultaneous emergence of inflation and unemployment, not least because, in Keynesian terms, policy solutions to one could only intensify the other. Instead, politicians found that state spending had itself become a further cause of inflation, as massive public sector wage bills were not matched by the production of sufficient commodities in the manufacturing sector, and as productivity in the service parts of the public sector remained stubbornly low. Nor could they easily use enhanced supplies of credit to fuel new economic expansion. Even the control of the money supply in total was difficult with the Eurodollar market so autonomous and the multinational banking network so extensive; and where controls could hold it was now clear that profit margins were too low, and outdated capital stock too abundant and underutilized, to allow extra money to pull forward investment and output rather than inflate prices. State welfare spending that fuelled inflation had itself become a barrier to private capital accumulation, and politicians found themselves trapped between political demands for extra state spending to maintain the generalized legitimacy of the system and the private corporate sector's need to reduce that welfare spending to facilitate price stability and accumulation.

The political life of the advanced capitalist world is now dominated by the diminished impact of Keynesian policies of credit control. Each successive recession from the mid 1960s required ever greater injections of money into the circuit of capitalist production and exchange to draw forward extra industrial output, and had additional inflationary consequences whenever that production faltered. This growing inflationary pressure meant that recessions had to be initiated sooner, and depressions allowed to run deeper, to keep inflation at bay. The weaker the productive base of the national capitalism, the sooner that recovery had to halt, and the higher domestic interest rates had to be maintained to attract speculative capital from abroad; but even governments in strong economies learnt in the 1970s that they 'had to moderate the application of the anti-crisis techniques so as to avert runaway inflation'[71] and to prevent their inflation rate leaping far higher than that of their keenest capitalist rivals. As the stronger economies pulled out of recession after 1974, they did so by seeing 'a new swelling of credit and international credit money'[72] but this time one directed increasingly to creditors in semi-colonial countries. By the end of 1977 the debts of these countries to the international banking network stood at US $250 thousand million: 'Brazil alone [in 1976] owed $14 thousand million to US private banks',[73] and the debts of Zaïre, Zambia and a host of other Third World non oil-producing countries were equally astronomic. In fact, 'the average Third World country now has an external debt of 29% of annual output, and debt servicing (interest and scheduled loan repayments) represents 16 per cent of exports'.[74] As the level of debt in the world system increased, so too did the vulnerability of the world banking networks that supplied that debt. Any flight from money into gold sparked by an inflationary surge, or any defaulting by a major international debtor (country or multinational company), threatened to bring a financial collapse of 1929 proportions; and the banking system had as a result to take an ever tougher line with debtor governments in an attempt to ease the rate of growth of international debt. No international agency or individual government had the economic resources or political will to underwrite those debts entirely, and yet 'nothing less than a total restructuring of the monetary system, and with it the destruction of the existing volume of virtually unredeemable credit [could] provide the conditions for a new phase of capitalist economic recovery and expansion with price stability'.[75]

In all these ways, banking instability added its impact to that of diminishing labour productivity and inter-imperialist rivalry to lessen the capacity of governments to alleviate their own class struggles through Keynesian policies of demand management. As the need grew for governments to spend to bolster the legitimacy of an economic and social system in deep crisis, the very depth and character of that crisis blocked the capacity of governments to make that spending without adding still further to the crisis they wished to alleviate. Here in its essence was the paradox of politics bequeathed to the governments of the capitalist bloc by the end of the long boom in the 1970s.

Politics in recession

From 1974 politicians everywhere in the OECD operated within very tight economic constraints. World trade was either stagnant or growing only slowly, and competition between economies was intense. An era of liberalized trade was being replaced by one of growing protectionism. An era of fixed exchange rates had given way to one of floating rates and competitive devaluations. Relative price stability had given way to inflation, labour shortages to mass unemployment, low interest rates to high ones, and growing state spending to an era of cuts in welfare provisions. The crisis was not world wide, but fell most heavily on the older industrialized powers and the oil-less underdeveloped world; and even between them a new international division of labour was emerging, initiated by the growing propensity of multinational companies to locate at least the labour-intensive part of their manufacturing processes in certain low wage economies of the Third World. There at least, industrial output was growing rapidly. These Third World economies raised their share of world capitalist output from 10 per cent in 1950 to 20 per cent by 1978, as the export of capital by multinationals consolidated new 'dependent' industrial economies in the repressive political conditions of South Korea, Singapore, the Philippines, Brazil and Taiwan: dependent in the sense of being locked into (and therefore dependent upon) international processes of production and sales on a world scale. In this regard it is significant that multinational 'corporations in 1970–2 accounted for nearly 70% of the manufactured exports of Singapore, 43% of Brazil, 30% of Mexico, 20% of Taiwan, 15% of South Korea and at least 30% of the Argentine'.[76] The result there was intensified labour exploitation; and in the decaying centres of advanced capitalism, a process of 'deindustrialization' that constrained the space for political manoeuvre still further.

Politicians in the weaker capitalisms found that companies could be sustained, if they could be sustained at all, only by extensive government aid, and by assistance in weakening the power of labour movements. Politicians there found too that they could not run fully-employed economies by persistently inflating levels of home demand, because to do so just made prices rise disproportionately at home, sucked in foreign imports, and undermined the export potential of their own national companies. Instead they found that to the degree that the resulting balance of payments deficits could be financed by foreign loans, the terms of those loans, as well as reasons of national competitive strength, obliged them to pursue price stability before full employment. That in its turn committed them to challenging not the power of private capital, whose dominance had produced the crisis, but its subsidiary causes: high levels of welfare spending and working class industrial strength. As we shall see in Part Three, in Britain at least the political casualty of that was the hitherto dominant political Centre, as the programmes of both Left and Right radicalized in the face of the bankruptcy of the Keynesianism that had underpinned the state

policies of the boom years. In fact the general political legacy from the 1970s recession in many weakening capitalist powers was some version of the British scenario: a socialist 'alternative economic policy' of the Labour Left variety facing a resurgent monetarism *à la* Thatcher, with the social forces able to resist the latter significantly weakened by the spread of mass unemployment.

These issues will be discussed more fully in Part Three. All that has to be grasped now is the extent to which the character of the capitalist world economy, the social and economic processes at work within it, and the logic of its periods of expansion and depression, remain key sources of information for the student of British politics. It is in that world order, as we have seen, that are to be found the origins of so many of the economic problems, social processes, and private groups and institutions that shape political life here. It is in that world order that we can locate the origins of many of the economic *problems* that beset the British state (economic recession, unemployment, inflation, international competition and deindustrialization); many of the *institutions* that impinge on the British state from outside (international financial agencies, multinational corporations, competitor economies and their governments); and many of the *social processes* altering the internal shape of class relations in Britain (not least the rise of a white collar 'salariat', the bitter relations between ethnic groups, and the particular sexual division of labour). None of these problems, institutions and processes can be explained solely in such international terms, but each of them has to be situated in that wider international context before it can be fully understood. We must keep this permanently in mind as we move now to look in detail at the impact of more localized economic and social processes on the character of recent British political life.

3   The weakness of the British economy

Very large sections of British political life have been dominated of late, not simply by world recession, but by the particularly poor performance of the British economy in that recession. This poor performance has become a major political issue, on which the fate of governments has regularly been settled; and it has in addition coloured many other aspects of political activity, by restricting the tax base for social expenditure, by generating only a restricted supply of usable commodities, and by accentuating a whole range of class antagonisms, from poverty to racism and beyond. Those problems, and that restricted tax base, await us in Parts Two and Three. What we must examine now is the character and scale of the economic weakness that lies behind them.

The rhythm of boom and slump in the world economy has overlain both the visibility and the trajectory of British economic decline. In the boom years the British economy grew sluggishly by international standards, but more steadily than it had done at any other point this century. Between 1951 and 1973 the average annual rate of economic growth in Britain was 2.8 per cent, and that was enough to guarantee full employment and rising living standards for a generation, and to bring thirteen years of unbroken Conservative rule after 1951. The return to power of Labour in 1964 was the first major political consequence of the growing signs of relative economic decline – a decline which in the 1960s manifested itself in the form of balance of payments crises, threats to sterling, government-induced deflation in response to

both, and as a result, rising unemployment. As the British economy lost its hold on world trade (between 1950 and 1979 the share of world trade captured by commodities manufactured in Britain fell from 25.5 per cent to 9.7 per cent) the penetration of the home economy by foreign imports rose steadily, giving balance of payments deficits in 1957, 1961 and 1966–7, and undermining foreign confidence in the exchange rate of the pound (and hence in sterling's role as capitalism's second reserve currency). The pound was devalued against the dollar in 1967 (from US $2.80 to US 2.40), and after 1971 (when exchange rates floated) it lost value still further (sinking to less than US $1.60 against a weakened dollar in the financial crisis of 1976). In 1961, 1966–70 and 1976 governments deflated the economy to ease balance of payments pressures, and so reduced still further an already sluggish rate of economic growth. The level of industrial production in Britain at the very end of the long post-war boom (when ironically Britain was on a three day week under government orders) was not attained again until late 1978, and by 1982 the economy had returned to deep recession once more. Unemployment (which had been 331,000 in 1966) stood at 3.19 million by July 1982. Industrial production had fallen by 15 per cent in just one twelve-month period after December 1979 – a rate of decline significantly faster than in even the worst years of the Great Depression (5.5 per cent in 1878–9) or between the wars (6.9 per cent in 1930–1). And this is not to be explained as a general feature of late capitalism. Elsewhere in the OECD, economies averaged a 3 per cent annual growth rate after 1975, and productivity rose by anything from 14 per cent to 29 per cent. Not so in Britain. Productivity here rose only by 5 per cent per annum between 1974 and 1979, and 'no other advanced capitalist country . . . experienced a fall [in output] in recent years [that was] remotely comparable'.[1]

A significant percentage of the spectacular industrial collapse of the early 1980s has been a direct product of Thatcherism, but it is not all to be dismissed in that way. On the contrary, the roots of economic decline run deep and far back, and have been closely associated with three other features of political and international life that are worth commenting on. The first has been the rise of strong overseas competition. It is not simply that the British economy has stagnated. It is rather that it has fallen back into the second league of capitalist powers, left behind (and increasingly squeezed from foreign markets) by the revival of West German, Japanese and French capitalism. This relative decline is clear in the figures in Table 4, which show that 'UK growth has lagged behind that of other capitalist economies for more than a century' and 'that the shortfall since the second world war has been much larger and more sustained than that of any earlier period'.[2]

Alongside this economic decline has gone a diminution in the world role of the British ruling class, and a loss of that imperial glory which was so important an element cementing the loyalty of the vast mass of the British people after 1870 to the highly unequal class structure over which those ruling groups presided. 'No country's fall from international power has been more dramatic than that of Britain. Fifty years ago Britain controlled an Empire containing one-fifth of the world's population. Today it is a fairly unimportant member of the western alliance and the European Economic Community.'[3] Economic life here between 1947 and 1976 was dominated by government attempts to keep sterling as a reserve currency – the symbol of Britain's world role – on the basis of an economy that no longer had the competitive edge to justify it; and sterling crises faded from the political agenda only with the arrival of North Sea oil and only when sterling's reserve status had finally been abandoned in the face of foreign reluctance to accept pounds in lieu of stronger currencies or of gold. Political life in the same period was shaped by a retreat from empire, and the reluctant acceptance by the governing élite that their influence on the world stage could only operate – if it could operate at all – either through a special relationship of subordination to the United States or as part of a stronger alliance of European states. Though the move from empire to Commonwealth was accepted without defeat in a major land war, it was forced by sustained nationalist and

Table 4 *Annual rate of growth of GDP at constant prices*

	1870–1913	1922–9	1929–37	1951–73	1973–9
France	1.6	4.4	−0.5	5.1	2.9
Germany	2.8	4.2	2.6	5.9	2.3
Japan	2.5	2.9	4.8	9.5	4.0
USA	4.1	3.3	−0.2	3.5	2.3
Italy	1.5	2.9	1.4	5.2	2.3
United Kingdom	1.9	2.6	2.0	2.8	0.8

Source: G. B. Stafford, 'The class struggle, the multiplier and the Alternative Economic Strategy', in M. Sawyer and K. Schott (eds.), *Socialist Economic Review 83* (Merlin 1983), p. 3.

guerrilla struggle that lasted half a century (from India after 1910 to Cyprus in the 1950s) and even then did not bring any automatic dismantling of the extended military apparatus consolidated in the heyday of imperialism. The trauma of Suez in 1956, and of economic decline thereafter, brought a scaling down of overseas military deployment – a retreat from East of Suez in the 1960s – but to date British military expenditure remains disproportionately high (second in volume within NATO to that of the USA, though Britain is now only eleventh in the league table of prosperity within that alliance), and governments are still capable of launching ambitious military projects against second league powers, as in the Falklands crisis of 1982. The pathetic sight of repeated prime ministerial attempts to assert Britain's special relationship with the United States in the face of American indifference, and the cult of Dunkirk and Churchill in which at times politicians immerse themselves, are just two symptoms of the political tensions created in this period of adjustment to the loss of world power.

Finally, in setting the context for a discussion of the origins of Britain's economic decline, it is worth remembering too just how long that decline has gone on, and for just how many decades it has preoccupied politicians, commentators and academics. 'Since 1910 at least it has all been "crises", save for those few years in the fifties when we had it so good (a slogan invented, characteristically, just when it had become plain that the post-war UK boom was over and we would soon be back to crisis as usual).'[4] The political discussion of economic decline in the 1960s and 1970s echoed earlier debates in the 1890s and 1920s, and in so doing stood as evidence of the longevity of the problem and of the intractability of the processes producing it.[5] In that sense contemporary politics in Britain is still engaged in a process of adjustment to the loss of world domination that first occurred a century ago, as economies with higher rates of productivity began to consolidate their own world role.

The figures on productivity rates in various economies are particularly striking, and take us to the heart of the economic problem faced now by governments seeking industrial regeneration. The figures in Table 5 make very clear how pitifully slowly, in comparative terms, industrial productivity in Britain grew even in the twenty-five years prior to 1914, and how slowly that productivity has grown still in the twenty-five years just gone. What the figures do not make explicit, but which we need to see too, is that prior to 1914 that weakness in productivity was hardly disastrous, because in absolute terms British industrial capital still 'enjoyed a higher level of productivity than most of its competitors' and because the proportion of goods traded internationally was low by modern standards. Neither of those things are true today. In 1970 'UK industrial productivity was approximately one-third of the US level, two-thirds that of France, West Germany and the smaller northern European economies, and about the same as the Italian level'.[6] It is not surprising then that by 1970 Britain had slipped from the position of leading capitalist economic power to one characterized by low wages, low profits and low investment, and one in which the quality and cost of its manufactured exports were increasingly unimpressive by international standards. It was this process of rapid

Table 5 *Phases of productivity growth, 1870–1976 (annual average compound growth rates)*

	1870–1913	*1913–50*	*1950–76*
France	1.8	1.7	4.9
Germany	1.9	1.2	5.8
Italy	1.2	1.8	5.3
Japan	1.8	1.4	7.5
United States	2.1	2.5	2.3
United Kingdom	1.1	1.5	2.8

and persistent economic decline that government after government was called upon to rectify, and which in its intractibility brought government after government to electoral defeat. For between 1959 and 1979 no government managed to win the election that closed its first full five-year term of office; and that too must be taken as an index of economic decline and its political consequences.

Elements of decline

Commentators have often noted, for the 1890s no less than the 1980s, that there are qualitative as well as quantitative elements in Britain's economic decline. The quantitative ones are striking enough. The percentage of GNP being invested in manufacturing plant and equipment in Britain is, and has been for a long time, low by international standards. Table 6 gives the results of an OECD survey for the period 1955–68, which shows clearly that the United Kingdom's annual average investment as a percentage of GNP falls well short of the Western European norm. The figures for 1973 are even more dramatic: 18.5 per cent of GDP invested in the USA, 20.9 per cent in Italy, 24 per cent in France, 24.6 per cent in West Germany, and 36.6 per cent in Japan – but only 19.8 per cent in the United Kingdom.[7] So is not surprising that 'one study in 1978 estimated that the fixed assets /worker in manufacturing in the UK was only £7,500, compared with £23,000 in West Germany and £30,000 in Japan'.[8] If home investment has been low, capital export has at times been just the reverse. 'Britain's annual investments abroad began actually to exceed her net capital formation at home'[9] as early as 1870, and were running at 7 per cent of GNP by 1914, when domestic investment was only 5 per cent. Capital exports, which eased significantly between the wars, have also grown again of late, particularly after the Conservative government removed controls on capital movements in 1979. These two features of the

Table 6 *Average annual investment: total GNP (percentage, measured at current prices)*

Norway	29.4
Netherlands	24.3
West Germany	24.2
Austria	23.8
France	21.6
Italy	20.9
Belgium	19.7
Denmark	19.5
United Kingdom	16.4

Source: S. Hughes and J. R. Davies, *Investment in the British Economy* (Heinemann 1980), p. 17.

British investment experience have inspired regular demands from the Left for the control of capital exports, the public ownership of financial institutions, the expansion of state-directed investment, and the scaling down of military expenditure at home and overseas, as key elements in the restoration of industrial grown and full employment.

Critics of that 'alternative economic strategy' have been able to point to a number of features of that investment pattern which complicate life significantly for the Labour Left. They have pointed to the fact that investment funds have never been in short supply. Capital exports have been all but matched by imports of capital (particularly American) since the mid 1960s, and 'the overwhelming view expressed in evidence to the Wilson Committee . . . is that the availability of external finance has not been a significant restraint on industrial investment in the UK'.[10] Critics have shown too how the gap between investment levels here and in competitor economies has *narrowed* of late, at the very time when the gap between growth rates has *widened*. And they have also been able to show that, where investment levels have been the same between industries in different countries, the output/unit of investment has been systematically lower here than elsewhere. So they have argued that capital export is less a cause than a symptom, better seen as an intelligible response by financial institutions to deep seated blockages to productivity growth in Britain, blockages 'whose origins lie deep in the social system'[11] and in particular in the quality of, and relationship between, managerial practices and trade union power in British industry. In this argument there is a tendency to play down tensions within the capitalist class between financial and industrial interests in favour of an emphasis on a tension between capital and labour.

Both sides of this debate can contribute to our understanding of the nature of Britain's economic decline, and the choice between them is false and misleading. British governments have been defeated so far in their pursuit of industrial regeneration partly by the character of the political élite to which they themselves belong, and partly by the particular balance of class forces that surrounds them – by characteristics, that is, of both capital and labour that block easy industrial change, and whose origins lie deep in the history of capitalist industrialization in Britain. It is not just that the economic problem faced by governments is intractable here because of its longevity. It is also that that longevity is itself a reflection of the fact that it was in Britain that capitalist industrialization began, and that governments still face problems arising from that early beginning.

The fact that Britain industrialized first has had very long term consequences, both here and abroad. Early capitalist industrialization in Britain gave industrial capital here, in the middle of the nineteenth century, a brief period of world domination. In mid century, 'one-third of the world's output of manufactured goods came from Britain. Britain provided half the world's coal and iron, half the world's cotton goods, almost half its steel. From this position Britain conducted one-quarter of the world's trade, and built up a massive commercial and financial predominance'.[12] That lead was unique, and was lost as

soon as competitors appeared, but the fact of its temporary existence gave to British industrial interests a particular attitude to economic growth and to state action quite different from the attitudes of similar industrialists elsewhere.

The response of the British ruling class, and its industrial section, to the challenge to its industrial dominance from the industrial bourgeoisies of 'second wave capitalisms' was critical. It did not use that challenge as a spur to industrial innovation, and to the creation of a 'growth culture' geared to industrial expansion and the redeployment of investment into new technology. For given its already existing world position, internal composition and perceived interests, that route was already closed; and no amount of agitation by the new Liberal 'modernizers' could bring the realignment required. Instead, and because it was already immersed in its role as the world's hegemonic power, the British ruling class retreated 'into the protective cocoon of . . . Empire',[13] pursuing 'further imperial advantage, taking advantage of privileged markets and connections; and . . . expand[ing] and exploit[ing] financial resources and skills focused in . . . the City'.[14] It did not, as did ruling classes in Germany and Japan, use the state to initiate a drive to industrial growth. Instead politics in Britain took a liberal form. Governments restricted themselves primarily to fiscal policy – not least to the management of the National Debt – and did not become heavily involved in the direction and encouragement of industrial activity on any scale. Nor did the state deliberately orchestrate a national culture geared to economic expansion. Instead capital was left largely to its own devices, because that was how industrial growth had succeeded before 1870, and because powerful political and economic interests had emerged that wanted it to remain that way. The dominant culture remained a hybrid, a mixture of pro-capitalist liberal individualism and pre-capitalist conservative/aristocratic strands of thought that favoured status over enterprise, and the amateur over the scientist. In that culture, as we shall see in the next chapter, industrial capital learnt to fill a distinct but subordinate place.

That 'political space' occupied in Germany and Japan by right-wing forces – of state aid to, and protection for, industrial growth – was left vacant in Britain, as the political project of capital was defined as 'laissez faire'. Indeed one reason for the moderation of English labourism lies here, in that this 'statism' was left free to be occupied as 'socialism' by a cautious Labour Party after 1900, and was only later to be challenged by the Conservative Party under Baldwin as free trade was reluctantly abandoned between the wars. Even then the Conservative movement to the centre was hesitant and ambiguous precisely because of the force of financial interests within the Conservative coalition. What never emerged in British politics was a powerful Conservative coalition of class forces demanding state-initiated industrial regeneration. Instead that project became associated in the public mind with the programmes of the Left, and (except in moments of deepest industrial crisis) was resisted as such even by industrial capital which might have benefited most from it.

Financial and industrial capital

The relationship between sections of capital, and their various political needs, is a vital and complex one, as we shall see in the next chapter. Yet the complexities need not distract us from the essential simplicity that underpins them. For as Britain industrialized after 1760, industrial capitalists did not draw on bank capital to anything like the degree that their industrial competitors elsewhere were to do later. Instead, the world monopoly position enjoyed by mid nineteenth-century British industrial capital, and the manner in which that industrialization had been financed

initially in pre-banking days, provided surpluses enough to (and the habit of) sustaining expansion from industry's own turnover and reserves. Banking capital, as it emerged and to the degree that it centred itself in London, was thus from the beginning distant from industry and more concerned with overseas activity, continuing its eighteenth-century involvement in the financing of world trade and state expenditure, acting as broker to foreign industrialists and governments seeking loans from those British surpluses, and as a channel through which British savers could tap the super profits of early European and American capitalist take-off. It should not be forgotten that by 1914 the British middle class was closer to being a class of 'rentiers' than at any time before or since; and that the City, unlike equivalent financial institutions in Germany and the United States, in the crucial years to 1914 remained preoccupied with 'the circuits of commercial and banking capital particularly at the international level'.[15] What is most striking about the practices of City institutions in that period is that they do not approximate to 'finance capital' proper – do not, that is, involve either the organizational fusion of banks and industry or the associated establishment of control over productive activity by money capital. Indeed if that is a feature of banking activity in Britain at any time in our period, it is one which is coming to some prominence only now.[16] Historically the City has not played that role. Instead, in the years up to 1914 City institutions played a crucial role in the export of portfolio capital; and both before and since that period, the City has concentrated much of its activity on commercial dealings, one stage removed from any direct involvement in the encouragement of productive investment either here or abroad. Indeed, 'from the 1830s to the present day – with the exception of the period from the late nineteenth century to 1914 – the City's earnings from insurance, the foreign exchange and money markets, the financing of trade, freight and commodity broking etc (that is, commercial activity) has *exceeded* the income from interest and dividends from overseas investments'.[17] As Geoffrey Ingham has said:

The City-industry separation can be seen, in fundamental terms, as a consequence of a potential contradiction between the commercial and wholesale banking practices of the former and the requirements of industry. The structure of the City's money, securities and other markets is oriented to the rapid turnover of marketable assets, rather than the *direct* involvement with the financing of industrial production. This disjuncture has been continuously manifest in two ways. First, in the low level of long-term external finance for productive industry, and secondly, in the political implementation and defence of policies designed to maintain London as an open, unrestricted marketplace with a currency strong enough to be a basis for international mercantile and banking transactions.[18]

Initially, that foreign and commercial activity by the banks served the interests of industrial capital too. By expanding economic activity abroad, banking capital created markets overseas for British-made consumer and capital goods, much in the way that Marshall Aid created demands for United States products in the immediate post-war years. But in the long term, as with United States hegemony after 1945, contradictions emerged, and the arrangement worked against the interests of British-based industrial capital. For as the foreign industries consolidated themselves, their demand for British products fell away, and their presence as competitors at home and abroad grew. Industrial capital in Britain began to lose its markets, to find itself with less easy access to banking credit than its emerging competitors, and to face a political class in which financial interests had a strong voice – and in which those financial interests were not geared to the protection and development of the national industrial base as their first priority. Instead, the interest of financial institutions in the strength of sterling, and the reliability of London as a capital market, won crucial political support *against* the interests of nationally-based industrial capital at key moments (most famously with the return to the Gold Standard in 1925). By keeping sterling's exchange rate high this weakened still further the capacity of a by now vulnerable industrial sector to compete effectively abroad, and this both added extra incentive for the bankers to stay well clear of industrial investment, and made the City's invisible earnings an ever more vital component of an otherwise weakening balance of payments, so strengthening the political leverage of financial interests still further.

Nationally-based industrial capital in the twentieth century has lacked any political leverage equivalent to that enjoyed by the City. As we have seen, the response of industrial interests in Britain to the rise of new industries based on electricity and steel after 1890, and to the arrival of considerable foreign competition, was not to innovate rapidly or to intensify labour processes, so much as to turn to the protected markets of the empire and to move only slowly out of the industries of capitalism's first long wave (cotton, coal and iron) into those of its second. Indeed 'a list of the ten largest manufacturing companies for 1914 shows four textile firms, three food, drink and tobacco companies, one construction supplier and only one firm each from engineering and chemicals'. The firms which were by then growing to dominance in American and German capitalism 'simply were not the dominant sections of British industry, let alone British capital. The core of heavy manufacturing industry – metal engineering, electronics, chemicals, steel – was already by the late nineteenth century a subordinate section of British capitalism'.[19] For after expanding manufacturing industry as a proportion of the economy very rapidly between 1770 and 1830, the 'weight' of industrial capital in the economy as a whole then stagnated for a century, to revive again only in the very changed conditions of the 1930s. Between those dates the 'lead' enjoyed by British-based industrial capital was lost, and lost permanently; as an entire ruling class failed to realize with sufficient speed that 'industrialisation as it unfolded had created new conditions for successful accumulation, in particular the continual raising of productivity not by individual skill, or by numbers, but through the constant revolutionising of techniques and the reorganisation of production'.[20]

Industrial capital's preference for traditional methods and traditional technologies went hand in hand with a particular management style and a particularly subordinate political position. It is very clear that managerial practices differ distinctly between national capitalisms, and that British management practice has been very slow to adopt 'the more precise and sophisticated . . . practices required for modern industry'.[21] This, when taken with small-scale investment and a reluctance to move from old areas of technology to new, has been and remains an important source of low productivity, against which successive governments have railed, but which neither they nor any other social agency has set out systematically to transform. Banking capital was probably best suited to be the agency for such a transformation, by the practices it could impose through the boardrooms, and yet, as we have seen, it had interests elsewhere that prevented this being an imperative for it. Indeed, financial interests were often more concerned to protect themselves against programmes of industrial regeneration that might threaten their international role than they were in canvassing for just that regeneration; and financiers found the protection of money capital's freedom of manoeuvre relatively easy to maintain 'in the critical decades before 1914, (as) northern industrial interests settled into a subordinate role, under the sway of London based financial and imperial interests'.[22]

The reasons for this late nineteenth-century subordination of industrial capital remain unclear and controversial. At the very least, as we shall see in Chapter 7, the subordination of industry to finance reflected changes in the relative strengths, and economic bases, of the constituent elements of the mid Victorian power bloc – a bloc in which the London-based commercial bourgeoisie had occupied a secondary role to that exercised by land and industrial capital. As rents and profits both fell dramatically in the Great Depression after 1873, the great landowners and key sections of the industrial bourgeoisie seem to have turned to new sources of investment: 'in urban property, government issues, stocks and shares, overseas investment, the finance and insuring of trade and revenue from invisible exports (i.e. on the movement of trade, rather than on producing things to trade). . . . One of the main consequences of this' was that 'the influence of the manufacturing classes began to decline, and with it the entrepreneurial drive which had sustained Britain's earlier growth. The financial, imperialist and investment sectors became the leading ones'.[23]

Thereafter, British-based industrial capital fell further and further behind its competitors. Only the disruption of international competition between 1945 and 1956 gave British industrial capital one last moment of unthreatened glory, one that did not survive the reappearance of West German and Japanese industrial might. Since then, as we know, the competitive position of home industry has weakened perpetually, with 'its periodic troubles provoking ever wilder schemes for Great Leaps forward, and ever increasing cynicism when, inexorably, those faltered into a few nervous sideways steps'.[24] For by the mid 1950s, of course, neither 'indicative planning', 'incomes policy', 'entry into Europe' nor any other 'wild scheme' could avoid the consequences of the fact that industrial activity in Great Britain was significantly undercapitalized, locked in outmoded technologies, lax in its management policies and too small in its scale of industrial organization. Amazingly, as late as 1965, industrial capital in Britain still lacked a single spokesman organization – and it took a Labour government to force the creation of the CBI, and to encourage industrial mergers in the 1960s (through the IRC) in a belated search for competitiveness through size. Much senior managerial energy went into that merger process, more indeed than went into the redeployment of investment into modern and technologically sophisticated machinery. As West German and French industrial investment grew apace, investment here followed in volume but not in kind, as industrial capital stagnated in decaying industries and outmoded production processes. Why this should have been so remains a matter of controversy and doubt, but a number of factors 'appear to have inhibited mechanisation. Two related ones are the low rate of accumulation . . . which tend[ed] to involve [only] small scale additions to existing plant (and so) inhibit(ed) the integration of radically innovative techniques. . . , and the lack of an aggressive competitive environment'[25] in the critical years before 1960. A third factor appears to have been the defensive strength of the workers in British manufacturing industry.

Union strength

Industrial capital faced, as finance capital did not, a certain kind of labour movement. The character of this will be the subject of Chapter 5, but it is clear that early industrialization enabled a labour aristocracy to consolidate a set of craft skills which were doggedly defended by highly sectionalist trade union activity of an industrially militant, but politically conservative kind between 1890 and 1914, and again in the very different and more favourable bargaining conditions of the post-war years. In both periods the degree of

worker resistance meant that 'UK exporters found it to their advantage to avoid conflict with workers over an accelerated remoulding of the structure of production, and instead redirected sales to the new or protected markets often with the aid of capital exports'.[26] The first attacks on these craft skills by industrial capital after 1890 were prompted by growing competition, and were enough to move the trade unions from Lib-Labism into the new Labour Party. A more generalized attack on working practices and jobs by a weakening industrial capitalism after 1918 brought the General Strike of 1926. The failure of that strike weakened worker resistance to rationalization in the 1930s, but the fact that it happened at all was a testimony to the strength of class feeling, organization and militancy in the labour force faced by industrial capital. That organization and militancy – if not the width of class feeling – was strengthened by wartime sacrifice and full employment after 1940, to give British industrial relations a characteristic pattern that will be discussed in detail in Chapter 5 – one in which small groups of well-placed workers resisted managerial attempts to erode jobs, working practices and living standards, and one in which politicans felt obliged to promise ambitious programmes of welfare provision to attract working-class votes. Industrial capital in the post-war years found no effective strategy for dealing with that working-class power until Thatcherite recession became available in the late 1970s, and until then, trapped between growing competition from better-capitalized overseas producers and labour militancy at home, industrial profits collapsed and capital fled to easier industrial climates abroad.[27]

The governing élite

Industrial capital was burdened too by a particular state and ruling class. That class hung on to its world role tenaciously, as its junior members embroiled themselves in financial linkages in the empire and later in Western Europe. This 'external orientation' of key sections of the state élite, as we shall see later, was partly a product of the social background, experience and connections of the personnel who occupied key positions in the structure of the state. But more importantly, it was also a product of policy commitments, to the maintenance of Britain's world role, consolidated in the nineteenth-century period of industrial dominance and reinforced by the experience of twentieth-century war. Those policy commitments persisted unchallenged, even by the bulk of the political Left, until 1956 at least, even though they brought with them patterns of industrial decay of an accelerated kind.

We shall discuss the full character of the state machine – its internal power structure, its personnel, and its policies – in Part Three; and we shall also discuss then the particular weakness of the Left in Britain in the post-war years, in spite of its years in 'power'. Here it is enough to note that, even in its nineteenth-century heyday, industrial capital in Britain never dominated the personnel of the state, who remained 'wedded to imperialism. A network of bankers, financiers, colonials, ex-colonials, foreign investors and entrepreneurs – now reinforced by British multinational companies' directors and shareholders – these are the backbone of private and public life: Whitehall, the Tory party and the boardrooms'.[28] This 'southern London-based élite, first mercantile and then financial in its interests',[29] developed no large-scale practice of moving between government and industry, of training industrial leaders, or of steering industrial investment behind nationally specified goals. Instead, it pursued foreign and financial policies that ate away at the national industrial base, by obliging industrial recovery to be achieved in the tiny space left by heavy military spending and by successive attempts to protect sterling, and by obliging radicals to apologize in advance for questioning the near axiomatic equation of national strength with the exchange rate of the pound.

This association of the national interest with the maintenance of a military role abroad, and an over-valued currency, was not inevitable. It arose from a congruence of interests between sections of the governing élite and those of the City. British governments after 1945, for their own purposes, strove to maintain their status as a world power in the changed conditions of United States dominance, by sustaining both a substantial military presence abroad and an associated 'special relationship' with Washington, and by consolidating Britain's own commercial and financial dominance in the Commonwealth and empire – using sterling as a second 'reserve currency' in trading relationships organized through London. It was in this way and for these reasons that the sterling system, 'resting on fixed exchange rates and London's role as banker' came to be seen by successive governments as 'the key support for Britain's role as a world power',[30] and it was in this way too that in spite of Keynes' misgivings, 'the stability of the international financial and commercial system that was created under Anglo-American supervision at the end of the war' came to be held as 'essential for the operation of the sterling system and thus for the maintenance of Britain's international role'.[31] Victory in 1945 obscured more basic truths, blinding politicians to the need for 'a full scale attack on the structural inadequacies of the economy'. As West Germany and France, among others, were driven by military defeat to 're-examine their national economic and industrial policies, the British successes encouraged them to believe that existing policies and techniques were sufficient for peacetime purposes',[32] and so an opportunity was lost to restructure British industrial capital in the 1950s – an opportunity that, once lost, never came again.[33] As Stephen Blank has correctly observed of government policy in this period:

while emphases differed and evolved through time and changing conditions, basic commitments did not. What these came to involve was the creation of an interlocking network of policies which related to the preservation of Britain's role as a world power. Included were the restoration of sterling's international transaction and reserve functions, fixed exchange rates, overseas investment directed particularly towards the sterling area, government spending and lending in the Commonwealth and sterling area, and the maintenance of a British military and defence presence in those areas. . . . [As a result] for much of the post-war period domestic and international economic policy was dominated by and subordinated to the goals of foreign policy, goals which Britain was incapable of realising. Yet the attempt to achieve these goals led successive governments to sacrifice the domestic economy again and again. By the end of the 1950s a vicious circle had evolved in which efforts to maintain its international position became themselves the very cause of Britain's continuing international vulnerability. Efforts to create new policies and institutions whose purpose was to confront the problem of the domestic economy and to improve domestic economic performance foundered on the unwillingness of political leaders to abandon the most cherished symbol of Britain's international position by devaluing the pound.[34]

There were times, of course, when the political options seemed wider, particularly when financial interests were discredited and a radical Labour government emerged. There is no doubt, for example, that the hold of the Treasury on government policy weakened in the 1940s, and that later in that decade 'there was rapid growth in industrial production, with protection and intervention. But the possibility of the creation of sustained rapid accumulation was not realised because again governments subordinated domestic developments to imperial aspirations'.[35] Under intense American pressure, resources were swallowed instead into the Korean war boom, free trade was introduced, and the position of the City was strengthened through a return to sterling convertibility. In all these ways an opportunity was lost to retool British manufacturing industry before the revival of West Germany and Japan. Instead of that retooling, it was in this period that:

Britain's special relationship with the USA was inspired by the vision of refurbishing Britain's old imperial role in changed world conditions. The Atlantic alliance afforded a secure framework within which the colonial empire could be converted into a neo-colonial empire and the overseas operations of British big capital could be resumed and extended. In the conditions of the 1940s and 1950s, with Britain's main economic rivals apart from the USA temporarily out of action, and judged on its own terms, this strategy for preserving the waning force of British imperialism made sense. It became an incubus on the development of British capitalism only when the conditions in which it was conceived disappeared with the redistribution of world economic power and the re-emergence of significant inter-imperialist rivalry in the 1960s. The problem was that, as a set of institutions, policies and assumptions the imperial structure possessed remarkable powers of survival. The chronic nature of Britain's post-war economic crisis owes much to the tenacity of this imperial legacy.[36]

Even under Labour governments, Treasury and Foreign Office pressure to defend sterling, to allow the export of private capital and to maintain an overseas military presence, took their toll, adversely affecting the balance of payments and requiring cutbacks in domestic demand by governments to ease the pressure of imports. It should not be forgotten that 'the immediate cause of the sterling crises in 1947, 1949, 1951, 1955, 1957, 1961, and between 1963 and 1967 was generally, though not invariably, a deficit on the balance of payments [which] occurred not because exports were too low but because government spending overseas and private investment overseas were too high'.[37] Labour governments no less than Tory ones operated within the dominant ethos: 'Britain had to stay great; this meant putting sterling first; that in its turn implied balance-of-payments constraints and man-handling the industrial sector to fit'.[38] The result was a process of cumulative industrial decline (low returns inspiring low investment, low investment inspiring low productivity and low wages, low productivity and low wages bringing low returns) from which politicians strove to break in vain.

The whole external mentality of British finance capital, and of the British governing élite's interest in world power, were mirrored among successful industrial capitalists themselves in the boom years. Large-scale industrial capital went international. 'The opportunities that Britain's imperial trading and financial connections provided led to the development after 1950 of some vast and very successful international businesses.'[39] As the British national economy lost its international standing, British-based multinational companies grew in size and number. 'Among the largest 200 non-American companies, 53 were British, 43 Japanese, 25 German and 23 French' in 1970. 'By 1971 the value of foreign production by British business was more than double the value of visible export trade, whereas it was less than 40% for Germany and Japan';[40] and by then the clash of interests to which British governments were subject was less that between industrial and financial capital as 'between the new and often combined international operations of British industry and British finance, and the requirements of domestic expansion',[41] – between that of international capital on the one hand, and of nationally-based industrial capital and labour on the other.

As we shall see in Part Two, the material content of class relations in Britain has been intimately affected by the many-sided consequences of that cumulative pattern of industrial decline. The political agenda of an entire society has been structured by that content, and by the relationship of power between the classes that underpinned it. For what British politicians have faced in the post-war years has been a balance of class forces, and an inherited structure of basic policy commitments, that have eroded economic performance. The disproportionate weight of finance has blocked any state-led drive to industrial regeneration. The strength of working class industrial power has made any autonomous regeneration by industrial capital that much more difficult to achieve; and the absence of a state élite with this as its overriding priority has compounded the difficulty. Political options throughout the period took their shape from that balance, and from those basic commitments. Keynesianism, as a policy which favoured national industrial capital rather than finance capital, was run as an attempt to coalesce industrial and financial interests behind market-inspired economic growth. The failure of that strategy prompted radicals of both Right and Left to attempt to *shift* the balance of class forces in one direction or another; shifting it away from labour to capital under Thatcherism, or away from finance capital to a coalition of nationally-based industrial capital and labour under the Labour Left's 'alternative economic strategy'. The world recession strengthened Thatcherism in its attempts to weaken labour, but the weight of financial interests behind the monetarist coalition still blocked industrial regeneration; and the 'alternative economic strategy' has yet to be tried. But if and when it is, it too will have to confront the political leverage of capital, both financial and industrial, national and international, and the defensive political strength of the labour movement. It is to the documentation of these that we shall now turn.

4 The political power of capital

What follows in the chapters to come must be understood as growing out of the two interrelated narratives that we have now established, on the emergence, character and dynamic of capitalism as a world system, and on the initial supremacy and subsequent decline of British industrial capital within that system. In particular, capitalism has created and consolidated a certain kind of *labour process*, and an associated pattern of trade union organization and class struggle, which will be considered in detail in the next chapter. Moreover, capitalism has required, and so called into existence, a certain pattern of *class relationships*, and has in addition consolidated and amended already existing patterns of discrimination by gender, race and religion, which will be the subject of the whole of Part Two. Yet again and from its outset, capitalism required certain policies from its *state*, and has lately required state action of an extensive kind – action directed towards, among other things, that labour force and those class relationships; and so this whole aspect of the politics of capitalism will have to await consideration until we reach Part Three. But overridingly capitalism has at its core the new social force of *capital* itself, and it is with the character, development and interests of this here in Britain that we must begin.

The traditional image associated in the public mind with a term like 'capitalism' is that of factories, industrial output, and the making and selling of goods – in a word, 'production'. But here we shall talk not of production but of 'accumulation', for the act of producing commodities in capitalism is not given its shape by technological imperatives, or by social requirements collectively understood, but by the need to accumulate capital. What is produced by capitalism is not just industrial goods. In fact, as we shall see, the production of services can also accumulate capital, as can agricultural output, trade between unequal partners, and even the moving about of money. In all these economic activities what is being sought is an enhancement of capital itself. It is this drive to accumulate which shapes and directs the entire productive effort, so if we are to grasp the nature of that shape and direction, it is with the accumulation of capital that we need to begin.

Capital is a social relationship of a particular kind, a social power that derives from the private ownership of the means of production in an economic and social system in which the bulk of the population have only their labour power to sell, and in which the reproduction of that labour power occurs through the purchase of commodities (wage goods) produced by similarly placed workers elsewhere or by other exploited classes. The surpluses which accrue from the organization of production and the sale of commodities by capitalists have a twin source. They arise either from a process of unequal exchange (buying cheap and selling dear) between capitalist enterprises in the metropolitan centres of the world system and non-capitalist systems of production elsewhere (slave modes of production, petty-commodity production, domestic labour systems, peasant producers and so on); or from the expropriation of surplus value from the labour force of advanced capitalism through the wage relationship of employer and employee that occurs in capitalism's dominant economic institutions – the private industrial firm and the bureaucratically-organized financial institution. Those surpluses – profits – held as private property by the capitalist class, manifest themselves in many different forms, being held by some capitalists as money, as means of production (machinery and raw materials), in the form of rent, or of stocks of as yet unsold commodities. This distribution of capital in these different forms is its most public feature, but it should not be allowed to obscure capital's common source in the relationships of exploitation which will be discussed in Part Two.

Yet the fact that capital can and does exist in different forms, and that, as we have seen, it is created in systems of production and exchange that involve regular and unavoidable competition between capitalists (competition that is still organized within and between the boundaries of nation states) means that politicians normally face not capital, not one united social force, but rather many capitals – many national capitals, many fractions of even one national capital, many sectors of any one fraction, many firms within any one sector. This means that the politics of capital are at once a mixture of unity and division. As we shall see, these many and disparate capitalist units are capable of showing a remarkable degree of unity if a general threat to the social privileges of capital and of the class that possesses it is perceived, particularly if that threat comes from the labour movement and the other exploited classes on whose perpetual subordination capital depends for its very existence. But this basic unity of class interests should not blind us to the fact that, more normally, politicians operate within a plurality of pressures from the world of capital, and accordingly face a multiplicity of potentially conflicting demands from it.

That plurality of demands, and the multi-plicity of units and differing interests between the sections of capital that it reflects, is not a random plurality, but is firmly anchored in any period in the particular development of capitalism as a whole. The overriding features of contemporary British capital, for example, may be said to be five: the dominance of finance capital over industrial capital; the growth of monopolies and multinational companies in the industrial sector; the persistence of small and medium size firms in each industrial sector; the relative predominance of old and stagnant industries over new and growing ones; and the general crisis of under-investment, low profits and dwindling competitiveness across the entire industrial sector regardless of size. Each of those features reflects both general trends in capitalist development and particular elements of the British experience of capitalism. The rise of finance capital and of multinationals, the emergence of monopolies and the existence of old industries must all be understood as products of the nature of capitalist development discussed in Chapter 2, and in particular of the way in which the long waves of capitalist development, and their punctuation by severe crises, resulted in the ever greater concentration and centralization of capital, altered the organic composition of that capital away from labour-intensive processes to capital-intensive ones, and generated new growth sectors in each long wave to replace the growth points of the wave that had gone before. Moreover, the fact that industrial capital in Britain remains disproportionately anchored in those old industries, and is subject now to a generalized crisis of under-investment and competitiveness, has to be seen as the product both of the downturn in the world economy in the 1970s and of the cumulative pattern of class stalemate and state-inertia discussed in Chapter 3. The result, as has been said already, is that British governments face powerful financial institutions with a long tradition of political influence, a multinational industrial sector of more recent origin, and a national industrial economy in considerable difficulties. What we need to do is to look carefully at each of these in turn, and then to examine their cumulative impact on the policy options available to politicians now.

The power of financial institutions

It has often been observed that 'within the total productive circuit of capital . . . capital takes three basic forms . . . money capital, commodity capital and productive capital.[1] The banker, the merchant and the industrialist are the three characteristic figures of the capitalist class; and because money plays so crucial a role in the circulation of capital, individuals and institutions who deal exclusively in money have long occupied a critical place within the capitalist system as a whole. By lending to individuals, to companies and to states, financiers have acted to redirect the surpluses which merchants and industrialists have extracted from actual production processes with which the financiers themselves have had at best only an indirect relationship. Such finance capitalists, taking a share of total surplus value in the form of interest, play several crucial roles within capitalism: facilitating the circulation of goods by providing the means of exchange; lending money capital to permit the purchase of means of production; easing the concentration and centralization of the ownership of those means of production by financing the purchase of stocks and shares; and creating the credit money which alone has enabled post-war capitalism to offset the tendencies which brought it to crisis and to near-disaster between the wars. Indeed, at each stage in the development of capitalism, the role of the circuit of interest-bearing capital in its own right, and hence the power of financial interests within the capitalist class, has grown: from the relatively marginal usurer of pre-capitalist feudal Europe, to the limited banking function of early industrial capital,

and to the great banking networks of capitalism's monopoly stage.

That development has been enough to encourage many commentators to label the modern economy 'finance capitalism', one in which there has been 'an articulated subordination of commercial capital, industrial capital and banking capital' in which 'it is banking capital which dominates the other forms of capital'.[2] But since on that argument, no meaningful distinction can now be drawn between the interests of the banks and the big international industrial monopolies, it still seems premature and overdrawn for the British case at least; and it seems more appropriate to stress instead the economic and political influence of financial interests as a separate section of capital – influence which has served to weaken the competitive strength of nationally-based industrial capital, and which has yet to be successfully challenged by any other sector of the ruling class or by any coalition of the Left.[3]

Convention cites 'the City' as one of the centres of power in contemporary Britain. But 'the City' as a term is a shorthand for a complex of financial institutions: clearing banks and merchant banks, discount and finance houses, building societies, pension funds and insurance companies, the Stock Market and other security and commodity markets, overseas banks based in London, and the Bank of England. Historically, the City's centre of gravity in its early years lay in the Bank of England, the Stock Market and the discount houses. These were joined in the nineteenth century – as London became the financial centre of the emerging capitalist world – by the merchant banks formed in and after the Napoleonic Wars; and the twentieth century has seen the rise to prominence of the four big clearing banks, the building societies and the pension funds. Merchant banks remain vital parts of the City – managing the vast investment portfolios of the pension funds and dealing in the new Eurodollar market. The

City is still 'far and away the largest insurance market in the world',[4] earning in 1972 £300 million of overseas currency on that activity alone.[5]

So complex a structure as this cannot be expected to have a single set of interests. Instead, competition is rife between certain of its sections – not least between the banks and the building societies for personal savings – and policies suiting one section may not suit another. Even the high interest rates that bring the London clearing banks additional windfall profits can, via their impact on sterling's exchange rate, 'make it difficult for insurance companies and insurance brokers, as well as industry, to sell their service or goods abroad', and the leading insurance companies, after all, 'depend more heavily on their overseas premium earnings than on domestic UK premium income'.[6] So, like industry, 'financiers are "a hostile band of brothers", united by common interests, divided by competition and suspicion'[7] – and their common interests require organization before they can be expressed.

This organization and representation is performed by key financial institutions, in this case primarily by the Bank of England. Recent changes within the City – particularly the growth of pension funds and insurance companies with their own Whitehall connections, the rise of the building societies to a position of prominence because of the spread of owner occupation, the rise to prominence of the Committee of London Clearing Bankers, and the arrival of many foreign banks in the City – are now eroding the capacity of the Bank of England to speak for the City as a whole, or to maintain its monopoly on the channels of communication between financial institutions and governments.[8] Yet the Bank of England remains the City's foremost spokesman, and has pressed regularly for policy that reflects the general needs of the London financial institutions as it understands them: free capital movement in and out of the UK; a stable exchange rate for sterling; high interest rates; the limitation of state direction of industry, and domestic deflation whenever City interests were threatened by an overheated home economy. These demands have reflected in part a genuine concern for the local economy. Since some City interests have major local industrial connections, 'those who speak for the City' have had 'to take a view on what would be good for industry and commerce as a whole'. That influence has 'time and again been exerted on the side of discipline: the long term strength of industry' depending 'on the City's customary view, on there being sufficient competitive pressure upon it to hold down wages and to press industrialists to rationalise, reduce employment and raise productivity'.[9] The cost of that pressure to local industry, as we have seen, has at times been great.

What we need to grasp now, however, is that there have also been times (not least in the early 1980s) when such a policy has cost banks and pension funds dearly. Yet City institutions have continued to press for tighter monetary controls, high interest rates and a strong pound because of their own prior need to maintain London 'as an international financial centre vis-à-vis those of New York, Frankfurt and others. At crucial conjunctures this has required policies to maintain a relatively high exchange rate (although this is not a permanent policy) and to ensure high interest rates irrespective of their effects upon industrial profits and accumulation'.[10] Indeed the interests of the City in general have taken the shape that they have both because of the City's dependence on the growth of a very particular kind of trade (in commodities, money and securities on an international scale) and because of the way in which that trade can flourish only if underwritten by government policies of a quite definite kind. For trade in money and securities requires 'conditions which are not typical of trade in general. Most important of these is the need for an acceptable and, preferably *guaranteed* international means of payment. And, of course the guarantee is politically generated by the budgetary prudence and the legal enactment of monetary regulations on the part of the nation which undertakes this role'.[11] It is for these that the Bank of England has repeatedly pressed.

What is striking about this political pressure is that it has been effective, in spite of its deleterious effects on the competitive position of British industrial capital. 'On the political level, the City has exercised a dominant position in the determination of economic policy, which is to say that its perceived interests have generally, though not exclusively, been the guiding thread for economic policy even when faced with opposition from the political agents of other groups within the dominant class or those of the subordinate classes.'[12] City interests prevailed over industrial ones in the opposition to free trade after 1906, in the decision to return to the gold standard in 1925, and in the way in which the 1931 financial crisis was handled. City interests benefited disproportionately from the retreat from planning after 1948, and from the way in which successive post-war governments strove to maintain a world role for Britain based on the use of sterling as a reserve currency, on the liberalization of capital markets, and on the maintenance of the sterling area.

It cannot be said that City interests prevailed in total; 'on the debit side must go credit policies which show a truly Keynesian hostility to the rentier. Governments have persistently intervened in favour of domestic and industrial borrowers, with the result that for a large part of the post-war period real interest rates have been negative'.[13] Yet this, and the persistence of exchange controls until 1979, cannot obscure the fact that the steadfast determination of both Labour and Conservative governments to maintain the exchange rate of sterling until the early 1970s, at the cost of heavy internal deflation, reflected systematic and consistent City pressure. Nor can it obscure the fact that the decision to follow that by seeking entry to the EEC occurred at the very time when the City was replacing its own dependence on sterling with an equally international preoccupation with the Eurodollar. What is striking about these policies is not only their congruence with the interests of key sections of the City, but their centrality to the whole of economic life. It is not just that the City exercised an influence way beyond its numbers. It exercised an influence where it mattered most, on the basic framework of government economic policy as a whole.

The ability of financial interests to establish and sustain so dominant a role politically can best be explained under three headings: the resources of the financial institutions, their history and their opponents.

The resources of the City

The centrality of the functions performed by City institutions, both to the smooth running of government and the health of the domestic industrial economy, gives City interests a particular 'presence' in the minds of governments, and leaves left-wing governments in particular open to sanctions whose potency in the short term cannot easily be matched either by industry or by labour. Late capitalism has sustained itself for so long only by the development of a credit cycle increasingly autonomous from industrial production, whose perpetual 'priming' has been vital to governments seeking industrial growth. Yet when governments have sought to contain the money supply instead, again they have had to deal directly with the financial institutions. 'For within the British system it is not the State which directly creates money but the financial system itself. The State does not directly print money, instead it creates "financial instruments" through its borrowing requirements'[14] on the basis of which the banks lend.

Both the general economic policy, and the funding of their own programmes and personnel, is possible only for as long as the banks are willing to buy government securities – and any deviation from orthodox policy directly threatens that willingness. Moreover, in a weak national capitalism with serious balance of payments problems, financial institutions gain an extra set of sanctions: able (indeed obliged by their own requirement for profits) to move currency out of sterling if policy seems to them unsatisfactory; able to point to their capacity to contribute 'invisible earnings' (£2307 million in 1978 alone)[15] to give their policy demands extra weight; able to call for higher interest rates to attract in foreign currencies to cover trading deficits accrued by industrial capital; and always in the last resort the avenue governments must use to the international banking community which alone can provide short and medium term credit to cover persistent balance of payments deficits – credit that comes again on bankers' terms. Labour governments in particular tend to experience the full range of sanctions – coming in with policies that make City institutions wary, and then being pulled back to the 'orthodoxy' of high interest rates and deflationary economic policies by runs on sterling, currency crises and IMF loans. It was in this way in the 1970s that, as the City lost that part of its leverage which had historically rested on sterling's role as a reserve currency, it found its policy preoccupations reinforced by the 'increasing intervention of the IMF in the determination of economic policy'.[16]

The IMF presence here merely reinforced the impact on public policy of financial institutions whose position in the circuits of capital gave them an immediate leverage in the councils of the state which neither industrial capital nor labour could easily match. As Coakley and Harris have correctly written, 'the exchange rate and interest rate are the levers of the City's power: they are measures of its pivotal role in the economy'.[17] This power

to influence exchange and interest rates illustrates the specificity of financial institutions as compared with other firms and bodies: for whereas any firm importing or exporting, or even any worker holidaying in Benidorm, may have an indirect influence on the demand/suppply balance for foreign exchange, the financial institutions' position and role in the economic structure is to concentrate financial balances in their hands and thereby dominate the exchange markets and credit markets. It is they, rather than industrial firms or other agents that act in the wholesale money and foreign exchange markets where interest and exchange rates are set.[18]

It is financial institutions too who enjoy a 'pivotal role in determining the adequacy, price and direction of finance for industry' and who are thereby in a position 'to influence industry or control it in some circumstances'.[19] This too gives financiers an advantage in the pursuit of political influence that other sections of capital and labour find difficult to roll back.

The City's historic dominance

If Conservative governments clash with finance capital less often than Labour ones, this is partly because of the close personal contacts that financial institutions maintain with Conservative politicians. In the nineteenth-century heyday of the merchant bank, these social connections were *the* mechanism of control operated by finance capital on the state: in Moran's words, 'an informal highly developed social network connecting the Treasury, the Bank of England and leading merchant bankers', in which 'leading merchant banking families and leading political families, especially those in the Conservative Party, inhabited the same small world'.[20]

These social linkages were themselves a

reflection of the centrality of financial interests to the power bloc then dominant around the British state, a centrality which put financial concerns at the heart of both the social and ideological self-definitions of an entire ruling class. The City is still warrened by a myriad of interlocking directorates between financial institutions, between such institutions and large manufacturing firms, and between both these and the political élite. Many senior civil servants end up in financial institutions: as Aaronovitch observed long ago, 'the top men in the Treasury move in and out of the City freely; their policies are well known to suit finance capital, and their subsequent careers show where their affinity lies'.[21] By the 1960s, 'the bulk of Conservative M.P.s were almost certain to have interests in finance rather in one of the older professions or manufacturing industry';[22] and the proportion of Conservative Party funds coming from finance and property companies has increased significantly of late, to constitute probably over 30 per cent of all company funds reaching the Party in the early 1980s.[23] Moreover, these personal connections have been consolidated (and to a degree supplemented as the City has grown in size and diversity) by the spokesman role played for the City by the Governor of the Bank of England and by the Treasury.

The dominance of the Treasury within the machinery of the state gives the City its political edge, and the Treasury's own defeat of ministries such as the DEA is itself a contributory factor to the persistence of City influence, leaving, as it does, the City's advocates in a privileged position 'at the heart of the State apparatus where economic policy is formulated'.[24] The Governor of the Bank of England has at times been quite clear on his role – as spokesman for a set of private financial institutions in spite of his own position as head of a nationalized bank – and there are records enough of governors using their position to lobby ferociously, not to say frenetically, for City policies.[25]

The City's opponents

Yet it is also significant that that lobby has been very little challenged. What challenge there has been – from protectionism and Keynesianism before 1939 to state planning and the Labour Left's AES since 1945 – have been easily contained. This is partly a result of the limited degree of organization achieved by industrial capital, as will be seen later. It is also a consequence of Labour Party moderation which must be explained elsewhere.[26] But it is also a consequence of the quite remarkable degree to which both industrial capital and labour have shared in the general consensus on policy that has united the political élite and the City; namely that the overriding aim of government policy should be to maintain Britain's world role.

Both industrial capital and labour have been slow to perceive the threat to their objectives contained in this subordination to policies of high interest rates, free capital movements and a strong currency. No Labour government to date has stood out successfully against them, and it has really taken the modern Labour Left to the 1970s to begin to see how vital is this whole sector of public policy.[27] Industrial capital and its spokesman organizations remain largely uncritical of the general thrust of government policy, if willing to baulk at the occasional detail.[28] This 'ideological domination' of City interests has not in reality been a matter of City dictation, but rather of a congruence of interests between key sections of the political élite and key institutions of the City, buttressed by the manner in which 'the consequent delicate balance of payments situation served as a means of checking and reorienting government policy through periodic exchange crises'.[29] As Stephen Blank has put it:

rather than searching for the influence of one Department, the City or the Bank, it is more useful and accurate to think in terms of an 'overseas' or 'sterling' lobby within the government and administration, sharing the belief that 'Britain's international position and responsibilities constituted the primary policy objectives and that the international role of sterling was vital to this position. They also agreed that Britain's international position should provide the essential regulator for the domestic economy.[30]

In fact the assertion of a lobby is not a denial of City influence so much as a recognition of its form. For 'it remains true that financial interests had the greatest stake in the old system and constituted the basis of that lobby in the economy and class structure'. In this regard it is significant that it was 'only after their realisation that the City could carve a new niche in the advanced capitalist world as an international financial entrepôt, with or without an international British currency',[31] that economic policy shifted fundamentally.

The state now faces a financial sector with a particular character and set of interests. Within the City large concentrations of money capital now lie in just a few hands. City institutions as a whole 'have at their disposal the massive treasury of £562 billion, or just over £10,000 per head of the 1981 population. Of that £562 billion, £331.7 billion lies with the banks, £74.3 billion with the insurance companies and £63.8 billion with pension funds'.[32] The assets of Barclay's Bank alone in 1981 stood at £48.8 billion, making that bank the world's sixth largest. The Halifax Building Society – as the largest non-banking institution in the City – had assets that year of £11.9 billion. The Prudential – the largest insurance company – had assets of £10.9 billion. The largest pension fund had assets of £5.2 billion; and the top five building societies were together worth £34 billion. It is significant too that these financial institutions together now own 58 per cent (1979 figures) of all the United Kingdom listed ordinary shares (pension funds owning 17 per cent in their own right, insurance companies 16 per cent and investment trusts 10 per cent),[33] and it is clear that

just four major banks, seven insurance companies and nine merchant banks between them have a controlling interest in ten of Britain's top fifty manufacturing companies.[34]

For in the last two decades the relationship between industry and the City has grown closer, though still that relationship is not as close as elsewhere in the advanced capitalist world. 'Even a rather cursory inspection of the shareholding position of the largest 250 companies reveals a very high percentage still under ownership control', but nevertheless 'finance capital is now becoming much more involved in the control of domestic corporations'.[35] This is a significant change. As mergers have occurred within financial institutions, and among the largest industrial concerns, so the linkages between the two have been consolidated. 'Studies carried out in the 1950s and 1960s suggest that 10 or more "interest groups" had formed around major banks and insurance companies', and that 'groupings such as those centred around Morgan Grenfell (itself a subsidiary of Morgan Guaranty Trust), Rothschilds, Lazards, Barclays, Lloyds and Jardine Matheson are alliances which are occasionally subject to a common policy but which at least try to avoid competition within groups'.[36] Banks, both merchant and lending, seem to play a critical role here. John Scott has described the contemporary situation in the following way:

Clearing banks are the means through which finance capitalists can influence decisions which are made in all parts of the monopoly sector, and thereby exert a considerable influence over the dependent non-monopoly sector. This does not mean that they are agencies for control over industry by bankers. Finance capitalists, many of whom sit on bank boards, are recruited from banking, manufacturing and commerce, not solely from banking. In fact, full time bankers are normally outweighed in numbers by the many outside directors who sit on the bank boards. The banks are the means through which the major capitalist interests coalesce in order to co-ordinate the behaviour of the system as a whole. Each of the banks brings together a relatively distinct group of interests to form a bank-centred sphere of influence. These spheres – currently centred on Barclays Bank, Lloyds Bank, Midland Bank and National Westminster Bank – overlap with one another and their membership shifts over time, but at any particular moment they have a great significance in relation to the allocation of capital, the recruitment of business leaders and the flow of information. Share and loan capital comes from the insurance companies, pension funds, unit trusts and investment trusts, and capital is generally mobilised and syndicated by the merchant banks with whom those 'institutions' are associated. The clearing banks, aided by the merchant banks, oversee the allocation of this capital and help in the provision of personnel for the institutions and the enterprises in which the institutions are involved. The clearing banks co-ordinate the constellations of interests which are involved in the control of the majority of the larger enterprises, and the smaller merchant banks act as brokers between the institutions and the various spheres of influence.[37]

This means that no government hitherto has ever faced such a concentration of financial power in Britain, nor has any industrial sector here been so potentially subservient to financial control. But potential remains one thing and actual practice another. The extensive system of interlocking directorships through which finance and industry connect should be understood as a mechanism for linking, communicating and co-ordinating, rather than as a means of direct and detailed banking control over industrial policy. Such control is a possibility in individual cases, but more normally the presence of a major banking interest on an industrial board sets limits on the range of corporate strategy and the choice of senior personnel, but does not allow the bank total say. For 'banks and industry are involved in a relationship in which both sides hold strong cards and . . . their mutual lending and borrowing operations provide no basis for assuming that either controls the other'. 'The centrality of banks and other financial companies [here] is an index of their influence but not of their dominance.'[38]

In fact there is still very little direct evidence on the role played by financial institutions in the control of industry in contemporary Britain; and what evidence we do have suggests both that traditionally financial interests have kept an arms-length relationship with home-based industrial capital, and that that relationship is not changing quite as much as the figures on interlocking directorships and institutional share-ownership might suggest. Traditionally, the banks have lent little to industry, have lent for short periods only, and have favoured a 'consolidationist' rather than an aggressively 'accumulationist' industrial strategy.[39] Traditionally, too, the dominant coalition of interests within the City was merchant bankers and London clearing banks geared to colonial capital and so externally orientated. The new giants of the City still carry that orientation. 'British investors devote a greater proportion of GNP to overseas investment than any other major capitalist nation',[40] locked into the Eurodollar market, lending to big multinational companies, and investing large percentages of their portfolios in productive capital based abroad. It is still the case that the bulk of the City's profits come from these overseas sources of surplus value, and from alliances with multinational monopoly capital rather than with small and medium sized industrial enterprises geared more exclusively to the prosperity of the United Kingdom's economy.[41]

City interests still have no organic link to, nor any dependence upon, the strength of productive capital in Britain. If their policy demands help that capital, that is purely accidental and fortuitous; generally they do not. The overwhelming thrust of their policy demands, in alliance with the multinational companies to whom they lend, is still towards the 'internationalization of the UK economy', still to making London 'ever more a service zone to international capital – the conveniently offshore location for investment or reinvestment, insurance and speculation, guaranteed by both public and private institutions and underwritten by a famous social stability'. The domestic costs of that external orientation remain appallingly high: the downgrading of industrial capital here in Britain, the shutting of old factories, the laying off of entire industrial populations, the transformation of 'the Northern river valleys (into) assembly stages or branch units of American, German, Japanese (and eventually Korean or Brazilian?) enterprises'.[42] It is in this way that the political power of the City stands as the first major blockage to any successful strategy of industrial regeneration, let alone of socialist transformation.

The power of multinational industrial capital

If the City is the first blockage, multinational industrial capital is the second. For governments in Britain do not only face powerful financial interests. They also face an industrial structure that is itself divided into three major sectors: a public sector of utilities and run-down manufacturing industries, which we will discuss in Part Three; a sector of small and medium size companies wholly/mainly geared to the home market, whose political influence will be discussed in the next section; and a set of industries dominated by massive multinational monopoly companies. It is these industrial giants who also possess considerable sanctions in the battle for influence over national policy.

Monopoly, of course, is not new to capitalism. What is new is its scale, and the increasingly international nature of its operation. Nineteenth-century industrial capital everywhere was composed of many thousands of small firms, each in competition with one another; but that highly competitive universe rapidly gave way under its own logic to a concentration of production and centralization of capital that left the bulk of industrial output in fewer and fewer hands. In 1909, for example, in Britain the largest 100 industrial firms were responsible for only 16 per cent of total manufacturing output. Yet after important periods of mergers in the 1920s and 1960s, that figure had risen to 27 per cent by 1953 and to 42 per cent by 1975 (Table 7). It is probably nearer to 50 per cent by now. As a result, although it took 2000 companies to produce half Britain's total manufacturing output in 1913, in 1970 it took only 140. Small firms survive in large numbers, of course, but those are dwarfed in virtually every industrial sector by five or six major companies. The Department of Employment lists twenty-two such sectors, and in twenty of them six firms are now responsible for more than a half of the sector's total output. Even these figures possibly underestimate the dominant effect which these large companies have in the market. If Scott's calculations are correct, the top 100 companies in 1974–5 took as much as 62 per cent of the total turnover of the largest 1000 manufacturing companies in the United Kingdom, used 64 per cent of their total capital and captured 69 per cent of total profits. In the same year, the top fifty companies 'took 48% of the turnover, 49% of the capital employed, and 56% of the profits'. As Marsh and Locksley observed, 'Big is certainly dominant in the manufacturing sector'.[43]

Moreover, many of these large companies now operate on a multinational scale. Internationalism has also long been a feature of capitalism. World trade in slaves, metals and commodities was a crucial catalyst to early capital accumulation; and the pursuit on a world scale of outlets for capital, new sources of raw materials and new markets, became a defining feature of economic life in the West from at least the middle of the nineteenth century. Initially this 'imperialism' took the form both of physical conquest of colonies and

Table 7   *The share of firms in net output*

	1935 (per cent)	1958 (per cent)	1963 (per cent)	1968 (per cent)
Largest firms				
50 firms	14.9	24.7	27.9	32.4
100 firms	24.0	32.3	37.4	42.0
200 firms	n.a.	41.0	47.9	52.5
Largest firms' share in employment				
50 largest firms	15.0	21.2	24.3	29.4
100 largest firms	22.0	27.7	32.6	37.8
200 largest firms	28.0	35.5	42.0	47.1

Source: S. Aaronovitch and M. Sawyer, 'The concentration of British manufacturing', *Lloyds Bank Review* (October 1974), p. 23.

export of portfolio capital, primarily by individual savers, to buy the shares of foreign nationally-based and internally-oriented firms and the bonds of governments. As late as 1914, the number of genuinely international *firms* was very small: firms 'such as Unilever and Royal Dutch Shell were very rare, and more often nationally based companies tended to operate within the boundaries of protected trading areas and colonial empires'.[44] But since 1918, and especially since 1945, that has no longer been the case. There has been a significant increase in the export of productive capital, as firms have bought up or built productive capacity elsewhere in the world, and organized production abroad as well as in their home base. These international firms are no longer to be found just in railways, timber, mining and oil, but now dominate the entire secondary sector (including engineering, petrochemicals, pharmaceuticals, food processing, paper and printing). Within these companies, control has become increasingly co-ordinated on a world scale, with each national unit having to fit into a global corporate policy; and in certain industries (cars and light electronics in particular) we have seen not just the internationalization of ownership and control, but also the

internationalization of the production process itself, as firms have begun to build part of their commodities in one country, part in another, assembling them perhaps in a third. As a result, and increasingly, trade takes place between and within the subsidiaries of multinational companies, so that, for example, in Britain in 1968 22 per cent of all company exports, and 30 per cent of all exports from companies based here, originated in the multinational sector.[45]

Indeed the arrival of foreign investment in the United Kingdom economy on a significant scale in the 1960s acted to quicken the drift to monopoly, obliging British companies 'to merge in order to rationalise their activities and meet foreign competition',[46] and allowing multinationals to consolidate themselves in precisely those already oligopolistic sectors where they could 'exploit their technologically induced oligopolistic advantage before it [was] eroded by competition'.[47] In this way chemicals, electronics and pharmaceuticals, motor vehicles and engineering continued to bear the brunt of this invasion of foreign capital, and multinational companies as a result continued to show higher degrees of capital intensity (in terms of capital expenditure/employee) and productivity than were achieved by United

Kingdom-owned firms lacking foreign capital.[48] Initially the bulk of these multinational firms were American based and funded, and three-quarters of all foreign investment in the United Kingdom in the early 1960s was American in origin. Indeed, 'between 1960 and 1968 the value of US investment in the UK tripled'.[49] More recently, however, Western European and Japanese firms have played a greater and faster growing role in the multinational sector both here and abroad; and throughout British capital has been exported in far greater proportions, relative to GNP, than in any other major capitalist power with the exception of Switzerland.[50] This has meant both that the 'accumulated value of UK direct investment overseas was almost three times greater than the value of foreign direct investment in the UK in 1960, and (still) almost twice as great in 1970',[51] and that the United Kingdom remains second only to the United States in the scale of direct foreign investment by its national companies. So, whereas in 1957 more than three-quarters of the largest 100 companies in the capitalist world were United States based, and a half of the rest were British, by 1977 the United States share had fallen to forty-eight and the British to nine. Yet three of those were still among the largest twenty firms of all,[52] and United Kingdom firms still 'accounted for a third of all western European industrial com-

panies with a turnover exceeding £350 million'.[53] It is therefore hard to avoid the conclusion that while 'British capital has greatly expanded its overseas productive operations relative to its domestic investment in manufacturing, . . . foreign firms have preferred to export to the UK rather than set up new production units here'.[54]

All this has had a number of crucial political consequences, of which we might single out four. First, it has meant that British governments have faced an industrial sector, part of which at least has been dependent on foreign capital, under foreign control, and run as part of a multinational venture, and which therefore constitutes at least in potential a challenge to the government's national sovereignty. Second, it has meant that British governments have faced big British firms with significant interests overseas, able and willing to shift resources away from the United Kingdom if the conditions for profitability seem particularly disadvantageous here. Table 8 makes very clear the difference between these firms and their smaller equivalents. Third, yet ironically, it is not these home-oriented industries that have been the motor of economic growth. Instead, and precisely because multinational companies have concentrated their investments on the growth industries of the long wave, it has meant that governments pursuing economic growth have needed to

Table 8 *United Kingdom/overseas involvement of industrial and commercial companies*

Analysis by asset size involved	50 largest (per cent)	The rest (1450) (per cent)
Proportion of total assets of 1500 companies surveyed	48.5	51.5
Operating wholly in UK	7.4	40.2
Operating mainly in UK	50.4	48.1
Operating mainly overseas	38.2	10.7
Operating wholly overseas	4.0	0.9

Source: J. Hughes, *Britain in crisis* (Spokesman 1981), p. 29.

mobilize multinational firms in particular, in spite of their international interests, while facing a home industrial sector of a smaller scale – one that was less heavily capitalized, and one that enjoyed much more restricted access to overseas sources of credit, raw materials and markets. When we realize that as much as 20.9 per cent of all gross fixed capital formation in the United Kingdom economy in 1970 was made by local affiliates of United States owned multinationals (and 27 per cent if we include all foreign owned affiliates) the scale of the problem here becomes clear.

Fourth, because multinationals are very large, it has also meant that British governments, in common with governments in other capitalist states, have had to deal with companies whose budgets and scale of operation are enormous. The budget of General Motors – as the largest multinational – lies somewhere between the GNP of Denmark and Switzerland. The gross sales of ICI exceed the GNP of Eire. These are truly vast concerns, whose hold on the total United Kingdom national economy has actually been growing of late through direct investment and merger: and in this way the problem posed for British governments by the existence of the multinational corporate sector has been intensifying. The 'sector of what might be thought of as totally or predominantly British company operations has been under pressure' from the multinationals, and 'in the "giant" company area any policy initiatives have to deal with enterprises that are only partly committed to UK industrial operation, and which can flexibly deploy capital and credit within a multinational framework of reference'.[55] Moreover, it has been precisely in the sector of British industry dominated by multinationals that trade performance has deteriorated most rapidly in the 1970s, as multinational companies turned increasingly to other parts of their conglomerates for production.[56]

Both Labour and Conservative governments have found that big multinational companies have had individual needs and policy requirements which they were large enough to express directly to the government ministry concerned: for a particular kind of state aid, a certain sort of export guarantee, a particular industrial location and so on. The Conservative Party in particular has come to be heavily dependent on financial contributions from firms of this size and scale of operations. As much as 60 per cent of all traced contributions now comes from four sectors (finance and property, food, drink and tobacco, construction and electrical engineering) in which multinational companies play a significant part. Moreover, governments of both parties have found that these big multinational organizations, with their large capital outlays and skilled labour forces, have tended to prefer policies that kept labour costs low by co-option rather than by industrial confrontation, have pushed for wages policies to facilitate long term planning on costs and demands, and have wanted policies on capital costs and industrial taxation that minimized overheads and helped to fund research and development.

Multinational companies have joined City interests in arguing strongly against exchange controls and for stable exchange rates, against any blockage on the free movement of capital, too much direct government intervention in industrial management, excessive public ownership, and any strengthening of working-class industrial rights and social provision at the expense of private managerial prerogatives and privileges. Governments have found that multinational companies have also suffered in the intensified competition and dwindling markets of the 1970s recession, and are not above coming to the state to demand loans, assistance with restructuring and redundancies, and easier credit policies to permit the sale of their reduced output at inflated prices. The big multinationals have, in fact, been an important source of inflation in the 1970s, raising their prices and exploiting their monopoly position to offset the impact on their heavy fixed costs of a fall in total demand. Governments, for all their talk of money supply targets and so on, have been reluctant to see large companies collapse for want of demand. Local participation in the increasingly international circuit of industrial production has remained too vital, and the political and social consequences of widespread redundancies and factory closures too appalling, for politicians to allow multinationals to collapse in the pursuit of price stability.

British governments were slow to formulate clear policies on the new multinational companies. Because such companies were not really a major presence in the United Kingdom's economy until the late 1950s, initially governments did not see them 'as presenting problems different from those caused by the activities of purely national enterprises';[57] and instead tried to contain them by using the conventional mechanisms of industrial policy. On paper those mechanisms seemed extensive and potent enough, including as they did general controls on levels of demand through monetary and fiscal policy; the supervision and sponsorship of individual industries by separate government departments; the heavy reliance of certain industries on government orders for their products, and on government financial assistance in the form of investment grants and export guarantees; the creation of specialist institutions for direct industrial intervention (particularly the IRC and later the NEB); the existence of exchange controls for most of the post-war period; legal requirements on even foreign-owned companies to register under the Companies Act, and on all companies to gain government approval for the siting of new plants; their exposure to anti-monopoly policy via the Monopolies Commission; and even, under the Labour government of 1974–9, their incorporation in a system of planning agreements designed specifically to subordinate multinational corporate policy to government-specified national goals.[58]

But the sheer size and international scale of operations that characterized the multinational sector rendered many of these government controls ineffective. Some were just blocked by a refusal to co-operate. Planning agreements are a major case in point.[59] Some were not used by governments, because of the fear that multinationals would go elsewhere: tight exchange controls are an example. And some, when used, affected smaller firms while leaving the multinationals immune through size. This was particularly true of general monetary policy, as Stuart Holland has observed:

The essential part of the problem posed by the new multinationals lies in the extent to which they can suspend the normal constraints and incentives of the price mechanism in transactions between their subsidiaries in different countries. In such transactions, these companies are their own main market. By trading between subsidiaries they sidestep the market mechanism underlying Keynesian international trade models. Also, to the extent that their domestic market hold in individual countries represents a situation of joint/shared monopoly, they are not subject to the range of competitive constraints at home which used to characterise a market situation. In other words, their multinational activity is a global dimension reinforcing the meso-economic power which they now exercise in the home market.[60]

Instead of keeping a tight grip on industrial activity, governments have found themselves increasingly helpless as 'a system in which most trade is conducted between different firms in different countries (gave) way to a system in which trade increasingly is conducted between the *same* big league firms in different countries'.[61] In such a system, and even with exchange controls, multinationals were able to move resources freely across national boundaries by the use of *transfer pricing* (by buying or selling, that is, from an affiliate abroad at a false price that bore no relation to the actual costs of production involved). By this simple device alone, multinationals could (and do) exacerbate balance of payments problems, evade profits tax, weaken trade union power by creating a false impression of poor profitability, and filter out of the country any subsidy given by governments seeking to persuade them to invest locally. These administered prices pose serious questions of government control, 'for what is a mere question of "internal accounting" for the company represents imports and exports for the countries involved' and can (and must) 'affect therefore both the balance of payments and the level of income (with its fiscal and monetary repercussions within a given level of public expenditure) and consequently the pattern of growth of the whole economy'.[62] Indeed the possibility of 'national sovereignty' in economic affairs becomes highly problematic in an age of multinational capital; and this is less a problem of 'conspiracy' and 'agency' by big companies than of structural forces released on both governments and companies by the logic of capitalist competition itself. For multinationals are no 'freer' than states here to ignore the dictates of their situation, and are instead obliged to engage regularly in 'transfer pricing' to counteract their own problems of intensified competition and dwindling profitability on a world scale.

For the same reasons, multinational companies also speculate against currencies and enjoy privileged access to foreign sources of credit, which also erode the sovereignty of national governments even in advanced capitalist societies. They, and not the 'gnomes of Zurich', are the major movers of 'hot currency' as they struggle to protect the value of their liquid assets in the uncertain world of floating exchange rates. Once they have decided that a currency is over-valued, their sale of it brings its price down in a self-fulfilling spiral – to the point even, as in 1976 with the pound, when the decision of the government to buy sterling,

to protect its value at the cost of using up most of the remaining national reserves of foreign currency, actually made matters worse, as even more multinationals took this as a heaven-sent opportunity to unload their sterling before the bottom really fell out of sterling's price. Governments rarely have the reserves (and governments in weak national capitalisms never do) to outstay the multinationals in this ludicrous spiral of falling confidence; yet that exchange rate helps to determine levels of inflation and employment, and to stave off major foreign loans with their associated cuts in public sector jobs and welfare provision. Governments are thus left helpless before the multinationals in a currency crisis, and cannot even control their access to credit via restrictions on bank lending, since the multinationals can and will turn to the vast Eurodollar credit system which prefers to lend to them because of their size and the diversity (both geographically and in product terms) of their output.

The result of this concentration of private industrial power in these multinational giants is perhaps now obvious. Governments just find that it is very difficult to shape economic life as they planned. They find it hard to protect exchange rates against speculation or to control levels of investment via monetary policy. Indeed, in the latter case, when they try, they only hit those small and medium size firms which are denied the multinationals' access to Eurodollar lending, and so actually increase the relative market strength of the giants they would control. They find it hard to guarantee that subsidies given will actually be used for the purposes they require, rather than be syphoned away into another (and foreign) part of the conglomerate. They find it difficult to encourage firms to increase their exports, if (as in the case of the three non-United Kingdom owned British car firms) that would only involve a local affiliate of the multinational eroding the market position of another affiliate elsewhere; and they find it difficult to stop multinationals running down production here (by increasing their reliance on the import of components from those foreign affiliates). Governments find it difficult too to increase levels of corporate taxation, strengthen workers' rights and direct industrial investment without driving multinational industrial capital away to 'safer' political climates, and are likewise wary of tightening exchange controls for fear of precipitating just such an adverse redistribution of productive capital (and hence jobs and output). Of course, the dependence of multinationals on state assistance, and their inability to shake themselves free of the need for state action to protect their capital, gives governments a degree of leverage, particularly with multinationals in serious competitive difficulties. Yet the existence and power of the multinational sector erodes the effectiveness and legitimacy of the nation state, and it is the multinational in trouble which is least predisposed to tolerate high levels of corporate taxation and government direction. This is the contradiction that lies at the heart of the multinational company and the state in late capitalism.

Government policy on the car industry illustrates the general problems faced by politicians here. Foreign ownership of British-based car production grew apace in the 1960s, Chrysler taking over Rootes, General Motors already owning Vauxhall, and Ford already an American-based concern. Government policy perpetually chased the multinationals. A Labour government in 1968 encouraged British manufacturers to unite in British Leyland to gain a comparable size, and nationalized British Leyland in 1974 when it could no longer compete successfully as a private concern. But even when they had nationalized it, governments were driven by the logic of competition in an over-capitalized market to act as any private multinational would have done: streamlining production, cutting jobs, and eventually joining with a small foreign car company (Honda) in its own kind of joint venture with multinational capital. Chrysler failed in that competitive struggle, and a British government was obliged to subsidize it heavily in 1975, only to see Chrysler then sell its United Kingdom holdings to a French car firm, running down its United Kingdom labour force dramatically in the process. If governments could not control weak multinationals, nor could they control the strong. Henry Ford actually flew in in person to tell Prime Minister Heath to toughen his labour laws in 1971, and a later Labour government was forced to abandon its sanctions against the Ford Motor Company (when they had made a wage settlement in excess of the government's norm, after a long strike) because of the need to attract new Ford investment to Wales. Negotiating with multinationals, in Harold Wilson's words, was like negotiating 'with a gun at your head'; and government controls were really only 'a sledgehammer to catch an eel', all powerful on paper, but largely impotent because of the sheer scale of multinational operation and the dependence of governments on the multinationals for growth and employment.[63]

No less than the City, the power of multinational capital poses problems both for governments who would reindustrialize Britain and for those who would transform it into a democratic socialism. For the first, the dilemma is clear. The logic of market forces on a world scale is creating – through the agency of multinational companies – a new international division of labour that is de-industrializing Britain; and governments can pull back multinationals only if they can create conditions for private capital accumulation that are more attractive than those available in South-East Asia and Latin America. That project seems to foreshadow low wages, restricted trade union rights and intensified working conditions here that will in turn necessitate a violent confrontation with organized labour; and which will, at best, leave 'the Northern river valleys', as we observed before, the assembly points for foreign capital. Yet if instead socialism is to be our goal, the labour movement has to find a way of combatting the international power of capital, which will deploy its resources away from a strongly social democratic economy with high taxation, and may even (as in Chile) actively encourage dissent from the opponents of socialism inside the country. It is to the serious problems that this poses for the Left that we shall return in the final chapter.

Small-scale capital

British governments also face political pressures from small and medium size businesses of many types: small industrial firms, retail outlets, self-employed independent craftsmen and even co-operative ventures. The significant feature of these businesses is their lack of size, and their associated market vulnerability in an age of monopoly capital; and what goes with that – their need for state help and yet their inability to catch the ear of governments except by indirect means. Because they are too small to be able to approach a ministry on their own, small and medium size businesses are obliged to win what political influence they can through membership of the Conservative Party, by conventional lobby techniques (letters and visits to MPs, deputations to Whitehall and Westminster, campaigns through the media and so on), by federating with similar firms in trade associations, and even, on occasions, by lobbying jointly with the unions in their industries for particular state policies and aid.

Such companies are particularly vulnerable to both the general character and detailed thrust of government policy, and it is over this sector of business more than any other that politicians in power can genuinely claim to 'govern'. Such firms are invariably disproportionately dependent for their profits on the buoyancy of the home market, and on the availability of domestic sources of credit at cheap rates for their capital accumulation. Yet it is precisely these features of national economic life which are most open to government influence through changes in monetary and fiscal policy. It is small and medium size businesses whose total labour costs (and therefore profit margins) are particularly sensitive to legislation reflecting trade union pressure: on factory conditions, employment contracts, health and safety at work; and who lack the financial resources to absorb easily significant increases in National Insurance contributions, corporation tax and other government levies. Indeed, in general it is from managers in this size of firm that the heaviest political support has come for anti-union legislation, precisely because they cannot easily cope with a situation in which they are trapped between strong unions, fierce competition, and unsympathetic government policy. It is this sector of industry which is likely to rely heavily on state aid to industry, and to need particular protection from ministers in trade negotiations with other governments: on tariffs, import controls, unfair competition and the like. Such businesses are most vulnerable to any decision by government to cut back their own spending in critical sectors (say road building) or to withdraw orders from companies in breach of pay policy (as did the Labour government with its 'black list' of firms in 1977–8).[64] With government orders currently absorbing 30 per cent of total manufacturing output, this alone can, for certain industries and firms, be a sanction of quite draconian proportions. When trade unions press for better minimum conditions, it is often small and medium size businesses which argue hardest for exemptions (as we saw under that same Labour government); and it is from this sector that so many 'lame duck' industries have come in search of state aid as Britain's industrial decline has accelerated. Indeed the recent record level of bankruptcies among small private businesses is one clear indication of how this sector of industry at least has no monopoly of political power.

This is not to say that small and medium size business is without political resources, or without defences against state pressure. The capacity of any government to direct even small companies is limited by the politicians' lack of detailed knowledge about the way in which the economy works at the level of the firm, by the sheer complexity and changing character of industrial life, and by the legal independence of the firms they face. Governments rely too on the co-operation of businesses of all sizes for the collation of statistics, the raising of taxes, and the implementation of detailed industrial policy, and are dependent on the energies of businessmen for the achievement of economic growth. Since any private firm is quite free to 'ignore all the advisory services and financial inducements provided by government in an attempt to stimulate it into behaving in new ways',[65] this ability of the firm to maintain its independence can frustrate government policy in serious ways. Ultimately, of course, a government can force a company to its requirements by legal compulsion of various sorts, but only at the very high price of putting into jeopardy the voluntary co-operation of other companies on whose activities politicians and civil servants continue to depend.

Moreover, small and medium size businesses provide much of the personnel, and voting base, of the right-wing of the Conservative Party. '32% of constituency chairmen in the Conservative Party in 1969 were small and medium proprietors'.[66] Small and medium size businesses fund the party heavily,[67] and sustain (along with bigger companies) other organizations seeking to defend free enterprise.[68] Such businesses too are well organized in trade associations which have close relationships with appropriate government departments and easy access to senior politicians; and large numbers of them belong to the Institute of Directors and to the CBI and look to them for protection before the

state. 44 per cent of the CBI's company membership in 1974 was made up of firms employing less than fifty people, and another 33 per cent of firms employing between fifty-one and 200 people. Although this is no index of the actual distribution of power within these peak organizations, it remains the case that the needs of small and medium size businesses will be heard there. For even where large firms dominate a trade association, the interests of smaller firms often still come to the fore precisely because the monopolies choose to 'shelter behind the needs and interests of small business in seeking to secure wage minima or price controls geared to the situation of the marginal firm rather than to that of the large enterprise'.[69]

It often comes as a surprise though, particularly to those of a left-wing persuasion, to find that the CBI (and its predecessors the FBI, the EEF and the NABM) is relatively ineffective in shaping government policy – even under a Conservative government – and that its greatest successes tend to occur on the detail of legislation rather than on its general thrust. Analysts of the CBI have been forced to conclude that much of its influence 'does not come in the form of obtaining dramatic reversals in government policy, but rather through a "drip, drip, drip" process, a gradual wearing away and modification of government programmes so that the final version bears little resemblance to the original intention'.[70] Indeed the CBI cannot always manage even this. After all, it is not long since Sir Terence Beckett (its Director-General) threatened to 'take the gloves off and have a bare knuckle fight'[71] with a Conservative government over its policy on interest rates and domestic deflation – a threat quickly withdrawn but all too reminiscent of the strained relationship that tends to build up between trade unions and Labour Cabinets in the last years of Labour administrations. For

in many ways a Conservative Government poses

more strategic problems for the CBI than a Labour Government. On the one hand, Labour Governments (up to now at any rate) have been more open to influence from the CBI, as the experience of the last Labour Government shows. Indeed the more right wing members of such governments may see the CBI as a welcome ally in their battles against the left. . . . Conservative Governments pose different problems. In many respects they are more likely to do what the CBI wants, and there are therefore fewer areas in which policy can be 'shifted' in such a way as to produce tangible benefits which can be displayed as trophies to the membership. In other respects, when they do not do what the CBI wants, they tend to be less open to influence than Labour Governments. There are a number of reasons for this tendency: because Conservative ministers are more likely to have boardroom experience, they feel more confident about asserting what industry really needs; Conservative Governments are anxious not to be seen in the pocket of big business for electoral reasons; and, if anything, they are more likely to listen to the City than the CBI, whereas the Labour Party has a special respect for manufacturing industry. Moreover, if a Conservative Government does not do what the CBI wants, it is more difficult to attack them openly, for fear of upsetting those CBI members who are loyal Conservative supporters.[72]

This lack of leverage by peak organizations of business is often explained as a consequence of their traditionally low-key style of lobbying – their class-based embarrassment at anything more excessive than a deputation, a phone call, a letter and a glass of sherry. Indeed for this very reason the CBI has recently widened its activities: launching an annual conference on TUC lines, and even participating in regional demonstrations, to increase its visibility and hopefully its impact.[73] But businessmen still look uneasy doing this in an English context. For what Stephen Blank has called the 'political culture' of British industry still dictates a low political profile for businessmen. The origins of that culture lie far back,

not least in the accommodation made between the rising industrial bourgeoisie and the English aristocracy after 1832, and the particular experience of world monopoly prior to 1880. The cultural residue of this Victorian dominance remains with us still: a residue that is in essence 'a mercantile, old bourgeois *weltanschauung*, and not a neo-capitalist one. Many of its impulses are frankly hostile to "capitalist" ideas in this narrower, more modern sense'.[74] Aristocratic attitudes to the 'unsuitability' of business as a profession are still evident. *Laissez-faire* policies are still seen as self-evidently preferable and safe; and there persists a sense of the unconstitutionality of excessive pressure group power, even by the CBI, in the face of particularly a Conservative government's right to specify the 'national interest'. Certainly the CBI could hardly be said to show, in its style and activity, 'the aggressive self-confidence that seems to have been typical of the business community in the USA and West Germany, where business has been widely seen as the backbone of the nation'.[75] Nor do businessmen walk too easily in the corridors of power. Civil servants and businessmen for most of this century have not moved in the same social circles. Nor have many civil servants had any background or experience in industry. And though that is changing now, and the public status and visibility of senior industrialists has no doubt risen of late, it still remains the case that the business lobby in Britain has fallen victim so often to what Peter Nettl called the 'élite consensus' – sets of procedures, values and attitudes specified by the civil service, and more designed to enable Whitehall 'to colonize' industry than to strengthen industry's voice in Whitehall.[76]

However, style is by no means even the major determinant of influence here, and visibility (and protest), as we shall argue with the unions later, is as much a sign of impotence as of power. The CBI and its predecessors have had so muted an impact on the general drift of government economic policy much more because of industrial capital's subordination to the hegemony of financial interests, to their belief that what is good for the City is good for Britain. They have lacked leverage too because of divisions of interest and opinion within their own constituency: by size, industrial sector, and on policy. 'The size of firms, the product produced and the raw material utilised, methods of financing, competition, the degree of labour or capital intensiveness, whether an industry deals internationally or is primarily oriented towards the domestic market, labour relations – all create differences of interests between industries and even within a single industry.'[77] With such divisions, it has never been possible for any one organization of businessmen to specify without challenge what capital's real policy needs actually are – and this has both restricted the CBI's ability to speak out clearly in new directions without precipitating weakening resignations,[78] and has left an area of autonomy for politicians, able to listen to just some sectors of capital in specifying those needs for them. The divisions within the business lobby are at their most acute on the question of general state strategy. The CBI continues to be riven by those

'two clusters of capitalist opinion' on the role of the State that can be identified in rivalry with each other throughout this century. (One) has favoured cutting concessions to labour, and relying more on a combination of market forces and penal law to ensure labour discipline. The other school of thought has sought both to extend state activity in aid of business . . . and to secure the 'partnership' of organised labour for these ends through concessions and through the firms' institutionalisation of ostensibly voluntary collective bargaining.[79]

The centre of gravity of CBI policy has oscillated between these two extremes over the years, taking a hard monetarist line when facing an interventionist Labour government, but driven by the impact of Tory monetarism after 1979 to swing back towards tripartism and calls for government intervention in industry. Yet in doing that, the contradiction between the specific needs of particular businesses and the general need of the capitalist class as a whole has continued to build an unavoidable ambiguity into the heart of CBI policy, obliging it to contain its dislike of the monetarist 'medicine' (of high interest rates and domestic deflation) precisely because it dislikes the 'illness' (of inflation and strong trade unionism) even less.

It is exactly at those moments when this clash between the particular and the general is at its least evident that CBI leverage is at its peak. What the CBI is best at is blocking wilder excesses of trade union and Labour political radicalism – at 'policing the boundary' of trade union power while leaving the broad settlement of government policy in the hands of multinational industrial capital and financial interests – some of whom, of course, are CBI members, but for whom the CBI (which is 'still essentially an organisation for manufacturing industry')[80] is not the vital channel of political representation.[81]

Moreover it should not be thought that the political influence of even small business is to be measured by CBI successes in the lobby. The power relationship of capital to government is of a subtler kind, less visible and more potent than simply the interaction of lobbyist and lobbied. Whether lobbied or not, governments simply find, on a regular basis, that – other things apart – they need a healthy private industrial sector if they are to finance their own programmes and if they are to be re-elected. As a result policy 'drifts' business's way unless powerful forces operate to turn it otherwise. The question of 'challenge' is crucial here. For what gives capital its power is not just the activity of capitalists and managers, but the all pervasive impact on our society of 'the anonymous forces of property and the market',[82] and the passive enjoyment of advantage and privilege, obtained merely because 'of the way things work', and because those ways are not exposed to serious challenge. As Westergaard and Resler have rightly said:

In any society the patterns of people's lives and their living conditions take the forms which they do, not so much because somebody somewhere makes a series of decisions to that effect; but in large part because certain social mechanisms, principles, assumptions – call them what you will – are taken for granted. Typically of course these mechanisms and assumptions favour the interests of this or that group *vis-à-vis* the rest of the population. The favoured group enjoys effective power, even when its members take no active steps to exercise power. They do not need to do so – for much of the time at least – simply because things work their way in any case. In a capitalist society the social mechanisms and assumptions which are generally taken for granted in this way are those, in the first instance, of private property and the market. It is they which largely determine the living conditions of the people and the use of resources. And they clearly favour the interests of capital: they confer power on Capital in a very real and tangible sense. But the proof of that power is not to be found only, or even chiefly, in the fact that capitalists and managers make decisions. It is to be found in the fact that the decisions which both they and others – including government – make, and the sheer routine conduct of affairs even without definite decision-making, in the main have a common denominator: an everyday acceptance of private property and market mechanisms. It is taken for granted, 'in the ways things work', that profit should be the normal yardstick of investment in most areas of activity; that the living standards of the propertyless majority should be set primarily by the terms on which they sell or once sold their labour, and so on . . . the point of emphasising the place of anonymous social mechanisms in power is to draw attention to the controlling role of assumptions which are often not stated, simply because they are taken for granted in practical affairs. The power of capital, to repeat, is revealed much less in positive acts of decision-making – involving conflict and choice between alternative policies – than in the everyday, for much of the time unquestioned, application of those assumptions which give priority to private capital accumulation and market exchange in the use and distribution of resources. Power is to be found more in uneventful routine than in conscious and active exercise of will.[83]

The CBI then is left with the job of blocking any challenge to such 'uneventful routines' that comes from the labour movement. Its capacity to do that, as we shall see in the next chapter, derives in part from the ambiguities in the trade unions' own position, since they too require a healthy and competitive private economy to guarantee jobs for their members, and are as a result riddled with contradictory policy requirements of their own. Yet there are times when trade union militancy and Labour Party political radicalism is seen by business as a whole to threaten the rights and privileges of private capital, and then the CBI comes into the forefront of industrial politics as a defensive spokesman: most recently and potently over industrial democracy and planning agreements under the Labour government of 1974–9.[84] But except in the face of such a challenge, the CBI can claim no monopoly for its views on the side of capital. Instead, it always operates in a context in which powerful financial interests and multinational industrial capital are pressing their specific claims, and in which genuine disagreements exist even within the CBI on how industry can best be helped by the state. As a result, the CBI is normally weak when faced by monopoly capital, but defensively strong when faced by anything other than the most politically radical labour and trade union movement. To show how that operates, it is to the political power of labour that we turn now.

5 The political power of organized labour

As we have already seen, and as others have established at greater length,[1] the very existence of capital, and its growth over time, arises directly out of the creation and sale of commodities produced by others – by men and women without capital, by those with only their labour power to sell. This fact alone structures the universe faced by politicians in a capitalist society such as ours in a quite simple and overwhelming way, by placing on the agenda of political life not simply the interests, power and demands of those who own or control capital, but the interests, power and demands of those whose labour is its source. The relationship between labour and capital, as we shall see in Part Two, is a complex yet ultimately contradictory one, and the class structure it sustains in capitalism's monopoly stage is equally differentiated and obtuse. What we must recognize now is that these complexities are built on, and derive from, what is still the defining base of the capitalist mode of production: a labour process geared to the extraction of surplus value from labour by capital in the context of a perennial and anarchic struggle for advantage between capitalist firms. The very existence of trade unions, and the general interests and demands they articulate, originate in that labour process, and in the social relationships of production within which it occurs. If therefore we are to understand the particular character and influence of contemporary trade unionism in British politics, we have to grasp both the general character of the capitalist labour process and the dominant experiences of labour within capitalism at this late stage of its development.

Industrial production under capitalism is geared to the self-augmentation of capital, to the extraction of surplus value from labour power, and its realization in the form of profits, by the repeated bringing together – by the capitalist class – of the means of production (raw materials and machinery) and labour power in order to create new commodities. Capital can grow only through this process, and only then if, within it, it can perpetually increase the rate of extraction of surplus value: in absolute terms (by extending the working day or intensifying the pace of work) or in relative terms (by perpetually revolutionizing the process of production by the application of new machinery and techniques). For the labourers who actually produce the commodities, and whose surplus labour generates profits, this perpetual pressure to intensify the rate of exploitation gives to the work experience under capitalism a particular flavour – one that is not predetermined by any 'technological necessity' endemic to industrialization itself, but which arises directly out of the particular social relationships surrounding the production process under capitalism.

For the accumulation of capital by the expropriation of surplus value creates and requires a necessary set of *inequalities* at the point of production: inequalities in work experience, in rewards and in status and power within the workplace which alone creates the set of social relationships within which capital can be accumulated. Workers under capitalism find (to greater or lesser degrees, depending on their particular position in those social relationships, as we shall see in Part Two) that in selling their labour power they are actually obliged to submit themselves to an authority structure (within the capitalist firm) geared to extracting from them as high an 'effort-wage' bargain as it can. They find too that, because they own neither the things they make nor the tools they use, their labour power is treated as a commodity, and that they themselves are just as subordinate as the machinery with which they work to the prior requirements of capital accumulation. They find, in other words, that the work rules, job content, factory organization and pace of effort to which they are subject on a daily basis are not fixed by their needs, but are subordinate to the service of other goals (profits, sales, competitiveness, the full utilization of machinery and so on). They also find that, subject themselves as they will to the prior dictates of capital, capital in return gives them no security or stability in their industrial universe. On the contrary, and necessarily so because of the uncontrolled nature of the competitive struggle between capitalists, even the most loyal workers of the most paternalistic employer find their settled work routines threatened regularly by new technologies, their job security never certain because of fierce competition, and their wages perennially in need of defence and augmentation in the face of managerial pressure to hold costs to a minimum.

These instabilities have been features of life under capitalism from the beginning, but have manifested themselves in different ways at each stage of capitalism's development. So now, at this stage of late capitalism, the labour process has a particular character, the full detail of which will be discussed in Chapter 7, which is an important source of the class experiences and interests with which politicians must come to terms. For the moment, however, it will be enough to notice that the post-war labour process has been characterized by a persistent managerial pressure to erode existing skills, to spread machine-minding, and to proliferate new supervisory relationships geared to the full exploitation of heavily automated production processes. Of late, workers have experienced too a considerable pressure on their workplace organization and its associated degree of control of aspects of the work process, as multinational industrial capital in its profits crisis has sought to resolve its own competitive difficulties by intensifying the rate of exploitation of its workforce. What was accepted as a satisfactory distribution of power between management and workers in one period is suddenly unsatisfactory in the next; and jobs that seemed secure for a generation suddenly vanish in the face of intensifying competition, dwindling markets and new processes. From these detailed developments, as from the general character of capital–labour relations, two things follow that are of central importance for the political universe of the capitalist state: the nature of workers' interests, and the character of worker organization.

Precisely because of the existence and dominance of just such a set of social relationships and market processes, labour in general is *given* its interests. What it has to strive for – in the most general terms – is predetermined by the position of wage labour in the class structure of a capitalist society and by the nature of the capitalist labour process. To survive at all, workers need to maintain, if not to augment, their wages, their employment security, and whatever limited degree of control they have managed to achieve over aspects of the work process. Yet they have perpetually to strive for these in the face of capitalist processes that continually threaten to erode them: managerial pressures on wages and effort levels; the competitively-induced necessity for new technologies and the destruction of old skills; and the instabilities of capitalist recession and crisis. The general position of labour under capitalism puts labour on the defensive, but requires of it action if its position is not persistently to be eroded. It is from this imperative to act that the union function itself necessarily arises.

The British trade union movement

Trade unions are the creatures of industrial capitalism, and, unless deliberately repressed by the state, occur everywhere that capitalist social relationships establish themselves. For in their essential functions, trade unions are a major and common organizational response to the particular experience of work under capitalism. As we have seen already, that way of organizing production is unique in at least two senses. It leaves its productive class wholly dependent on their money wage for their own reproduction; and it subjects that class to the particular rigours of a labour process that is subordinated to the prior need to accumulate capital. Therefore, capitalism invites a response by those who work for it: a response essentially hostile and one that quickly becomes collective – as workers invariably come to recognize their common need to act together (as a work group if not necessarily as a class) to gain at least some minimal degree of control over the terms of their employment and the conditions under which they work. In pursuit of that control, they are then often led into an involvement with wider social issues, because of (and to the degree to which they come to see) that those terms and conditions are themselves the product of the particular structures and processes dominant in the society as a whole. But whether that widening of involvement occurs, and whether (when it does) it takes a socialist or a non-socialist form, it remains the case that at the base of industrial capitalism workers invariably form unions that are preoccupied in the first instance with the winning of some degree of immediate job control.[2]

What is most striking about that preoccupa-tion is the way in which it has always been opposed, certainly by many employers and for long periods also by the state. The story of nineteenth-century trade unionism in Britain was that of the struggle to win the legal right to exist in a form which made effective union action possible – a struggle which culminated in the 1906 Trades Dispute Act. Twentieth-century unionism has been preoccupied with translating that right into a reality, with winning the right to negotiate with employers and to be consulted by the state. The centre of gravity of that struggle – in the sense of the actual issues involved – varies over time, but the need for the struggle does not. Trade union procedural rights ebb and flow with the relative strength of the class forces deployed around them; and rights once won have to be defended if they are not to be lost. There are still employers who refuse to negotiate with unions at all. That is what the dispute at Grunwick's was all about. There is still opposition from employers generally to any significant widening of the range of issues negotiated with, and rights enjoyed by, workers and their representatives; and governments still intervene (and indeed do so increasingly) to alter the structure of labour law and the degree of consultation granted.

All this has a direct and central bearing on the character of trade union politics. For it means that trade unions enter the political arena in an inherently defensive and reactive way. Their very right to be there is itself an issue to be fought for and defended; and once won, has to be used to seek some redress to a structure of power which, left to itself, would exclude them and their members entirely. If they enjoy power now, it is power that is limited, that has been hard won, and that can be easily lost; for they began, and essentially remain, as outsiders, lobbyists, pressure groups industrially on capital and politically on the state, perpetually obliged to come from behind. There are union successes of course, as we shall see, and 'defeats for powerful capitalist interests as well as victories. After all David did overcome Goliath. But the point of the story is that David *was* smaller than Goliath and that the odds *were* heavily against him'.[3] We need to keep this truth before us if we are to grasp the actual character of the trade unions' limited impact on contemporary British politics.

For as a dwarf in the politics of giants, trade unions often find their actions are a disappointment to socialists, who look to the working class as the agency of socialist change, only to find in the union movement a brake on their more ambitious aims. Trade unions are only rarely revolutionary bodies. At times, certain of them have professed to be. Syndicalism had its moment early in the century,[4] and throughout unions have shown a propensity to support programmes of wider social reform. Indeed, as we shall see in Part Three, working-class pressure as a whole has been a vital factor democratizing the liberal state, and extending its welfare functions – in political developments which reflect *both* the limited but real social power, *and* the genuine subordination and exploitation, consolidated around the working class by its place within capitalism. But the impact of capitalism on the politics of labour has not all been in one direction. For capitalism does not just unite workers in a common labour process. It also divides them, by industry, skill, race, gender and religion. Those divisions surface in the sectionalism, and at times in the sexism and racism, of certain trade union policies. They certainly give to those policies a preoccupation with the moderate, a propensity to operate within the prevailing system while leaving unchallenged its organizing assumptions. The characteristic trade union demand, after all, is for better wages, not for the end of the wage system; for the protection of demarcated roles, not for the replacement of the division of labour; and for a greater say in the degree of labour control and grading, rather than for any end to the hierarchial and supervisory structures through which capitalism expropriates its surpluses.

Indeed, it is possible to match our figure of circles of power in Chapter 1 (Figure 1) with a figure (Figure 3) of issues on which workers and their unions seek influence, with the actual right to organize at the centre of the circle, and the question of capitalism itself at the edge. Between them are wages and working conditions, factory acts, levels of investment, general economic policy, social reform and the distribution of power. Put in that way it is possible to see clearly both that union power declines rapidly as soon as you leave the centre of the circle, and that the very question of how wide union interests spread is itself one of the most variable elements in the history of labour movements. On some occasions, and for rare moments, union activity has expanded even to the edge of the circle; but more normally it has not. Union preoccupations have been more restricted and moderate, and therefore, as will be argued, have suffered even at the centre of the circle by the social power of the institutions and processes

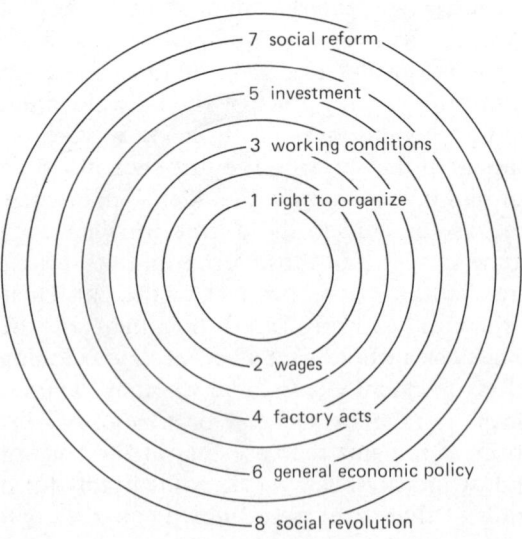

Figure 3   *Issues on which workers and unions seek influence*

beyond, which unionism has not tried with sufficient consistency to reach. Be that as it may, the existence of such a circle of possible trade union demands serves to remind us that, although capitalism defines for unionism the *range* of its political interests, it does not define what part of that range will actually predominate. Although structural forces within capitalism (of a material and cultural kind) pull unionism towards the moderate demands at the circle's centre, whether or not they stay there is fixed, not by capitalism, but by the rhythm of class struggle and the quality of leadership to which the unions are themselves exposed. The politics of unionism, no less than of industrial capital, have themselves to be organized and shaped by men and women whose lives bear the structures of capitalism but which are not totally predetermined by them.

The power of the trade unions

Seen in that context, the British trade union movement has been, and remains, remarkable both for its organizational strength and for its political moderation. Industrial capital in Britain faces a set of unions of considerable size, enjoying (as we shall see) a distinct but limited degree of industrial and political power, and wholly Labourist[5] in their political practices. All that is a product of the particular historical experience of capitalism in Britain. Unions in Britain originated in, and have grown from, three broad periods and bases. First, skilled workers and miners consolidated their unions after 1850. This was followed by the rise of the general unions of semi-skilled and unskilled manual workers from the late 1880s; then by the spread of public sector and white-collar unionism, the latter particularly in the post-war years, as the state itself became a major employer of labour.[6] Throughout that growth, the underlying political moderation of a working class protected to a degree from the worst excesses of rapid capital accumulation

by the nineteenth-century world monopoly position of British industrial capital, and then by imperialism, enabled the craft and general unions to ally together in the loose federation of the TUC, and to consolidate their organizational and electoral links with the Labour Party, to the exclusion of more radical forms of working-class politics.

The subsequent, and much more recent, involvement of the TUC in tripartite negotiations at state level (which will be discussed more fully in Part Three) was enough to persuade the remaining white-collar unions to affiliate to the Congress after 1960, after a brief flirtation with an independent white-collar federation of labour (COPPSO).[7] This has left the British state facing a uniquely united and politically moderate set of unions, within which a series of recent mergers has combined with a particular pattern of occupational growth to produce a restricted number of large craft-based, industrial, general or white-collar union bodies. The recent recession has reduced their numbers somewhat, but they remain large and concentrated, as Table 9 shows.

The long waves of capitalist development have had their impact too on the centres of gravity of this united labour movement. Its key actors in the period up to 1926 were to be found in the mines, in heavy industry and in cotton. By the 1950s those industries were in decline (the number of miners, for example, fell from 704,000 in 1947 to 287,000 in 1971); and in the long post-war boom unions consolidated themselves instead among workers in light engineering, motor vehicles and electronics, and in the new public sector bureaucracies. Their presence and power here was challenged in its turn by the severity and character of the 1970s recession, as unemployment returned to engineering, as cutbacks in government spending threatened public sector wages and jobs, and as the rising cost of oil gave miners a renewed base for wage militancy. This differential experience between

Table 9   *Union membership in Britain*

	a *Labour force*	b *Union membership*	*b as % of a*
1976	23,713,000	12,376,000	52.2

TUC membership in 1979   12,128,078

Unions with over 250,000 members

	1962		1977	1979	1982
TGWU	1,318,274	TGWU	1,929,834	2,072,818	1,700,000
AEU	982,182	AUEW	1,412,076	1,483,419	1,020,000
GMWU	786,138	GMWU	916,438	964,836	866,000
NUM	545,329	NALGO	683,011	729,405	796,000
USDAW	351,371	NUPE	650,530	712,000	704,000
NUR	308,050	EETPU	420,000	420,000	395,000
ETU	252,851	USDAW	412,627	462,178	438,000
		ASTMS	396,000	471,000	428,000
		UCATT	297,264	320,723	275,000
		NUT	289,107	291,239	224,000
		NUM	259,966	254,887	250,000

(TGWU: Transport and General Workers' Union; AUEW: Amalgamated Union of Engineering Workers; GMWU: General and Municipal Workers' Union; NALGO: National and Local Government Officers' Association; NUPE: National Union of Public Employees; EETPU Electricians' Union; USDAW: Union of Shop, Distributive and Allied Trades; ASTMS; Association of Supervisory, Technical and Managerial Staffs; UCATT: Union of Construction Workers and Allied Trades; NUT: National Union of Teachers; NUM: National Union of Mineworkers; NUR: National Union of Railwaymen)

Source: K Coates and T. Topham, *Trade Unions in Britain*, (Spokesman 1980), pp. 7, 43, 111; and C. Leys, *Politics in Britain* (Heinemann 1983), p. 115.

sectors and over time serves to remind us that different unions enjoy differing degrees of industrial and political leverage. Traditionally in Britain, militancy was highly concentrated in just a few industries (particularly coal-mining, cars, shipbuilding and engineering), and took the form through the 1950s of short unofficial strikes involving relatively few people. Before the Second World War, any militancy that survived the Depression was normally directed at private employers, with the state intervening directly only occasionally – and often as a distinctly partial mediator – so that trade union power became a 'political' issue only when governments chose to make it so, or when strikes reached a scale (as in 1926) that crossed the boundaries of one industry alone. But since 1945 the state has been a major employer in its own right, so strike action on wages and working conditions could no longer be kept apart from wider political questions, try as unions did to keep it so.

It is important to understand that the daily practice of British unionism became 'politicized' by the extending role of the state, and not by an increase in any radicalism in the union function or leadership. Indeed, official trade unionism has been slow to adapt its thinking to the qualitatively new situation created for it by greater state involvement in the economy; and to this day trade union leaders are 'happier' striking against private employers than against the government, with whom they prefer to maintain a more 'constitutional and pressure group' relationship. For by the 1960s and 1970s the state not only employed large numbers of workers directly (and proved capable, as an employer in its own right, of shutting coal-mines, steel plants and car factories); it also intervened directly in the private economy in the pursuit of nationally-specified economic goals. In the process, the distribution of militancy changed. Particularly after 1966, as governments of both parties sought to redress the dwindling competitiveness of British industrial capital by a mixture of incomes policies, new labour laws and cuts in their own spending, a new pattern of militancy emerged: more concentrated in the public sector, involving new groups of workers, including the white-collared, and taking the form often of long national stoppages.

Indeed, to understand the relationship between the unions and the state in the 1970s recession it is vital to grasp the degree of industrial power which certain sections of the union rank-and-file had established in the years of the long boom that preceded it. For there is a very real sense in which government policy since at least the 1960s in the field of industrial relations has been geared to first containing, and then reducing significantly, that degree of industrial power. By the mid 1950s, at the very latest, it was conventional across British industry as a whole for employers (often in federations) and unions to negotiate national minimum terms and conditions of service, just as in the public sector similar national negotiating structures had long been consolidated. This constituted a significant industrial advance for the unions when compared with the depression years of the 1930s, as first war-time production, then a post-war Labour government and rapid economic growth, combined to leave labour in short supply and union recognition by employers largely achieved. The issues allowed in negotiation were still narrow, and certain employers still resisted negotiating at all; but that battle at least was largely over and won as the boom consolidated itself.

Full employment also brought more significant changes of power at factory level across British industry in this period. Because labour was scarce, competition in the product markets relatively light, and work groups well organized with their own shop stewards, employers found it in their own short-term interests to buy industrial peace by negotiating a wide range of issues locally with those stewards: the pace of work, bonus payments, levels of manning and overtime, individual cases of discipline, and so on. These practices were particularly well developed in the growth industries of the boom, where labour was a small percentage of total costs, and where the regular introduction of new semi-automated production techniques and differentiated products provided ample scope for negotiating on new working practices and rates of pay.

The result, at local level, was a diminished capacity by management to increase the rate of productivity, the persistence of small unofficial strikes whenever they tried, and a significant degree of wage drift – as earnings rose more rapidly than did nationally negotiated wage rates. It was these developments which caught the attention of governments from the mid 1960s, as the dwindling competitiveness of British manufacturing capital became apparent. Unions, stewards and work groups found themselves subject to a series of hostile government initiatives: calls on union officials to control their stewards; incomes policies with productivity strings; legal changes to outlaw the tactics used by stewards in their pursuit of local power; and, when all these failed, deliberately deepened recession to create a 'better' market climate for renewed managerial attempts to regain industrial control, and for renewed moves by the state to tighten labour law in ways which eroded the solidarity of work place action.[8]

It was the response of the unions to that process of state attrition of their newly gained industrial power that brought unionism itself to the heart of British politics after 1966, and created the image of union rule. For it is clear that, in the relatively easy labour conditions of the boom, the state lacked sufficient power itself to destroy easily the basis of shop steward power. The rigidities of incomes policies tied to productivity deals bred resentments in the public sector between 1966 and 1969, because public sector workers had fewer practices to sell and stewards to defend them, and because state policy there more easily held them back in the struggle for wages. A Labour government fell in 1970, discredited by the resulting public sector strikes. That government had already failed to introduce legislation attacking the power of shop stewards, through a union-orchestrated back-bench revolt in the Labour Party. When a second attempt at legislation (the 1971 Industrial Relations Act) was defeated by a wave of strikes (by dockers, railwaymen and others), and a Tory government fell in 1974 after an unsuccessful confrontation with the miners, the 'negative' power of unionism was visible for all to see. Indeed, under the Labour government of 1974–9, trade unionism in Britain enjoyed a unique and brief period of political ascendancy, as that government – in its first social contract – traded the promise of wage restraint by the unions for union-inspired legislation and White Papers on as wide a range of issues as the unions had yet achieved: industrial relations reform and industrial democracy, social welfare provision, investment and planning agreements, and withdrawal from the Common Market. Yet from 1975 that moment of power passed, as the unions found themselves on the downturn of what has been called 'the cycle of union influence'.[9] The unions after 1975 delivered wage restraint, but the Labour government was obliged, by heavier pressures from industry, the City and the international financial community, to renege increasingly on its part of the contract. Expenditure was cut in the public sector. Planning agreements and industrial democracy were abandoned. EEC membership remained, and unemployment was allowed to rise.[10] When the Conservatives returned to power in 1979, to replace a Labour

administration itself discredited by yet another 'winter of discontent' after four years of pay restraint, even the legal changes won in the Labour government's 1975 Act were undermined by new legislation in 1980 and 1982. For by then the depth of the recession induced by government monetarist policies had brought unemployment to over four million,[11] left employers (in British Leyland and elsewhere) free to recapture direct control of working practices, and left first the civil servants and then the health workers without any significant support from private sector workers as they battled alone (and ultimately unsuccessfully) against a government determined to cut public spending and to hold down wages across the economy as a whole. By 1982 even the unions' right to sit on the advisory committees that surround the state was being challenged by the Conservative government.[12]

Union power in contemporary capitalism

This story of threatened industrial control and volatile political leverage tells us much about the character and determinants of union power in contemporary capitalism. The unions do not approach the state without political resources. When labour is scarce, and competition in the product markets of an industry easy, unions can expect to make significant gains locally, and may not even need to mobilize their membership for national political activity at all. The changing organic composition of capital in the industries of the long boom lessened managerial resistance to trade union wage demands, and provided the base on which a well-organized and self-confident working class could defend and extend its living standards and power by militancy, if need be even against the state. Even when those easy market conditions began to be eroded, and governments entered the field of industrial relations seeking to reduce the power of stewards and unions, workers still possessed the capacity to discredit a government electorally by a series of industrial disputes inspired by unpopular incomes policies. Three times in the 1970s governments fell that way; and although the need to strike indicated clearly in each case how far government policy had moved away from the wishes of the unions, still the capacity to resist incomes policies gave the unions a powerful veto on (and therefore a base from which to negotiate about) a central area of government economic management.

Here the relationship between the unions and the Labour Party was particularly significant. The close ties between the unions and the Party in the 1970s gave its political leadership a particular sensitivity to trade union needs, especially when the Party was in opposition. The relationship between the two has long been close, and the unions' formal powers within it apparently overwhelming. Trade union funds provide between 40 and 70 per cent of Party finances; unions sponsor between 30 and 40 per cent of all Labour MPs, and enjoy majority voting power at the Party's conference and on its NEC.[13] Historically of course, the unions have never exploited that formal position to the full, preferring to keep away from the detailed settlement of Labour Party policy for so long as the parliamentarians kept their distance from the unions' own sphere of activity – namely wages and industrial conditions. For two generations after 1931, union bloc votes sustained the dominance at conference and in the NEC of a Right and Centre party leadership, through a process of mutual consultation in which the union leaders were definitely the junior partners. But as even Labour governments began to legislate on wages in the 1960s, and after the 1969 clash on the government's planned legislation on union powers, a new generation of trade union leaders emerged, determined to play a bigger role in Labour Party decision-making. They were able to do so, not least through the newly created Liaison Committee, in part because of their formal position in the Party's structure. Even then their involvement was restricted by their own concern for trade union unity (large and significant unions in the TUC, like NALGO and the NUT, are not affiliated to the Labour Party), and by their own sense of the supremacy of Parliament. Yet union involvement in policy-making grew in the early 1970s, and for once gave weight to the left-wing critics of the previous Labour government. By the early 1970s, leading members of that government had come to recognize that there were votes to be won from parading their special relationship with the unions. As a result trade union demands figured centrally in the 1974 manifestos and in the post 1979 'Alternative Economic Strategy'.[14]

In power, however, the relationship between the unions and the Party has a distinct habit of going into reverse; and it certainly did in the 1970s. For with a Labour government in power, the loyalty of union leaders, and of the bulk of union activists, to 'their' government undermines their resistance to policies of retrenchment made necessary by the continuing weakness of British industrial capital. This was clear after 1974. It was not simply that the Labour government then met powerful counter-pressures from capital. It did, and they were very effective: on planning agreements, industrial democracy, levels of government spending and unemployment. More vitally, it was also that the concessions made by the Labour government to the unions (on social security payments and trade union procedural rights), when taken with the persistent strength of work groups and shop stewards at factory level, eroded still further the competitive edge of industrial capital, and so accentuated the economic weakness from which capital derived its political leverage in the first place. In power and over a long period, a Labour government gave the unions not so much influence as a set of debilitating paradoxes. It gave them a *political* one, that to resist Labour government retrenchment by industrial action was only to pave the way for the arrival in power of an even less sympathetic Conservative government. It also gave them an *economic* one, that (regardless of which party was in power) the trade unions needed a healthy economy in which to negotiate, and yet found that their own power was a barrier to the reconstitution of that health so long as the economy was locked in a capitalist system which in crisis needed to achieve significant increases in the rate of extraction of surplus value if its profit rates were to be sustained. Lacking any practice in, or familiarity with, the politics of replacing capitalism, trade unions operating within it found themselves not with political power but with an eroding influence, obliged to struggle ineffectually merely to slow down the impact of the recession on their members, at the price of seeing the relative competitive edge of British industrial capital in that recession weaken still further.

The character of trade union power

We are now in a position to specify more accurately the character of trade union power. It is the power of a Sisyphus, not of a Hercules. The basic asymmetry in the distribution of power in capitalism dominates unions just as much as it does their members. The individual worker faces an employer who is armed with immensely superior sanctions (that is why unionism arises in the first place) and that asymmetry does not go away for the union's presence. Without unionism, the worker is subject to dismissal and loss of wages, sanctions that are necessarily traumatic for his or her life situation, but which are only marginal to the costs of the employer. Even when unionized, work groups still face an authority structure in industry that is in private hands, in which the thrust of managerial policy goes on automatically unless unions act quickly to stop it. Even at this level then, union power is necessarily negative and reactive, no matter

how easy the conditions of bargaining happen to be. In the broader context, union power is still of that kind, still engaged in attempting to shape and reverse processes initiated elsewhere, ones that are carried through quite automatically by market forces and private managerial structures unless the unions are strong enough to block them. It is in that sense that union power generally has the quality of Sisyphus, perpetually obliged to push the ball up a hill down which, left to itself, it would roll automatically.[15] The tide of power for capital, as was argued in Chapter 4, runs with the gradient of market forces in capitalism. That of the unions does not, as Figure 4 indicates. As a result unions have to work with immense industry to move government policy in their direction, and to keep it there, once moved.

Even when organized for that task, the unions' terrain is difficult. If, as many of their critics imply, they enjoy enormous 'potential' power, it is a potential 'whose realisation is beset with immense difficulties'.[16] The unions' ultimate sanction, the strike, is negative and reactive in character, and is profoundly difficult to maintain in the face of powerful material and cultural forces that always operate on strikers and their families. For the unions lack resources of the kind exercised by capital.

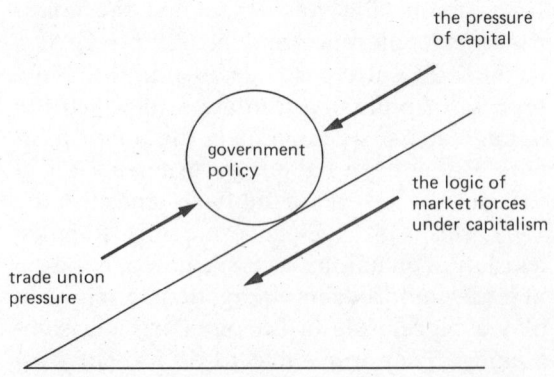

Figure 4   *Union power*

There are no labour 'gnomes of Zurich', no labour equivalent of the World Bank, the International Monetary Fund or the OECD, to ensure that governments desist from taking measures detrimental to wage earners and favourable to business, or to press for policies which are of advantage to 'lower income groups' and which are opposed to the interests of economic élites. For wage earners in the capitalist world, international solidarity is part of a hallowed rhetoric which seldom manifests itself concretely and effectively; for business, it is a permanent reality.[17]

It is capital, not the unions, that enjoys power 'in the day-to-day economic decision-making of capitalist enterprise. What a firm produces, whether it exports or does not export; whether it invests, in what, and for what purpose; whether it absorbs or is absorbed by other firms – these and many other such decisions are matters over which labour has at best an indirect degree of influence and more generally no influence at all'.[18] It is for this reason, as Ralph Miliband has correctly observed, that 'governments are so much less concerned to obtain the "confidence" of labour than of business'.[19]

Instead, unions face centres of power, in sections of the civil service, in industry and in the City, that are well organized and class conscious. Assertive trade unionism can and does provoke from these élites counter-activity of a powerful kind. Money moves abroad, investment is redeployed, industrial plant run down, anti-union parties and propaganda well funded. This latter is particularly important in the British case, for unions here operate in a culture largely influenced by, and sympathetic to, the preoccupations of these capitalist centres of power. The force and orchestration of anti-union feeling is enough to undermine all but the strongest consolidation of support for industrial action, and leaves union leaderships for the bulk of the time with a politically conservative and only sporadically industrially militant membership. A full dis-

cussion of the determinants and content of class consciousness in Britain must wait until Chapter 7. What we need to grasp here is only the extent to which the gap between official orthodoxies and actual industrial experience tends to produce a volatility and transcience in mass consciousness, to the detriment of any politically radicalized and sustained trade union leadership. In the pursuit of power, union leaders operate on a much 'shorter leash' than any optimistic theory of working class socialist consciousness would allow. As Richard Hyman has noted:

Large numbers of workers are recognising for the first time the need for collective self activity to protect their living standards and working conditions; but this activity does not reflect any *general* questioning of the relations of production in capitalist society. The hegemony of bourgeois ideology is evident in the findings of public opinion surveys: the majority of trade unionists are willing to criticise the unions for economic difficulties, blame workers for most disputes, and support legal restrictions on the right to strike. Such findings follow naturally from the purely sectional consciousness of most organised workers: they are ready to accept the condemnation, by press and politicians, of *other* workers' strikes. Though they are unable to accept the dominant ideology in relation to their *own* activity, this activity is itself – whether or not it results in concrete gains – often transient; rarely does it result in any enduring revision of consciousness.[20]

It is this volatility and moderation of consciousness that union leaders then compound by their own active commitment to parliamentarianism and to the Labour Party. That too acts as a powerful force limiting the range of tactics and demands advocated before the state by contemporary union leaders. Particularly with a Labour government, as we have seen, such as set of beliefs immobilizes the unions at the very moment when their defences need to be at their strongest, as Labour governments cut public spending, wages and jobs under external financial pressure and industrial competitive decline.

This set of dominant values is but one main feature of the whole structure of inequality faced by trade union leaders as they approach the state, the full impact of which is to leave them (and stewards at a lower level)[21] particularly vulnerable to incorporation. Under that pressure, union leaders are not usually 'bought off' by the promise of easier life styles after retirement, but are more normally drawn away from their memberships by a different working routine, different social contacts, and by sustained managerial pressure to act as 'managers of discontent', educators of their members in the 'realities' of economic life. The very fact that those 'realities' under capitalism preclude the easy complementarity of rapid capital accumulation and strong trade unionism, means that there is a perennial tendency in trade union politics to succumb to that pressure; and for leaders and their members to act quite voluntarily to hold back militant demands and tactics in the short term, in the hope that the resulting revival of corporate profits will bring easier times ahead. Given the intensification of world recession and the growth of fierce competition from better capitalized and even less unionized workforces, that hope of course invariably proves to be forlorn. But it never stops the strategy of short term restraint from reappearing with uncanny regularity, to rob the unions of even their vestigial defensive power.

For the unions are the victims of the incompatibility of their needs with a weak capitalism. Now, as always, unions tend to ask for little, but a little that is still too much. They want job security as well as high wages and some degree of control over the work process. They want price stability, but also government expenditure on welfare provision. They even, at times, seek some redistribution in the wider distribution of social wealth and power. Yet they are caught by the logic of market forces in a weak capitalism. Job security requires industrial competitiveness, and hence high productivity. Price stability requires that government expenditure does not outstrip the growth of that productivity in the industrial sector. Both competitiveness and productivity require in their turn that management intensifies labour processes, exploitation rates and levels of accumulation. None of that allows for the rising wages, job control and social welfare that unions seek too. The tragedy of unionism in contemporary capitalism is not its power but its relative and growing impotence, and those who see and describe it otherwise play their own part in quickening the pace at which any vestigial union power erodes.

There is much in the contemporary world to worry the advocates of trade unionism. The rise of multinational industrial capital presents even greater problems to unions seeking industrial power; and the crisis of profits in the multinational sector puts existing degrees of job control at risk. The new international division of labour that those multinational companies, in their profits crisis, are initiating, weakens union leverage in Britain still further, by threatening militant workers with an even quicker loss of jobs. The severity of the present recession is also eroding industrial militancy, as workers hang on to jobs only by tolerating intensifications of work routines and cuts in real wages that they would not have tolerated in easier times. The recession is hitting the unions directly, both by denying them a militant membership on which to resist it, and by bringing them close to financial disaster as their membership numbers decline (the TUC, for example, lost a million members in 1981 alone).

The drift of industry out of the inner cities, and its relocation increasingly in rural and suburban areas, eats away too at trade union industrial power at the very moment when the desperate plight of the urban poor cries out for strong organization of the union type. For de-industrialization is ripping out the traditional heartland of industrial militancy: 'the dock industry, an important exemplar, organising centre and training ground for activists has been all but wiped out in Liverpool, Hull and London's East End; the heavy engineering industry has been battered in Manchester, Coventry, Tyneside and Clydeside; the steel industry has been decimated in Sheffield and South Wales; the West Midlands foundry, car and car components industries have suffered huge job losses'.[22] What is left in the inner city is the big concentration of public sector employees, 'the local councils, hospitals, universities and polytechnics. With highly sectionalised workforces, elaborate status hierarchies and little muscle, these cannot be the leading cohorts of the future. On the contrary, and as the recent health workers' dispute has plainly demonstrated, they are critically dependent upon secondary support on a scale not ordinarily given'.[23] The inflationary nature of the contemporary crisis, moreover, means that they will need that support more and more. For the stagflation of the 1970s has drawn governments into economic activity in ways which threaten union power, encouraging them to cut back their own social expenditure, so directly reducing public sector employment and the social wage; and obliging them, in the pursuit of a healthy industrial base, to lend state power to the side of management in their assault on shop stewards and work groups. The full character of that attack is a topic for Part Three of this book, for it helps to set the political agenda of the Left in the 1980s. But its existence already makes two things about trade union power abundantly clear. First, the unions' capacity to establish *permanently* a powerful leverage on the state runs quite counter to the imperatives on state action emerging from late capitalism in its crisis. Second, as a result, and no matter how hard and unclear the actual way forward is, there seems no avoiding the conclusion that the only guarantee of enhanced and permanent union power lies in the attempt to replace that capitalism in crisis by a democratic and socialist polity. That too is a topic to which we will return in the final pages of this book (Chapter 11).

Part Two: The Social Context of British Politics

6   Class and politics in contemporary Britain

So far we have talked about the economy. In particular we have discussed the processes to which that economy is subject, and the major concentrations of institutional power (from multinational corporations to trade unions) to which it gives rise. We have attempted to establish the characteristic political demands and resources associated with each. But if we are to understand the state in full, and contemporary politics as a whole, we must move on. For what politicians face is far more than an economy, however complex. They face an entire *civil society*, a multifaceted social structure built around and based upon that economic activity, but a social structure none the less that stretches far beyond these economic processes, and contains and generates sets of experiences and interests far removed from economic activity itself. Indeed, our ability to understand properly the political significance of the economic forces we have just described obliges us to situate them in the wider social formation in which they actually operate, and through which they enter the consciousness of politicians and the terrain of the state.

The spheres of political life we have examined so far have had at their centre the process of *capital accumulation*; but even as an economic system capitalism (and the accumulation at its core) requires far more than a social division of labour within the factory and the office. The labour that enters that factory or office has itself to be *reproduced* on a daily basis, in a social 'space' far removed from the sphere of wage labour as such. The goods made in that factory, and distributed through that office, have then to be sold and *consumed*, so that profits can be *realized* to finance a further stage of accumulation. Given the visible gap between the social or communal nature of production and the private appropriation of profit, the structure of ownership and command that surrounds accumulation has also to be *legitimated* in the eyes of those subject to it. It is in the sphere of civil society as a whole, 'on that site where individual subjects reproduce their material conditions of life',[1] that such patterns of reproduction, realization and legitimation takes place. It is there too, in civil society, in that 'set of social relationships that lie between the economic structure and the state', that the social division of labour consolidated around the accumulation process meets, shapes, and is in its turn shaped by patterns of social division that predate capitalism, or that are called into existence not by capitalist accumulation as such, but by the processes of reproduction, realization and legitimation that surround and sustain it.

What the social division of labour that is consolidated around the accumulation process does is to create *classes*, and to give those classes a propensity to hold interests of a particular kind. However, classes do not emerge from a blank page of history. They do not emerge, that is, unmarked by their origins, or by what has gone before. Nor are the experiences of individuals within them (and the set of self-definitions and preoccupations those individuals gather) unaffected by social processes released upon and around them in their social roles, not just as workers, but as parents, consumers, citizens and lovers. On the contrary, and as we shall see, capitalism and its classes were born into a world already shaped by patterns of social inequality based not just on class but on gender and religion, and to a lesser extent, on race too. Capitalism then set in motion processes which incorporated those already-existing social divisions into a complex articulation with the new polarities of its own social order. In addition, and as it developed, capitalism also consolidated differential patterns of consumption ultimately derivative upon the inequalities of its own class division – relations of 'distribution, exchange and consumption' in the sphere of circulation that constitutes 'the crucial mediator between the sphere of production and the social relations of civil society'[3] as a whole. As it developed, capitalism also called into existence sets of political institutions and structures of legitimation that shaped (without totally determining) both the experience of life for its own subordinate classes and their characteristic patterns of thought and reaction.

What that means for us now is that a full analysis of the social context of British politics requires that we chart not only the dominant patterns of *exploitation* but also the related systems of *oppression* in contemporary British capitalism. What we have to note first is that the accumulation process at the heart of capitalism generates *classes*, sets of social relationships organized around the *exploitation* of wage labour and the expropriation of surplus value; sets of social relationships, moreover, which generate struggles within and between dominant and subordinate classes. But classes do not exist alone, because the accumulation process does not exist in isolation. Instead, and because of capitalist production's own need for associated spheres of reproduction, consumption and legitimation (and because, as we will see later, capitalism

also exists only in articulation with other non-capitalist modes of production) we will find that complex patterns of *oppression* (by gender, race and religion) exist alongside, and are integrated within, the dominant relationships of class exploitation. These patterns of oppression generate not class struggles, but *popular-democratic* ones – mobilizations of sections of the oppressed which relate in complicated ways to the struggles within and between classes over the accumulation of capital itself. For radicals absorbed within these popular-democratic mobilizations, the wider questions of class struggle and capitalist-replacement may seem secondary and irrelevant, or even distracting and divisive. For Marxists, however, although the accumulation process can be said to be 'determining in the last instance', the primacy of the social tensions generated by capitalist accumulation ought not to obscure the fundamental nature of the related patterns of non-class oppression without which capitalism cannot survive.

Once this is recognized, the task facing the Left both at the theoretical and practical levels becomes clear. Theoretically, the job of the Left is to understand both exploitation and oppression under capitalism in their complex inter-relationship. Politically, the job of the Left is to forge an alliance between the exploited and the oppressed. Indeed, it is this recognition which gives shape to subsequent chapters. For such a view suggests that our task next (in Chapter 7) is to chart class relationships and class struggles before, in Chapter 8, looking at the associated patterns of oppression and popular-democratic resistance that go on alongside. In Chapter 9 we shall examine the whole area of ideas, consciousness, legitimacy and social stability; before, in the final chapters, drawing attention to the problems and opportunities presented both to the state and to the Left by this interaction of exploitation and oppression in contemporary British politics.

What we must do first is to build on what we have established already, clarify our sense of the relationship between accumulation and civil society, and locate the major social divisions of labour that link the two. In other words, before examining the complexities of civil society, we must establish their base in the class structure that surrounds the accumulation process. Since our ultimate focus is on politics and the state, a diagram of linkages may be of value here (Figure 5). So far we have looked at the flows of influence from a capitalist economy to the state. Logically, given that this is capitalism and that we are interested in the state as such, two other tasks face us before even that simplified relationship can be said to be mapped in full. We need, that is, to explore the reciprocal relationship of the state to the economy (Figure 6), and to fix the intervening relations of social class (Figure 7). The first of these tasks will be dealt with in Chapter 10; the second in Chapter 7.

The fact that there is a gap between those two, that Chapters 8 and 9 need to exist, reflects a recognition within the structure of the argument here that capitalism is more than a process of accumulation and class division. Since processes of reproduction, realization and legitimation also go on, and since the total social formation within which the capitalist mode of production is dominant is a complex totality, that also has to be mapped and its

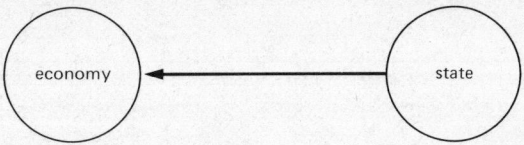

Figure 6   *The relationship of the state to the economy*

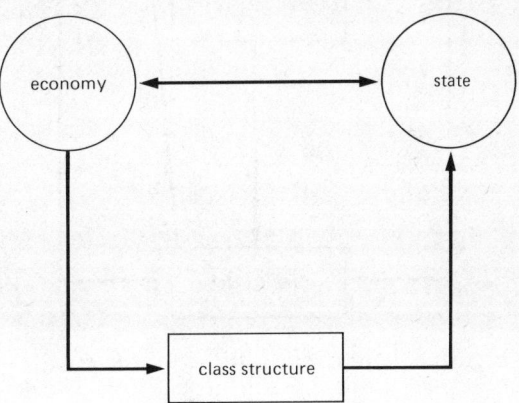

Figure 7   *The relationships of social class*

political significance charted. Civil society as a whole ought properly to be inserted into the figure as follows, in order to make clear that the completion of the task before us actually requires that we supplement the study of 'A' and 'B' with the examination of 'C', 'D' and 'E' (Figure 8). Modern politics operates on a terrain 'C', in which the state seeks to enhance the credibility of its own position and the legitimacy of the social order as a whole, in the face of class struggles and popular-democratic mobilizations generated by the problems and inequalities experienced within the accumulation, realization and reproduction processes of late capitalism. To understand those in turn requires a systematic examination of 'D' and 'E'. We need to understand at 'D' the way in which reproduction and consumption are

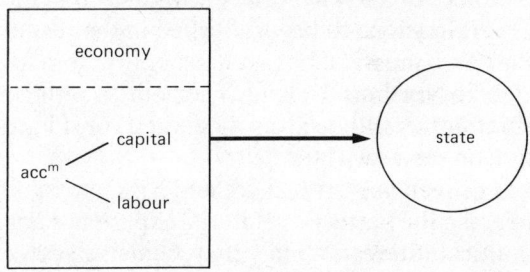

Figure 5   *Flows of influence from a capitalist economy to the state*

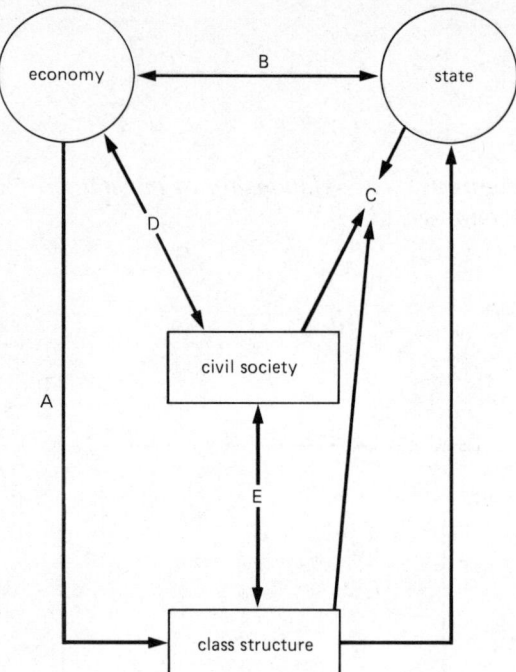

Figure 8   *State, class and civil society*

shaped by contradictions within, and the stages of development of, the accumulation process itself. We must also examine at 'E' the class 'structuration' of those reproduction and consumption patterns, and the reciprocal impact of religion, patriarchy and racism on the social division of labour surrounding accumulation as such.

That is the overall task of Part Two. Our most immediate problem is where to begin. The choice of starting point is itself a theoretical statement. Entry points in analysis are never neutral between theoretical paradigms. Consistent with the Marxist framework used so far, I suggest we begin not with civil society as such, but with accumulation. I suggest this in spite of the recognition that, in a society like ours, people's experiences are affected by many things that do not have anything to do directly with accumulation by how old they

are, by their gender, race, religion, or where they live. People are not reducible to the work they do, or to their position in (or absence from) the social division of labour surrounding production. On the contrary, individuals have to be understood 'in the round'.

For example, people in their forties and fifties are obviously at a different point in their individual life cycles from those in their twenties: there is a *generational* dimension to politics that taps wholly different memories, experiences, expectations, preoccupations and timescales. There is a *gender* dimension too. The experience of men and women differs so markedly in every tiny detail of living that no automatic congruity of political interests can be assumed between them. If congruity exists, it will need to be explained, and the pattern of its absence charted equally. Experience in this society too is structured differentially by *ethnic background* and by region. To be black is to carry a range of disabilities in virtually every aspect of public human experience, from work and leisure to housing and health. Likewise there are significant *regional* variations in the distribution of employment, social capital, class structure and political traditions – a regional factor visible even within English politics (in the divide of north and south), even more potent in the incipient nationalisms of Scotland and Wales, and at its most acute in the particular politics of religion, nationalism and class in the six northern counties of Ireland. Indeed, so acute is it there that it is necessary now to say that the generalizations to be established in the rest of Part Two must not be taken to apply automatically to Northern Ireland. The politics of those six counties will be given a detailed consideration on their own later.

Yet even in Northern Ireland it is impossible to grasp the pattern of material experience and political interests simply by rehearsing such a list of discrete social factors as age, gender, ethnicity, region or religion. For the impact of such factors on people's lives, and certainly on their politics, arises out of the relationship each establishes with the otherwise all-pervasive influence of *class* in British society. Governments face a population structured primarily by the differential experiences, organizations, patterns of collective behaviour, attitudes and interests sustained by the class structure into which they are embedded. That structure is a complex one, as we will see. The impact of class is subtle and many-sided. But the complexities and subtleties are themselves rooted in a quite simple fact: that this society is a capitalist one, in which the experience of individuals is moulded primarily by the terms upon which they sell their labour power. Those terms are *socially* determined, historically transmitted, necessarily unequal and persistently the terrain of disagreement and struggle. That is not to deny that this society is also patriarchal and racist, nor to denigrate the importance for its contemporary politics of the uneven regional impact of imperialism, even within the United Kingdom. It is rather to stress that to grasp the differing experiences of men and women in this society it is necessary to locate those men and women in a social structure which is both capitalist and patriarchal. Likewise, to locate the differing experience of black and white (both male and female), it is necessary to locate people of all ethnic backgrounds in a social structure which is not simply capitalist and patriarchal, but racist as well.

Because that social structure is hierarchial, we would do well to start at the top. Because that hierarchy is capitalist in origin, we would do well to start with class. Because it is patriarchal, we ought properly to begin (if we are coming from the top) with men; and because it is racist a view from the top must take us first to the whites. That is, we must first establish the character of the dominant set of social relationships, the class relations and associated interests of white males, before exploring the relationship between that class structure and its agents, and those of the super-exploited – women of any colour, and men and women of any colour but white. For we shall find that the life experience of white men is fixed by their class position, and by their dominance over women and the non-white. The life situation of white women is fixed partly by their class, but also by the restricting impact of a patriarchal culture and its sexist social practices. We will find too that black males are restricted further by a parallel process of racism; black women by racism and sexism too. We will also find the impact of class everywhere.

In short we shall find a hierarchy of social privilege in every sphere: between men, between women and between blacks – but hierarchies in which the centre of gravity of each is lower, as we move from white men through white women to blacks. This is expressed in Figure 9. The experience of, say, a black female in this society (at 'X') is a cumulative product of being locked into related and unequal social structures by class, gender and colour. To be black, female and working class is to face as restricted a range of social chances as any in this society. To be white and male and upper class is to face the greatest. To be white, female and middle class is to occupy about as central a location as you can find. Since to grasp the whole, it is

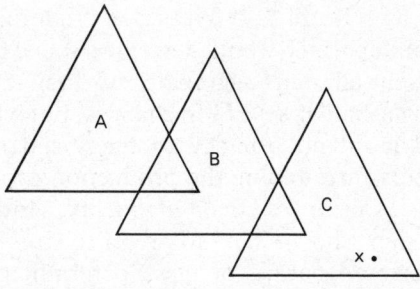

A inequality by class
B inequality by gender
C inequality by race

Figure 9   *The hierarchy of social privilege*

necessary to study the parts, let us start at 'A' and build in 'B' and 'C' later. Let us look first at the class structure and associated political interests of white male non-Irish Britain.

The problem of class

To write about class at all is to enter an arena of enormous controversy. Like all controversies, what is striking about this one is how so many of the participants within it are so keen to stress their areas of disagreement that they fail to concede first the consensus which alone makes the controversy possible. What is common to them all is the recognition of inequality, of the existence of strata within British society, broad bands of social positions (occupied by generation after generation of people), within which broadly similar sets of life chances are experienced. Britain is stratified, like all societies hitherto, into relationships of superiority and subordination, where people at the top, because of their social position, have differentially favourable access to the scarce goods of the society (and not just to its consumer goods, but to its psychic and immaterial ones: power, prestige, control and status).

The disagreement in the literature turns on how best to describe and explain this inequality. It is in this sense, as Peter Calvert has it, that 'class [is] an essentially contested concept'.[2] There is a Weberian tradition of scholarship which would describe a social class as essentially an aggregate of individuals sharing a similar set of life chances, but which would grant no primacy to the social relationships surrounding the production process as the source of that inequality. Indeed Weberian scholars tend to prefer to stress the multifaceted nature of class determination, the way class position is fixed by market forces, and the existence of separate sources of inequality beyond class and the market – inequalities of status and power.[3] Against that there is a Marxist tradition which is unhappy

with any notion that has class as simply reflecting and embodying inequalities in the *distribution* of the social product, and which argues instead that class relationships arise in the process of *production* that precedes such distributional struggles.[4] From the Marxist tradition comes the argument that the social relationships surrounding the production process are the primary ones, in the sense that they texture all the rest of the social relationships in the society; and that those social relationships of production are, in their essence, relationships of conflict and contradiction. In other words, a Marxist sense of class would suggest that the whole social structure has at its core the need to produce the artefacts vital for the sustenance of life, that in each society that production process is sustained over time by stable sets of social relationships, and that in all class societies (including capitalism) those relationships take an exploitative form. Although production is a collective act, what characterizes class societies is that the surplus produced is expropriated as the private property of a non-producing minority. No matter how complex actual class relationships become, through their centre necessarily runs a conflict between the producers of wealth and its expropriators that colours the whole of political life in that society.

Now I have deliberately used opaque terms ('textured', 'essence', 'core' and 'colour') to try to transmit the recognition that the impact of these basic clashes of interest between classes in the production process is a highly mediated one, filtered into political life through a mass of intervening attitudes, practices and institutions that it is the purpose of this part of the book to chart. It would be far too easy (and totally misleading) to assume that the sale of labour power by itself predetermines the self-definitions, sense of self-interest and broader social identification of those doing the selling. Clearly it does not. Workers in very similar class positions can and do hold very different definitions of their situation and interests at any one time, and those definitions can and do change in time. How class position is mediated into class consciousness and action will therefore be one of the vital themes running through this chapter, through Chapters 7 and 9. The strength of a Marxist approach lies in its insistence that class positions do exist independently of the consciousness of the individuals who occupy those positions, and in its associated assertion that those class positions arise because production in any society is always organized in a particular way; that there is a *mode of production* in which a certain set of social relationships is dominant and defining.

That in turn suggests that to understand the dominant set of social relationships now, we must locate the dominant mode of production. To do that, we must explain and trace its emergence over time, and fix precisely the interaction of the new mode of production (and its emerging social classes) with previously dominant modes and their social classes. We have already completed much of that task, establishing in Part One that the dominant mode of production in Britain is capitalist (in which the determining social relationships are those of wage labour and private property). We have already seen both the way in which that capitalism emerged from feudalism and the way in which it has itself been subject to internal processes of development and change.

We are now in a position to see the class structure of contemporary Britain as a product of that historical process, and in its constituent elements to be still composed of social classes created in the transition to capitalism, and in the internal development of capitalism once dominant. Figure 10 attempts to capture that truth in a schematic way, suggesting that the present class structure can best be seen as an articulation of three things: the legacy of feudalism and the character of its transition to capitalism (which has left us with a particular aristocracy, a certain set of agrarian social classes and elements of a petty bourgeoisie of small shopkeepers and artisans); the constituent classes of capitalism itself (a class of merchant capitalists, industrialists and eventually financiers, and a proletariat constituted from a displaced peasantry and destroyed artisanate); and social strata called into existence by developments within capitalism (developments that enlarged white collar employment in the private monopolies and the state bureaucracy, that moved proletarian employment from heavy industry to light, and consolidated the dominance of financial and multinational interests in the ruling class). Table 10 gives a numerical specification of the actual occupational distribution in 1971, and some measure of how that distribution has changed this century.

Class structure and inequality

If we look at the pattern of inequality associated with the contemporary class structure, certain things are very clear. The first is the imbalance of effort and reward within the production process itself.[5] For governments face a society in which those groups of men and women who experience the most adverse working conditions, the longest working hours, the most socially disruptive and personally wearing industrial routines, and who experience the lowest degree of job security and control – are characteristically less well paid than are other groups who produce less in easier and more certain conditions. Manual workers in particular work on average longer hours, do more shift work, have tighter controls on the timing and content of their work, and have a higher propensity to work in conditions that are noisier, subject to greater temperature extremes and supported by lower quality provision of canteens and lavatories, than do white-collar and managerial staff. At the same time they are more subject to industrial accidents, shorter holidays, smaller

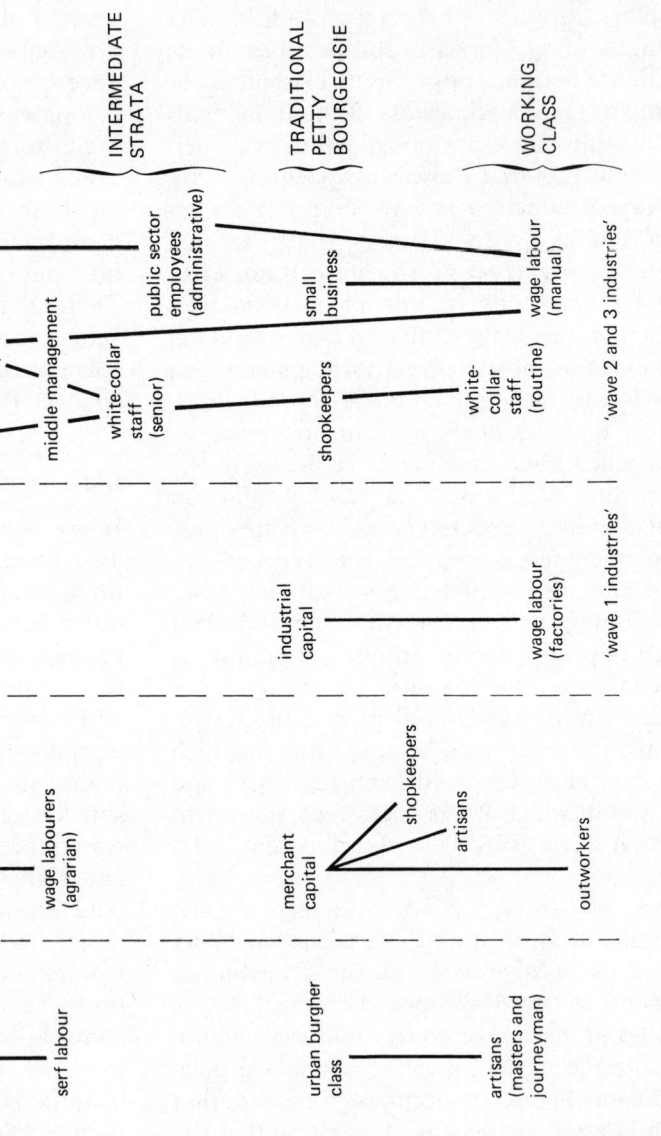

Figure 10 *British class structure as a product of historical process*

Table 10   *The occupied population of Great Britain by major occupational groups, 1911–71*

Occupational groups	Number of persons in major occupational groups 1911–71 (thousands)						
	1911	*1921*	*1931*	*1951*	*1961*	*1966*	*1971*
Employers and proprietors	1,232	1,318	1,407	1,117	1,140	832	622
White-collar workers	3,433	4,094	4,841	6,948	8,479	9,461	10,405
Managers and administrators	631	704	770	1,245	1,270	1,514	2,085
Higher professionals	184	196	240	435	718	829	928
Lower professionals and technicians	560	679	728	1,059	1,418	1,604	1,880
Foremen and inspectors	237	279	323	590	681	736	736
Clerks	832	1,256	1,404	2,341	2,994	3,262	3,412
Salesmen and shop assistants	989	980	1,376	1,278	1,398	1,516	1,364
Manual workers	13,685	13,920	14,776	14,450	14,021	14,393	13,343
Skilled	5,608	5,572	5,618	5,617	5,981	5,857	
Semi-skilled	6,310	5,608	6,044	6,124	6,004	6,437	
Unskilled	1,767	2,740	3,114	2,709	2,037	2,099	
Total occupied population	18,350	19,332	21,024	22,515	23,639	24,686	24,370

Note: In the 1966 sample census and the 1971 census the employer and managerial status categories given are 'self-employed with and without employers' and 'managers'. In contrast with 1961 this distinguishes employers from managers but it does not distinguish the self-employed (without employees), which are included in the groups according to the nature of their occupations, from the employers and proprietors. People of both employer and self-employed status are included in the employer and the proprietor occupations and in the higher and lower professional groups in the table so that no division of the 'self-employed with and without employers' was necessary. For the other groups in this table, however, the 'self-employed with and without employees' were divided into employers and self-employed according to the 1951 ratio of employers to self-employed in these groups. The 'employers' were then added to the 'employers and proprietors' group and the 'self-employed' added to their appropriate groups (skilled, semi-skilled, etc).

Source: R. Brown, 'Work', in P. Abrams (ed.), *Work, Urbanism and Inequality* (Weidenfeld and Nicolson 1978), p. 74.

pensions, less secure earnings, greater unemployment and a quite different level and pattern of earnings during their working life – one that peaks early and declines into poverty in old age, unprotected by the increments and occupational pensions characteristic of middle management and state-employed professionals.[6] Earning levels too are quite definitely skewed against the manual working class, and here the experience of even 'affluent workers' is quite typical. Miners now (and car workers in an earlier epoch) have to work long hours, shifts, at weekends and under bad conditions, to accumulate a wage packet comparable to or at least near that common among middle management and profession-

als. Even then they have much less guarantee (as car workers have already found, and miners fear they are poised to find) that such a level of affluence can be sustained in the face of intensified competition and shifting government policy in the areas in which they work.

In the professions, rising earnings often go hand in hand with an enriched and more satisfying job. Among even those limited sections of the manual working class for whom high earnings are a possibility, the reverse is invariably the case. Indeed 'one could summarise this evidence by stating that white collar workers have careers whereas blue collar employees simply do jobs'.[7] As a result governments find that 'cash' is itself *the* preoccupation to which manual workers look in order to justify the excesses of working conditions and hours to which they are repeatedly and unavoidably put.

Two other features of inequality are associated with, and indeed arise from, that pattern of earnings and working conditions at the point of production. The first occurs in the area of consumption, of both private and social goods and services. For governments face too a society in which the access people enjoy to the cultural and material products of their collective act of labour (housing, consumer goods, social services and cultural facilities) is differentially and unequally allocated; in which that allocation is determined by the position occupied by individuals in the class system of ownership and command. The working class's lack of property and dependence on the sale of their labour power, gives them a 'vulnerability' to poverty in recession, personal sickness and old age that middle-class people characteristically lack. It is from their ranks that 'are, so to speak, recruited the unemployed, the aged poor, the chronically destitute, and the sub-proletariat of capitalist society'.[8] Poverty is now with us on a very large scale. So too is wealth. By 1979 ten million people were living on or at the edge of poverty, put there by low pay, unemployment, age, sickness and the absence of a main breadwinner.[9] Indeed, the main recent and quite monumental study of poverty in Britain found that even before the onset of deepening recession, at least one person in four lacked the means likely to be necessary for ordinary life by common current standards.[10] As the recession deepened, poverty spread still further. In 1980, the Low Pay Unit found that 4.7 million full-time adult workers and nearly 2.8 million part-timers earned less than the Unit's low pay definition of £75 a week, in an overall distribution of income that was still as unequal as it had been in 1886.[11] By 1982, with anything between 3.8 million and 5 million people unemployed, the total number of people in paid work in Great Britain was lower than at any time since 1939.

Alongside that poverty stands the persistence and monopoly of wealth, the ownership of substantial chunks of private capital by the few. House ownership and the possession of consumer durables may have become more widespread, and have penetrated to a degree the skilled strata of the working class. Televisions and stereos may have an even wider distribution. But the ownership of shares, and the possession of private wealth and income in total, remains stubbornly unequal. In 1977 the top 1 per cent of the population still received 5.4 per cent of total personal income, the top 10 per cent 25.8 per cent, and that was equivalent to the share taken by the bottom 50 per cent (Table 11). In the same year the most privileged 10 per cent still owned 89.6 per cent of all privately-owned shares, 84.1 per cent of all land, and 37.5 per cent of the housing stock by value.

The bottom 80% (of the population) owned less than a quarter of total personal wealth in 1975: this was less than the top 1% of the population in the same year. The next 4% of the population owned almost as great a share of total personal wealth – just under 22%. The top 5% then, owned some 46% of total personal wealth, just less than twice that of the bottom 80% of the population [Table 12]. However fast the distribution has been changing, the top wealth holding groups still undoubtedly have a disproportionate share of the total.[12]

Moreover, people at the top of the social pyramid do more than eat better and live longer than those lower down. They also enjoy more power. For governments still face a class-skewed distribution of political resources. We have seen this already in our examination of the influence of capital, and we will see it again when we look at the class who rules through its ownership of that capital. All that needs to be said now is that a ruling class exists, one indeed that still retains effective control over the rules under which the

Table 11 *Blue Book estimates of the distribution of income before and after tax, United Kingdom, 1949–78/9*

| | Percentage shares of total income | | | | | | | |
| | Before tax* | | | | After tax* | | | |
	Top 10%	Next 30%	Middle 30%	Bottom 30%	Top 10%	Next 30%	Middle 30%	Bottom 30%
1949	33.2	34.9	31.9		27.1	36.9	36.0	
1954	30.1	38.0	21.6	10.3	25.3	39.3	23.8	11.6
1959	29.4	38.4	22.5	9.7	25.2	39.8	23.7	11.2
1964	29.1	39.0	22.4	9.5	25.9	40.1	22.4	11.6
1969	28.0	38.9	22.8	10.4	24.3	39.2	24.5	12.0
1970–1	27.5	40.0	22.3	10.2	23.9	40.4	23.8	11.8
1973–4	26.8	39.7	22.6	10.9	23.6	39.9	23.7	12.8
1976–7	25.8	40.5	22.7	11.0	22.4	40.6	24.1	12.9
1976–7**	26.2	40.6	22.4	10.8	23.2	40.6	23.6	12.6
1977–8**	26.2	40.7	22.3	10.7	23.3	40.9	23.3	12.6
1978–9**	26.1	41.2	22.3	10.4	23.4	41.1	23.4	12.1

* The shares may not add up to 100 per cent because of rounding.

** These estimates differ from those given above in that they are before the deduction of mortgage interest.

Sources: Royal Commission (1979a), Table 2.3 and *National Income and Expenditure* (1980), p. 113; (1981), p. 116. (Compiled by John Westergaard, and published in *New Socialist* (January–February 1984), p. 32.)

Table 12 *Trends in the distribution of personal wealth up to 1973, England and Wales*

Percentage shares of personal wealth owned by given quantile groups of the population aged 25 and over, assuming that persons not covered by the estate duty returns have no wealth; at specified dates between 1911 and 1973

| | Percentage share of personal wealth | | | | | |
Quantile group	1911–13 (%)	1924–30 (%)	1936–8 (%)	1954 (%)	1960 (%)	1973* (%)
Top 1 per cent	69	62	56	43	42	27.6
2–5 per cent	18	22	23	28	33	23.7
6–10 per cent	5	7	9	8	8	15.9
11–100 per cent	8	9	12	21	17	32.8
Cumulative basis						
Top 1 per cent	69	62	56	43	42	27.6
Top 5 per cent	87	84	79	71	75	51.3
Top 10 per cent	92	91	88	79	83	67.2

Note: *The figures for 1960 and 1973 are, strictly speaking, not comparable but they do not alter the gist of the argument.

Sources: J. Revell, 'Changes in the social distribution of property in Britain during the twentieth century', 3rd international conference of economic history, Munich 1965; and Royal Commission on Wealth and Income, *Report No. 1*, p. 102. (Cited by R. Brown, in M. Abrams, *Work, Urbanism and Inequality* (Weidenfeld and Nicolson 1978).)

majority of us work, the ideas and information to which we are characteristically subject, and the means of coercion (from work discipline and redundancy to the courts, police and army) on which ultimately the stability of an unequal social order depends. In fact, for all its complexity, the basic character of the class structure faced by successive British governments is remarkably simple, particularly at the top. For there is a concentration of extraordinary privilege. These people, and these people alone

have wealth, and the near total security in life, the latitude of choice, the ease in everyday management and manipulation of people and things around them, which all go with wealth. They have power: less because they actively direct affairs – though many of them do that – than because the anonymous regulation of affairs by principles of property, profit and market is in tune with their interests. . . . The persistence of such acute inequalities of material conditions and security is indeed . . . a product of the persistence of capitalist power. . . . The continuing inequalities of wealth, income and welfare that divide the population are among the most crucial consequences – the most visible manifestations of the division of power in a society such as Britain. Those inequalities reflect, while they also demonstrate, the continuing power of capital – the power, not just of capitalists and managers but of the anonymous forces of property and the market.[13]

Of course the precise impact of these inequalities of industrial experience, material reward and social power has been mediated and moderated by the degree of organization and militancy displayed by institutions created and sustained in the main by the working class. But as those institutions repeatedly discover, the allocation of social rewards and power against which they are obliged to struggle is neither random nor accidental, nor is it one reflecting patterns of human need or any genetically transmitted distribution of aptitudes and skills between individuals. On the contrary, and as I have argued elsewhere:

some men and women face one set of life chances (and other men and women face other and more limited sets) because of their different position in the class structure of a capitalist society. It is because some people successfully lay claim to the ownership of the means and the product of the collective act of labour, and because these same people occupy positions of command within the private (industrial, financial and administrative) hierarchies that constitute the central owning institutions of contemporary capitalism, that they can monopolise the greater part of the social product, and can transmit the advantage of their class position more or less easily to their offspring. Conversely, it is because the majority of men and women in the society do not own either the means or the products of their collective labour, and because they occupy subordinate positions in the private hierarchies of command, that they experience a different and more limited set of life chances. It is because the manual working class (and increasingly the routine white collar worker) occupy the bottom positions in these hierarchies, and are totally denied property rights over the means and the products of their collective labour, that their experience of the instabilities and inequalities of such a social order are so extreme. And it is because capitalism and inequality are inseparable in this way that the removal of the latter [as we shall argue in Part Three] cannot be divorced from the question of socialism itself.[14]

Yet it is not simply for socialists that this pattern of inequality holds the key to much in British politics. It remains the major factor structuring political loyalty throughout the system. Class remains basic to the whole voting relationship, for all the volatility of recent voting patterns that we will examine later. Its existence remains an important source of inspiration for radicals, and its defence a major preoccupation of right-wing forces and the social élites they service. The differential experience and rewards it contains help to explain the differing responses politicians meet to policy initiatives in a multiplicity of areas. It means that the pursuit of broadly-based support for policy in areas as disparate as industrial relations and health, education and transport, remains just that – a pursuit, that must be continually recreated in the face of differential experiences which, in their persistence, perpetually erode such alliances at their core. Indeed, it also makes clear that the protection of such a web of inequality is itself a political project of vital importance to privileged groups; one whose success over a long period stands as a remarkable testimony to the effort which political forces of the Right and Centre have expended on that task alone. Why they should have succeeded so well is the subject of Chapter 9. That they have succeeded is clear from the evidence of this chapter. In doing so, they have moulded and survived sets of political interests at each level of the class structure that we shall now explore.

7 The position and interests of white males in the class structure

The ruling class

From what we have established already, two things should now be clear. The first is the power concentrated within British society in just a limited number of large economic enterprises: in the main financial institutions of the City and the larger industrial concerns. The second is the persistence within the social structure as a whole of immense privilege in the hands of a few. What must now be recognized is the relationship between those two things: *the monopoly of privilege by the privileged within the monopolies* – the existence, that is, of a propertied class, understood as a 'group of intermarried families enjoying superior advantages deriving from the use of capital and rooted in control over capital'.[1] It is also important to understand the relationship between the group of corporate controllers at the core of that class and the wider social layers within the ruling class who are heavily dependent for the maintenance and reproduction of their wealth and privileges on the persistence of such tight and restricted corporate control.

Of course, to argue for the existence of a ruling class based on the ownership and control of capital is to fall foul of three very conventional and widely held views on the character of industrial power and social privilege in Britain. First, it is to clash with those who have argued that the force of class inequality has been eroded by the 'decomposition of capital', by a managerial revolution that has separated ownership from control.

That, we are told, has left the effective direction of industrial activity in the hands of professional managers who are themselves wage labourers, sellers of their own labour power, recruited from a wider social base than ruling class theory will allow and motivated by a quite different orientation to work, profits, power and the state from that dominant among industrial controllers in an earlier period of owner-capitalism. In stronger versions of this thesis, such managers have become the new ruling class. But in less strident and more sophisticated presentations of the managerial thesis, 'opinions differ as to the power of the corporate elite when compared to other social groups, but . . . the general conclusion among managerialists seems to be that it is much more limited than that of the (supposedly) now defunct capitalist class'.[2]

To argue for the existence of a ruling class is also to run foul of those who maintain that industrial power has not simply moved from owners to managers, but has drifted even further down into the 'technostructure' of large corporations, leaving those in formal control so dependent on the expert advice of their subordinates that to focus on top people in top positions is no longer necessarily the best way to find out who exactly is taking the important industrial decisions.[3] This point may itself be cited as but one example of a wider criticism of élite studies in general and ruling class theories in particular, that they are weakened by the methodologies that construct them, characterized as these are by a propensity to rely on evidence that is easily measurable and visible (what Ivor Crewe called 'the tired old variables'[4] of social background, education and formal corporate position), as though these automatically told us anything of importance about the interests, perspectives, loyalties and strategic power of the élites concerned.[5] Indeed in certain hands those variables are not simply dismissed as tired, but as actually misleading – serving, so it is said, to obscure the very real extent to which the ruling class has not simply changed but has been replaced by a 'more amorphous and differentiated set of "leadership groups" ' recruited from a meritocracy of 'clever grammar school boys' – leadership groups lacking the common ties and capacity to transmit privilege between generations that is characteristic of 'proper' and full-blown upper and ruling classes.[6]

The arguments about managerialism, technocracy and meritocracy have a certain force, but what they oblige us to do is to refine, rather than to abandon, theses that stress the political importance of the persistence in Britain of concentrations of private power and privilege anchored in the ownership and control of capital. There has undoubtedly been a managerial revolution of a kind, which has altered the character of the propertied class without leading to its dissolution. It is a managerial revolution that has been brought into existence by developments within capitalism itself. The concentration and centralization of capital in particular, has been associated with the emergence of a new sort of industrial manager, as part of an elongated, more rigorous and more scientifically-based supervisory structure than that common in the small-scale, family-controlled and individually-run enterprise dominant in Victorian capitalism. Indeed this 'extension of managerial control, in the sense of the effective power of managers to determine the policies which govern the fate of the large-scale corporation, is a characteristic phenomenon in all neo-capitalist economies'.[7] But as we shall see, the

separation of ownership and control has not been total. Family firms remain a significant if diminishing element in the British corporate structure; and even in public companies 'in which stock ownership is widely dispersed, ownership of relatively small blocks of shares can be sufficient to allow those who own them to intervene effectively in the running of the corporation'.[8] 'Rather than the dissolution of the propertied class, we have seen its "managerial reorganisation" [with] the privileged class of propertied families [becoming] increasingly autonomous from *particular* proprietary interests, though its members continue to monopolise positions of strategic control in modern capitalist enterprises.'[9] For, as we have seen, company ownership in Britain this century has been characterized by the growth of institutional stock-ownership, and although that makes for extra complexity in tracing patterns of formal and actual control, it remains the case, as we shall see, that it is particularly in such 'capital owning' institutions that senior positions remain restricted to a tiny social group. So here too, far from the demise of owner-capitalists signifying a major democratic shift in the locus of industrial control, their replacement by institutional stock ownership might more properly be seen as 'one of the most significant mechanisms in the modern economy whereby ownership of private property is tied directly to economic power'.[10]

The 'driving out' of the individual shareholder by the arrival of massive pension funds and insurance companies run by professional managers does not signify the end of a capital-owning ruling class. It simply means that at last financial institutions are coming to play a greater role in shaping the activity of locally-based industrial monopolies, by the consolidation of a linked set of industrial and financial interests centred on the clearing banks in particular. The result, in class terms, is the emergence of a propertied class whose divergent interests free them, to a far greater

extent than in the past, from disproportionate dependence on any one company/
sector, but whose wealth and privileges remain wholly dependent on successful capital
accumulation somewhere, whether here or
abroad.

The financial controllers at the heart of the
system are very few in number – John Scott has
them as somewhere between 200 and 400
people. They continue to be drawn in the main
from a very restricted social background, but
even where they are not, they, and the
managerial strata of which they are the centre,
continue to be locked into capitalist patterns
of activity and privilege. The goals of managerial activity remain quintessentially capitalist
– to accumulate capital and realize profits
through the organization and exploitation of
labour power; and 'to imagine that the
personnel manager, production manager or
supervisor has any choice than to extract
surplus value as efficiently as posssible from
his labour force is quite absurd'.[11] Indeed, if
anything, managerial freedom of manoeuvre
here is more restricted than that enjoyed by an
earlier generation of owner-capitalists, because of the intensity of corporate competition
now and because of the way in which managerial career patterns in the contemporary
world are so dependent on the success of their
particular corporation in that competitive
struggle. In any event, as we shall see in a
moment, very senior managerial personnel
continue to be drawn from a highly restricted
social background, to own industrial shares
themselves to a disproportionately large extent, and as a result of that and of their senior
positions, to be among the wealthiest and most
highly paid individuals in the community.
Senior managers may have arrived, but they
remain very much part of the 'global function
of capital'[12] and of the social universe of those
who own it. 'That there occurs conflict
between shareholders and managers cannot
be denied'; but 'rather than indicating that
managers and owners increasingly move apart

in their outlook on and attitudes towards
society in general and towards the enterprise
in particular, what evidence there is suggests
something quite different: that an overall
homogeneity of value and belief, and a high
degree of social solidarity, as manifest in
interpersonal contacts, friendships and marriage ties, is more noticeable than any marked
cleavages'.[13] The differentiation of function
within the complexities of global capital
should not blind us to the 'social unity of
managers and owners'[14] that has consolidated
itself around that function.

If the argument on a managerial revolution
is overstated, then that on the rise of a 'new
technocracy' – a new power-centre deep in the
specialist layers within the executive hierarchy
– is simply wrong. Indeed, all the evidence
would suggest that it is the very 'specialism'
associated with the role of technical experts in
industrial decision-making that leaves them
unable to influence policy beyond their
sphere; and that key decisions on investment
policy, industrial location, product range and
labour practices continue to be settled at
board level. Of course, power there, as
elsewhere, 'is always limited, hedged in by
numerous constraints';[15] and the occupation
of high office, in industry as in politics, is not
automatically synonymous with effective control. Not all the members of any one company
board occupy and exercise executive power:
perhaps as many as a third of all directors of
large companies in the United Kingdom may
be non-executive in function, 'gate keepers'
assessing proposals submitted by fellow directors and lower management, and as such
subject to 'manipulative strategies' targeted
on them by their subordinates. Indeed, Pahl
and Winkler would have us believe that those
who sit on many boards – the 'overlapping
directors' who link industrial and financial
concerns at board level – may be particularly
easy to manipulate because of their multiplicity of interests, may be 'controlled, not
controlling'. As they have it: 'capital is not

synonymous with control. Contact is not synonymous with influence'.[16] Yet such a possibility does not destroy the force of the argument on interlocking directorships so much as alter its content. The thesis is not that these men dictate the detail of industrial policy, but only that they are in a position to set the limits within which it operates. The power of finance over industry, as was suggested in Part One, is the power to veto and to shape, the power to allocate resources rather than to exercise operational control on a detailed basis.[17] As John Scott has observed, 'the power of such non-executive directors rests precisely on the fact that executives have to work extremely hard and very efficiently in order to present the board with a limited set of options. If the non-executive directors were powerless, then such manipulative strategies would hardly be necessary. The need to manipulate is a sign of the relative *weakness* of the executives, not a sign of their power'.[18] For this reason, it remains 'legitimate to treat the board of directors as the institutional locus of strategic control, so long as it is not assumed that all board members are equally important'.[19] In the process we may distort the reality of industrial decision-making to a degree, capturing in our sample 'men who (have) effective power and others who (have) only the trappings of office'.[20] But to discard the notion of a corporate élite entirely would be to distort still more, by obscuring the extent to which control over the allocation of resources in large industrial and financial institutions in Great Britain remains in the hands of a tiny, interconnected and highly conservative minority.

If we then locate and characterize such a corporate élite in part by the 'tired old variables' of social background and education, it is because the corporate élite themselves continue to attach enormous significance to just those things, recruiting themselves in the main from a very restricted social strata, and using the privileged parts of the education

system as the major mechanism by which they transmit their privileges to their children. Studies of élite recruitment demonstrate this over and over again, showing that senior personnel in the key financial institutions, in industry and in the 'older' sectors of the state – the army, the judiciary and the Anglican bishops – continue to be drawn in the main from a very privileged and restricted social group. They show too, as we shall see, a particular if limited degree of social mobility; but that social mobility operates for individuals moving into élite structures in which the aristocracy, and the children of the rich, occupy a dominant position. This is particularly true of large financial institutions, in twenty-seven of which, for example, Richard Whitley found that 80 per cent of their directors had been to fee-paying schools, 87 per cent had been to Oxbridge, and 46 per cent were members of London's most 'prestigious and aristocratically connected clubs'[21] (the figure of attendance at fee-paying schools for the population as a whole is, in contrast, 2.5 per cent). Whitley found too that 93 per cent of his twenty-seven major financial institutions were linked by interlocking directorships, and that twenty-six of the twenty-seven firms were linked by kinship of an aristocratic kind. Although he found significantly lower scores on all these dimensions for large industrial companies, it remained the case that even there 66 per cent of company directors had been to fee-paying schools, 66 per cent had been to Oxbridge, and 28 per cent belonged to the top nine London clubs. In the board rooms of both industry and finance, it should be recognized, 'there occurred a decline between 1900 and 1970 in the proportion of individuals of upper class origin, but the trend is more consistent for industrial directors'. Most of the change, however, 'is accounted for by the increase in the percentage of directors, both industrial and financial, drawn from "upper middle class" backgrounds', particularly professional ones; and it seems reasonable to conclude that although 'boardrooms have been rather more widely recruited in recent years than in the past . . . the broadening of recruitment has been largely restricted to the upper echelons of the class structure. There is little evidence that this élite has opened to men whose origins are to be found in the working or lower middle classes'.[22]

Instead, what is striking is the linkage of big industrial and big financial institutions through interlocking directorships, and the way in which members of the aristocracy occupy a disproportionately large number of those linking positions. Only the remaining family or tycoon-based industrial concerns seem to have escaped this degree of aristocratic integration. For the rest, as Table 13 shows, the upper class origins and public school education of key executive figures remain remarkably consistent. Indeed it should be noted that the compilers of this table were unable to locate 'among the chairmen of the merchant banks' even 'one case of an individual emanating from a background outside the upper class',[23] so dominant is this pattern of inherited privilege here. 'Banking is clearly the most fixed and unchanging in terms of the class background and educational experience of its chairmen.'[24] This contrasts to a degree with a non-financial sector such as retailing (which is much nearer the industrial 'norm', with 67 per cent of its directors privately educated and with few aristocrats on its boards).[25] But this is a detail, and overall the picture is clear. To quote Richard Whitley again:

it appears that very large industrial and financial firms do recruit their Board members from a narrow segment of the population. These directors undergo a remarkably similar educational experience and, to some extent, have similar social circles as evidenced by club membership and kinship links. They tend, in other words, to be members of the same culture, or at any rate to have the background for sharing a common culture.[26]

In industry therefore, as well as in finance, individuals with aristocratic backgrounds, and people enjoying inherited wealth, monopolize very senior positions. Indeed, 'at the apex of society the links between members of the elite are genealogical – what Simon Haxby in the 1930s called "the cousinhood" – lower down, the initial links are provided by parental acquaintance, residential proximity and shared education'.[27] Around the industrial

Table 13   *The social origins and educational backgrounds of company chairmen*

	Working class (%)	Middle class (%)	Upper class (%)	Unknown (%)	Public school (%)
Clearing banks	—	3	74	23	86
Merchant banks	—	—	89	11	76
Misc. manufacture	1	13	59	27	54
Breweries	2	11	75	12	76
Iron and steel	2	11	55	32	70
Railways	—	11	86	3	70
Shipping	—	10	67	23	62
Oil	—	13	47	40	57
Retail	—	32	21	47	21
Mean	1	10	66	23	Total 65

Source: P. Stansworth and A. Giddens, *Elites and Power in British Society* (Cambridge University Press 1974), pp. 83, 84.

and financial élite, the 'great and the good' across the society as a whole continue to be drawn from a similarly restricted and privileged social background. As late as 1959, for example, 'a third of all (army) officers of the rank of Lieutenant-General and above had aristocratic or gentry connections. Despite the trend towards a reduction in the upper-class component, it is striking that, overall, even taking the lowest estimate, a third of all army leaders between the 1910s and 1950s had upper-class origins or connections'.[28] Indeed it was possible for 'a market research team (to report) that nearly half of the successful candidates for a commission came from public schools'.[29] The army they joined in 1960 was still led by thirty-six Lieutenant-Generals, Generals and Field Marshals, twenty-nine of whom had been to public school.

In 1965, 65 per cent of all senior judges came from upper middle, professional or landed families, and among new judges appointed between 1970 and 1975, 68 per cent had been to public school and 74 per cent to Oxbridge. In fact, 'four out of five full-time professional judges are products of public schools and of Oxford or Cambridge';[30] as are 85 per cent of all English bishops. As late as 1960 70 per cent of all English diocesan bishops could be said to have been recruited from upper middle-class backgrounds, and as many as 34.9 per cent of them to have kinship connections with the landed peerage.[31] Indeed, 'until only very recently there was not a single senior army officer, Anglican bishop or high court judge who had a manual worker as father'.[32] The trend remains clear that, as the army and the church have lost their appeal to the ruling class as a whole, they have turned increasingly to the recruitment of their own children, and not to wider social groups, for their very senior personnel.

Of course, social background is no dictator of interests, nor education the predeterminer of adult attitudes. After all, Tony Benn's father was a peer, Roy Jenkins's a trade union

official. Fee-paying schools should be thought of rather as one of two mechanisms – inherited wealth is the other – by which one generation transmits its privileges to the next, by placing its children in senior positions in crucial institutions and by reproducing and consolidating in them a particular élite culture. The participation of élite groups in fee-paying education is too all-pervasive to permit us to discount its importance. On the contrary, as Table 14 shows, 'the public schools and the ancient universities are crucial mechanisms for the integration and recruitment of both the establishment and the wider business class'.[33] For 'one thing which is clear is that the maintenance of the old ruling class as a sociological entity depends upon the preservation of a separate form of education where that class's values can be fostered and maintained'.[34]

Yet even so we should not ignore the impact of democratic pressures, institutional growth and social mobility on the changing position of the privileged in British society. Democratic pressures have opened certain élite positions to people of lower social background. As we shall see in more detail in Part Three, Parliament and government are the major examples here. The working class entered Parliament through the Labour Party and still do, although since 1945 the Labour Party's own internal selection processes have shifted the centre of social gravity up to the lower middle class – higher, that is, than in the heyday of direct working-class representation in Parliament, but still significantly lower than in other centres of private power in industry and finance.[35] The growth of government activity and the expansion of its bureaucracies after 1945 created what John Goldthorpe and his colleagues have called a new 'service class' beneath the élite,[36] recruited during the long boom years from working-class and lower middle-class backgrounds through the channel of grammar school and university education. From that class too have risen to positions of

Table 14   *The public school background of élite groups*

	Total	Percentage from public schools
14 year olds in England and Wales (1967)	642,977	2.6
Conservative MPs (1970)	330	64.4
Conservative Cabinet (1970)	18	77.7
Royal Navy (Rear Admirals and above, 1970)	76	88.9
Army (Major Generals and above, 1970)	117	86.1
RAF (Air Vice-Marshals and above, 1971)	85	62.5
Ambassadors (1971)	80	82.5
High Court and Appeal Court judges (1971)	91	80.2
Church of England Bishops (1971)	133	67.4
Directors of forty major industrial firms (1971)	261	67.8
Directors of clearing banks (1971)	99	79.9
Directors of merchant banks (1971)	106	77.4
Directors of major insurance companies (1971)	118	83.1
Governors and directors of the Bank of England (1971)	18	55.5

Source: T Noble, *Modern Britain: Structure and Change* (Batsford 1975), p. 314.

prominence in industry and commerce particularly gifted or fortunate individuals whose success gives the lie to any argument that the British élite structure is totally closed. Indeed it is possible to chart, as does Table 15, a slight fall in the total monopoly of key élite positions enjoyed in the post-war years by the product of the public school system.

However, those individuals, as they have risen (and indeed normally as a prerequisite of their rise) have been socialized into traditional élite values and interests, and have converted themselves into transmitters of privilege to their own children. For this reason among others, it can be said that the rise of a fortunate few, and the consolidation of a new service class, has not removed the privileges of the propertied élite. Instead it has helped to reproduce those privileges, by introducing much needed new talent at the top, and effective administration in the middle, of key controlling institutions. For even with the expansion of middle management positions in both the public and private bureaucracies, the *relative* chances of people from different social classes reaching the top have remained virtu-

ally unchanged during the past sixty years. So in John Goldthorpe's seven-class study, for example, 'he found that those born into classes 6 and 7 remained more than three times less likely, and those born into classes 3, 4 and 5 more than twice as unlikely, to end up in classes 1 and 2 as those who had been born into the top two classes. These relative inequalities remained consistent throughout the period covered by the survey (roughly 1918 to 1972)';[36] so that overall, 'in most institutions the evidence suggests that there has been a broadening of the social base of entrants to lower positions of leadership, but little change at the top'.[37] At the top, now as before, a propertied class remains firmly in control.

Politicians in Britain face a propertied class of immense self-confidence and power – a tiny group of people who control financial and industrial resources, who are personally wealthy, who are linked socially to one another through kinship and clubs, who possess in the private education system a mechanism for transmitting their privileges, and who enjoy easy access to governments because of their formal position and their personal and social

Table 15   *Grammar school education in eight élite groups*

	1939 (%)	1950 (%)	1960 (%)	1970–1 (%)
Civil service (under secretary and above)	6.6	25.5	25.8	31.4
Ambassadors	0.0	11.8	9.5	12.0
High Court and Appeal Court judges	5.0	6.1	10.3	9.5
Royal Navy (Rear Admirals and above)	19.0	6.3	5.0	12.9
Army (Major Generals and above)	4.6	10.2	4.2	8.3
RAF (Air Vice-Marshals and above)	0.0	5.5	8.6	23.5
Church of England (Assistant Bishops and above)	4.5	11.5	15.1	17.9
Directors of clearing banks	3.9	5.8	10.1	9.0

Source: T. Noble *Modern Britain: Structure and Change* (Batsford 1975), p. 320.

linkages to senior civil servants, MPs and Cabinet ministers. John Westergaard's description of this class still seems to me to be the best:

The dominant grouping is that of a small, homogeneous *élite* of wealth and private corporate property – politically entrenched in the leadership of the Conservative Party; strongly represented in, or linked with, a variety of public and private bodies; assured of the general support of the press, if not at the overt political level of the publicly controlled mass media; its members sharing for a large part a common, exclusive educational background, and united by fairly close ties of kinship and everyday association. . . . It is an élite which, while its economic base is that of financial and industrial capital, yet has its own uniquely British features, in part inherited from the agrarian-mercantile nobility and gentry of the pre-industrial era. It is neither a tightly closed group – indeed much of its viability may derive from its absorbtive capacity – nor a monolithically united one. But internal divisions remain generally confined to particular issues, and do not develop into major fissures of a durable kind.[38]

Instead, and on the contrary, 'the business class as a whole is characterized by a high degree of social cohesion',[39] and constitutes a veritable establishment, a whole network of self-confident, privileged and interconnected people, consolidated around a limited number of important institutions, and productive of a climate of values, opinions and preoccupations that constitute the 'common sense' of the entire ruling class.

At the centre of that class are the directors, top executives and principal shareholders of the largest industrial and financial concerns, who with their immediate families number perhaps 25,000 to 50,000 people. 'Around this core, and linked to it through kinship, education and culture, are those people of property who have retired from business or who followed careers outside the business world . . . in the civil service, the law, the church, the army, the universities and other similar occupations' including 'large scale landowner-ship and farming'.[40] Here in total stands perhaps 1 per cent of the population – differentially dependent on finance, industry, rents or the professions, but commonly dependent for their privileges on the maintenance and success of the monopolies, and on the preservation of highly unequal rights and rewards as between senior management and the rest of the workforce, and between the professions and the rest of the white-collar salariat. It is these people who have wealth and inherit it. At least half the men and probably two-thirds of the women among the rich in one generation can be seen to have inherited the bulk of their wealth from the generation before them.[41] It is these people who have the highest incomes and who own the vast majority of privately owned industrial shares.[42] It is after all significant that the government's Top Salaries Review Board had terms of reference that stretched out to take in 'chairmen and members of the boards of nationalised industries, the higher judiciary, senior civil servants and senior officers of the armed forces'. It is these people too whose children monopolize fee-paying education, and who benefit in fact from a 'cycle of privilege'[43] that reproduces itself through the inheritance of wealth, the public schools, the monopoly of key occupational positions, and the 'informality and social connectivity' that keeps the privileged in touch with one another and with what is going on and is available for exploitation. It is these people who socialize together, inter-marry, and maintain close personal connections with the senior echelons of the Conservative Party.[44] It is these people too who, although internally divided by their differential dependence on distinct sections of capital and its associated professions, are united in a common sense of their own class position and interests against any challenge from without, and who possess – as we shall see in Chapter 9 – a quite literally hegemonic sense of their own right and suitability to rule.

The precise character of this propertied class now is the product of a long historical process through which the English pre-industrial ruling class accommodated itself to the rising force of industrial capital, and in which the centres of gravity and power of capital itself shifted as small-scale liberal capitalism gave way to the dominance of the monopolies. Therefore, within the ruling élites we find an accommodation and a mix of aristocracy and business, a mix consolidated between 1870 and 1914 by the way in which landed wealth transmuted itself into financial capital, and big industrial concentrations separated themselves from small, to create a *plutocracy* of the

very rich. That plutocracy was united within a class culture that stressed aristocratic values of the 'gentleman' and the 'amateur', but it never lost sight of its own dependence on successful capital accumulation through trade, finance, and to a lesser extent, industry both here and overseas. The result of that fusion of capitalist and precapitalist ruling groups, and the transformation of the wealth of the aristocracy from one exclusively based on land to one in which financial dealings played a major role, was to leave a power bloc in which aristocratic elements occupied a disproportionate place, precapitalist values and social practices retained high status, and the symbols of aristocratic rule – particularly monarchy, landownership and titles – continued to fascinate senior industrial personnel. Yet it was a power bloc that was, for all its aristocratic trimmings, profoundly capitalist in its interests and activities, one whose centre of gravity lay with the 'industrial and financial bourgeoisie, which constituted the hegemonic class or fraction, despite feudal survivals in the state and in the aristocratic features of the dominant ideology'.[45] For what occurred after 1873 was not the replacement of one ruling class by another, but the fusion of the old and the new, and the transformation of both. So possibly by the turn of the century, and certainly between the wars, 'among the larger industrial organisations we see the emergence of a national economic élite, whose background and educational experience does not differentiate them in any obvious way from that of those men in the dominant positions in the spheres of politics, the civil service and the Church'.[46]

In fact, within the privileged élites, different 'power blocs' consolidated their dominance at different periods as the relative strengths of different fractions of capital rose and fell. 'This concept of a power bloc is an important one. It allows us to replace the highly simplified concept of a more or less homogeneous or unified ruling class with the alternative, and historically much more accurate concept, of a ruling bloc or alliance, composed of different fractions. Political changes, then, occur first through the opening up of internal differences *within* the power bloc, by a change in the balance between the different elements within the alliance of forces, and through a shift from one section to another in terms of its leading element.'[47] The power bloc of mid Victorian liberalism was a fusion of northern-based small-scale industrial capital in coal, steel, railways and textiles, and the Whig section of the land-based aristocracy. That power bloc gave way by 1914 to a plutocracy of big landowners and big bourgeoisie, within which rentier and financial interests increasingly eclipsed manufacturing ones, and in which the dominant sections of the bourgeoisie became 'merchants, bankers, shipowners, and stock and insurance brokers',[48] usually in the City of London, rather than manufacturers and industrialists – a bourgeoisie, that is, that was heavily tied to colonial and other overseas processes of surplus extraction. We have had occasion already to stress the importance of this shift in relationships within the power bloc in explaining the twentieth-century weakness of British-based industrial capital. It is worth stressing again that the history of late Victorian Britain should be read 'as first the containment, then the defeat, of industrialism by an older, more powerful and more political bourgeoisie'.[49] For as Rubenstein has argued, 'mid Victorian Britain contained two middle classes: by far the larger and wealthier based on commerce and London, the other on manufacturing and the North of England. Together with the landed élite, those contested for the benefits of wealth, status and power', a contest which by 1914 had been resolved 'by the collapse of the three old élites, and their merger into one élite, dominated by the South of England and finance, with its London-based associates of great influence in twentieth century society, like the Civil Service and the professions, the familiar "Establishment" of fact and fiction'.[50]

As we have seen in Part One, this London-based financial élite has remained the dominant element in the power bloc ever since, in spite of challenges from sections of industrial capital. Indeed, during the 1920s, 'the prevalent coalition of interests was that between banking capital on the one hand and colonial and mining capital on the other. Coal and steel capital belonged to the same coalition, but this position was partly forced upon them by the deflationary policies imposed by the other two. Of the dominant coalition, only the coal and steel capitalists directly confronted the British working class, as the other two fractions depended for their expansion on the exploitation of workers and peasants elsewhere in the world. Politically this coalition remained a dominant force until well into the nineteen fifties'.[51] Since then, with the rise of new mass consumer industries, the decline of the relative competitive strength of British industrial capital, and the consolidation of the multinationals, a new power bloc has been formed between City interests no longer tied exclusively to colonial and mining capital, and the largest multinational industrial concerns. And as the internal composition of the power bloc has shifted over time in line with the relative strengths of different sections of capital, other sections of the privileged have found themselves as a result relatively disadvantaged and distanced from the state. They have also found, and they continue to find, that although the power bloc may press for specific policies not entirely to their liking, it also defends the general interests of the privileged in ways that suit them only too well. Indeed, the success of the privileged here has been remarkable, and 'suggests perhaps that the continuance of degrees of inequality almost unparalleled in the industrial world may be explained by the considerable powers of resistance which the privileged may call upon to defend their property and position'[52] – even against governments of radical political persuasion.

For there can be no doubt that what governments face in Britain is a ruling class in the quite conventional meaning of that term. I realize that to demonstrate such a proposition is a complex matter, and that to show that a particular class 'is a ruling class it is necessary to specify the modes in which its economic hegemony is translated into political domination: which means examining, among other things, processes of recruitment to élite positions in the major institutional spheres, the relations between economic, political and other élites, and the use of effective power to further definite class interests'.[53] The totality of that exercise is one project that runs through this volume as a whole. We have already established in Part One the political leverage of financial and industrial capital, and in Part Two the restricted nature of recruitment to, and the high degree of social integration within, the élites who control that capital. It remains for us in Part Three to look at the linkages of the state to the personnel, institutions and policies of these privileged groups.

Then, as now, our argument will not be made any easier to establish by the low visibility of these élites – their 'social and cultural anonymity'[54] which is itself a key feature of the way élite power is exercised and élite privilege protected in the liberal democracies.[55] But lack of visibility here, like the obverse and striking visibility of trade union activity, is not a reliable guide to where the effective control of this society actually lies. If by a ruling class we mean 'a group which provides the majority of those who occupy positions of power, and who, in their turn, can materially assist their sons to reach similar positions',[56] then British governments definitely face such a class. If by a ruling class we mean, in addition, that the basis of élite privilege rests on the ownership and control of capital – a dependence on capital, moreover, which gives the élites *both* a set of common interests in its accumulation and realization

and the resources to press those interests effectively on governments of any political persuasion, then again we have a ruling class in contemporary Britain. Furthermore, if by a ruling class we mean also a class capable of persuading the vast majority of the people for most of the time that its privileges are inevitable and legitimate, and that its interests are those of the nation as a whole; if, that is, by a ruling class we mean a class with truly hegemonic power, then again, as we shall see in Chapter 9, British governments do face such a class. They are not merely confronted by a collection of relatively discrete élites without cohesion, without a consciousness of their common interests, and without a willingness to act collectively to defend those interests if threatened. Instead, the power of the ruling class in Britain is so entrenched because it is so hegemonic, so buttressed on a daily basis by the common acceptance by all of us of the inevitability and legitimacy of certain basic relationships – of property and the market – that serve, unless challenged, to reproduce automatically the patterns of privilege and power on which the social position of the propertied class depends.[57]

The privileged in this society have a set of interests in common as members of a class: interests in the maintenance of private property; in the protection and enlargement of that sphere within which market processes can dominate the production and distribution of resources; in the protection of élite privileges and the limitation of effective democratic control and social reform; and in the existence of traditional institutions and social practices, and the associated diminution of any shift in class power downwards towards the dispossessed. Those common interests exist alongside, and in times of challenge take precedence over, divisions of interest within the privileged on a range of more specific matters. The visibility of these divisions, in the absence of such a challenge, need not mislead us into thinking that the ruling class has itself decomposed. On the contrary, given the nature of the capitalist mode of production, where any one capital is necessarily locked into contradictory relationships not just with labour but with other capitals also, such a pluralism of cleavages and interests is inevitable and to be expected. So too is a certain autonomy for the state, as it mediates between the different fractions of capital and handles the political pressure of labour; and a certain instability in both the constituent elements of the power bloc, and the manner in which those private interests shape state policy, is also to be expected. All this we shall see in Part Three, when we discuss the shift in the locus of ruling-class political control from the social connections of the establishments to the corporate structures of the late capitalist state; and when we explore the possibility of state autonomy being taken to its limit in the election of a government determined to service the interests of the dispossessed and to move against the privileged. For the arrival of such a government would not disprove the existence of a ruling class, but rather would challenge its power. The resulting conflict would throw into greater relief what, in quieter times, is one of the central but silent truths of British politics: that the existence of separate élites in a capitalist society such as ours does not prevent them from constituting themselves as 'a dominant economic class, possessed of a high degree of cohesion and solidarity, with common interests and common purposes which far transcend their specific differences and disagreements'.[58] If politics is to be your vocation in late twentieth-century Britain, it is with the power of this ruling class that you will have to contend.

The intermediate strata

The social layers beneath the propertied class are immensely complex. At the base of the class structure, as we shall see later, is a class of manual workers – the traditional 'proletariat' that Marx saw as the gravediggers of capitalism. Between that class and the capitalists whose graves they were to dig persists a complex set of intermediate strata, which shade imperceptibly into the propertied ruling class at the top and the proletariat at the bottom. These middle strata are themselves both old and new, established and marginal, as John Goldthorpe's much cited figure, reproduced as Figure 11, suggests.

What all these social strata have in common is their middle position in the class structure. They are neither workers nor capitalists, members of neither of the constituent classes of the capitalist mode of production. In fact their relationship to that mode of production is complicated, and differs between the various strata within the middle class. One element – a traditional petty bourgeoisie of shopkeepers and self-employed artisans (owners of small-scale capital which they work themselves) – derives from, and reproduces within modern capitalism, that earlier form of simple commodity production 'which was historically the form of transition from the feudal to the capitalist mode'.[59] As we shall see, they share much in common with a class of small capitalists, and a professional strata (in the law and medicine, and latterly in accountancy, engineering and the like) whose traditional privileges predate industrial capitalism in

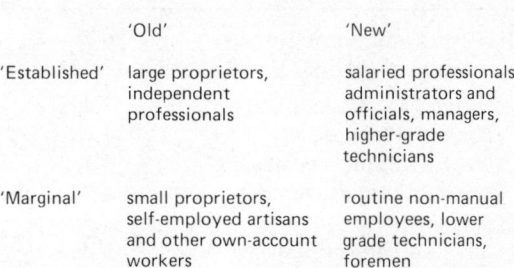

	'Old'	'New'
'Established'	large proprietors, independent professionals	salaried professionals, administrators and officials, managers, higher-grade technicians
'Marginal'	small proprietors, self-employed artisans and other own-account workers	routine non-manual employees, lower grade technicians, foremen

Figure 11 *Components of the middle class*

Source: J. Goldthorpe 'Comment', *British Journal of Sociology,* **29** no. 4 (December 1978), p. 437.

origin, but which have had to be constituted afresh in modern times through new forms of financial arrangements within (or alongside) both the public and the private ruling bureaucracies. And in those bureaucratic structures there now exists a new middle class – 'salary earners' rather than 'profit takers' in G. D. H. Cole's useful distinction[60] – a strata of managers and middle level state bureaucrats called into existence by the concentration and centralization of capital, the rise of the monopolies and the extension of the state – a 'service class'[61] which in turn supervises a vast array of clerical and other non-manual workers whose social position was traditionally middle class, but who are now being extensively proletarianized.

The rise of these new middle strata is *the* major development in the class structure of contemporary capitalism, as Table 16 suggests. It is a vital element in the changing class position of many male workers and also, as we shall see in Chapter 8, a key element in the contemporary class location of many women workers. The traditional petty bourgeoisie has fared less well. As the Bolton Committee on small firms found in 1971, 'the declining share of small enterprises in economic activity is a universal process but . . . has gone further here than elsewhere'.[62] In fact by then, less than 8 per cent of the occupied population 'ran their own businesses and employed others, or were simply self-employed'; and commercially these were important only in 'agriculture, forestry and fishing (about 63% of all occupied), construction (26%), distributive trades (18%), and miscellaneous services (19%)'. That still left '1.25 million small firms in the U.K. giving employment to 6 million and contributing nearly 20% of the GNP';[63] but it meant that the self-employed were no longer a larger stratum than the new middle class, which now takes in 'between ten and twelve per cent of the economically active male population'.[64] The intermediate strata as a whole constitutes anything between 30 and 42 per cent of the population, depending on whether or not routine white-collar workers are counted here or in the proletariat proper. Indeed, on the widest definition, it seems safe to say that by 1978, 46.3 per cent of the employed population as a whole were employed in non-manual occupations, and 'that by 1985 the proportion of non-manual workers

Table 16   *Major occupational groups as a percentage of the total occupied population*

	1911	1931	1961	1971	No. of persons (000s) 1971
Employers and proprietors	6.7	6.7	4.8	2.6	622
White-collar workers	18.7	23.0	35.9	42.7	10,405
Managers and administrators	3.4	3.7	5.4	8.6	2,085
Higher professionals	1.0	1.1	3.0	3.8	928
Lower prof. and technicians	3.1	3.5	6.0	7.7	1,880
Foremen and inspectors	1.3	1.5	2.9	3.0	736
Clerks	4.5	6.7	12.7	14.0	3,412
Salesmen and shop assistants	5.4	6.5	5.9	5.6	1,364
Manual workers	74.6	70.3	59.3	54.7	13,343
	100	100	100	100	24,370

Source: R. King and J. Reynor, *The Middle Class* (Longman 1981), p. 81.

is expected to be over 50%'.[65] Non-manual labour then, and the intermediate social position it has traditionally occupied, constitute an important element in the contemporary class structure, an element which we need to be able to grasp theoretically, and to chart empirically, if we are to understand the full character and origins of the different class interests faced by the state.

At the level of social theory, the problem is how to characterize all these strata, and indeed whether to treat them as a class at all. Commentators on both the Right and Left have agreed on the significance of the question down the years, while continuing to proliferate a multiplicity of divergent answers to it. For many Conservative thinkers, the English middle classes have embodied all that is desirable in values, practices and political stability, such that their decline has been bewailed as 'the' problem of contemporary society.[66] Others, of similar or related persuasions, seeing not so much a decline as a transformation of the middle class, have perceived the new middle class either as a 'managerial revolution', a new ruling class or, if not quite that, at least a revitalized and irrepressable social force.[67] Theoreticians on the Left have had problems of a different kind. The persistence, and indeed growth, of middle strata has often been cited by critics of Marxism as proof of the irrelevance of Marx's writings to the twentieth century, standing as they do in such stark contrast to the famous projection of *The Communist Manifesto* that 'our epoch, the epoch of the bourgeoisie, possesses however this distinctive feature: it has simplified class antagonisms. Society as a whole is more and more splitting up into two great hostile camps directly facing each other: Bourgeoisie and Proletariat'. Marx's defenders these days tend to trade quote for quote, citing Marx's anticipation of the white-collar revolution in his less well-known critique of David Ricardo, that 'what he forgets to emphasise is the constantly growing numbers

of the middle class, those who stand between the workman on the one hand and the capitalist and the landlord on the other'.[68] But what they too have to concede is that Marx never incorporated that second position fully and satisfactorily into the drift of his own political sociology, with its emphasis on class polarization and simplification; and that as a result Marxists have faced, and continue to face, serious problems both in conceptualizing the middle strata and in consolidating the pattern of class alliances within the revolutionary project which their continued existence inevitably makes necessary.

In fact many Left theoreticians have settled into one of the three positions on this issue isolated by Frank Parkin, namely minimalist, maximalist or intermediate.[69] According to one view, the middle class proper is actually very tiny, since the bulk of white-collar workers (including here very senior management) sell their labour power, and are therefore objectively members of the working class.[70] According to another view, common to European communist parties of late, the intermediate strata are just that – strata, which, because of their exploitation by the big monopolies, can be expected to ally easily with working-class forces in the struggle for popular reforms.[71] Critics of this position within the communist movement, most notably Nicos Poulantzas, have challenged it directly, seeing in that formulation the danger of constructing alliances with anti-socialist forces, and denying that any linkage between the middle strata and the working class can be expected to occur in an automatic or easy fashion. Instead Poulantzas has argued that the middle strata constitute a *class*, and indeed a large one, in which the new elements share sufficient of the ideology of the traditional petty bourgeoisie to constitute in effect a new petty bourgeoisie, a class which 'at every level . . . exercises specific authority and ideological domination over the working class',[72] and as such a class which will in the main ally with capital and not with labour. Poulantzas is, of course, aware of processes of proletarianization at the base of the middle strata, but is still keen to stress that, because those being proletarianized 'are members of another class . . . they must be won by the working class'. They do 'not automatically adopt the class position of the working class'[73] and indeed even if won to that position can be lost again. Poulantzas for his part has been criticized by others, not just for treating the new middle strata as a class, but also for tying them back to the traditional petty bourgeoisie; so that there is plenty of other Marxist literature around which is prepared to treat the new managerial and administrative strata as a distinct class – either as a new professional–managerial class with interests of its own,[74] or as a new working class likely in the end to be the catalyst of socialist revolution.[75]

In the face of such a plethora of strata and theories, and given the different and often mutually incompatible political consequences of the various theories available, it is vital here to move slowly and with caution. In particular we must not assume within our categories a unity of interests and purpose between strata that neither the base of their social position nor their actual political practice in fact confers. Indeed, it seems more useful to follow the writings of Carchedi and Wright, in observing that we need to differentiate between the old and the new in the intermediate strata, and to locate the *contradictory class locations* of each.

For capitalism clearly permits the continuation of a traditional petty bourgeoisie of shopkeepers and artisans, people who produce commodities (and are therefore subject to the market) but who employ little or no labour as they do so, depending instead 'primarily upon family labour, on the sweat of wives and children',[76] Capitalism also clearly reproduces generation after generation of small businessmen – capitalists who employ labour, but whose scale of operation is tiny relative to the monopolies, and whose free-

dom of manoeuvre (and indeed survival) is intimately determined by economic rhythms established in the monopoly sector. Within contemporary capitalism too we find a set of professions – traditional ones like medicine and the law, and new ones like accountancy, engineering and architecture – which have managed to turn their monopoly of a particular labour skill and qualification into a basis for privileged remuneration, and whose capacity to maintain that privilege turns now on their ability to extract a 'super wage' from either individual clients, private capital or the state. The professions within the middle class, unlike small business or members of the petty bourgeoisie, live off surplus value that they do not themselves create; yet they do so now in different ways. The mixture of feudal and capitalist modes of remuneration varies. Many doctors mix a salary with private practice. Solicitors and lawyers, in the main, continue to depend on private fees. Others, like engineers, strive still to consolidate qualifying associations that can strengthen their bargaining position as wage earners. As such, these professions are still at the centre of the intermediate strata, and their interests and politics run in different directions through it. For to the degree that the traditional professions in particular continue to recruit from the upper class and to use nepotistic mechanisms of closure at the entrance to their professions, they can be expected to see themselves as part of the propertied class, beyond the intermediate strata. And to the degree that professionals sell their skill as a commodity (create and exploit, that is, their 'intellectual capital') they can be expected to identify with the self-employed among the middle class. But to the extent instead that they have either become functionally interconnected to processes of capital accumulation and profit realization or been forced into a wage relationship, particularly with the state bureaucracy, they can be expected to stand nearer – in interests and perspectives – to the new 'service class' of private and public sector middle managers and administrators.

Clearly, late capitalism has brought enormous changes in the scope and content of management, changes whose basic character needs to be recognized if the material base of the 'new' middle class is to be grasped in all its complexity. Three things at least have happened. First, the owner-capitalist of the traditional kind has been replaced increasingly by what Carchedi has called 'the function of global capital':[77] that is, 'the development of capital has transformed the operating function of the capitalist from a personal activity into the work of a mass of people . . . the management functions of control and appropriation have in themselves become labour processes'.[78] At the same time the control of individual workers over the totality of the production of a commodity has been replaced by the rise of the *collective worker* – a situation in which output occurs through a complex division of labour tightly supervised by managerial agents. In this way 'the labour process has become the responsibility of the capitalist' for whom it is now essential that 'control over the labour process pass(es) from the hands of the worker into his own'.[79] Finally, at this stage in the concentration and centralization of capital, 'whereas at the level of *production* relations the appropriation of surplus value involves the direct surveillance and coercion of labour in the effort to increase productivity and lower costs, the process of *realization* introduces new mechanisms of control which have the function of 'watching over capital, of checking and controlling the progress of its enlargement'.[80] It is these three processes, 'the progressive loss of control over the labour process on the part of the direct producers; the elaboration of complex authority hierarchies within capitalist enterprises and bureaucracies; and the differentiation of various functions originally embodied in the entrepreneurial capitalist',[81] which has brought into existence complex hierarchies of managers and supervisors, clerical staff, research scientists and engineers, accountants, technicians and sales personnel.

As we shall see in detail in Part Three, late capitalism has also called into existence a parallel set of state functionaries, some of whom serve capital directly by playing an immediate role in private capital accumulation and realization (in ministries of technology, nationalized industries and in departments of finance); some of whom are directly concerned with maintaining existing patterns of social inequality (in the police, army and judiciary), and some of whom are engaged in welfare functions which partly sustain social peace and partly help to reproduce labour power. People employed in these hierarchies find themselves, as do employees in the extended managerial hierarchies of the private sector, engaged to varying degrees in the function of global capital and in that of the collective worker, and as such 'have one foot in the bourgeoisie and one in the proletariat'.[82] Such individuals occupy 'contradictory class locations' which help to sustain varied and volatile social interests and political involvements. As a result, we need to be able to locate those contradictory locations and to isolate the main groupings of class interests to which they give rise.

In fact, following Erik Olin Wright, we can 'analyse the class relations of capitalist society in terms of three processes underlying social relations of production: control of labour power, control of the physical means of production, and control of investment and resources'.[83] The two constituent classes of the capitalist mode of production – the bourgeoisie and the proletariat – can then be located at the polar ends of each of these, with the traditional petty bourgeoisie alongside them, enjoying formal control of only the second and third of those processes (and in practice finding now that even that limited degree of control is heavily constrained by monopoly power).[84] The relationship between these three constituent classes can then be expressed diagrammatically as in Figure 12.

What Wright then suggests is that the bulk of the new intermediate strata can be located at different positions *between* these three, occupying 'contradictory locations' ('positions which are torn between the basic contradictory class relations of capitalist society'):[85] between the bourgeoisie and the proletariat in the case of white collar and managerial staff; between the bourgeoisie and the petty bourgeoisie for small business; and between the petty bourgeoisie and the proletariat for semi-autonomous workers of the skilled craft and lower professional kind who still retain some degree of control over their immediate labour process. What situates each of these is the 'structural ambiguity'[86] of their position, their partial enjoyment of some or all of the three processes of control underlying the figure, and their partial exposure to those control processes at the hands of others. In each case, their contradictory location must be seen as a 'variable, rather than an all-or-nothing characteristic'.[87] To take the axis 'bourgeoisie–proletariat' as an example: foremen are nearer to the working class in their contradictory location than are middle managers, and senior managers shade away into the

propertied bourgeoisie proper, as we have seen. Middle managers and technicians are the most contradictory in their locations here, controlling 'various pieces of the labour process' while being themselves wages earners excluded from any control over investment and resources.[89] Wright quotes Braverman to illustrate this:

If we are to call this a 'new middle class' as many have done, we must do so with certain reservations. The old middle class occupied that position by virtue of its place outside the polar class structure: it possessed the attributes of neither capitalist nor worker; it played no direct role in the capital accumulation process whether on one side or the other. This 'new middle class' by contrast, occupies its intermediate position not because it is outside the process of increasing capital, but because, as part of this process, it takes its characteristics from both sides. Not only does it receive its petty share of the prerogatives and rewards of capital, but it also bears the mark of the proletarian condition.[90]

He then suggests Table 17.

The result is Figure 13, which shows the

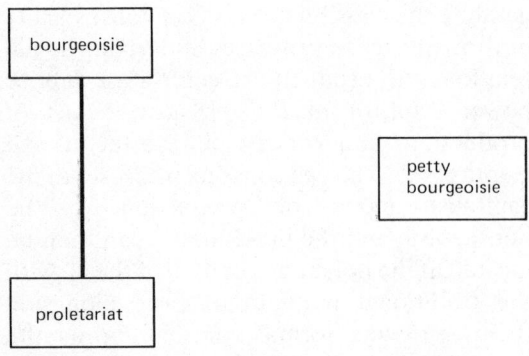

Figure 12   *The relationship between the constituent classes of the capitalist mode of production*

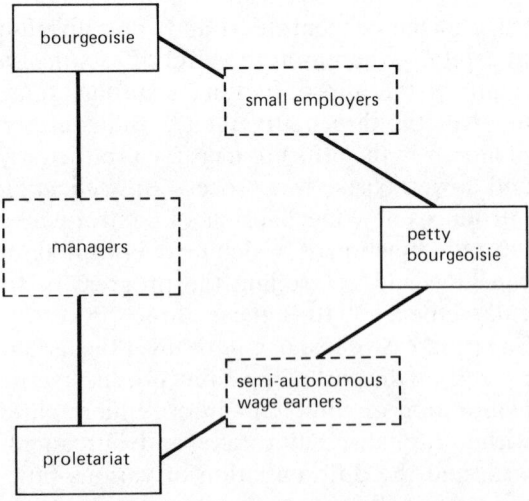

Figure 13   *Contradictory class locations for key sections of the intermediate strata*

Table 17 *Contradictory locations within class locations*

	Substantive social processes comprising class relations			Juridical categories of class relations		
	Economic ownership	*Possession*		*Legal ownership*		*Wage labour*
	Control over investments, resources	Control over the physical means of production	Control over the labour power of others	Legal ownership of property (capital, stocks, real estate, etc.)	Legal status of, being the employer of labour power	Sale of one's own labour power
Bourgeoisie						
Traditional capitalist	+	+	+	+	+	–
Top corporate executive	+	+	+	Partial	–	Minimal
Contradictory location between the proletariat and the bourgeoisie						
Top managers	Partial/minimal	+	Partial	Minimal	–	Partial
Middle managers	Minimal/–	Partial	Minimal	–	–	+
Technocrats	–	Minimal	Minimal	–	–	+
Foremen/line supervisors	–	–	Minimal	–	–	+
Proletariat	–	–	–	–	–	+
Contradictory location between the proletariat and the petty bourgeoisie						
Semi-autonomous employees	–	Minimal	–	–	–	+
Petty bourgeoisie	+	+	–	+	–	–
Contradictory location between the petty bourgeoisie and the bourgeoisie						
Small employers	+	+	Minimal	+	Minimal	–

Note + Full control Minimal Residual control
Partial Attenuated control – No control

Source: E. O. Wright, 'Class boundaries in advanced capitalist societies', *New Left Review*, **98** (July–August 1976), p. 33.

contradictory class locations for key sections of the intermediate strata. To this we can then add the bulk of state employees. For it is clear that certain sections of public sector workers participate directly in, or work directly to assist the private initiation of, processes of capital accumulation, and thereby reproduce the managerial–proletarian axis of Figure 13.[91] It is clear that other sectors of state employment are more properly located outside capitalist market processes altogether, engaged, as we have said, in the reproduction there of the social cohesion of the capitalist mode of production as a whole, and of the labour force in particular: producing use-values rather than exchange values, and often enjoying considerable degrees of job autonomy as they do so. Their relationship is expressed in Figure 14. Formulated in this fashion, the clustering of interests within the intermediate strata begins to take a certain shape. It suggests that the complex social structure of late capitalism is productive of not one middle class set of interests but of at least *three*: a petty bourgeois, small employer, independent professional cluster at 'A'; a professional–managerial 'service class' cluster at 'B'; and a proletarianized white collar and semi-autonomous cluster at 'C'. That is certainly the case in practice in contemporary Britain, as an examination of each will quickly show.

The traditional petty bourgeoisie

The political interests of the traditional petty bourgeoisie are structured primarily by contradictions between their position and that of the dominant social classes and processes consolidated by late capitalism: namely monopoly capital, organized labour and state policy. It is clear that late capitalism has a

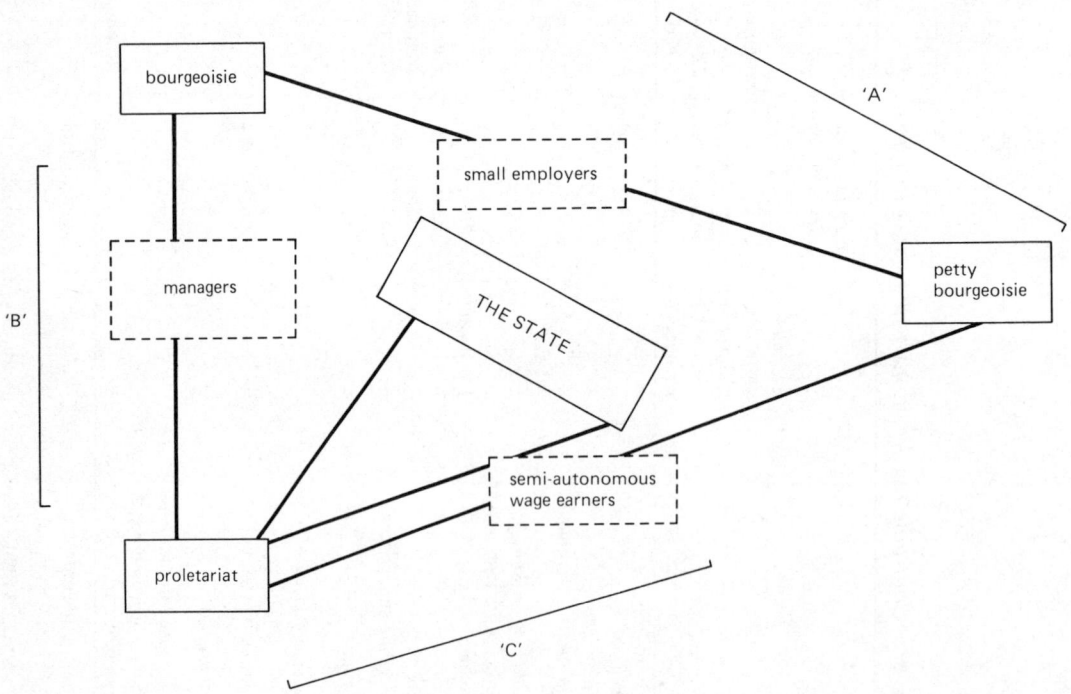

Figure 14   *Clustering of interests within the intermediate strata*

space for small business, which is capable of reproducing itself perpetually beneath the monopolies. Small-scale business is an important source of technical innovation in late capitalism, a valuable training ground for less qualified labour, and a protective front to monopoly power – permitting price levels to be artificially sustained with resulting 'super profits' for the larger concerns.[92] Independent business activity of a tiny scale is also a vital channel of social mobility, a 'buffer between capital and labour . . . (and) a bridge and a mediator between them'.[93] In this way small scale business has both a material and an ideological role within late capitalism; yet it is one which is experienced by small business itself as inherently precarious, involving 'long hours, exiguous rewards and poor conditions'.[94] 'Small businessmen have long regarded themselves as on the verge of extinction and prey to large collective predators in the jungle of modern monopoly capitalism: big business, organised labour and a powerful interventionist state.'[95] These fears are far from groundless: for although the stratum perpetually reproduces itself, individuals within it do regularly go to the wall. This is the section of the community, after all, that has the virtual monopoly of bankruptcies, and which is often denied the protection of limited liability enjoyed by larger joint-stock concerns. This is the stratum too whose lack of political leverage relative to big business we have already documented in Chapter 4, a lack of leverage reflected in the whole drift of post-war government policy in favour of big capital: with nationalizations, state purchasing, aid for restructuring, taxation on profits and state regulatory controls all favouring larger concerns, and all buying industrial peace at the price of intensifying the difficulties of small-scale enterprise.

'The sense of precariousness, of contingency' tends to lead, throughout this stratum, 'to the awareness of life as struggle, and to ambiguity in their relationship to others in the major classes. Small capital is menaced from above and below'.[96] Indeed, the centre of gravity of petty bourgeois politics has shifted down the years exactly in line with that growing menace. 'From radicalism in the early part of the last century, the petty bourgeoisie seemed to have moved to support Liberalism by the 1890s and after the rise of a Labour Party and the demise of Liberalism in the early decades of the twentieth century, the general allegiance of the stratum moved to the Tories.' Under pressure, that is, both from corporate capital and labour, the traditional petty bourgeoisie 'has been progressively squeezed' and 'has migrated across the political spectrum from left to right'.[97]

This shift is reflected most strongly in a particularly virulent opposition, among the petty bourgeoisie, to 'the Labour Party and all it represents'.[98] The characteristic ideology of the traditional petty bourgeois remains powerfully anti-corporatist, setting high store on 'autonomy' and 'independence', disliking bureaucracy, control, intervention and change. As Roger King has it, the traditional petty bourgeoisie in the main 'share a persisting dislike of higher taxation, bureaucratisation, the growth of government power, and the decline of individualism . . . (and) are hostile to anything which smacks of bureaucracy, planning and socialism'.[99] Empirical studies would suggest that the dominant political orientation of this stratum is best described as 'radical individualism' – strongly anti-collectivist, powerfully anti-union, and distrustful of big business and state activity. Here is one social base for the revival of the New Right in Conservative thinking in the 1970s, a social force with a 'compressed' view of the middle class (that is, seeing it squeezed between the monopolies and labour),[100] that has proved to be 'consistent if somewhat grudgingly Tory' in its political allegiance, a powerful ally of that section of the Conservative Party committed to 'rolling back the State' and disciplining the unions;

and as such, a force that also remains suspicious of the power and preoccupations of the new middle class of salaried and professional managers who are locked into bureaucratic employment in the monopolies and the state.

At certain moments of capitalist crisis, and in other places, this stratum has been mobilized by the extreme Right (by the Nazis in Germany in the early 1930s, and by the Poujadists in France in the 1950s). Even in Britain, the Conservative Party before Margaret Thatcher's rise to leadership was felt by many small businessmen to be too responsive to big capital and labour. It was this dissension that fuelled much of the revival of middle-class pressure groups in the 1970s, as we shall see. For then, and before, it was from this section of the community more than from any other that governments of all political persuasions met sustained, if generally ineffective, opposition to any growth of 'state intervention in the market with its levying of new taxes, its growing power to license occupations, to inspect business premises and business records . . . its attempts to regulate the relationships between employers and employees'[101] and its propensity to extend local rates and National Insurance contributions.

Open at times of capitalist crisis to anti-capitalist appeals, because of its tensions with the monopolies, this stratum is no easy ground for the Left. For its natural political propensity is to seek a reversal of historical trends, a radical conservatism – a return to an era of small business, weak unions, individualism and self-help – that is far easier for the extreme Right to mobilize than it is for the Left to harness. This is particularly so because of the extent to which what underpins petty bourgeois radicalism is 'an outrage to the moral assumptions quite as much as actual deprivation. Few are really being forced out of business, none are starving, but many are aware of widespread changes, social and political, as well as economic, which threaten

them'.[102] Indeed, latterly the Thatcherite wing of the Conservative Party has exploited those anxieties extremely well, extolling a set of virtues (Sir Keith Joseph's 'social responsibility; hard work; thrift; a desire for self-betterment and family betterment: the long view in preference to immediate gratification; independence of spirit combined with readiness to co-operate; rationality; constructiveness'),[103] that are particularly attractive to the owners of small businesses.

The present leadership of the Conservative Party have been led in this direction in part because of the prior mobilization of this stratum since 1974 by a set of new organizations: by the short-lived Middle Class Association; the National Association of Ratepayers' Action Groups; the National Federation of the Self-Employed; the Association of Self-Employed People; and the more upper class National Association for Freedom (now the Freedom Association), not to mention the briefly canvassed vigilante groups Civil Assistance and GB 75.[104] These organizations were all convinced, in their various ways, that the general drift of policy, particularly under a Labour government wedded to corporatism, had got to be resisted with vigour and determination. In spite of the fact that the very 'individualism' of this stratum was, and is, a barrier to any effective collective action by it, we still saw in the 1970s the growth of a veritable middle class movement of protest against welfare capitalism and its corporatist decision-making structures, a movement inspired by Labour government initiatives on employment protection, industrial arbitration, trade union and industrial relations reform, and by the 8 per cent National Insurance contribution levied on the self-employed in 1975. Mary Whitehouse's National Viewers' and Listeners' Association, though formed earlier, also needs to be situated here, as a predominantly 'middle aged and middle class'[105] response to the hedonism of the commercial culture of late capitalism, and to the more sexually liberated style of living consolidated especially among the middle class young in the heyday of the long boom. For the NVALA constituted one leading element in the moral wing of a 'middle class revolt' linking small business, owner occupiers and outraged Christians, a revolt whose activists were willing in the 1970s for the first time to experiment with a whole range of new tactics in pursuit of influence: 'street demonstrations, conventional parliamentary and Whitehall lobbying, . . . attempts at tax strikes, forms of civil disobedience in the deliberate obstruction of civil service work, the use of the courts to challenge governments and the setting up of a system of referendums among business enterprises'.[106]

The new 'service class'

As I have already had occasion to mention, there is an influential tradition of scholarship on the Left that would argue, admittedly with great sophistication and an awareness of the complexity of things, that those traditional petty bourgeois values and preoccupations (its 'ideological sub ensemble' as it is known in the trade) are shared by the new stratum of managers, technicians, engineers and state bureaucrats to such an extent that these new figures in the middle class must be thought of as a new petty bourgeoisie, in the same class as the old.[107] Leaving aside for our purposes any discussion of whether classes can properly be located through the ideologies to which their members are prone, it is quite clear that, even at the ideological level, these similarities of perspective between the old and the new in the intermediate strata apply only in the most superficial way. For while it is true that 'individualism characterises the ideology of both the new and the old petty bourgeoisie, the individualism of the two categories is extremely different. The individualism of the old petty bourgeoisie stresses individual autonomy, be your own boss, control over

your own destiny etc. The individualism of the new petty bourgeoisie, on the other hand, is a careerist individualism, an individualism geared towards organisational mobility'. For while the 'archetypal traditional petty bourgeois is the "rugged individualist" who makes his/her own way outside of the external demands of organisations', the archetypal 'new petty bourgeois is the "organisation man" whose individualism is structured around the requirements of bureaucratic advancement'.[108] It is to the impact of those bureaucracies that we shall turn now.

We have noted already how, in late capitalism, the hitherto relatively undifferentiated activity of capital accumulation has become increasingly complex and fragmented. We have seen that 'the many and varied tasks and operations within the capitalist function – the provision of finance, marketing, supply of raw materials, control of the labour force, etc – have increasingly been dealt with by specialised sectors dealing with a particular aspect of the capitalist function'. We have seen too how 'within these sectors, the capitalist function is fulfilled by *agents* who do not necessarily own the means of production'.[109] Indeed, what has happened increasingly through the history of industrial capitalism, if we follow the Braverman thesis, is that 'management' itself has become at one and the same time both a vital and expanding function and a labour process in its own right, 'as the never ending search for the rationalisation of production under conditions of monopoly capitalism' has brought with it 'increasing managerial control over the labour process', a control ever more confined, as time goes on, 'to smaller groups of executives assisted by computerised and mechanised labour saving devices'.[110] In the pursuit of surplus value, that is, capitalism has generated a managerial function to create and supervise an increasingly differentiated set of production tasks in the labour process of the working class, and has then subjected that very managerial function to exactly similar processes of fragmentation and routinization.

This has meant that capitalism has called into existence, in its private managerial hierarchies, and in the state bureaucracies that underpin them, a new 'service class' – a stratum of men (and it is usually men) on whose loyalty and initiative the propertied class depends for efficient capital accumulation, and to whom, though employees themselves, authority and responsibility have necessarily to be delegated. As John Goldthorpe has observed, 'these employees, in being typically engaged in the exercise of delegated authority or in the application of specialist knowledge or expertise, operate in their work tasks and roles with a distinctive degree of autonomy and discretion; and in direct consequence of the element of trust that is thus necessarily involved in their relationship with their employing organisation, they are accorded conditions of employment which are also distinctive in both the level and kind of rewards that are involved'.[111] These privileges serve then to buttress the identification of this service class to capital. They act as 'secondary structural factors' in Crompton and Gubbay's term,[112] and are both material and psychological in form. That is, it is this class whose identification with capital is reinforced by high incomes (and by the resultingly privileged consumer patterns and house ownership), by bureaucratically specified and relatively upwardly open career patterns, by high status at work, and by considerable power and discretion there. As a result, it is this stratum which lives off the exploitation of the working class in the most direct and obvious way – not as capitalists as such, but as a stratum 'who receive from the bourgeoisie a fraction of the social surplus value . . . who receive as income – through whatever form (salary, commercial profit, commissions) a sum of money greater than the value of their labour power' (what Carchedi calls 'revenue' as distinct from 'wages').[113]

Yet they remain a 'service' rather than a 'ruling' class in three crucial ways. The first is that they do 'serve' others: no matter how effectively the most successful members of the service class manage to slide into the propertied class proper (by capital ownership and marriage) it remains the case that the service class as a whole face *above* them a different class who 'owe their positions not to processes of bureaucratic appointment and advancement but to their own *power*, whether the bases of this are economic, political, military or whatever'.[114] Yet for all their subordinate position, the new managerial cadre remain a stratum apart even from the more routine white-collar workers immediately beneath them, precisely because they enjoy more income, authority and prestige, and more basically because the service they perform for capital is the systematic extraction of surplus value, from white-collar and manual workers alike. Their existence as a stratum, and the relative success and failure of individuals within it, turns precisely on their ability to increase the rate of exploitation of their subordinates in the interests ultimately (in the private sector) of capital accumulation, and (in the non-productive parts of the state sector) of the cost-effective reproduction of social peace and labour power vital to that accumulation process. It is in this sense that, in late capitalism, 'the manager, rather than the capitalist rentier, is the central figure . . . is capital personified'.[115]

Yet for all that, this new service class remain 'agents' of capital, employees themselves, in a contradictory and structurally ambiguous position. One way of recognizing that is to remember that the differentiation of functions within 'global capital' has been made necessary, and has precipitated, the further differentiation of job elements within the labour process from which surplus value is expropriated – has brought into existence, that is, not just 'global capital' but also the 'collective labourer'. The production of commodities in late capitalism is then possible only to the extent that those highly specialized and segmented tasks can be properly co-ordinated. This in its turn means that the managerial hierarchy face two imperatives, not one: not simply to supervise, control and exploit labour power (the function of global capital), but also to co-ordinate a complex labour process (which is really part of the function of collective labour). Different managerial positions involve different mixtures of those two things; and this is one source of the stratum's structural ambiguity. In the pursuit of either, the managerial function itself is experienced by those who perform it as a labour process, a job like any other, subject just as they are to processes of rationalization and higher managerial control. This is the second source of structural ambiguity for the managerial stratum. What has happened historically, as we shall see below (p. 132), is that greater and greater parts of the lower managerial hierarchy (routine white-collar workers, foremen and supervisors, even technicians and lower management) have over the years been 'doubly proletarianized' – as their jobs have been drained of any function associated with capital, and as they have themselves been increasingly treated as just another form of wage labour. The result of that has been to open them to trade unionism and to some relationship, however tenuous and tense, with the rest of the labour movement. What we must grasp now is that it has also pulled them away from the 'service class' proper, from their more senior colleagues whose immersion in the function and privileges of global capital continues to predispose them to a particular kind of conservative politics.

Members of the service class, in the main, 'would seem to stand, like the growing middle class already envisaged by Marx, as a collectivity with a major interest in, and commitment to the status quo'.[117] They can be expected to act in ways 'characteristic of members of privileged strata: that is, that they

will seek to use the superior resources that they possess in order to preserve their positions of relative social power and advantage, for themselves and for their children'.[118] Their function and whole work experience may be expected to bring them into conflict with the working class, and make them generally antipathetical to political programmes designed to achieve any significant increase in working-class industrial power. Their own career patterns seem likely to predispose them to values of 'hierarchy and meritocracy';[119] and to give them a predeliction for policies which strengthen the bureaucracies.' For although advancement within hierarchies may be an individual matter, the advancement of a particular career hierarchy may be of importance to one occupation or profession . . . the advancement of career hierarchies as such'[120] will be of concern to them all. It is this section of the middle class, therefore, that may be expected to be most open to policies that extend the bureaucratic structures of welfare capitalism and its corporatist decision-making forms, though even here enthusiasm for welfare bureaucracies is less likely to be found in that section of the service class employed by private capital than it is among the bureaucrats of the state. What is likely to be common to them, though, is an enthusiasm for big capital and for state involvement that will be in tension, not just with the political project of labour, but with the political predilections of the petty bourgeoisie as well.

One other feature of this stratum is also significant politically, and that is its power. It is this stratum which 'mans' the civil service and controls industrial production on a day-to-day basis. It is used to being listened to, to issuing orders, and to being obeyed; and as a result can be quick to mobilize if it feels its privileges threatened. It is this stratum too whose children benefit most from state education, and which as a group make the fullest use of the welfare services. It is also this stratum which continues to be well represented in every area of public debate – from economic policy and school reorganization to nuclear defence – a debate in which, on the other side, it is as likely as not to meet representative figures of that final section of the intermediate strata – its unionized and radical wing – whose structural position and politics we must also chart.

The middle-class Left

If the bulk of the intermediate strata constitutes difficult terrain for the Left, its white-collar and 'autonomous worker' section does not. On the contrary, this section has been the source of the most rapid growth of trade unionism since the war, and at times has been open to political radicalization by the Left to a degree absent even from the more traditional part of the organized labour movement. Indeed, if Labour voting is taken as an index of radicalism, the middle-class Left – constituting as it does some 30 per cent of all middle-class votes – is in percentage terms as significant a political fact in contemporary Britain as is working-class support for the Conservatives.

At least three things have happened to this segment of the intermediate strata which have brought its people close in identification to the rest of the labour movement, and have predisposed at least a section of them to regular bouts of political radicalism. One process, affecting the bulk of routine white-collar workers (from clerical grades to scientific and technical staff) has been the 'double proletarianization' to which I referred earlier. White-collar jobs of traditionally high status and obvious managerial content have grown vastly in number (from 3.75 million to 7 million between 1931 and 1971), have been drained as they grew of all but the most vestigial element of a managerial role, and have – and this is where the 'double' occurs – been subject to the very processes of de-skilling,[121] routinization, bureaucratization, exploitation and unemployment hitherto the monopoly of the manual working class. The precise impact of these processes has varied at different levels in the white-collar hierarchy, and overall white-collar conditions of employment remain distinctly better than those experienced by the bulk of manual labour.[122] In fact the process of proletarianization has been most acute at the base of the white-collar pyramid, so that there 'it seems almost certain that the large majority of white-collar employees, especially clerical and secretarial employees, have – at most – trivial autonomy on the job and thus should be placed within the working class itself'.[123]

There is an important sense in which the precise positioning of white-collar workers on this class boundary is an exercise more in semantics than in politics, although 'to the extent that clerks maintain their position at the fingertips of the extended arm of managerial authority, despite the relative decline in their social prestige and the similarity of their income levels with manual workers' there is still just a case for saying that 'they will remain marginally and tenaciously members of the middle class'.[124] Yet whether they constitute the bottom level of the intermediate strata, or are best thought of as working class, or whether they are 'partly within the working class, partly on its fringes: not distinctively outside it, as conventional usage still implies',[125] the practical result remains the same. That is, subject to the proletarianization of their working conditions, such white-collar workers have recently joined unions at a quite spectacular rate, and have been obliged to look to those unions for strike action in the pursuit of better pay and conditions. Moreover, because so many white-collar workers are directly employed by the state, or where they are not, have been so visibly affected by repeated government attempts at incomes control down the years, the period since 1961 has seen a tendency for unions of white-collar workers to federate with those of manual workers in peak organizations lobbying the state (especially the TUC),[126] to strike even against the government when that lobbying was unsuccessful,[127] and to be willing in certain cases to play a greater role within the Labour Party (ASTMS is an obvious example) in the hope of influencing the policy of governments yet to come (Table 18).

Of course we need to be cautious here, not to overdraw or misrepresent the change. Industrial militancy is not the same as political radicalism. Nor is union membership an automatic indicator of class consciousness.[128] Instead, the centre of gravity of most white collar unions most of the time remains industrially moderate and politically conservative, as NALGO's recent 8:1 rejection of Labour Party affiliation served to remind us. Many white collar trade unionists retain status preoccupations and antipathies to manual unionism that are reflective both of their own ambiguous class position and of the social ethic associated with their job in earlier periods when its managerial content was greater. Many white-collar workers join trade unions 'with the aim of preserving their separate status and material interests, and the actions of white collar unions more generally seek to defend or improve differentials with manual workers'.[129] As such these white collar trade unionists should be seen for what they are – 'reluctant militants'[130] – pursuing sectional interests as doggedly as any craft union

Table 18 *Union membership and density*

	1948	1964	1974
Union membership (000s)			
White-collar	1934	2684	4263
Manual	7398	7534	7491
Union density (percentage)			
White-collar	30.2	29.6	39.4
Manual	50.7	52.9	57.9

Source: R. Price and G. S. Bain, 'Union growth revisited: 1948–1974 in perspective', *British Journal of Industrial Relations,* **14** no. 3, p. 347.

of skilled manual workers. As Roberts and his colleagues found in their sample of technicians, 'expressions of solidarity with the manual working class were conspicuous only by their absence'.[131]

Yet even so, what is striking about the available empirical evidence is both the way it demonstrates the willingness of all levels of white-collar workers to unionize, and the manner in which it underlines the greater propensity of workers at the base of the white-collar hierarchy to identify with the industrial and political ambitions of the manual working class. As Roberts has it, 'white collar proletarians . . . are not mythical creatures'. Although they remain a minority among white collar workers as a whole, 'there are thousands of them, and they can be found in the exact circumstances that previous exponents of the proletarianisation thesis have identified': 'in relatively depressed socioeconomic conditions . . . (and) typically employed in routine jobs'.[132] It is these white-collar workers in particular who find themselves threatened by the way in which state employment is itself under threat. Just as the long boom flourished on state spending and private economic growth, so the return of recession has brought generalized unemployment in the private sector and calls to 'roll back the state'; and that has put in jeopardy white-collar jobs hitherto deemed secure for life. White collar workers so threatened are open to new political initiatives, from the Right as well as the Left, and objective conditions favouring a left-wing response only 'become greater as we approach the barrier of manual labour, with the repetitive type of labour performed by commercial employees and office workers'.[133] But if the rank and file can and do go either way politically, the activist strata in these unions has not. Instead the recession has pulled into local leadership positions within their unions an activist strata whose political sympathies are often Left Labourist or even more socialist, an activist strata which, as a result, is significantly more left-wing in its politics than is the bulk of its own rank and file.

Indeed, white collar trade union activists remain an important component of the new middle-class Left, one of three elements there. For late capitalism has also allowed the consolidation of a new *artisanate* outside the bureaucracies – a set of often college trained young people denied access to bureaucratic occupations because of the recession, who have turned instead (and by preference in many cases) to petty commodity production (in wood, textiles, paint and so on). Self-employed, these people are free of the exploitative pressures of the capitalist labour process; although as commodity producers themselves, they are still dependent on small and local markets, and as such sensitized to wider social processes, particularly at the local level. Such artisans have long been a source of a radical anti-capitalist culture. 'By the very nature of their work, and the specific perm-eability that it presents to working class agents', artisans 'have always displayed an objectively proletarian polarization, far more than have the small retailers. Artisan produc-tion was the cradle of revolutionary syndical-ism, and its traditions of struggle are still very much alive'.[134] They certainly were in the heyday of the anti-capitalist struggles in Britain between 1790 and 1830.[135] Artisan radicalism flourished again in the arts and crafts movement of the early twentieth cen-tury; and it was these people too whom Orwell dismissed so caustically in the 1930s, when he observed that 'one sometimes gets the im-pression that the mere words "socialism" and "communism" draw towards them with magnetic force every fruit juice drinker, nudist, sandal-wearer, sex-maniac, Quaker, "Nature Cure" quack, pacifist, and feminist in England'.[136] Their reappearance as a signi-ficant social force on the Left in the late 1970s was signalled by the rise of ecology and other radical environmental parties; and reflects the fate of a generation of the young, educated unemployed – alienated from capitalism by education and work experience, and kept at a distance from the socialism of the organized labour movement by their class position and their own exclusion from the 'solidarizing' experiences of wage labour.[137]

As a component of the middle-class Left, the new artisans are prone to hostility to trade unionism as a social practice, and to revolu-tionary socialism as a liberating ideology, be-cause of their distance from the proletariat. This is a problem internal to the Left to which we shall return in the last chapter. Yet for all that, many of the new artisans are politically active in radical causes, and certainly consti-tute a vital part of the activist wing of such popular-democratic mobilizations as CND and the women's movement. For as Cotsgrove and Duff found when they examined their 'strong environmentalists', the anti-capitalist and anti-industrialization themes in contem-porary 'green politics' derive from a quite distinct and radical sub-culture. So that where the public at large set highest store by 'law and order', followed by satisfying work, economic growth, differentials, and rewards for achieve-ment, in contrast environmentalists appear to prefer a society which above all attaches importance to 'humanly satisfying work, in which production is selective rather than aiming to satisfy the demand for consumer goods, which sets limits to economic growth, and emphasises participation as against the influence of experts'.[138] It is this 'alternative culture' that continues to be one of the most visible elements in the politics and life-style of the new anti-authoritarian middle-class Left.

George Orwell was able to dismiss these people in the 1930s because they were so few in number. Their greater significance now arises in part from the alliances which they have built with others of their generation and class – those who did find employment, particularly in the welfare bureaucracies of the state. As Cotsgrove and Duff found, what was particularly striking was 'the high proportion of environmentalists in (their) sample occupying roles in the non-productive service sector: doctors, social workers, teachers and the creative arts'.[139] For late capitalism has also consolidated a stratum of almost exclusively publicly-employed semi-professionals, people whose whole job experience and training is at one remove from the commodity production and exploitative labour processes of capitalism proper. These are people who, as far as capitalism is concerned, are employed in the reproduction of labour power: materially through health care, culturally in education, or socially, in welfare provision of various sorts. Since each of these spheres has a 'function' for capital, individuals working within it can still, and often do, identify with capital, with the 'service class' and its conservative politics. Since there is a labour process of a bureaucratized kind within each sector, this identification is particularly easy and marked among senior administrative grades within each welfare bureaucracy. But many of their subordinates adopt different politics. For the very distancing of this stratum from market relationships, and from a labour process of a capitalist kind, permits and facilitates the consolidation here of a critical attitude to the dominant capitalist processes, institutions and classes that surround them. As Cotsgrove and Duff put it:

To the extent that schools, hospitals and welfare agencies operate outside the market place, and those who work in them are dedicated to maximising non-economic values, they constitute non-industrial enclaves within industrial societies and are the carriers of alternative non-economic values. And they may well provide a more congenial environment for those for whom the values and ideology of industrial capitalism do not win unqualified enthusiasm and unquestioning support. In short, those who reject the ideology and values of industrial capitalism are likely to choose careers outside the market place. Moreover such occupations can offer a substantial degree of personal autonomy for those who have little taste for a subordinate role in the predominantly hierarchial structures of industrial society.[140]

Moreover, this relative autonomy, and the lengthy education through which they have gone, also seems to have left these welfare bureaucrats with the political skills and self-confidence of the middle class as a whole, and encourages them to move with relative ease from passive critique to organized political intervention. Higher education seems to have played a crucial preparatory role here, exposing a generation of predominantly lower-middle class students to critical thinking, and consolidating a commitment among them to universal ethics and personal fulfilment through work and life that the reality of late capitalism in crisis has found harder and harder to match. 'Undoubtedly leftism is one strong outcome of increasing "universalism" – with proletarianisation as a major reinforcing factor here.'[141] In the years of economic expansion these state-employed professionals consolidated their own organizations and increased their own demands for autonomy and control. With the return of world recession, and that 'fiscal crisis of the state' (which will be discussed in Part Three), those professional demands came into increasing conflict with state calls for greater managerial control and accountability in the public services. As O'Connor has described it: 'the fusion of economic base and political superstructure and the fiscal crisis have led to the "rationalisation" of state jobs, the introduction of efficiency criteria, the waiving of professional standards, and in general the transplantation of capitalist norms from direct production in the private economy to the state administration'.[142] All that has had a radicalizing effect on a significant number of welfare bureaucrats, creating in them a sense of dissatisfaction that required only a catalyst to transform it into direct political action. The deepening crisis of capitalism was such a catalyst for many in the 1970s, encouraging them to colonize a succession of constituency labour parties, and to give to each a Bennite or even a Militant face. The way in which that capitalist crisis was associated with the escalation of the arms race acted as an even more powerful catalyst to the middle class left in the late 1970s, mobilizing far greater numbers into the revitalized Peace Movement. Of course, so many CND members are there as single-issue campaigners, reluctant to link their opposition to nuclear weapons with other campaigns on unemployment, trade union rights and the defence of civil liberties.[143] But many peace campaigners do make those connections; and these radicals are invariably drawn from the three sectors of the middle-class Left I have mentioned: trade union activists in the white-collar unions, new artisans and welfare bureaucrats. It is this 'specific fraction of the middle class whose interests and values diverge markedly from other groups in industrial societies',[144] whose values challenge the dominant modes of contemporary legitimation, and which as such pose a radical challenge to Conservative governments in the last two decades of the century.

It is clear that the Left stands fair to benefit – in terms of support – from the processes isolated here: from the increasing proletarianization of the intermediate strata, and from 'a heightening radicalism by well-paid professional and intellectual employees whose opposition to existing patterns of power is engendered by the dissemination of critical thinking in higher education and the growth of public sector occupations which foster hostile attitudes to the market individualism of competitive capitalism'.[145] Elsewhere in the intermediate strata, more conservative views more normally prevail, sustained there by their adherents' involvement in the function of global capital, or by their reliance on patterns of self-employment threatened by the strong **trade unionism**, high taxation and labour

codes of welfare capitalism. It is true that, as a result, the 'middle class in Britain today is a less established, less unified middle class'[146] than it once was, and as such is less closed to the Left than hitherto. It is also true that, in a sense, 'the new middle class are up for sale' politically – subject to only a 'shallow anchorage (in their) political loyalties':[147] volatile, and vulnerable to differing political initiatives because of their contradictory class locations. Precisely because they stand in so intermediate a position between the two great social classes of capitalism, there is a sense in which 'self understanding' across the intermediate strata as a whole has a propensity to come only 'from the refraction of the ideological positions of both major social classes through the common structural position of its members'; and in that sense to be, *par excellence*, 'a field of struggle between bourgeois and working class ideology'.[148]

This alone is enough to ensure – as we shall see in Part Three – that a crucial preoccupation of the Conservative state lies in the maintenance of its hegemony here; just as it is also the case that the Left cannot avoid challenging that hegemony if it is to win popular support for its project. For the building of a popular coalition for socialist change requires the establishment of a socialist counter-hegemony among the intermediate strata no less than among the working class as a whole. The problem for the Left is that the structural location of the intermediate strata, though contradictory, is weighted heavily in favour of capital. Small businesses and the service class are easier ground for the Right than for the Left, more easily winnable to 'authoritarian populism' than to 'democratic socialism'. Therefore capitalist institutions, processes and ruling classes continue to have a generalized legitimacy in spite of the deepening economic crisis to which those institutions have been subject since the end of the long boom. For this reason, if for no other, this relationship between the intermediate strata and the struggle for socialist change will face us again in the last chapter of this volume, when we explore the possible strategies for left-wing advance available in the 1980s.

The working class

At the base of the male white class structure in contemporary Britain stand nearly 10 million manual workers, the bedrock of the traditional labour movement. As industrial capitalism established itself in nineteenth-century Britain, it was workers of this kind who were at the forefront of the struggle for union recognition, political representation and social rights. As artisans and hand loom weavers succumbed in their different times and places to proletarianization, the centre of gravity of the new working class shifted to the coal mines, the factories, the foundries and the railways. From the 1850s craft unions, and from the 1870s unions of miners, managed to establish a precarious hold on employer recognition and rank-and-file support. From the late 1880s they were joined by general unions of the semi- and unskilled in the docks, the public utilities and the expanding transport system. By 1921 1,591,000 men worked in transport, 1,888,000 in engineering and shipbuilding, and 1,204,000 in the mines. As these industries went into decline between the wars, new sources of employment eventually rose to absorb a fresh generation of manual workers: in light engineering, vehicle construction, chemicals and food processing.

Of course, to describe the process in that way is already to do at least two things. It is to put at the heart of the definition of the working class the reality of *change*. As Braverman has it, the term 'working class' 'properly understood, never precisely delineated a specific body of people, but was rather an expression for an ongoing social process' in which 'immense changes'[149] and associated insecurities remain the dominant features. It is also to grant significance to two of the great divisions of experience and interest *within* the manual working class that have coloured its politics throughout: the divisions of industry and of skill. Table 19 shows the changing distribution of the occupied population between industries since 1948, and makes clear its shifting centre of gravity: from heavy engineering to light, from traditional industries to new, and from wholly private employment to significant employment by the state. What the figures do not indicate so clearly, but what is also true, is the growing tendency behind them 'to the concentration and centralisation of capitals, the expansion of labour processes that are based on production line technologies and forms of control . . . the shift of labour out of direct production and into circulation and distribution, and the expansion of labour within the state'.[150] What the figures do record, however, is the persistence within that changing occupational distribution of hierarchies of skill – as men with long craft traditions, established apprenticeship schemes and degrees of job autonomy work alongside others who lack even those limited protections against the full rigours of an unregulated labour market. The modern working class still contains its printers, skilled engineers, electricians and train drivers, though its numerical centre these days consists far more of heavily unionized semi-skilled workers in factories employing 500 people or more.

We shall discuss below in more detail this whole question of 'skill'. What must be understood first is the extent to which manual workers in this society, for all the sources of division within them, share a largely common set of industrial experiences and a largely common set of social rewards and life chances. For all the rise in real incomes since the war, 'inequality at the workplace' remains 'systematically related to social class. There are major differences in the character, security, conditions and fringe benefits at work as between manual and non-manual grades. And among manual grades, the unskilled are

Table 19 *Industrial distribution of employment in United Kingdom, 1948–74*

Industry	Old Basis			New Basis		
	1948	1971	Percentage change 1948–71	1971	1974	Percentage change 1971–4
Education	521	1,485	185.0	1,517	1,748	15.2
Insurance, banking, and finance	432	998	131.0	991	1,130	14.0
Professional and scientific services	806	1,514	87.8	1,492	1,645	10.3
Paper, printing, and publishing	472	638	35.2	609	598	−1.8
Distribution	2,093	2,703	29.1	2,679	2,810	4.9
Local government	720	899	24.9	932	1,005	7.8
Food, drink, and tobacco	731	893	22.2	798	784	−1.7
Metals and engineering	3,739	4,534	21.3	4,329	4,118	−4.9
Chemicals and allied	447	538	20.4	494	484	−2.0
Gas, electricity, and water	329	386	17.3	386	352	−8.8
Other transport and communications	1,221	1,362	11.6	1,364	1,314	−3.7
Furniture and timber	294	308	4.8	279	290	3.9
Entertainment and sport	238	249	4.6	272	284	4.4
Construction	1,375	1,416	3.0	1,389	1,429	2.9
Footwear	116	100	−13.8	95	87	−8.4
Hotels and catering	710	590	−16.9	714	824	15.4
Clothing	498	411	−17.5	369	346	−6.2
National government	717	590	−17.7	608	624	2.6
Textiles (excluding cotton)	708	525	−25.8	543	475	−12.5
Cotton	293	156	−46.8	146	121	−17.1
Mining	803	426	−46.9	418	365	−12.7
Railways	576	267	−53.6	247	224	−9.3
Agriculture, forestry, and fishing	868	369	−57.5	450	428	−4.9

Source: G. S. Bain and R. Price, 'Union growth revisited: 1948–74 in perspective', *British Journal of Industrial Relations*, **14** no. 33, (1979), p. 344.

markedly more disadvantaged than the skilled and partly skilled'.[151] At the bottom of all the hierarchies of industrial command and state direction in late capitalism, manual workers in particular still experience (as we saw in Chapter 6) relatively restricted levels of earnings (Table 20), disproportionately difficult working conditions, and highly restricted degrees of job autonomy and control. Vulnerable in recession to unemployment, and in times of intense competition subject to perennial work pressure, it is this class which experiences the full rigours of the capitalist labour process, and whose politics, as a result, can be expected to show the ravages of that experience.

So to understand the material base of contemporary working class political attitudes and interests, we need to have a full sense of that labour process. Here the recent work of Harry Braverman, for all its limitations, is an important source.[152] For as he has made clear,

capitalism as it developed imposed particular and changing pressures on those who worked for it.

In the earliest stages of capitalist industrialization – when industrial capital was in its *manu*facturing as distinct from its later *machino*facturing stage – the expropriation of surplus value by the capitalist class occurred largely through the bringing together of labour processes in which workers retained significant degrees of control over the actual process of production, but in which long hours were common as the major source of profit. As others have described it, 'in manufacture each worker or group of workers still [had] some degree of control over the content, speed, intensity, rhythm, etc. of work: and the integration, the balancing or harmonising of the collective work [was] still empirical. It [was] still worked out on the basis of observation of actual work, rather than calculated beforehand on the basis of knowledge of the

Table 20 *Occupational class averages of wages and percentages for all occupational classes, men 1914–15, 1922–4, 1935–6, 1955–6, 1960*

	1913–14 % of av.	1922–4 % of av.	% of 1913–14	1935–6 % of av.	% of 1922–4	1955–6 % of av.	% of 1935–6	1960 % of av.	% of 1955–6	% of 1913–14
Men										
Professional										
Higher	410	372	91	392	105	290	74	298	103	73
Lower	194	204	105	190	93	115	60	124	108	64
Managers, etc.	250	307	123	272	89	279	103	271	97	108
Clerks	124	116	94	119	103	98	82	100	102	81
Foremen	141	171	121	169	99	148	88	149	101	106
Manual										
Skilled	124	115	93	121	105	117	97	117	100	94
Semi-skilled	86	80	93	83	104	88	97	85	97	99
Unskilled	79	82	104	80	98	82	102	79	96	100
Men's average (current weights)	115	114	99	115	100	119	103	118	99	103
Mean deviation (per cent)	67	73		70		48		49		

Source: R. Brown, 'Work', in P. Abrams (ed.), *Work, Urbanism and Inequality* (Weidenfeld and Nicolson 1978), p. 92.

machine functions'.[153] Then, as competition intensified, working-class resistance increased, capital centralized and as the mass of capital grew apace, the expropriation of surplus value shifted in form, and came to rely heavily instead on the application of machinery to production – in a move known in Marxist political economy as one from the expropriation of *absolute* surplus value to that of *relative* surplus value. Indeed in general terms it is possible to chart over time the introduction of ever *wider* and ever *deeper* waves of machinery to production: with the generalized spread of powered machinery after 1880; of assembly-line production after 1918; of transfer automation from the 1940s; and, even now, of computerized automation.[154] At each stage, the role of labour power in the production process diminished, with dramatic upturns in the productivity of labour being bought at the price of leaving more and more of the actual production process dependent on machinery. This shift – from the 'spinning jenny to the micro-chip' – represented a significant increase in human control over nature, a quite immense leap in the productivity of human effort; but because of its immersion in capitalist relations of production, it also represented the growing domination of capital over labour, of 'dead' labour over 'living', which in its turn did two things of importance to the capitalist labour process. It brought the steady erosion of skills, and the steady extension of managerial controls over that deskilled labour.

In other words, as capitalism developed, it destroyed generation after generation of labour skills, built into its labour process a propensity to fragment jobs into increasingly tiny and unskilled components, and subjected that highly specialized labour to ever greater degrees of managerial supervision. We have already seen the impact of that on the managerial end of the class structure, as the supervisory hierarchy lengthened and then in its turn became subject to similar processes of deskilling and proletarianization. What we have to grasp now is its impact on the industrial experience of manual workers: deskilling them by consolidating the division of mental and manual labour (in Braverman's phrase, splitting 'conception' from 'execution'); and exposing them to tight managerial control and pressure – to the 'real' as distinct from the 'formal' subordination of labour to capital. The result of this cumulative 'imposition of work discipline, the subdivision of labour, the control of work methods through monopolisation of knowledge, and mechanisation'[155] has been, in Braverman's words, the 'degradation of work in the twentieth century', its total subordination to the rhythms and requirements of capital-in-the-machine, and the creation of that situation – much commented upon by industrial sociologists – in which the vast reservoirs of skill and potential that exist in a modern labour force are systematically under-utilized. To give only one rather graphic example: Blackburn and Mann found as many as 85 per cent of the unskilled manual workers in their study exercised less skill at work than they would if they drove to work. Indeed, 'most of them expend more mental effort and resourcefulness in getting to work than in doing their jobs'.[156] Little wonder then that for Braverman, 'the "progress" of capitalism seems only to deepen the gulf between worker and machine and to subordinate the worker ever more decisively to the yoke of the machine'.[157]

This analysis, in Braverman's hands, is used to indite capitalism. For as he argues, the pressures to which workers are subject is not fixed

by capitalism from the point of view of the satisfaction of human needs. Rather, powered by the needs of the capital accumulation process, it becomes a frenzied drive which approaches the level of a generalised social insanity. Never is any level of productivity regarded as sufficient. In the (car) industry, a constantly diminishing number of workers produces, decade by decade, a growing number of increasingly degraded products which, as they are placed upon the streets . . . poison and disrupt the entire social atmosphere – while at the same time the cities where motor vehicles are produced become centres of degraded labour on the one hand and permanent unemployment on the other. . . . Like Captain Ahab, the capitalist, can say 'All my methods are sane, my motives and object mad'.[158]

Yet for all the force of his vision and critique, Braverman still has his critics, and rightly so. They argue that his case, though in its essentials accurate, is 'over-determined and under-differentiated'.[159] They point to the over-romanticization of nineteenth-century craft control in Braverman's description, and his failure to see that Victorian management could (and modern management still can and does) use the autonomy of those craft unions as yet another way of increasing their control over the capitalist labour process. Where Braverman sees a unidimensional drift to 'scientific management' of the Taylor kind, they see the persistence of a choice of managerial strategies, even a resistance by management to Taylorism, with the incorporation of a labour aristocracy into a subordinate managerial position as still popular with managements facing strong union organization. They point too to the way in which the destruction of a set of skills by one generation of machinery still enables the consolidation of a new if different set of skills in the next. As Lee has it, 'experience repeatedly showed that the machines created craft jobs and tasks to offset ones which had been lost', in general shifting 'the manual skill requirement from production to job planning and maintenance'.[160] They point, in other words, to the rhythm of skilling and deskilling, and to the way in which the establishment of a 'skill' (just as much as the establishment of a 'profession' in a higher class) is itself the product of social struggle and achieved recog-

nition. 'For what counts as "skilled work" or a "skilled trade" depends in some substantial degree upon what can be *made* to count as such.'[161]

They point moreover to the way in which the systematic introduction of machinery not only deskills, but also 'creates . . . competencies and other opportunities for bargaining leverage arising from the complex co-ordination and interdependence of the collective labourer'; and in periods of rapid accumulation at least, when the introduction of machinery does not produce massive unemployment, how 'it depletes the reserve army of labour and provides a basis for powerful worker organisation'.[162] They point, that is, to the way in which the pressure to deskill and to increase managerial control can be, and often is, met by industrial resistance and working-class struggle. It is not so much a process as a fight, the intensity of which is quickened both by the strength of labour organization and by the severity of the competitive pressures experienced by management. This is important in the British case, since that struggle has dominated post-war industrial relations in the growth sectors of the boom; with the significant degree of working-class job control achieved there in the years of full employment being subject to steady managerial pressure (and state harassment) from the mid 1960s, as the competitive problems of the car industry, the docks and light engineering began to intensify.[163]

Indeed, Braverman's critics have pointed out too that these attempts by management 'to develop forms of grading and wage payment (as in the car industry) which most effectively compel the exercise of specific dexterity and experience to maximise intensity and productiveness'[164] have been at their most acute of late in just such industries – in the sectors of capital accumulation dominated by the monopolies – where vast quantities of fixed capital have had to be worked with ever greater intensity to prevent a quite cataclysmic collapse of profits. Workers in smaller firms, less heavily capitalized, have met different and less acute pressures; and have often been vulnerable to unemployment quite directly because of their dependence on sales to the monopolies, while not themselves being able to protect their own jobs by any intensification of work routines on their part alone. The picture that emerges then is of a monopoly sector increasingly bent on deskilling and intensifying the work process, and a dependent small business sector subject to random and growing unemployment, with the workers in both sectors experiencing industrial decline as a quite direct threat to their work routines, their living standards and their jobs.

There is a sense in which, by now, none of this should surprise us. For these are just the most recent manifestations of tensions between capital and labour that are endemic to this mode of production.[165] As we have had occasion to mention before, since capital can be accumulated only through the expropriation of surplus value from labour power, the system's relentless pressure to quicken that rate of accumulation necessarily comes through to workers in the form of perennial pressures to alter adversely their wage-effort bargain: to lengthen the working day, or to intensify the pace of work, or to subordinate labour to ever more sophisticated and demanding machinery. Though that new technology can create new jobs (and even new skills), and though managerial strategies for labour control are not as single-mindedly authoritarian as Braverman implied, these qualifications have to be thought of as counter-tendencies to the otherwise quite 'general process of deskilling and the erosion of worker autonomy in the labour process'[166] that applies generally in late capitalism, as work is experienced as a *class* relationship of conflict, subordination and exploitation. For the 'three basic structural features of the capitalist organisation of the labour process . . . (the division of intellectual and manual labour . . .

hierarchial control . . . fragmentation or de-skilling of labour)'[167] operate to the extent that working-class resistance to them is limited and muted. The pressures to deskill and control are there throughout, taking different forms as the pattern of class struggle around them ebbs and flows. Moreover, the instabilities of competition between capitalist firms, what Marx elsewhere called 'the essential locomotive of bourgeois economy', is experienced by workers as a further source of pressure and insecurity, as it builds into the system the perpetual necessity to innovate, to abandon old capital, to destroy old working practices, and to shift the weight of expenditure in production from labour to machinery. The work situation of the manual working class under capitalism is thus necessarily one of inequality, uncertainty and change; and politicians must as a result face workers who have to battle even to maintain existing levels of pay, conditions and job security, and who are conscious of how precarious their hold on all those things necessarily has to be.

The danger, of course, of leaving the argument at this point is that it might be thought too general and too timeless, too insensitive to variations and changes in the work process and class relationships of a complex and developing capitalist society. It is clear enough that the actual working situation of manual workers does differ significantly: that some work in small firms, with limited amounts of capital equipment and close proximity to their employer; that some work in large and highly bureaucratized structures, as often as not employed by a multinational corporation or the state; that some work on highly automated production lines, others in continuous process industries, yet others in small batch one-off production. Blauner's fourfold typology of productive techniques still applies: 'craft industry . . . where there is a low level of mechanisation and skilled labour predominates; "machine tending" industries, with a higher degree of mechanisation, where the worker merely "minds" the machine; industries involving "assembly line" techniques, with a very advanced level of job fragmentation and highly routined and specific tasks; and "continuous process" industries . . . involving automatically controlled production flows, in which the labour task concerns only the monitoring and maintenance of the machinery'.[168] Indeed a liberal strand of recent scholarship has argued strongly that the emergence of more modern production systems of the continuous flow kind, accompanied as these are often said to have been by sophisticated personnel management and generalized affluence, can be expected to have softened class tension significantly, lessened alienation and consolidated a sense of 'team spirit' in place of the divisions between 'them and us'. So, 'in the case of process technologies in general, and of the chemical industry in particular, we find sociologists . . . stressing that physical drudgery is giving way to a new type of "meaningful" work. In optimistic vein, it is even sometimes suggested that the chemical industry represents the shape of an already emerging future: a future which will bring dignity to what is euphemistically called "blue collar work", which will see a reduction in so called "alienation" and so on'.[169]

Yet the evidence, though patchy, does not in the end support that. Even in the relatively 'clean' work situation of a process industry like chemicals, 'for every man who watched dials, another maintained the plant, another was a lorry driver, and another two humped bags or shovelled muck'. 'In fact about 50% of the work involved in chemical production in Britain is still classified as demanding virtually no skill from the worker.'[170] Indeed, in general 'the reality is that "affluence" and pleasant work has become nothing like as widespread as was supposed. And whereas some people have become comparatively well off, this has cost them in other ways . . . affluence . . . doesn't alter the work they have

to do or the hours they have to work; nor the fact that while at work they have to conform to a system that is (capital's) system'. 'Capital's grip is tightening on all those employed . . . whatever their factory position – workers, foremen, managers – the rationalisation and economising affects them all.'[171]

All this has long been enough to give manual workers as a whole a sense of their common position and common interests, as we shall see. But the form that that perception takes is also coloured by what is new in the present experience of this perennial class tension. What is new, and unique to this crisis, as far as manual workers are concerned, is this: that the present recession has come after a generation of full employment, when jobs and slowly rising affluence had come to be widely believed as guaranteeable for everyone. Also the recession has come very abruptly in the 1970s and has run very deep (taking unemployment to over 4 million). The recession (just as the boom before it) is widely believed to be within the responsibility of politicians, because of the enhanced role played by the post-war state in the whole field of economic management. To the perennial tensions of class, that is, the present crisis has added the political dimensions of broken expectations and failed governments.

Contradictory class pressures

It was just this sort of experience that Marx anticipated would drive the proletariat into a sense of its common class interests, and would bring those interests into alliance with the revolutionary socialist project. He predicted that not only would selling labour power become the dominant experience of living under capitalism, but that in addition the conditions of inequality, insecurity and alienation associated with that sale would invite initially a pattern of industrial unrest from the working class, then its political mobilization, and ultimately a generalized commitment throughout the proletariat to the revolutionary replacement of capitalism by socialism. History has not yet produced that scenario; but the absence of a large and successful revolutionary proletariat in Britain ought not to blind us to the way in which the development of the capitalist labour process has created the ground for just such a development. That it has also released processes and forces working in the opposite direction serves only to underline the important political fact that contradictory class pressures are no monopoly of the intermediate strata. They are part and parcel too of the experience of 'working class-ness' in late capitalism.

For it is overwhelmingly the case that the terms and conditions on which labour power is sold do dominate life for male manual workers in our society. As we have seen, the work experience of manual labour is profoundly shaped by capital's need to expropriate surplus value from it, and hence to sustain managerial pressure on the work process and complex hierarchies to supervise it. We have seen too that inequalities at work transmit themselves in complex ways into the whole fabric of social life. This is a society stratified by class, and it is lived that way by the men within it. For these inequalities in their work experience, and in their social rewards, power and status, are experienced collectively, as class inequalities, and have long sustained collective, class-based institutions and responses. The collective experience of shared inequalities generated in the past, and continues to generate, powerful collective loyalties. The fact that, in essence, these inequalities derive from a division between the producers of wealth and its expropriators has long tended to pull collective loyalties in Britain into the simple polarity of class and into an antagonistic mould. Of course, as we shall see in a moment, there is sufficient heterogeneity in working-class work experience, status and rewards to sustain institutions, attitudes and patterns of political involvement that cut across this class division. But it must be understood that they do just that – they cut across a more *basic* division of class established by the social relationships of exploitation called into existence by capitalism.

This class division surfaces in the reality of British life and politics in many ways; in part in the attitudes men have to work. Survey after survey, in industry after industry, records a uniform picture. The bulk of manual workers most of the time are heavily alienated from the work they have to do. They are fully conscious of class divisions at the point of production. They fully recognize the extent to which the whole process of labour under capitalism is something they do for someone else; and that it is something to be endured, and to be traded off against what level of earnings, and whatever minimum input of effort, the local labour market and local managerial policies will allow. Job satisfaction varies, of course, between levels of skill, between occupations and over time, and workers share a definite interest in the competitive viability of their firm which may reach a point of identification with its owners and managers. Indeed:

since the war sociologists have taken it into their heads to interview workers and ask them whether or not they consider the factory to be like a football team. Affirmative answers have been taken as an indication of a lack of class consciousness. This however misses the fundamental point about capitalist production. It isn't an either-or question, of being like a football team *or* being like two opposing camps. Factory production involves *both*. Because production has a social basis the factory obviously can be seen, at some level, as a collectivity with management operating in a co-ordinating role. The contradictions of factory production, and the source of contradictory elements within class consciousness, is rooted in the fact that the exploitation of workers is achieved through collective, co-ordinated activities within both the factory and society generally.[172]

For this 'dualism' in their industrial perspectives cannot obscure the degree to which the bulk of manual workers 'work to live, rather than live to work' ('wind me up at 8.00 a.m. and that's that. I'm just here waiting for the buzzer')[173] and look to maximize their benefits in the trade off between wages and effort that capital obliges them to make and to remake on a daily basis. As the Ford workers at the Rouge River plant in Detroit once graphically put it, 'we come here for eight hours. Do we have to work as well'. And even in a modern process plant, 'the only dignity most workers find in work is in *not* co-operating voluntarily and spontaneously, in *not* acting out their potential, and their dissatisfaction with a society which forces them to waste their lives finds its expression in different individual forms, especially in absenteeism'.[174]

The reality of class tension is evident too in the pattern of industrial resistance to the initiation of any significant adverse change in that trade off between wages and effort. Worker resistance is as old as capitalism itself,[175] and the creation of heavily capital-intensive production processes in late capitalism has opened the way to new and often highly effective forms of worker resistance (from systematic slacking and industrial sabotage to go-slows and the lightening strike). British workers have been particularly effective at all this; and their defensive class power is (and has been for a generation now) at the heart of the problem of accumulation experienced by British industrial capital. As Michael Mann put it, 'what then are the enduring achievements of the British working class? To mention the principal achievement is generally considered bad taste: the inalienable right of the British worker to work less hard than the workers of any other major industrial power'.[176] The daily struggle for control across British industry has been met by 'the elaboration of subterranean traditions of shopfloor resistance' by manual workers, who have long resisted, and where they can continue to resist,

managerial and state attempts to tighten supervision and quicken the pace of work. The years of the long boom were, *par excellence*, also 'the period of the growth of informal shopfloor action – unofficial disputes, the growth of shop steward power in representing shopfloor interests, the tendency of "wage drift" through local control of output and bonus schemes as well as the more individual strategies of sabotage, absenteeism and high labour turnover'.[177] If unemployment now threatens that power, as it does, there is no escaping from the fact that the Conservative government have been led to push unemployment so high precisely to break a degree of working-class resistance and defensive power that derive so effectively from a class-based industrial tradition. The British working class this century has repeatedly demonstrated a distinct sense of its own class position and interests, undivided (outside Ireland) by any significant divisions of religion and politics. Manual workers have used their trade unions, work groups and local shop stewards in a guerrilla campaign against the encroachments of both governments and management, normally in isolated struggles without wider class dimensions, but also, at times (in 1926, or at Saltley in 1971) as part of a much wider coalition of working class industrial interests. The British working class has also repeatedly thrown up a layer of industrial activists and political mobilizers, the bedrock of Labour (and to a lesser extent communist) politics for more than three-quarters of a century.

Such class attitudes and practices have not, however, except on those rare occasions, widened into anything approaching a revolutionary socialist perspective. On the contrary, as we shall see in Chapter 9, the dominant political orientation of the British working class has been *Labourist*, committed to a form of parliamentary politics in which class interests are submerged into a general national project of social reform and economic reconstruction. What we need to establish now is how, at the industrial and social level, the sense of alienation and class general to manual workers coexists quite happily with sets of attitudes, institutions and practices that erode that sense of class unity and class radicalism.

For capitalism not only unites workers. It also divides them. It divides them as an unintended by-product of its own uneven development; and it divides them consciously, as a mechanism of control and exploitation. 'The labour movement has always, historically, reflected in its diversity and sectoral divisions, the ways in which workers are inserted into competing enterprises, into particular kinds of labour process, a particular division of labour, a particular organisation of the capitalist firm or enterprise, and a particular division of grades, crafts, skills.'[178] Capitalism's fragmentation of skills has permitted the consolidation of craft unions with a vested interest in the maintenance of differentials, and this is but the most extreme example of a general feature of capitalist control systems: that capital controls through hierarchies, and consolidates support by the differential allocation of tiny status distinctions, so establishing a 'hierarchy fetishism' – a set of discretely different practices, positions and rewards which the occupants then struggle to maintain in their own self-defence. In this way capitalism has always mixed contradictory tendencies: *homogenizing* labour (by concentrating 'larger numbers of workers in the enterprise, the mass-collective worker, based on the maximisation of scale, advanced mechanisation, "fordist" developments in flow-line and fast-assembly processes, and the dilution of older craft-related skills') while *redividing* labour as it does so (creating 'at each stage, a new division of labour, new hierarchies of supervisory and technical function, new distinctions and divisions').[179] Skilled craftsmen in particular have a freedom, a dignity and a market power that, however inadequate, give them a basis for self-confident trade unionism that the unskilled and semi-skilled characteris-

tically lack. As Stuart Hall has observed, this has crucial political consequences, 'for this "fractioning" and diversity is the real, empirical experience of the class: the class in its singular, already-unified form, is really a political metaphor'; and this 'working class "sectoralism" . . . has helped to sustain the reformism and the economism of the labour movement by stimulating competition between different sections of the class, turning it inward into compromises and negotiations within the class'.[180]

In addition, capitalism has always developed unevenly. It has done so regionally and between industries. It now does so between its monopoly and non-monopoly sectors, splitting even its manual working class, here as in the United States, 'into the more highly paid workers in the more mechanised sectors of industry and lower paid workers in labour intensive areas'. 'This bifurcation . . . is reproduced by patterns of uneven and combined development in different branches of the economy. This development is *uneven* because mechanisation does not take place at uniform rates across branches of industry: it is *combined* because the process of mechanisation in one area contributes to the labour intensive character of others.'[181] It is also political, as we will see in Part Three, because the state is so heavily involved in its reproduction.

In fact we might usefully anticipate certain of the arguments in Part Three, in order to establish one of the important consequences of the growth of state employment in late capitalism. As we will see later, state spending reinforces the uneven development of capitalist sectors by disproportionately strengthening the monopolies. In the process it also creates a distinct area of public employment – both in its own administrative and welfare bureaucracies and in those parts of manufacturing production that it chooses to nationalize. The latter at least, for our purposes here, should be thought of as similar to the private monopolies in their pattern of investment, productivity and unionization. That monopoly sector is able to invest on a large scale and to reap significant increases in productivity as a result. The unions within it are in their turn able to 'hang on' to a disproportionately large share of that enhanced return because (and to the extent that) their monopoly employers can pass on any increased wages in the form of higher prices. (Indeed only intensified international competion *between* monopolies has eroded that capacity in many British-based corporate and publicly-owned giants of late.) Workers in smaller firms, however, lack that 'productivity bonus' and find unionization difficult – because their firms are small and scattered and their employers more hostile. Public sector employees in non-manufacturing parts of the state sector face a similar problem of low productivity while, because of the bureaucratic and political nature of their employment, finding themselves able to unionize on a scale comparable to workers in the monopoly sector.

The result of all this is a quite uneven pattern of unionization even among manual workers, a pattern fixed by the sector of capital and the state in which manual workers are employed. Table 21 shows this clearly.

This differential pattern of unionization is itself a reflection of more complex processes. For the uneven development of capitalism produces quite distinct types of work situation and bargaining context, which Patrick Dunleavy has captured neatly in Figure 15.

Dunleavy is keen to use these sectoral distinctions as a guide to variations in attitudes to politics *within* classes. He suggests, for example, that 'the objective effect of the growth of the union/non-union cleavage . . . is apparently to strengthen support for Labour amongst the unionised minority of the electorate, while constituting a basis for anti-Labour voting amongst the non-unionised majority, including a minority of manual workers. The public/private cleavage, operating through the

unionisation influence on alignments, seems to fulfill a similar role'.[182] Whether this is so must, in the absence of extensive research, remain only a hypothesis. But what is certain is that the cumulative impact of status differences, sectoral distinctions and uneven development is the immersion of manual workers in a multiplicity of overlapping and partly competing labour markets, each with very different wage rates, frequency of employment, and so on.

The skilled craftsman is in a different labour market from the semi-skilled assembly worker, and both are qualitatively stronger – in self-confidence, bargaining power and unionization – than the migrant agricultural labourer, the waiter or the assistant in the tiny corner grocery store. The manual working class face at least a division between core and peripheral modes of employment, a fragmentation into a *primary* sector of core workers whose retention is vital to the company's survival, and a *secondary* sector of the more peripheral, less secure and well-paid – the super-exploited layers of late capitalism. This is indeed one of the crucial linkages between the male white class structure and the super-exploitation of women and ethnic minorities; for it is in these peripheral secondary labour markets that female and black employment is so often concentrated. The reproduction of that pattern of super-exploitation is then reinforced and reproduced by class struggle between white skilled workers and their employers. For 'class struggle carried on in an organised way by certain sectors of the labour force conjoins with managerial strategies to generate labour market segmentation. Employers are inclined to acquiesce in recognising sheltered labour market positions especially in internal labour markets; or they are in some part forced to acquiesce by the power of certain sectors of the labour force'.[183]

Here then is one major source of division within the working class: a consciousness of

Table 21   *Densities of union membership in selected industries, 1974*

Industry	Size of workforce (000s)	Density of union membership	Predominantly industry is in:
Distribution	2810	11	
Construction	1429	27	
Hotels and catering	824	5	Market sector
Other professional services	470	3	
Agriculture	416	22	
Clothing	346	60	
Wood and furniture	290	35	Indeterminate
Leather	44	46	
Engineering and metals	4118	69	
Food, drinks, tobacco	784	51	
Insurance, banking, etc.	681	45	
Paper, printing, publishing	596	72	
Chemicals	484	51	
Entertainment and media	190	65	
Building materials	172	40	Corporate sector
Rubber	127	56	
Sea transport	91	100	
Footwear	87	79	
Glass	75	79	
Pottery	61	94	
Post Office/telecommunications	510	88	
Gas, electricity, water	352	92	
Coal mining	314	96	Public corporations
Railways	224	97	
Port and inland waterways	82	95	
Air transport	80	94	
Education and local government	2752	86	
Health	1175	61	Public services
National government	624	91	

Source: P. Dunleavy, 'The political implications of sectoral cleavages and the growth of state employment', *Political Studies*, **23** (1980), p. 370.

sectional interests, a preoccupation with localized gradations of status, a focus on the maintenance of differentials, and a reluctance to be drawn easily into wider class mobilizations. Even among the unskilled, sectional divisions can still hold. Blackburn and Mann found their sample of unskilled manual workers 'divided, not into stable, quasi-hereditary strata, but into two non-stable groupings: employment organisations and age-seniority cohorts. Both divert potential class action; the first into "free collective bargaining" which can only reinforce the market nature of capitalism, the second into an essentially conservative posture of sitting tight and quiet, waiting for promotion'.[184] They correctly criticize many Marxist accounts of the British working class for treating 'the potential existence of a united

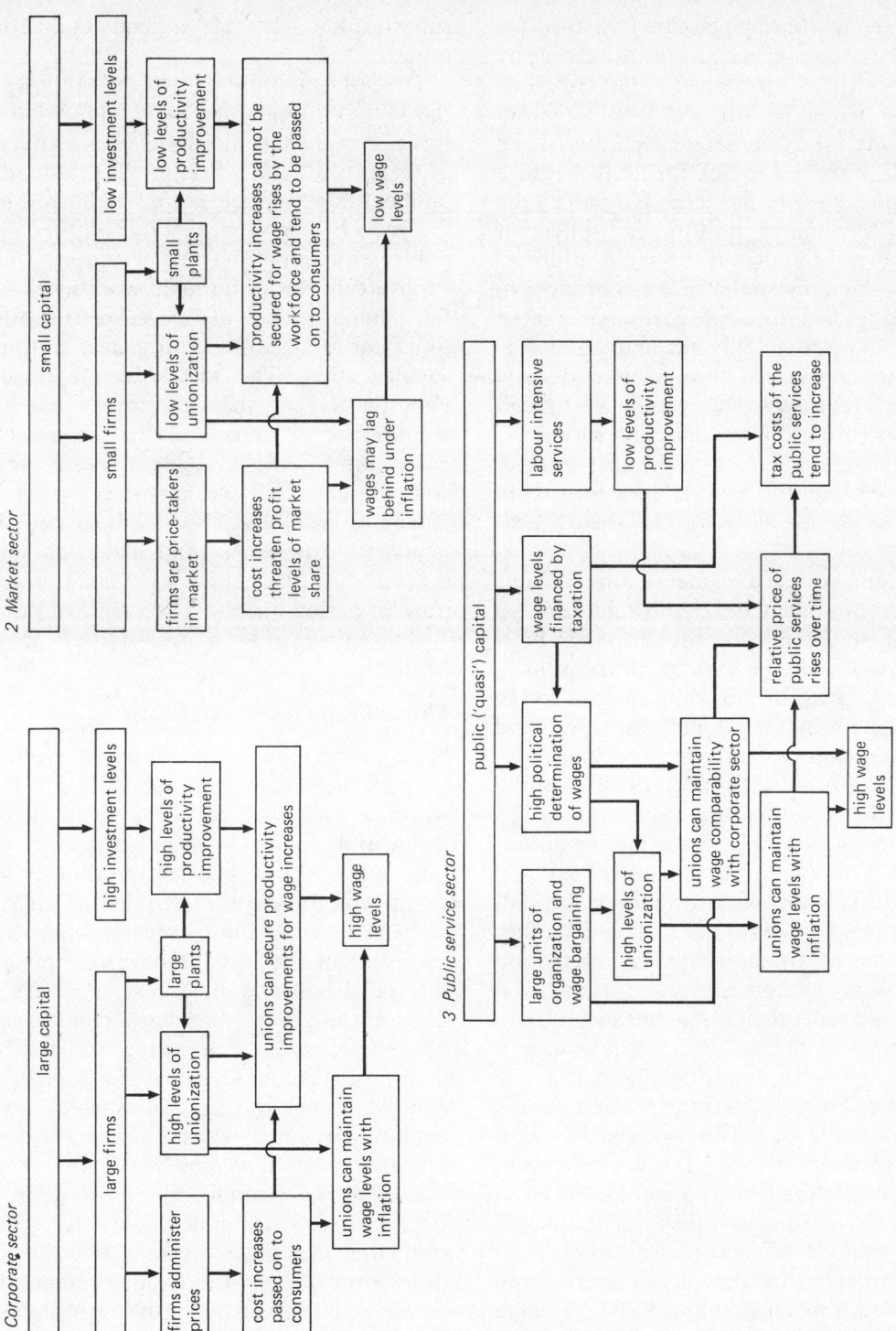

Figure 15   *Origins of divergent labour interests between capital sectors*

Source: P. Dunleavy, 'The political implications of sectoral cleavages and the growth of state employment', *Political Studies,* **23** (1980), pp. 380–1.

homogeneous working class (as) "natural" –
and its actual emergence (as) thwarted only by
employee-divisive strategies'. For in such
accounts 'equally "natural" sectionalism
among workers is consequently ignored'.[185]
This is a grave error: for precisely because
there is no *automatic* mechanism by which the
sense of a common position as 'sellers of
labour power' can drown the sense of difference that the terms of that sale can produce in
the working class, so sectional responses often
become a more intelligible short-term response to managerial threats than do any
wider class responses. This is true even though
the result is to reinforce divisions within the
working class, to set worker against worker,
and to reproduce the material base for sexism
and racism in the heart of the British proletariat.

The fact that such a segmentation of labour
markets hits women and ethnic minorities so
hard suggests that factors other than the labour
process itself continue to shape the consciousness and activity of the white male working
class. Quite what those processes are, and
what the political significance of their consequences will be, is the subject matter of the
chapter that follows. All that needs to be
noted now is that those other factors do not
drop out of the air, but are themselves part and
parcel of the complex articulation of capitalism with other modes of production and other
mechanisms of stratification. The articulation
of capitalism and domestic labour is a critical
element in gender divisions in this society; and
the relationship of capitalism to colonialism is
vital to the fate of minorities, both Catholic
and ethnic. The detail, for the moment, is less
vital than the legacy. The legacy is this: that
the consciousness of the male white proletariat
is shaped not only by common features of
working class-ness and by the divisions engendered by segmented sets of labour markets. It
is also moulded by the racism and sexism
endemic to a social structure in which white
males as a whole derive benefit from the
super-exploitation of women and ethnic
groups.

The political problems which that poses for
the Left is a topic for Chapter 11. When we
reach it we shall also note again that the
availability of the working class for radical
politics has been made more problematic over
the years by two other features of its contemporary situation. The first is the systematic
exposure of the white male working class to
the dominant values of their propertied rulers,
to an entire hegemonic project of enormous
sophistication. The second is the material
underpinning of that in recent times: the
creation of a whole culture of privatized
entertainment, atomized life styles and eroded
communities, that weaken still further any
common sense of class which is sustained by
industrial experience, and makes far more
difficult than Marx anticipated that process of
transformation necessary for socialist politics
– that move from a class-in-itself to one
for-itself.

The politics of the working class

For some on the Left all that has been enough
to persuade them that the politics of the
working class will never be revolutionary.
White male manual workers have more to lose
than their chains. The less pessimistic have
simply noted the contradictions and volatility
of working-class consciousness and political
involvement that result from the cumulative
impact of these contradictory pressures. Indeed working-class attitudes to industry, society and politics have been much researched of
late. Over two decades now sociologists have
gone into factories and housing estates to
explore particular theses, equipped with particular expectations and conceptual apparatus. They have often gone in to explore the
impact of new technologies or rising living
standards on political loyalties; to explore the
differential impact of work and community on
working-class attitudes, or to see the extent to
which manual workers hold the kinds of social

imagery and sense of class interests anticipated by traditional Marxism. For all the limits
of their methodology,[186] what they have found
has not necessarily brought much comfort to
the Left.

Certainly there is no evidence of the
existence of qualitatively different social
perceptions and political proclivities that
might set apart manual workers as a distinct
bloc from a whole range of routine white-
collar workers. Indeed and instead, manual
workers share with the intermediate strata a
largely private set of perceptions and goals:
with family prosperity, the education of their
children, and the security of their jobs. Like
many white-collar workers too, most manual
workers pursue those private goals in a highly
instrumental way: relying on trade unions, for
example, because of their recognition of the
importance of collective bargaining to their
individual job and wage, but feeling no
emotional commitment to the union as a class
institution. The union is supported simply
because it is necessary, and the wider political
issues pursued by union leaders and activists
are largely of no concern to the bulk of manual
workers. Huw Beynon's chemical workers are
typical here, in experiencing their 'union as a
service organisation: a deductor of taxes and a
provider of facilities. Something important.
Something to fall back on. But not *their* union.
In no sense did they feel that their membership
of the TGWU made them a part of something
– in no way did they see themselves being
involved in a union *movement*. And this
absence, this sense that unionism ought to be
something more than it was, was fundamental
to their frustration with "the union"'.[187]

For such instrumentalities are quite compatible both with collective action (in the form
of industrial struggles of various kinds) and
with a retention of a powerful sense of class.
'The signs are fairly firm that manual workers
– the majority, in particular, who accept the
self-appellation "working class" – are inclined
to underline size of income, sometimes ownership of property, in contrast to non-
ownership, sometimes the capacity or incapacity to exercise power to pull strings – as essential criteria of class division. . . . There is enough
established fact and plausible interpretation
here to allow a conclusion that blue-collar
workers' views of the world have a recognis-
able quasi-Marxist tinge to them – though
rarely, in Britain, with any active revolutionary twist. That fits well enough too with the
fact that politics for the Labour majority
among manual workers involves defence or
promotion of class interests.'[188]

When car workers were surveyed in the
early 1960s, that sense of class predisposed the
vast majority of them to vote for the Labour
Party, as in some real sense still the party of
the working class. But 'only exceptionally did
this appear to result from any strong feelings
of class loyalty and solidarity. Motivations
were instrumental. Workers joined the union
and voted Labour for pragmatic reasons; as
means towards enhancing their own private
interests'.[189] Since the connection being made
here was mainly an instrumental one, it was
also brittle; and two decades later many
'affluent' car workers voted Conservative in
1979, rejecting a Labour government which
had pegged their wages, supported their
managements and orchestrated unemployment in their industry. Even before such
volatility in voting became a more general
feature of the manual working class as a
whole, the Conservative Party had always
drawn a significant working-class vote; particularly from workers outside the trade union
movement, and also (more controversially
perhaps) from workers in smaller industrial
plants. Historically a deference vote, there is
evidence too that Tory working-class voting
has become increasingly instrumental in its
motivation of late. Certainly the Right exploited the contradictions of social democracy
to good effect in 1979 and 1983, gaining the
electoral loyalty of up to one-third of all trade
union members in the 1979 poll and –

amazingly – of more skilled manual workers than the Labour Party in the General Election of 1983.

That Conservative success itself reflected the penetration of a whole set of official orthodoxies deep into the consciousness of many manual workers, long before the events of the 1970s precipitated the crisis of support for Labourism. This 'penetration of orthodoxy' into popular consciousness is so vital a feature of contemporary British politics that we shall discuss its content, mechanisms, origin and significance in Chapter 9. What we need now is simply a summary of certain of its most significant consequences: its impact on the language and standards workers bring to life and politics; on the generalized opinions they hold about what does, and does not, constitute legitimate political behaviour; and its impact on their sense of what are the important issues in contemporary political life. Time and again surveys demonstrate the degree of superficial consensus between classes on all these dimensions of popular consciousness a consensus reflective of the interests and preoccupations of the ruling strata. Manual workers characteristically deploy the category of 'nation' before that of 'class', and accept the right of governments to specify the 'national interest'. They invariably, when asked, limit their sense of 'fairness' to fine variations of income and reward without challenging the wider inequality of power that surrounds them. They characteristically associate the 'market' with 'freedom' and the 'state' with 'bureaucracy' and 'constraint'. They characteristically accept the convention of bourgeois politics that makes trade union militancy against governments illegitimate, but IMF pressure not, and share the whole gambit of ruling-class platitudes: that unions have too much power, that the Russians are a military threat and the Americans are not; that law and order are the central issues of the day, and even that unemployment is unavoidable and public expenditure wasteful. If that was

not bad enough for the Left, survey after survey also shows 'the decline in the general appeal of socialist ideas to the majority of the working population outside the committed within the trade unions and the Labour Party'.[190]

So there is a very real sense in which 'the moment – the moment of transition to the *idea* of socialism quite as much as a transition to socialist practice – has been at least temporarily lost';[191] and that as a result the task facing the Left among the manual working class is as tough as its task before the intermediate strata. It has to scrape away layers of official orthodoxy in popular consciousness, and deeply-rooted elements of nationalism, sexism and racism that shape the minds of working-class voters just as much as they do the consciousness of other strata. That this is even a possibility arises in the main from what else is there in working-class experience and popular consciousness. For the surveys also show divisions of opinion between workers, and volatility over time – both in their view of the class structure and of their interests and actions within it. Some workers are 'deferential'. Others are more 'traditionally solidaristic', in the language of the trade. Others are neither. Workers industrially quiescent in one period may be extraordinarily militant in the next (Goldthorpe and Lockwood's car workers are a case in point);[192] and as their militancy varies, so too do their attitudes to a range of questions on the legitimacy of governments, the need for reform, and the adequacy of the consensus. Indeed, if surveys of working-class attitudes do permit generalizations, one of the strongest would be that while many workers may 'accept' the current order 'pragmatically – even with resignation – that is not to say that they give it their enthusiastic, "normative" support. Instead positive and negative views *co-exist* in working class consciousness: pragmatic attitudes towards labour on an everyday level' alongside values that 'tend to be hostile to the system rather than supportive of it'.[193] As Richard Hyman has observed:

A wide range of studies have clearly demonstrated the *inconsistencies* inherent in most workers' social attitudes. Typically they do not question the dominant attitude when formulated in abstract and general form: it is precisely at the level of the overall political economy that the class which is the ruling material force of society is most manifestly also its ruling intellectual force. Yet in respect of their concrete and specific experience they fail to endorse the full implications of the dominant ideology, adopting cynical attitudes towards those in positions of authority and engaging in actions . . . unacceptable to those who are wholeheartedly committed to the prevailing ideological perspective.[194]

In other words, we must recognize too the existence of a counter-culture, the consciousness of a gap between official orthodoxies and actual experience, that is there for the Left to tap. Roberts and his colleagues definitely found the general existence of what they called 'the proletarian worker' – a kind of manual worker who was quite simply much more prone than other manual workers 'to vote Labour, favour further nationalisation, argue that the trade unions have too little power, disapprove of Enoch Powell's views on immigration and race relations, oppose the re-introduction of capital punishment, and to approve of "Women's Lib" in general and married women working in particular'.[195] Seventy-eight of the 164 manual workers in their sample could be so described, concentrated particularly among those 'born into blue-collar families (living) mainly on working class council estates and . . . knit by friendships into work-based communities'.[196]

Indeed this particular survey suggested a bifurcation of working-class social imagery and political attitudes, since a significant proportion of their sample had a quite different, more obviously 'middle class' set of attitudes and loyalties. Robert and his colleagues see enough in working-class industrial experience to prevent working-class total incorporation and acquiescence, but little to sustain the faith of revolutionaries. For them, 'the working class remains an unstable and continuing challenge but not a revolutionary threat'.[197] Even though that seems too frozen a conclusion, then at least it is clear that the experience of manual work in late capitalism does not encourage the easy formulation of coherent alternatives in the minds of workers – far from it. They are too busy, too pressed for that – too aware at times of the psychic cost of thinking of alternatives beyond their reach. Nor in any case these days are they normally exposed to the presentation of such alternatives by any credible force on the Left. Huw Beynon reported one steward at Fords on that: 'as far as changing the nature of society goes, or even the organisation of an industry, they don't know, "If we thought about that we'd go crazy. I just can't afford to think about thinks like that. Sometimes I ask myself, 'where are we going. Where does it all add up to?' Then I'm in another meeting or on a case. We leave it to people like you tha'. Ideas about a new society and tha'"'.[198] In those circumstances, the daily pressure of work under capitalism for men like that is such as to encourage a retreat into private goals and pursuits beyond work, and to develop a fatalism, a sense of resignation, in the face of what seems to be the unavoidable.

What the daily reality of capitalist excess does do is to breed resistance, and with resistance comes – at least for a time – a slightly wider consciousness of options available: 'changes of mood' that 'draw on and give expression to the underlying reservoir of class attitudes which, while it may be deep below the surface, is never totally exhausted'.[199] The bedrock of that alternative is there permanently, in the coexistence in working-class consciousness of values and attitudes not in harmony with ruling ideas: on the excessive power of Big Business, on the way the legal system favours the rich, on the dislike of tight supervision, on the sense of being treated at work 'like a robot, like a moron', and on the general inadequacy of all politicians. At the heart of this counter-culture stand 'the co-existence of active dissent, distrust and grudging acceptance of routine' which must not be read 'for mere passive withdrawal from the values of official society. This last is certainly there. But there is also more: the elements of a mood of subversion, with a half formed diagnosis of the sources of injustice'. 'This is not of course a clear and consistent ideology of labour opposition to capital. It is an ideology of dissent, but at half-cock . . . an amalgam of . . . contradictory features' in which 'both the range and the sources of inequality are seen only rather dimly' – one weakened as yet 'by a common sense of incapacity to do anything very effective to change things'.[200]

It is an alternative, moreover, which gains some resilience from the daily struggle to survive. By saying this, I do not wish to over-romanticize 'struggle'. I am well aware that, as we observed in Chapter 4, 'there is very little evidence to support the . . . belief that participation in a major industrial struggle naturally generates an "explosion of consciousness" with lasting consequences'.[201] It is just that this struggle keeps alive the 'space' for an alternative and necessitates the perpetuation of some 'gap' between working-class attitudes and total incorporation. 'Even if, as some writers have suggested, the working class is unable to generate a truly revolutionary consciousness from within itself and will be converted to socialism only with outside assistance, simply being a manual worker with all this implies for income and career patterns and treatment in the work situation can hardly fail to dispose many individuals towards a proletarian view of their place in society and an associated set of oppositional values.'[202] To quote Huw Beynon again, 'if the history of the car workers shows anything at all about the "new" working class it is that, faced with the complete absence of any meaningful political leadership, workers do not lapse into inactivity and acquiescence. They will . . . form their own organisations, or use existing ones, and fight over the issues that stare them in the face. For these workers experience the class struggle every day of their lives. If, in the way they cope with it, they produce a politically confused situation, that's just too bad'.[203] Quite how bad it is will be one of the topics of the final chapter of this book.

8 Gender, race and religion in the British social formation

So far we have explored politics in a capitalism dominated by production, and focused on men; white men at that. As was made clear at the start of Chapter 6, capitalism is not, and never has been, so simple and isolated a set of economic processes and social relationships. Nor, in consequence, can its politics ever be as simple and straightforward as might be implied so far by an analysis couched in the language of class and focused on the contradictions between capital and labour in the process of production. Alongside the areas of political tension which we have so far explored lie other related social terrains whose existence is testimony to the incapacity of a capitalist mode of production to survive alone, either historically – when it never has; or conceptually – where it never properly could. On the contrary, capitalism has always existed in a complex articulation with modes of production that are not capitalist, and with sets of social relationships which do not derive directly from the production process. That can be seen in relation to both *domestic labour* and gender divisions, and to *imperialism* and race and religion.

To take domestic labour and gender divisions first, it is clear that capitalism works at all only because of the existence alongside its wage-labour sphere of an area of social production – one not organized on capitalist lines – in which the labour power on which capitalism depends is itself produced. This sphere of *reproduction* – and the domestic labour process around which it is built – is thus an integral part of any capitalist social forma-

tion, and has been from the outset. As such it constitutes an important source in its own right of stable social relationships and persistent patterns of social experience, and hence of group interests and political demands. Moreover, capitalism emerged into a world already stratified, not just by class but also by gender, one in which a sexual division of labour had already locked women into a disproportionate responsibility for this sphere of reproduction. Capitalism, while slowly replacing the class divisions of feudalism with a new social division of labour of its own, took over, altered, incorporated and reproduced that pre-existing pattern of gender discrimination. Indeed, as we shall see, the spread of capitalist relationships gave those gender divisions a new and double twist: by separating the sphere of domestic production physically from that of commodity production, and locking women back into domestic labour in the main; then differentially drawing these already heavily-burdened women into the margins of wage labour in a subordinate relationship to the men already there, so exploiting them twice – as cheap labour in their own right, and as the unpaid producers of the cheap labour of others.

In that double exploitation, women have never been entirely alone. For capitalism is also inherently expansionist in its drive for accumulation. In that expansion it has established – by the force of its military power, then the penetration of its cheaply-produced commodities – relationships of superiority and exploitation over non-capitalist modes of production and over the societies and peoples responsible for them. British capitalism emerged into a political space in which geo-political imperatives in an age of feudal dynastic rivalries had already induced the full colonization of Ireland by the English state. The social divisions through which that colonization was consolidated over three centuries remain now to haunt the political options of a contemporary British state no longer locked into the same set of geo-political concerns. Capital in Britain was accumulated by way of the slave trade and the systematic plunder of the East. In its imperialist phase it locked whole economic and social structures in subordination to its political rule. As we shall see, that in its turn added new currents of racism to British political culture, and new patterns of discrimination by ethnicity and territorial background into the emerging class structure.

For these reasons, the social universe within which the political system has to operate is not one moulded simply by the social relationships of the capitalist labour process. Class relationships even there are 'shot through' with other modes of social differentiation, by gender and race, and even – in the occupied parts of Ireland at least – by powerful currents of religious affiliation. In reproducing capitalism, the state is obliged to reproduce those relationships also. In coping with the conflicting demands of the various social groups generated by that capitalism, the state finds itself facing powerful social interests that cannot easily be categorized in class terms, but which turn instead on the colour of a person's skin, the intensity and nature of his or her relationship to God, and on gender itself. The popular-democratic struggles to which those interests give rise constitute in their turn a challenge to the way that British capitalism operates, and can – depending on their character – threaten the stability and integrity of the system as a whole. They constitute therefore, no less than the class mobilizations of the white male working class, a vital

component in the potential coalition of the Left. For that reason, if for no other, they must be understood in their social specificity, their historical trajectory and their theoretical significance. The initial mapping of situation, history and significance for the social divisions of gender, race and religion is our task in the pages to come.

Gender divisions and political interests

The social experience of women in this society is homogenized by gender and fragmented by class, such that the lives, experiences and interests of women 'in modern Britain are only comprehensible when their place in this double stratification system (of sex and class) is understood'.[1] It is clear that all women, regardless of their social background, share a set of experiences in common. They are expected to take at best a disproportionate, and at worst a total, responsibility for the sphere of domestic production. With the exception of a very few rich women, the vast majority must not only produce the children, but rear them, and feed and clothe a set of oppressive and powerful males, and carry whatever responsibilities the state pushes on to them for the care of the sick and the old. In sheer quantity, this 'household labour, including child care, constitutes a large amount of socially necessary production', even though 'in a society based on commodity production, it is not usually considered "real work" since it is outside of trade and the market place'.[2] In a society organized around the division between production and consumption, the factory and the home, women are treated as 'naturally' home-based, responsible for the consumption but not the production of commodities, locked into processes of essential labour without status or pay, and in consequence left in the main dependent for their material livelihood on the wages of the man (father, husband or lover) with whom they live and whom they service.

This is not to say that women do not perform wage labour. Ten million of them do that as well; and when they do, their experience as wage workers outside the home has a number of features which distinguish it sharply from that of the men whom they sustain and on whom they are generally made financially dependent. When women enter the wage labour force, they do not shed their domestic responsibilities but carry them as well, acting as *dual producers*, inside and outside the home. Their involvement in wage labour is invariably broken, if they marry, by a period of child care that prevents their easy pursuit of career and promotion. 'Women are out of the workforce on average a total of about 7 years or 16–19% of the time between the ages of 20 and 59';[3] and on their return invariably occupy subordinate positions, experience low and generally unequal pay, and find themselves disproportionately locked into jobs which extend and reproduce the 'personal service' function that they perform in the domestic sphere. Even in wage labour, therefore, women find certain kinds of jobs (invariably low grade and menial ones) as specified to be in some sense 'naturally' theirs, so that 'for a large number of women (the majority) their labour outside as well as within the home is characterised by an entrenched sexual bias; a bias which in turn is reflected in the fact that it is women, almost exclusively, who do the work that involves the direct servicing of people's immediate needs'.[4]

As they perform these services and routine manual tasks, women are expected to cope too with an industrial environment that is not geared to their needs as dual producers, but is built around the model of a male forty-hour week that is possible for men only because of their servicing by unpaid female labour in the home. Even though there are now 900,000 single-parent families, the vast majority of which are headed by women, it remains the case that both married women with children and women rearing children alone are obliged to combine child care and low-grade paid labour without adequate help (in the form of crèches and nurseries). It is also significant that whenever help of his kind is made available, it occurs in the form – almost always – of the inadequately paid labour of other women. Men very rarely look after their own children as their main job, and they virtually never make a job out of tending the pre-school children of others. In fact, part-time work (with all its inadequate levels of pay and working conditions) is often all that many women can manage in so uncongenial an environment. Even single women find themselves locked into dead-end, monotonous and poorly paid jobs in the main, and married middle-class women returning to employment after a period of child care are often effectively proletarianized – being pushed into job grades far below those attained by the men whose children they have raised. At work as in the home, there is a 'woman's place' – and it is one which, if it allows women any vestigial degree of control, restricts that almost exclusively to the organization of children and other women, and not to the superintendance of men at all.

The vast majority of women therefore face a similar set of economic problems: 'low pay at work, unequal access to jobs and training, hidden unemployment, financial dependence on men (and an) excessive share of unpaid work'.[5] The vast majority of women, that is, find themselves trapped in a vicious circle, 'caught between low paid work in the labour process and financial dependence on men in the family'.[6] Even in the sphere of wage labour the isolation of women in domestic production, and the productivity of labour in the factory, cumulatively pull apart the experience of men and women; so that while the gender division of labour creates an initial imbalance between the sexes, the automatic working of market processes keeps it going without central orchestration. Yet in addition there is orchestration, through a set of social attitudes and practices that are so general as to require no central control. For single or married, childless or not, women in the home, at work, and in society as a whole are subject to a deeply entrenched and all-pervasive sexist culture: one in which men's desires dominate, men occupy central positions of power, and in which social assumptions and practices keep women in positions of subordination. Even the conventional language of public life is sexist, and women are perpetually reminded of their subordination by the assertiveness of men everywhere and by explicit acts of gender domination from pornography through sexual harassment to rape. It is not without its wider significance that when the women of Leeds were nightly threatened by an uncaught Yorkshire Ripper, it was women (the victims) and not men whom the concerned public authorities (predominantly male, of course) sought to curfew off the streets.

Yet common though that is to the experience of women as a whole, its impact on their consciousness and interests is mediated by the relationships between women themselves within the class structure of a male-dominated society. Quite what the class position of women actually is, is now the subject of considerable academic/political debate.[7] Clearly the social anchorage which a woman initially enjoys is normally fixed by the social standing of the man who fathers her. It will be anchored later, if and when she marries, by the social status of the man with whom she lives; and this will be true even when allowance is made for the independent social anchorage that paid employment brings to the married woman. During women's period of unpaid child care, the differential class position of their husbands brings qualitatively different life chances to women rearing children in one class as against those rearing them in another. There are, of course, cross-class marriages (in which the man and woman occupy different class positions) to complicate the picture; and we need to fix the class position of single women, mothers alone and widows. But even single women are locked into wage labour in a world dominated by men; and since those men are themselves hierarchially organized, so too are the women who are obliged to service them.

That servicing is important. It suggests that women 'have a dual relationship to the class structure', partly as wage earners in their own right, and partly as child bearers and child rearers, with their class position and experiences mediated 'to some extent at least by the configuration of the family, dependence on men and domestic labour'.[8] Yet even so, there are middle-class women and working-class women just as there are middle-class men and working-class men; and the experiences and preoccupations of one class are not necessarily those of another. 'Women in all classes are the victims of handicaps associated with their sex. But those handicaps take different forms at different levels of society.'[9] Middle-class women face – among other things – the problem of 'the right to work' – of broken careers and the frustration of wasted education. Working-class women have invariably *had* to work; and their problems – low pay, routine and monotonous work – have been qualitatively different. There are ruling-class women too. Capital is not exclusively male. There are women capitalists, just as there are women prime ministers. Not many, of course, but some; and certainly 'there is little to be said about sex inequalities as far as ownership of capital is concerned. Primarily for reasons of tax and inheritance, women have an almost equal share in the ownership of wealth: they owned about 40% of all private wealth in 1970'.[10] At the other extreme, women constitute a majority of the poor, partly because they predominate among the elderly, and partly because this society is so hard on women bringing up children on their own.[11] Those rich women did not necessarily control the capital they owned, of course, but the fact that there are wealthy women as well as underpaid ones must also be remembered.

It has to be remembered in order to guard against any easy assumption that women in politics will generate a common and uncontested set of political demands. There is much in the experience of women in this society that is so common and unique to their sex as to make such a programme at least conceivable, and to give to women of whatever social class, age and situation a set of concerns and attitudes that overlap. The duality of their class position may indeed, as Jean Gardiner has suggested, be a major determinant of women's consciousness of class: 'it may, for instance, lead to militancy in support of child care facilities and shorter hours, and against social service cuts, rather than to militancy in support of higher wages'.[12] But women are themselves divided. Not all women need child care. Not all want abortions. Women, like men, are divided in any one period of time by age, circumstances and class; and women are divided from one another over time by alterations in employment opportunities and social attitudes. If we are to understand the material base for the political interests of women in contemporary Britain, we also need to develop some detailed sense of what those differences and changes have been.

That is not easy to do, since much of what is involved in being a woman in a sexist society is hidden – 'the problem without a name' that Betty Friedan mentioned so long ago. What is measurable and recorded is not necessarily central to the reality it is meant to capture, but has to be used for want of anything better. The employment figures are a case in point. Women, as we have seen, work in at least two, and often three, spheres of production. They work at home in domestic labour. Many work as 'out workers' in their homes in a range of sweated trades; yet others – a majority indeed – also perform part-time or full-time wage labour too. Housework remains arduous, and for most women tedious and unrewarding. Its hours are long: seventy-seven was the weekly average in Anne Oakley's 1974 sample, and was found dissatisfying by 70 per cent of all the women she studied. As a job its content has changed as capitalist commodity production has penetrated its manufacturing dimension, bringing a range of small-scale machinery into the average home to lower the labour input into many of the basic services to be performed there, and turning the household into a site for the consumption of wage goods under the supervision of unpaid female labour. The arrival of that machinery has, in its turn, left that labour 'freer' to sell itself to the capitalist sector proper, the better to buy the wage goods through which both male and female labour power can then be reproduced.

In the post-war years, more and more women have gone out to work. 'Between 1881 and 1951 the percentage of women in the work force aged 15 and over was relatively stable, ranging between 25% and 27%, with higher fluctuations during the two World Wars.'[13] By 1971 that figure had reached 42.6 per cent, and by then 9.4 million women worked for wages. By 1976, 10 million women worked, 38 per cent of whom had dependent children. Women now constitute 40 per cent of the total labour force, and an overwhelming majority (59.4 per cent) of all married women have a paid job of some kind. In 1911 that figure was 10 per cent, and in 1951 had still only risen to 22 per cent.[14] Its doubling since then has been accompanied by the rise of part-time employment among women (both absolutely and as a percentage of all female labour). In 1951 13 per cent of all working women worked part time. By 1975 that figure was 41 per cent – a move from 784,000 women in 1951 to 3,152,000 in 1971. This compares sharply with the situation among men, only one in twenty of whom now work part time.

Women in paid employment are heavily concentrated in certain occupations – in certain industries and in certain grades. There is in fact a quite remarkable degree of occupational concentration among women workers that has no parallel in the world of men. Over half of all employed women are to be found in just three service sectors: in distributive trades, professional and secretarial work, and miscellaneous services (mainly hairdressing, catering, cleaning and laundries). Even among women employed in manufacturing industry, half work in just four sectors: food and drink, clothing and footwear, textiles and electrical engineering (Table 22). In this way, the 'distribution of women across particular occupations is extremely uneven: women comprise 64.8% of the education, health and welfare labour force, 73.4% of the clerical, 58.6% of selling, 75.5% of personal services (catering, hairdressing and so on)'.[15] In contrast, they constitute only 5 per cent of the legal profession, 2 per cent of architects and surveyors and 0.2 per cent of civil engineers.[16] Moreover, in both services and industry, women are rarely at the top. There is a sexual division of labour within occupations, with positions becoming more masculine as they go up the bureaucratic hierarchy. So that 'even where women work alongside men, they usually hold positions of lower responsibility and perform tasks of a less skilled nature. . . . Men are the employers, managers, top professionals and skilled workers in our society'.[17] In fact, men and women only rarely work alongside one another in that sense. Certain occupations are designated female ghettos, others masculine preserves, as Table 23 suggests. 'A 1980 study has revealed that 45% of women and about 75% of men work in totally segregated jobs',[18] such that 'almost two million women work in occupations that are almost entirely (over 90%) done by women: typists, secretaries, maids, nurses, canteen assistants, sewing machinists'.[19] In this way, the industries in which women are concentrated, their job specifications and their low status within the managerial hierarchy, make it very clear that 'the mass increase of women in paid labour has not involved the majority of women in forms of labour that clash with the cultural definitions of women's domestic identity'[20] prevalent in society as a whole. On the contrary, it has reinforced them.

Women are locked into these jobs, as we shall see later, partly by conscious male decisions, made in trade unions and in the offices of male personnel officers, partly because of the 'disabilities' they carry – as wage earners – from their responsibilities in the sphere of domestic production. The burdens of child rearing disrupt industrial and professional careers, partly by taking women out of paid labour altogether at child birth, and partly by restricting them to part-time

Table 22 *Percentage of total female working population accounted for by certain industries, 1959, 1969, 1979*

Industry	1959	1969	1979	1980(a)
Distributive trades[1]	18.3	17.4	16.5	16.8
Insurance, banking, finance and business services	3.8	5.3	6.5	7.4
Professional and scientific services[2]	17.6	22.4	27.1	27.6
Miscellaneous services[3]	13.4	12.6	14.6	15.2
Public Administration and defence	5.0	5.6	6.7	6.8
Total	58.1	63.3	71.4	73.8
Females as a percentage of all workers	34.1	37.2	41.3	42.0

Notes:[1] Includes retailing; [2] Includes teaching and nursing; [3] Includes hairdressing, laundries and catering
Source: Minimum Wages for Women, EOC (1980), p. 6; (a) Dept of Employment Gazette (April 1981), Cited in Unit 11 of Open University course D102.

Table 23 *Predominantly female occupations*

	All persons (thousands)	Women (thousands)
90% or over female occupations		
Hand and machine sewers, embroiderers	238	230
Nurses	432	394
Maids, valets, etc.	443	428
Canteen assistants	304	293
Typists, secretaries, etc.	770	759
75% and under 90% female occupations		
Shop assistants	969	786
Charwomen, sweepers and cleaners	522	456
Kitchen hands	122	100
Office machine operators	177	153
Hairdressers, etc.	159	124
Telephone operators	107	89
60% and under 75% female occupations		
Clerks and cashiers	2475	1546
Waiters and waitresses	113	82
Primary and secondary teachers	496	318
Packers and labellers, etc.	183	121
Bartenders	103	73

Source: Annual Census of Employment (June 1974). Cited by Hilary Wainwright in P. Abrams, *Work, Urbanism and Inequality* (Weidenfeld and Nicolson 1978), p. 169.

work as they cope with the tasks of rearing school children, tending the sick and the old, and feeding and maintaining male workers. It is their inability to 'meet the requirements of (a) long-term uninterrupted employment, (b) full-time work and (c) geographic mobility' that makes it difficult for them 'to qualify for and remain in employment in the "protected sectors" of the labour market'.[21] Nor, given their domestic circumstances and male sexism, is active trade unionism an easily available option to them. Instead, carrying these 'disabilities' and subject to a gale of sexist discrimination, women are pushed into the less protected 'secondary sectors' of the economy where productivity is low, employment scattered in small and isolated units, and the coverage of labour law less extensive and generous: there to experience poor working conditions, lower than average pay, and disproportionately high rates of unemployment.

Although women now constitute 40 per cent of the paid labour force, they earn only 25 per cent of the total wage and salary bill, and that despite recent legislation on equal pay and sex discrimination. Even full-time women workers only managed to improve their pay relative to men from 63.1 per cent to 75.5 per cent between 1970 and 1977, and there is some evidence that even that gain is being eroded now. Women not in full-time employment fare even less well. If they work at home, they can expect only a pittance. 'A 1979 survey found that nearly two-thirds of home workers earned under 60 pence an hour (less than a third of the national average hourly earnings); and as many as a third of homeworkers earned 20 pence an hour – a tenth of the national average.'[22] As part-time workers women are almost equally unprotected by labour laws and almost equally badly paid. 80 per cent of them earned less than £1.50 an hour in 1979, compared with 47.8 per cent of full-time women and only 12.5 per cent of full-time men. Even as full-time workers, the concentration of women in secondary labour markets gives them a particular vulnerability now. For in the contemporary crisis of capitalism, it is just those sectors which are subject to employer initiatives at mechanization, and which are particularly liable to closure and labour shedding in the pursuit of corporate viability and public sector economy. The automation of the office threatens secretaries now, just as cuts in welfare provision threaten workers in the health and education sectors. In sum, women, coming late and disadvantged into employment through the burdens of child care and the force of sexist discrimination, find themselves the least rewarded and protected section of the white labour force at work, and the most likely to be ejected back into domestic production alone as mass unemployment grows.

The reasons for discrimination against women

There is, of course, an enormous controversy about why women are so treated, and each position in that debate, as in others, has serious and different political consequences. For those for whom the gender division of labour is a *natural* one – an inevitable (even desirable) social outgrowth of innate physiological differences between the sexes – the political consequences are highly conservative, driving women back into the home and into the protection of the dominant male. For *liberals* of various persuasions, female subordination is one important political problem among many, needing political initiatives to rectify it. Like problems of other kinds it is ultimately resolvable by a series of discrete reforms. Radical and socialist feminists see the process of gender differentiation as more structurally rooted, and as irresolvable without fundamental social changes that would remove the sexist practices which reproduce female subordination on a daily basis. For *radical feminists*, the root of the problem lies in 'patriarchy', in a 'set of social relations between men which have a material base, and which, though hierarchical, establish or create interdependence and solidarity among men that enable them to dominate women'.[23] Since on this perspective men are the problem, the politics of sexual revolution invariably involve (to differing degrees) separatism, the withdrawal from heterosexual relationships, and a general disregard for direct participation in a public politics (either of the state or the revolutionary Left) that is dominated and directed by men. For *socialist feminists*, the problem is less patriarchy in general than capitalist patriarchy in particular – the inter-

play of sex and class in an exploitative society based on wage labour. For them, the task of revolution involves the transformation of politics through the creation of a new Left that is both anti-capitalist and anti-patriarchal, in pursuit of a socialism in which a sexual division of labour is no longer allowed to underpin the abolition of social classes.

Not all socialist feminists are happy with the concept of patriarchy;[24] yet there is little doubt that we need 'to preserve the sense of structured gender inequalities, antedating capitalism and class relationships, which the term patriarchy seeks to convey'.[25] For one thing that is quite clear is that the pattern of unequal experience between men and women is not natural but rather *social* in origin. There is no intellectual legitimacy in 'the constant slippage from women's role in procreation to women's supposed responsibility for childcare. There is no biological reason why women should be particularly or exclusively concerned with child rearing'.[26] Physiological factors may predispose the social division of labour in that direction; but such differences between men and women do not make it automatic and unavoidable that it should be women who carry the full responsibility for child care long after any breastfeeding stage is over. Yet that role has long been imposed upon them. The physiological division of labour between the sexes in the act of human reproduction has been used to sustain a social division of labour based on gender; and men have kept women in positions of subordination in the vast majority (though crucially not in all) of societies known to us as anthropologists, historians and social scientists. There was certainly a gender division of labour in European feudalism; and its intensification was an important source of the primitive accumulation process that fuelled the later emergence of industrial capitalism.[27]

Yet fortunately – since it would be a considerable undertaking – our job here is not to trace the origins of that gender division, nor to locate the detailed mechanisms that reproduced it with such tenacity throughout the pre-capitalist era.[28] What we need to observe instead is the way that women experience subordination under a capitalist mode of production. For the subordination of women within capitalist societies has its own history. In the end, if not initially, capitalism divided the productive unit from the domestic. It split the factory from the home. 'Historians correctly argue that a major consequence of the industrial revolution was the destruction of the family as a unit of production', such that 'each stage in industrial differentiation and specialisation struck also at the family economy, disturbing customary relations between man and wife, parents and children, and differentiating more sharply between "work" and "life"'.[29] So 'what marks out capitalism is not the subjection of women as such, since this predates capitalism, but the privatisation of domestic labour and the exclusion of women from social labour, which serves to reproduce the subjection of women in a specifically capitalist form'.[30] It is as well not to be dogmatic here. It may be that capitalism could have emerged without that gender differentiation; but the crucial thing is that it did not. On the contrary, coming into a world with an already existing gender division, capitalism 'not only took over and entrenched the differentiation of tasks, but divided the workforce itself into wage earners and those dependent upon the wages of others. Capitalism did not create domestic labour or the "feminine" areas of wage labour, but it did create a set of social relations in which pre-existing divisions were not only reproduced but solidified in different relations in the wage-labour system'.[31] At the end of that process, women had lost even the limited hold they had enjoyed – as businesswomen, craftswomen and general agricultural producers – on economic independence at the different levels of the class structure of late feudal Europe.[32]

Although the long-term effect of capitalist development was to lock women in new patterns of subordination, initially capitalism was quite indifferent to the gender (and indeed the age) of those who ran its factories. Women and children were often preferred, as easier to control and exploit in an already existing patriarchial society. But women progressively left the factory in each generation thereafter, unless wars intervened to pull them back temporarily; and they left under a combination of powerful (and predominantly male) social pressures. The replacement of labour by machinery from the 1880s reduced the need for unskilled manual labour as population growth and immigration enhanced that labour's supply. Male workers (particularly skilled ones) organized to exclude cheaper challenges to their monopoly, and drove women out of skilled employment altogether. They were joined by the 'enlightened' wing of a patriarchal bourgeoisie who saw only too well the advantages to their preferred social order of a well-regulated sphere of domestic production – and who were, in any case, disturbed by the sexual (and hence social?) freedom characteristic of women released from isolation in the home. All this is a 'lost history' which is only now being rediscovered by a new generation of committed feminist historians. They are finding that trade unions, employers and the state were all active here: restricting women's entry to paid labour and sustaining procedures that guaranteed that women were ejected first, if anyone had to go. Women were excluded from the professions and the universities. They were not hired when men were available, or they were obliged to leave paid employment when they married. Factory acts restricted their working hours, and the principle of 'first in, last out' left the newly returned young mother particularly vulnerable to unemployment. We have all seen those processes at work; and Heidi Hartmann has summarized them as follows:

when women participated in the wage-labour market, they did so in a position as clearly limited by patriarchy as it was by capitalism. Men's control over women's labour was altered by the wage labour system, but it was not eliminated. In the labour market the dominant position of men was maintained by sex-ordered job segregation. Women's jobs were lower paid, considered less skilled and often involved less exercise of authority or control. Men acted to enforce job segregation in the labour market; they utilised trade union associations and strengthened the domestic division of labour, which required women to do housework, child-care, and related chores. Women's subordinate position in the labour-market reinforced their subordinate position in the family, and that in turn reinforced their labour-market position.[33]

So we have to remember that the notion of a 'woman's place being in the home' has been, and remains, a *social* construction consolidated over a long period and perpetually reproduced. How 'social' it is can be seen in the speed with which it was abandoned in two world wars, when labour shortage again made the mobilization of women as wage labourers essential to those who rule us. Of course, working-class women never left the factories entirely, and middle-class women since the war have expanded into the public and private white-collar bureaucracies that have mushroomed in late capitalism. Yet women under capitalism have always experienced a more or less concerted male attempt to restrict, even to end totally, their involvement in wage labour. The form of that attack has varied down the years. The Victorians professed a serious concern about the morality of young girls exposed to factory life. The conservatives of the 1950s relied on medical claims that young children required the unbroken attention of a devoted mother. But the concerns and effects have always been the same: to reduce the threat posed by women to male monopolies of high status employment, to make available a cheap reserve of easily-harnessable and malleable labour for menial manual tasks, and to ensure that male labour power was forthcoming in a state and quality that was possible only through the unstinting and unpaid domestic labour of womankind.

Such female labour may not be technically a 'reserve army' in the classic Marxist sense.[34] Its use, as we have seen, is too hedged about by the patriarchial proscriptions that hold women down to enable women to compete for, and hence cheapen, every form of male labour. Discriminatory practices (such as seniority clauses) give women a disproportionate exposure to unemployment in times of recession, but the concentration of their employment in particular sectors leaves men elsewhere free of heavy female competition. In fact, as we have also seen, new technology and cuts in welfare spending are now destroying jobs in those sectors in which women are heavily concentrated – so that, far from the presence of women threatening to increase male unemployment, it is that participation by women which is now most threatened. Yet the subordinate position of women in the labour market, reserve army or not, does still facilitate capital accumulation and sustain social stability. It enables many jobs to be performed by labour paid only 'pin money'; it sets worker against worker on grounds of gender; and consolidates a section of the labour force socialized into relative docility by the pressures of their dual role, their involvement in unprotected part-time work, and their exposure to a sexist culture.

For it is not only male trade union pressure that excludes women from an equal involvement in wage labour, and which frees men from an equal exposure to the rigours of domestic production. In the sphere of work, definite employer attitudes play their part too, and these derive from the general consolidation of sexist values and practices in society as a whole. 'Household structure and familial ideology also play an indirect part in the limitation of women's participation in wage labour';[35] and these in their turn are reproduced by a particular pattern of education and socialization within the family and the school, and by the particular content of the contemporary media. They are also reproduced by a whole set of state practices which are worth documenting if we are to understand fully the origins of the present political demands of those groups of women now campaigning against sexual discrimination and the institutions and practices that sustain it.

The 'sins' of the state here are those of commission and omission, and stretch out from state institutions and personnel, through the assumptions of state policy, into the detail of that policy itself. The state is predominantly peopled by men, and Margaret Thatcher apart, is progressively so the higher one rises within its hierarchies. Its coercive apparatuses in particular are male in domination and sexist in practice; and that is nowhere clearer than in treatment by the police and the courts of domestic violence, sexual harassment and rape. It is clear too in the legal code's commitment to the distinction between the 'public' and the 'private', with the private sphere so often specified as the 'family unit' subject to masculine control. Within that private space it is the state which attempts to regulate sexual behaviour through laws on marriage, divorce, prostitution, rape, pornography and so on. Historically, the content of those laws has served to reproduce female subordination and to consolidate male power, both inside and outside the family.

One major pattern of welfare provision is built around the notion of the family unit, with its dependent female and its family wage. As a result, women (particularly single and divorced women) find themselves disadvantaged in their access to social benefits of many kinds. Four areas of legislation – 'supplementary benefits, national insurance, taxation and student grants – are particularly important ways in which the state supports this

dependence' of women on men, 'and discriminates against lifestyles that attempt to achieve relationships based on mutual independence'.[36] There is no space here to establish the detailed evidence to sustain that view, although that evidence is readily available elsewhere. What we must understand is the general truth that underlies the detail: that when seen as a whole, state policy in the welfare area serves both to reinforce female dependence on the male 'breadwinner' and to leave women (through this dependence) in a semi-proletarianized state when they do enter wage labour. As Mary MacIntosh has it, 'in the case of women, the social security system has worked in a curious way, on the one hand to establish married women as dependent upon their husbands (and therefore not entirely reliant upon wage labour), but on the other hand by restricting their direct eligibility for social security benefits, to make them more vulnerable to use as a cheap labour power when they do have to engage in wage labour'.[38]

Even in the heyday of the long boom, state provision of child care support to ease the burdens of working women was singularly underdeveloped. With the return of recession and a Conservative government, women now find themselves under increasing pressure from the state's 'family policy' and associated cuts in welfare provision to give up paid employment altogether; to take on a greater responsibility for the care of the sick and the old; to lose their precarious and limited rights to abortion and birth control, and to stretch a depleted family and social wage to accommodate the stresses experienced by both male and female members of their family as mass poverty returns in the form of large-scale unemployment. That unemployment has fallen disproportionately on women anyway; and they are being expected to live through this recession in a reincarnated form of the 'model woman' canvassed so widely in the 1950s: stuck at home, loyal to hearth and family, and suitably deferential to the opinions and directives of their male superiors.

Women's political response

Not surprisingly, the range of political responses to all this has varied dramatically. The vast majority of women have been effectively depoliticized. As isolated home workers, they have lacked the solidaristic supports of large and permanent workgroups, and as a result have been disproportionately exposed to the dominant culture, both political and sexist. Their role as dual producers has left the conditions of paid employment sufficiently marginal to their concerns to eat away at any systematic female participation in trade unions and industrial militancy. For young single girls, marriage and domestic production often looks an attractive proposition, softening any propensity to industrial racialism inspired by their deprived working conditions. For married women, the parallel existence of a man's wage reduces their full dependence on their own earning power; and the burdens of child-rearing and home-maintenance leave the married woman with little time to participate fully in unions and politics.

In any case, the institutions of a male dominated political world are at best indifferent, and more normally hostile and resistant, to their involvement and concerns, riddled as those institutions are by the attitudes and practices of a sexist culture. That culture is so all pervasive, the powers of men so entrenched, and the situation of women so difficult in the main, that the vast majority of women absorb large parts of that culture as their own. They then police and reinforce their own subordination. With greater or lesser degrees of enthusiasm and identification, they accept the 'space', the 'roles' and the 'attitudes' specified for them as naturally female, handling their resulting frustrations in individual ways (from sexual adventures and domestic power struggles to mental illnesses of various

kinds), and acting to reproduce those roles and attitudes in their children and their women friends. Many 'women have absorbed, unconsciously or consciously, as part of their self-conceptions, a cultural interpretation of their biological distinctiveness as women'.[39] It is not surprising that, as a result, many women who have been obliged in their own life and times to operate in the restricted space left to them by a sexist culture should feel particularly threatened by (and therefore very hostile to) a new generation of women who are less willing to tolerate a similar pattern of subordination.

The cumulative impact of all that down the years has been to keep most women out of public life altogether, and to denude the political agenda of many of the concerns and problems experienced by women at different levels of the class structure. When those in charge of the state look out at the organized political universe that surrounds them, the world they see is predominantly a male one. Women were not even there as legal equivalents of men until the British Married Woman's Property Act of 1882, nor as voters until 1919 and 1928. Thereafter, and when they voted, they were appealed to as consumers and house-maintainers, as the bedrock of the family structure which kept them weak, and in that context showed until recently a *slightly* greater propensity than men both to abstain and to vote Conservative (partly, one suspects, because they live longer, and the old have tended to be slightly more conservative as a general rule; and also perhaps partly because of the isolated and oppressed nature of their domestic role).[40]

It was hard for women to shake free of that image and to break out of that silence in order to impose a more powerful political impact. Sexism in trade unions, and the problems of child care, kept many women, as we have seen, from full participation in union affairs. Women are less unionized than men (35.6 per cent as against 71.2 per cent in 1976), because for many work has to be more marginal a concern, because those women working part time are as difficult to unionize as part-time men, and because it is difficult for women to get to and to shape union meetings and policy. So although 10 million women now go out to work, only 3,560,000 were in unions in 1976, and at senior levels in the union hierarchy the presence of women is rare indeed. In fact, until its 1983 reorganization, the TUC General Council reserved just two seats for the representatives of the women's conference. These were the only two women on the council, and this is not surprising when you realize that 'in 1975 a survey of 62 unions showed that there were 2259 full-time male employees but only 71 full-time women employees' in their pay.[41] 1027 delegates went to

the 1974 TUC for example, but only sixty were women,[42] and that included five from NALGO (out of twenty-five from a union of whose members half are women) and five from the NUT (out of twenty-seven from a union of whose members 75 per cent are women). The TUC, of course, has its own women's conference; and it contains at least ten unions with very sizeable concentrations of women members, as Table 24 shows. There is now some evidence to suggest that the mobilization of women within those unions and through the women's conference is beginning to alter the public positions and certain of the practices of national trade union leaderships. The 1983 reforms of the General Council increased the number of women's representatives to six, and one woman trade union leader (from NUPE)

Table 24   *Women in the unions (figures in brackets show how many women there would be if they were represented according to their share of the membership)*

Union	Membership			Executive members		Full-time officials		TUC delegates	
	Total	F	%F	Total	F	Total	F	Total	F
APEX (Professional, Executive, Clerical, Computer)	150,000	77,000	51	15	1(8)	55	2(28)	15	4(8)
ASTMS (Technical, Managerial)	472,000	82,000	17	24	2(4)	63	6(11)	30	3(5)
BIFU (Banking, Insurance, Finance)	132,000	64,000	49	27	3(13)	41	6(20)	20	3(10)
GMWU (General and Municipal)	956,000	327,000	34	40	0(14)	243	13(83)	73	3(25)
NALGO (Local Govt Officers)	705,000	356,000	50	70	14(35)	165	11(83)	72	15(36)
NUPE (Public Employees)	700,000	470,000	67	26	8(17)	150	7(101)	32	10(22)
NUT (Teachers)	258,000	170,000	66	44	4(29)	43	3(28)	36	7(24)
UNTGW (Tailor and Garment)*	117,000	108,000	92	15	5(14)	47	9(43)	17	7(16)
TGWU (Transport and General)	2,070,000	330,000	16	39	0(6)	600	9(96)	85	6(14)
USDAW (Shop, Distributive, Allied)	462,000	281,000	63	16	3(10)	162	13(102)	38	8(24)
Totals	6,022,000	2,265,000	38	316	40(150)	1,569	76(595)	418	66(174)

Note: All figures are approximate and the most recent that were available in November 1980.

Source: A. Coote and B. Campbell, *Sweet Freedom* (Picador 1982), p. 167.

was elected in her own right, the first time that this had happened since 1952. In addition, the TUC has now revamped its own 'Aims for Women at Work', has its own charter for the under-fives, and gave official support to the 80,000 strong demonstration against John Corrie's Anti-Abortion Bill in 1979. As Anna Coote and Beatrix Campbell correctly observe, that 'was the largest trade union demonstration ever held for a cause which lay beyond the traditional scope of collective bargaining; it was also the biggest pro-abortion march'.[43] In addition, they are able to record more moves within individual unions to support feminist demands and increase the representation of women workers in the unions. Yet it has also to be said that male trade union opposition to effective action on equal pay is still very evident, and that there is still much to be done before the traditional and well-entrenched sexism of British trade union practice is a thing of the past.

The same is true of the situation in the political parties. There is some evidence, certainly in the parties of the Left, that the presence of women is growing and that women's demands are being incorporated into party programmes. The Labour Party programme in 1983 contained commitments in the areas of equal pay, child care, sex discrimination, job segregation and maternity grants, and agitation continued right up to the election to alter its Alternative Economic Strategy in ways that would ease the burdens of working women. What is clear, however, is that these moves run counter to the general past tendency in the political sphere to under-represent women as candidates and to exclude from policy the particular concerns of women. Like every other major institution in contemporary Britain, the political parties (and indeed the system as a whole) 'systematically deny women power officially, yet rely heavily on the labour of women, given voluntarily and in their "free" time, to continue functioning'.[44] Something like 40 per

cent of individual Labour Party members and 50 per cent of Conservative Party members are women. But these percentages shrink as you move up the internal organization of each party: on the management committees of the constituency parties, as delegates to party conference (11 per cent Labour, 24 per cent Conservative); on national committees (18/24 per cent); as local councillors (around 20 per cent) as parliamentary candidates (9/10 per cent) and as MPs (currently down to 3 per cent).[45] Sex roles within parties have often kept women making the tea, and that usual mixture of women's extra burdens in child care, and general cultural opposition to powerful women, has combined to keep the vast majority of MPs male. Between 1918 and 1974 just over 1000 women stood for Parliament as against 22,000 men, and the House of Commons has never had more than 5 per cent of its membership female. In the 1974 elections, first twenty-three and then twenty-seven women were returned, and in the two elections since that number has fallen to nineteen and twenty-one.

Moreover, the women who have become MPs have entered a House of Commons whose procedures and timetable reflect the practices of the nineteenth-century upper-class male club, with neither the facilities nor the hours appropriate to an easy combination of politics and child care. Women get through, of course, even to the top, but only by shedding most of the responsibilities and many of the attitudes characteristic of women as a whole. Consider, for example, Table 25 which shows Cabinet membership in Britain from 1920. What is remarkable about it is the dearth of women, and the concentration of the few who do get through in relatively minor departmental posts. Margaret Thatcher is the great exception, but her rise to power has brought no parallel promotion of women to key positions. We have yet to see a woman Foreign Secretary, Chancellor of the Exchequer or Secretary for Trade and Industry.

Table 25 *Men and women in office, 1920–70*

	Cabinet		Ministers not in Cabinet		Under secretaries		Parliamentary secretaries	
	Women	Men	Women	Men	Women	Men	Women	Men
1920	0	20	0	9	0	9	0	14
1925	0	21	0	4	0	6	1[1]	11
1930	1[2]	18	0	6	0	7	1[3]	8
1935	0	20	0	5	0	8	0	8
1940	0	9	0	20	0	9	1[4]	13
1945	0	8	0	34	0	10	2[5]	21
1950	0	17	1[6]	15	1[7]	7	0	17
1955	0	18	0	16	0	11	1[8]	16
1960	0	19	0	20	0	11	2[9]	13
1968	1[10]	23	2[11]	31	2[12]	15	1[13]	19
1970	1[14]	18	1[15]	24	0	14	0	9

Notes
1 Education
2 Labour
3 Health
4 Health
5 (a) Health (b) Home Affairs
6 National Insurance
7 Scotland
8 (a) Health
9 (a) Health (b) Pensions
10 Overseas Development
11 (a) Home Office
   (b) National Insurance
12 (a) Colonies (b) Scotland
13 Public Works
14 Education
15 Scotland

Source: M. Currell, *Political Women* (Croom Helm 1974), p. 29.

What is happening here, in the political sphere, is reproduced across the élite structure as a whole. There, in general, top positions remain male: exclusively so in the Church of England and the armed forces, and almost exclusively in education, the judiciary and industry. The Anglican establishment is formally closed to women. So too is the army outside the WRAC. 'No woman has yet been appointed Lord Chancellor, Solicitor-General or Attorney General, nor has any woman yet sat in the Court of Appeal or on the Judicial Committee of the House of Lords.'[46] Nor has the government yet put any woman on 'the boards running the gas, electricity, coal, atomic energy, railway and aerospace industries, nor on the Post Office Board'.[47] Elsewhere in the quangos, boards and tribunals of the state, there is a small female representation; but at the top of a class society as at the bottom women find themselves under-represented.

Even in the apparently equal world of education, as is shown in Table 26, the same pattern of discrimination persists.

Yet despite these disabilities, in the past women have intermittently mobilized industri-

Table 26 *Women in the educational élite, 1973*

Post	Total	No. of Women
University vice-chancellor	44	0
Polytechnic principal	28	0
Medical school principal	24	1
Agricultural college principal	44	0
College of education principal	172	72
Member of the UGC	21	2

Source: S. Delamont, *The Sociology of Women* (Allen and Unwin 1980), p. 163.

ally, socially and politically. They are doing so again now. Beneath the general acceptance (even by women) of a sexist culture, it is possible to locate a discontent with male domination which is there to be tapped by a revitalized movement for women's liberation. Women, no less than men (as we shall also see in the next chapter) 'negotiate' the dominant culture – operating normally within its stereotypes, yet conscious of its lack of total fit with their experience of reality – so creating a 'space' within which radical alternatives have the opportunity to establish themselves. Women workers are conscious of the inadequacies of their pay and conditions, and at times have shown a determination to resolve them by industrial militancy which has shaken employers and government alike, and which has forced even male trade unionists into supportive action. Women struck at Fords in 1968 for equal pay; and it was the fight of Asian women workers for trade union recognition at Grunwick that filled the streets of London with the largest and widest display of working-class support for one industrial dispute since the war.

In each generation a certain percentage of politically active women have pushed for legislation from within the unions and the Labour Party, and a much wider mobilization of women occurred prior to the First World War in the Suffragette struggle for the vote. 'Since the 1920s, when women first entered parliament, there have been women's campaigns on equal pay, on various aspects of sex discrimination, on nursery schools, on family allowances, on the rights of divorced women, on taxation, on contraception, abortion and women's health, and on consumer protection of various kinds.'[48] The struggle for the vote was formally successful. The vote was won, but women still lacked the organized social basis on which to translate that legal right into a social and political reality. In pursuit of that, agitation within the Labour Party has recently culminated in the introduction of an Equal Pay Act (in 1970), the provision of statutory rights to maternity leave and pensions through two acts in 1975, and the establishment of an Equal Opportunities Commission in the same year.

In fact the pressure for legislative changes of this kind should be understood as part of a much wider remobilization around the issue of gender divisions. For the 1970s saw the re-emergence of a movement for women's liberation, initiated in the main by a predominantly middle-class, college-educated generation of young women who were radicalized by the gap between the content of their education and aspirations, and the reality of their options (and those of other women) in a patriarchal capitalist society. The women's liberation movement spent the 1970s working to find an appropriate structure, mode of activity and programme. Women identifying with it were active politically on many fronts: in the unions, the Labour Party, the revolutionary and non-aligned Left, pushing for better child-care facilities and full welfare rights for women, campaigning on industrial pay and conditions, struggling against sexist practices in the schools, the media and the state, and insisting on the reclamation by women of control over their own sexuality and reproductive powers.

Precisely because the women's liberation movement has eschewed the kind of bureaucratized and formalized politics that many politically-active women find intimidating and unproductive in the world of men, it is not easy to point to this or that organization as representative of the movement as a whole. The movement has built itself around the concept of 'sisterhood', in small groups of women engaged in consciousness raising and campaigning, and has been as concerned with politicizing (and revolutionizing) the power relations of private life as with mass politicing in the public sphere. Yet women have campaigned on a vast area of public issues affecting women, and the movement has formulated its own set of public demands. The first national women's liberation conference in 1970 issued four, around which it was felt that many women could rally: equal pay now, equal education and job opportunities, free contraception and abortion on demand, and free twenty-four-hour nurseries. Later conferences added demands for financial and legal independence for women, an end to all discrimination against lesbians, a woman's right to define her own sexuality, and freedom from intimidation and sexual coercion by men. But the women's liberation movement is just that – a movement not simply an organization – and debate continues within its constituent parts and internal journals on a whole range of questions concerned with strategy and policy. Indeed, like other sections of the Left, radical women mobilizing within the movement have yet to solve the problem that has bedevilled the Left elsewhere this century: of how to bridge the divisions of class and interest within its potential constituency created by the differential treatment of people by capitalism.

The different class positions of women make different immediate demands more attractive to some than to others. Working-class women are quite likely to respond positively to demands for better pay (even to an end to job segregation), to requests for more time free of both domestic and industrial production, and to initiatives to improve the quality of social support for the young, old and sick. They may even respond to calls to end the notion of 'the family wage' and to alter men's working conditions to facilitate male involvement in domestic production. Middle-class feminists, particularly the young college-trained, tend to add demands less obviously linked to the immediacy of working-class oppression: abortion on demand, the right to determine one's own sexuality, the destruction of the family unit, and the wholesale replacement of a sexist culture. There is a scale of demands here. Some are achievable without fundamental social change, but most require a transformation as profound as any

pursued by the Left this century. The scale of the task is itself a disincentive to radicals, and a source of comfort to sexists and conservatives of all shades; yet they would do well to recognize the seismic nature of the changes now going on within the political universe of women.

For as the women's liberation movement struggles to link working-class women and middle-class feminists, its mobilizing potential has been underlined by the capacity of the women at Greenham Common in 1982 to pull 30,000 other women to join them in a day of protest against the imposition of Cruise missiles in Britain. The growing involvement of women in paid labour in the 1960s and 1970s has provided a material base for the emergence of a new and self-confident form of women's politics. The public presence of the women's liberation movement itself – and the half-hearted reforms already squeezed from a reluctant state by its activity – have alerted many women to the nature of their problems and their openness to political solutions. The revival of the cold war in the 1980s has mobilized even more women, particularly those locked in domestic production and child care, who are now confronted with the threat of the physical destruction of the families for whom they care.

As the state now attempts to push women back into the home as one element in its solution to capitalist recession, it no longer faces an almost exclusively conservative and socially quiescent female population. Large sections of that population do, of course, remain in that frame of mind. But it also faces one in which significant numbers of women are conscious of the injustice and remediability of their lot, and in which a movement for women's liberation is growing and spreading again. 'Within every area of social life, from nursery and primary schools to the health service, housing, the unions and political organizations, women are identifying and challenging all the ways in which everyday activities and institutions are based on the secondary position of women.'[49] Because the terrain of sexual oppression is so all pervasive and diffuse, so too is the shape and scope of the struggle against it, and that is both a strength and a problem for the coming together of a coherent and potent Left. But there can be no doubt now that any Conservative state seeking to intensify gender oppression will meet serious and widespread resistance if it tries. Nor can it be doubted that the Left's whole understanding of what socialism is has been transformed by the women's liberation movement's insistence that a society without classes will still not be free so long as a gender division of labour persists within it. That is a major step forward for the Left that must not be lost.

The politics of ethnic minorities

White women are not alone in experiencing discrimination in this society. For so too do the non-white ethnic minorities who make up about 4.2 per cent of the population as a whole. Down the years waves of immigrants have periodically settled here, driven to these islands in search of safety and prosperity by political terror, ethnic discrimination or economic exploitation at home. When they have arrived, they have invariably been received with hostility by large sections of the indigenous population, and have been pushed into low paid employment, menial jobs and ghettos of inadequate housing. Although they have stayed, and had children and grandchildren born here, they have still had to live as a community subject to discrimination because of their original country of origin, or because of their ethnic background. There were no major migrations into England from Norman times until the Huguenots came at the end of the seventeenth century, but throughout the Medieval period Jewish settlers were invariably denied full political and social rights, and on occasions were hounded and subjected to pogroms. The Irish came after the famine of the 1840s: by 1851 the census showed '727,326 Irish immigrants in England, constituting 2.9% of the population of England and Wales,

Table 27   *Net migrant flows. UK, since 1964, by citizenship of migrants*

Mid-year to mid-year	Alien excluding Pakistan[a]	Old Commonwealth	Citizenship (000s) New Commonwealth & Pakistan[a]	United Kingdom Controlled[b]	Other	Inflow	Total Outflow	Net[c]
1964–5	+22	+ 1	+55		−136	223	281	−58
1965–6	+24	− 2	+42		−141	210	286	−77
1966–7	+30	+ 5	+45		−175	232	326	−94
1967–8	+23	−10	+55	+15	−128	241	286	−45
1968–9	+21	− 2	+48	+ 8	−144	227	296	−68
1969–70	+24	− 3	+37	+ 6	−146	224	306	−82
1970–1	+21	− 5	+33	+ 9	− 98	227	266	−39
1971–2	+15	+ 6	+16	+16	− 97	196	240	−44
1972–3	+22	+ 3	+13	+34	− 76	225	230	− 5
1973–4	+21	+ 6	+14	+10	−122	183	255	−72
1974–5	+18	−	+20	+13	−116	194	261	−67
1975–6	+12	+ 3	+29	+12	− 79	197	220	−23
1976–7	+ 2	−	+24	+ 9	− 63	181	209	−28
1977–8	+ 3	+ 1	+25	+ 6	− 71	162	198	−36
1978–9	+ 9	+ 4	+38	+ 4	− 49	194	187	+ 6
1979–80	+23	+ 3	+34	+ 3	− 67	205	209	− 4

Notes
a   Pakistani citizens are included with 'New Commonwealth' throughout, although Pakistan left the Commonwealth in 1972.
b   United Kingdom passport holders subject to immigration control from March 1968.
c   Excluding net immigration due to direct traffic with the Irish Republic.
Source: Social Trends 12, 1982 Edition (HMSO) 1981, Table 1.16.

and 7.2% of the population of Scotland'. In the years since, a regular flow of labour backwards and forwards across the Irish sea has been an important if subsidiary feature of English and Scottish life. The net inflow of Irish labour still averaged 30,000 a year between 1946 and 1959, although it fell significantly thereafter.[51] As they came, particularly in the nineteenth century, the Irish experienced the full force of English prejudice, with significant amounts of collective violence (riots and the like) by English workers against what they saw as an Irish threat to their own precarious hold on jobs and wages. Jewish refugees from Eastern European anti-semitism met similar hostility when they arrived at the turn of the century, as did the Chinese and to a lesser extent the Poles who settled here after the Second World War. Now the brunt of discrimination is experienced by people from the New Commonwealth – the West Indies, India, Pakistan and Bangladesh – who have settled here in the years since 1950.

This is a racist society. Discrimination experienced by black Africans, Asians and West Indians, although often similar in form to that experienced by Irish and Jewish settlers before them, has a qualitatively different base, as we shall see. Each year more people leave these shores than enter them, and a significant percentage of those who come are 'white' (of European stock) and are relatively easily assimilated. Not so those who are brown or black. The British social structure contained very few people with such skin colouring before 1945; but after the war, with labour scarce here, significant numbers arrived (Table 27). As Table 28 shows, the majority of the non-white minorities currently established in Britain come from the places just listed: India, Pakistan and the West Indies in the main – and only an estimated 11 per cent derive from 'Sri Lanka, Hong Kong, Malaysia, Singapore and other countries in Asia and Oceania'.[52] These West Indian and

Table 28 *Overseas-born population of Great Britain 1971*

Country of birth	Resident in Great Britain
Total Ireland	709,235
Irish Republic	615,820
Ireland (part not stated)	93,415
Total New Commonwealth countries	1,151,090
Nigeria	28,565
Barbados	27,055
Guyana	21,070
Jamaica	171,775
Trinidad and Tobago	17,135
Cyprus	73,295
Hong Kong	29,520
India	321,995
Pakistan	139,935
Malta and Gozo	33,840
Total European countries	632,770
Germany	157,680
Italy	108,980
Poland	110,925
Spain	49,470
Total other countries	979,990
America	131,540
China	13,495
USSR	48,095
Turkey	6,615

Note: Estimated populaton of the United Kingdom in 1976 was 57,000,000.

Source: Census 1971, Great Britain, Country of Birth Tables. Cited in C. Husband (ed.), *Race in Britain* (Hutchinson, 1982), p. 76.

Asian migrants arrived steadily through the 1950s, so that by the end of 1959 22 per cent of those who were to migrate had already arrived. Fear of controls quickened that flow dramatically between 1960 and 1962; thereafter the flow of migrants steadily fell. The West Indians came first, the African Asians last (after 1968), Pakistani and Indian migrants more steadily in between. Initially, the flow was mainly men. By 1964, 90 per cent of the Pakistani population in Britain was male;

since then the balance between the sexes has tended to even out,[53] although it still left a 2:1 ratio of men to women in the Pakistani and Bangladeshi communities as late as 1971.[54] With their arrival, the balance of 'foreigners' resident in Britain altered from its 1951 position (of 1.6 million people living in Britain who were born outside the United Kingdom, of whom only 0.2 million were born in the New Commonwealth) to the 1971 census report of 3.0 million (1.2 million of whom were from the New Commonwealth), and to the 1976 position of 1.6 million people of New Commonwealth origin.

When these people came, they met the full force of racist discrimination. Although they came 'voluntarily', the space into which they moved was heavily constrained, so that 'if the free market economy decided the numbers of immigrants, economic growth and the colonial legacy determined the nature of the work they were put to'.[55] They settled into, and were held in, the low paid and menial jobs which the indigenous labour force were happy to leave behind, and from which white labour could flee because of the expansion of employment opportunities in the years of the long boom. Often lacking the conventional social and industrial skills of the manufacturing world into which they were entering, and often living and working in their second language, the original migrants settled at the bottom of the industrial class structure. As mainly rural *émigrés*, they had very little choice, and were willing to tolerate the appalling conditions to which they were exposed, partly because living standards for them here were still superior to those they had left, and partly because the possibility of future assimilation and progress was offered to them. However, assimilation did not materialize, and on the whole the ethnic minority population stayed in low paid manual labour. They remained there because they were cut off from the special education and training they needed to roll back the disadvantages created by centuries of colonial exploitation, and were blocked in their promotion by white hostility: from the workers 'threatened' by their rise, employers in search of cheap labour, and a state inexorably racist in its central assumptions and practices.

White hostility kept black labour systematically under-represented in managerial and white-collar jobs. 'The job levels of Asian and West Indian men are substantially lower than those of white men',[56] and are centred in particular industries (textiles, building, vehicle assembly, shipbuilding, transport, catering and health care) in which 'low pay, shift work, unpleasant working conditions and unsocial working hours'[57] predominate (Table 29). Leaving aside Ugandian Asians as a special case, and 'excluding the health service area, few black workers are to be found higher than at the skilled manual level. . . . Not only are black migrants predominantly manual workers, but also . . . more than two-fifths of them are in semi- and unskilled jobs'. Black workers in this society find themselves disproportionately exposed to 'small scale productive labour in sweat shop conditions' (particularly if they are women), long hours and menial tasks 'under the enervating conditions typical of low skill work in the catering trades and service sectors', or to shift work in heavily capitalized routine assembly/textile industries (Table 30).[59]

Nor is that discrimination restricted to fields of paid employment or applied only to first generation migrants. Their children born here experience it just as powerfully, and are the first victims of a racist culture and of the cycle of urban deprivation and poverty into which that racism locked their parents. For the Indian, Pakistani, West Indian and Ugandan Asian immigrants find themselves discriminated against in housing no less than in employment. Their communities are heavily concentrated regionally. 49 per cent of black immigrant workers live in Greater London; another 22 per cent are in West Yorkshire, the

Table 29 *Job level analysed by country of origin – men*

	White	West Indian	Pakistani/ Bangladeshis	Indian	African Asian
Men in job market who have worked					
(unweighted)	996	634	495	508	226
(weighted)	1594	2896	1391	1867	1050
	%	%	%	%	%
Job level (socio-economic group)					
Professional/management	23 }40	2 }8	4 }8	8 }20	10 }30
White-collar	17	6	4	12	20
Skilled manual	42	59	33	44	44
Semi-skilled manual	12 }18	23 }32	38 }58	27 }36	24 }26
Unskilled manual	6	9	20	9	2
Not classified	1	1	1	—	—

Source: D. Smith, *Racial Discrimination in Britain: the PEP report* (Penguin 1977), p. 73.

Table 30 *Shift work by country of origin – men*

Base: working men Type of shift worked	Whites %	Minorities %	West Indians %	Pakistani/ Bangladeshi %	Indian %	African %
Permanent nights	1	3	1	8	4	3
Total night shifts	9	19	19	27	18	12
Day shifts	5	12	13	11	12	9
Total working shifts	15	31	31	38	30	30

Source: D. Smith, *Racial Discrimination in Britain: the PEP report* (Penguin 1977).

West Midlands and South East Lancashire. Within those regions the ethnic minorities live and work in the areas of greatest urban and industrial decay. Trapped in urban poverty, the majority of such immigrants experience the usual cycle of urban deprivation (low pay and poor housing, inadequate schooling, limited welfare provision, and a declining local economy which sustains these conditions). Throughout the long years of the post-war boom, these ethnic communities knew a level of unemployment that was always higher than the white average. When recession returned and jobs were scarce again, white attempts to re-colonize the jobs they had hitherto been happy to surrender (and the disproportionate destruction of those jobs by technologically-induced unemployment) brought the level of redundancy and poverty among the ethnic minorities to new and record heights (Table 31). 'Between November 1973 and November

Table 31 *Unemployment rates, 1971–81*

	1971	1973	1975	1977	1981
Blacks	7.5	5.3	7.7	7.9	17.2
All workers	5.2	3.6	5.5	5.8	9.9

Source: Race and Immigration, Runnymede Trust Bulletin, no. 159 (September 1983), p. 7.

1977, while national unemployment figures doubled, unemployment figures among ethnic minorities quadrupled. This trend is continuing. According to DE statistics, from February 1979 to February 1980, ethnic minority unemployment has risen four times as fast as overall unemployment.'[60] By the latter date, reports were emerging that gave unemployment among black school leavers as three times as high as that among their white contemporaries.[61] Certainly in Brixton after the riots, 'Scarman found that an estimated 55% of black males under 19 were registered jobless – while the actual level [was] undoubtedly higher due to non-registration'; and 'there are strong indications that these extremely high levels of young black jobless'[62] remain and are now firmly entrenched.

Of course, it is only a racist society that treats ethnic minorities as a homogeneous unit. They are not. There are vast differences of background, origin and culture within these oppressed minorities, and different characteristic responses to the experience of oppression. Indeed, West Indian and Asian settlers and immigrants have been forced into whatever degree of common identity they now share by the common racism to which they have been subject, for they arrived – if from the Caribbean – with a sense of themselves as from a particular island, and – if from the Indian subcontinent – as from a particular village, region or sect. Once here, it was their treatment at the hands of the indigenous population that consolidated them as West Indian or Asian. Even then, within the internal politics of particular communities, more localized sets of self-definitions continue to be of vital importance.

In general though, it can be seen that the tight internal cohesion and long-established independent cultural patterns of the Asian communities have turned those communities far more into themselves than is common among parallel West Indian ones, and have encouraged the internal orchestration of capital,

employment, housing and mutual support. Consequently, until and unless attacked from outside, Asian communities have remained culturally separate and have not pressed too strongly for political recognition. 'It has been argued that the Sikh, Hindu and Moslem cultures each provide a coherent positive identity for migrants faced with racism and discrimination, and that traditions of petty bourgeois enterprise make possible an alternative economic strategy when access to or advance within the category of wage labour is obstructed.'[63] So that, as Rex and Moore have said, 'we cannot feel absolutely sure that a substantial part of the Asian community may not come to have . . . a Jewish future in Great Britain. That is to say, we can envisage the possibility of some of those who are now accumulating capital while working long hours in foundries or factories investing that capital in their own commercial and industrial enterprises and achieving economic success'[64] of a limited kind.

This reminds us too that within each ethnic group there are distinct variations by class. The Asian community in particular has its own professional strata (of doctors and teachers) and its own small traders and landlords, consolidated partly by the communities' own needs for housing and commodities distinctive to their own culture, and partly by their experience of where racism ends in the surrounding white society. For the indigenous population, although too often unwilling to work or live alongside people of Asian, West Indian or African descent still quite happily buys commodities from them (eating their food and purchasing their textiles) with little sense of the inconsistency of their attitudes and actions. These independent tradesmen and professionals often play a vital spokesperson role for entire communities, and are one source of conservatism within the politics of the ethnic response. But the communities for whom they speak are not of their class. 'Smith's data for the early 1970s showed that only 8% of his "Asian" sample and 6% of his West Indian sample could be classified as "self employed".[65] The petty bourgeoisie may be evident in black politics, but they are not typical of black experience as a whole. The bulk of the minority ethnic populations are working class and poor, trapped in semi-skilled and unskilled jobs or (as in the case of young second-generation settlers) heavily un-employed and excluded from the labour force and the labour movement altogether. The distribution of the black population within the white class structure is not so uniform as to justify their specification as a 'sub class'. Their incorporation into mainly the lower section of the working class initially as migrant labour and their incorporation there, because of the racism of society as a whole, means that their situation is not reducible to that of white class membership. Instead, it has a definite 'racial' dimension that shapes its interests and politics in a way that parallels white class politics, and yet establishes for itself a space of its own.

The dominant pattern of racial discrimina-tion marginalizes the ethnic communities, and lowers the access of people at each class level to the set of life chances characteristic of white men and women of similar age, education and skill. But although the facts of discrimination are clear, the explanations of its tenacity and form are not: and here again the old theoreti-cal debates reappear to structure analysis and shape policy. For racists, the problem is simple. People of non-white races have char-acteristics peculiar to their ethnic origin which limit their intelligence and social capacity, and which in their turn both explain and justify the pattern of discrimination we have charted. But that position is as obscene as it is ludicrous. The overwhelming weight of evidence makes clear that there is no such thing as 'distinct racial types', that capacities vary within and across ethnic divisions, and that the consolida-tion of racial hierarchies is a 'social', not a 'natural' process, with its own origins in history, its own logic and its own dynamic.

Liberal scholarship and policy have long recognized that; and British liberals in particu-lar spent the 1950s and 1960s reacting to the arrival of New Commonwealth immigrants by asserting the existence of a 'problem' of 'race relations' that was to be resolved through the immigrants' assimilation into a richer cultural and political pluralism after an understand-able but hopefully brief period of tension between the 'hosts' and the 'strangers' newly arrived within their midst.

Radical scholarship – in sharply rejecting the legitimacy of a 'race relations' approach[66] – has seen the problem as more permanent and structural than that: stressing the way in which racial divisions arise out of the combined but uneven development of capitalism as a world system, as the legacy of a colonial division of the world into white metropolitan and non-white peripheral economies that has now been reproduced within the social formations of the metropolitan centres by the labour migrations of the long boom. Where radical and Marxist scholarship part company, however, has been in their differing specifications of the precise relationship between race and class – in their disagreement over the extent to which the racism engendered by capitalist expansion ought to be seen as a distinct phenomenon in its own right, either as partially resolvable within capitalist structures or as solvable only when linked in its independent politics to the wider struggle to transform capitalism as a whole. Among activists holding to the Marxist view, further disagreements persist on the precise status of the black working class (particularly the growing number of the black unemployed) – on whether black workers and black unemployed youth are best seen as a lumpen proletariat, underclass, racialized class fraction, reserve army of labour or sub-proletariat subject to super-exploitation and racial oppression. As usual, very different con-sequences for political strategy follow from each of these related but distinct specifications of the black relationship to white capital.[67]

The weight of historical evidence again suggests that it is in the development of capitalism as a complex economic and social phenomenon on the world scale that the roots of contemporary racism, as both an ideology and a set of social practices, must be situated. For it is clear that 'they came here because we went there',[68] that the availability of large reserves of rural labour in the underdeveloped parts of the world capitalist system stemmed directly from the colonial underdevelopment of large tracts of Africa and Asia by imperialist powers. Those powers destroyed natural economies there, and used force to demolish existing industry and trade that threatened their imperial privilege. Those same imperial powers plundered the wealth of their colonies to fuel their own processes of capital accumulation – directly through taxation (as with India) or indirectly through the unpaid labour of slaves in West Africa and the West Indies. The colonial economies created by this process were locked into subordinate relationships with the metropolitan centre, supplying the imperial heartland with essential raw materials and with indigenous cheap labour sustained by a primitive and underdeveloped agriculture. When boom conditions in the West made labour scarce, colonial labour supplies were a natural source to which metropolitan capitalist centres turned. This happened everywhere in the post-war boom, as we saw in Chapter 2. In Britain, labour was drawn from the West Indies to run transport and health services and from Pakistan to work night-shifts in the Bradford mills.

At times, the recruitment process was a conscious one. London Transport actually opened a recruitment office in the West Indies. Normally it needed no central orchestration. Rural underdevelopment 'pushed' people away in search of prosperity; and a dearth of labour in Britain 'pulled' that labour here, completing, as is shown in Figure 16, a circle of interconnectedness between colony and colonial power that had long been vital to

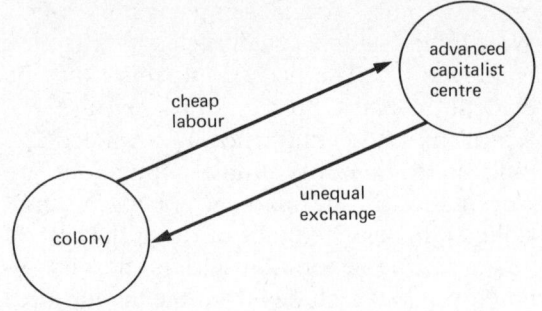

Figure 16   *The interconnectedness of colony and colonial power*

economic growth in the colonial centre. Indeed, only the arrival of extremely cheap and exploitable labour enabled large sections of the British textile industry in particular to continue in production at all. In its dramatic collapse in the recession of the 1970s and 1980s, the frailty of that industry was exposed for all to see at the very moment when the migrant labour which had sustained it for so long was experiencing the trauma of large-scale unemployment in a racist society. Having migrated to the metropolitan centre because of the way in which the nineteenth-century internationalization of capital had underdeveloped their home economies, the migrants became the first victims in those metropolitan centres of a new phase of internationalization by capital – one in which the partial redevelopment of carefully chosen Third World economies by multinational companies now undercut the under-capitalized and outmoded production systems of the metropolitan centre itself. In Stuart Hall's words, 'migrant workers now form the permanent basis of the modern industrial reserve army',[69] and more and more West Indian and Asian migrants are being forced into wagelessness through the collapse of the industries which their super-exploited labour had hitherto sustained, and through their own growing refusal to take the restricted number of 'shit jobs' left to them by the white power structure in the deepening recession.

However, colonialism left more than a relationship of dependence and exploitation between colony and centre. It left its own justifications too. It had to be legitimated in the centre by an ideology that would obscure its true character. Racism entered British political culture on a grand scale as the empire spread, through a barrage of self-justificatory rhetoric: the white man's burden, the simple nigger, the ignorant native, and so on. The categories of the language became imbued with racist symbolism that was there in embryo long before the colonial period. 'Black' gathered even stronger negative connotations, 'white' retained its positive ones. The humour of an entire culture gathered its racist over-tone, to match its established sexism. To the 'mother in law' joke came the Irish jokes, the Jewish jokes and those about the ignorant blacks. The mind of an entire people was polluted by the justificatory rhetoric of its imperialist rulers, to lie there – as intellectual filth – long after that empire had been taken down. Indeed, just as in the heyday of empire, the growing prosperity of the metropolitan centre that accrued through the unequal colonial exchange actually gave material 'proof' of black inferiority, so in the retreat from empire, the arrival of black migrants and the categories of a racist culture combined to identify easy scapegoats, and to divide the minds of the potentially radical coalition that might have turned that retreat into socialism.

This was no accident. The cultivation of racist and imperialist attitudes was a conscious and orchestrated feature of the ruling-class attempt to head off working-class protest at the turn of the century – one vital ingredient in the consolidation of its hegemony (of which more will be said in the next chapter). That ruling-class initiative was enormously success-ful. It was potent partly because of the quality of its orchestration, partly because there was a real material sense in which the interests of the British working class and those of colonial workers were divided and set against one another by the unequal exchange of the imperialist period. Living standards for all classes here were higher for the suppression of living standards in the colonies; and it is this division within the working class which racism has reproduced in Britain itself since 1948, as sections of those colonial workers have moved here to work and live. Indeed, racial divisions within the working class are, and will remain, one of the Left's most intrac-table political problems, because the super-exploitation of black workers has been estab-lished for so long, and runs so deep through society as a whole. As Paul Gilroy has said, 'black labour power has conditioned the most intimate structures of British daily life. "It is the sugar you stir, it is in the sinews of the infamous British sweet tooth, it is the tea leaves at the bottom of the British cuppa"'.[70]

The existence of such racial divisions has been beneficial to the existing social order in many ways. In the years of the long boom, immigrant labour facilitated capital accumula-tion. It provided a source of cheap labour, the costs of whose reproduction were not entirely born here. On the contrary, by drawing in the young, the male and the unmarried in the first instance, the costs of reproducing that labour could be pushed outside, on to the subsistence and dependent economies of the colonial system. Once here, that labour could be relied upon to work at menial tasks, under appalling conditions, for dismal wages. Its existence weakened indigenous labour by increasing the total number of workers, and by setting worker against worker. Then in time of recession, these migrants could be (more or less easily, depending on the country) repatri-ated, to lower the social costs here of rising unemployment. In fact, the 'problem' of ethnic tension in Britain is greater than elsewhere because that repatriation is not so easy in the British context. On the contrary, New Commonwealth immigrants came as citizens, possessing minimal civic rights that could not be easily or quickly denied. They stayed, to bear the costs of unemployment here, and with it the bitterness and growing confrontation of white racists and disaffected black youth alike. A bottom layer within the working class, the bulk of ethnic minority labour in this country experienced the poverty and insecurity of workers everywhere, but did so in a political climate within which other sections of the working class – equally insecure and long polluted by the rhetoric of empire – were as likely to turn against them as to stand with them in common struggle.

For the pattern of discrimination experienced by ethnic minorities, no less than that experienced by women, has perpetually to be reproduced; and it is. It is reproduced partly by the material situation in which white workers find themselves now, struggling to hold on to jobs and incomes in the face of recession and technological change. In that situation it is all too easy to see the newly-arrived black workers (and even their children born here, who are in truth as indigenous as white workers themselves) as a threat, to be resisted by conscious action. The very strength of that response across large sections of the white working class has rendered ineffective the formal commitments of the trade unions to the ending of racial discrimination. Instead, the lack of active trade union involvement in anti-racial struggles (and the lack of union enthusiasm for measures of positive discrimination such as quotas) has allowed employers the space to discriminate between workers by colour. Unions and employers together have established industrial relations procedures (not least in the protection of skilled jobs and the giving of seniority privileges in the event of redundancies) that have effectively discriminated against newly arrived ethnic workers. Those workers have joined trade unions in large numbers. 60 per cent of Asian male workers are currently unionized.[71] But they have found the bulk of their white

colleagues immersed in a racist culture which is so widely and deeply engrained in the 'common sense' of a post-imperial society that it surfaces perpetually in that society's media and education systems.

It also surfaces, and as such is reproduced, in the practices of the state. Each wave of immigration since the Jews has precipitated a new set of racist immigration curbs, from the 1905 Aliens Act through to the Immigration Acts of 1962, 1968, 1971 and 1982. It is true that those later acts were accompanied by legislative initiatives banning racial discrimination; banning direct discrimination in public places in 1965 and in housing and employment in 1968, and even banning indirect discrimination in those places in the 1976 Act. But that legislation has been difficult to enforce; and the commission charged with enforcement have been notoriously ineffective. Indeed, 'it has been argued that these committees have acted as a quasi-colonial buffer institution, supposedly serving as a forum for the articulation of specifically black grievances and thereby indirectly linking the black population to the political structure'. To the extent to which this is so, 'the result is that the community relations apparatus serves as an instrument of social control' rather than social change, 'ensuring and attempting to enshrine the political marginality of black migrants and their children'.[72]

In any event, the potency of such state agencies as vehicles of racial equality has been eroded by the obviously racist nature of the immigration controls that surround them. The state's posture, as a liberal institution treating its citizens with equality and justice regardless of their colour, has been rendered meaningless at the individual level by the racism of the immigration service and the police, and by the state's propensity to mobilize popular support by stressing a 'national interest' couched in terms of a special 'Englishness' whose content is blatantly white, imperialist and xenophobic. This question of the state's contribution to popular consciousness – the question of its hegemony – is a topic of such importance that we shall examine it in detail in Chapters 9 and 10. What must be understood now and instead is the way in which the administrative practices of the state are themselves heavily involved in the reproduction of racial discrimination.

Every liberal journal you open shows evidence of the daily reality of state racism: heart-rending stories of families divided by immigration officials, black kids beaten up in police cells, Asian men picked up in the street on suspicion of illegal immigration. One statistic perhaps captures some part of that, and certainly draws attention to a feature of police harassment that was to precipitate urban riots in the early 1980s. That is the arrest of black kids on suspicion – the so called 'sus law' that dates back to 1824. 'In 1977, for example, young Afro-Caribbean males, who made up only 2.2% of the total population of London, accounted for 44% of all "sus" arrests.'[73] What the black communities face in Britain is institutionalized racism, bureaucratic procedures and individual administrative decisions that single them out for particularly harsh treatment in employment, foreign travel, welfare provision and legal protection. Since the state itself is a major culprit in that institutionalized racism, the ethnic minorities cannot easily turn to its agencies for protection and support in the event of discrimination and racist attack. On the contrary, the politics of the ethnic minorities have increasingly had to become a politics geared not to seeking protection through the state so much as seeking protection against the state. In this the black communities have learned the hard way lessons about the awesomeness of state power that the rest of the labour movement is only now beginning to learn in earnest.

State policy here both reflects and accentuates the growing tension between white and black in a society in post-imperial decline. The Notting Hill riots of 1958 – 'this historic turning point in the post-war history of Caribbean labour in Britain' as they have been called[74] – brought a quick and racist response from the Conservative government, whose proposed controls ironically precipitated the very 'flood' of immigrants they were supposed to block, as people rushed here before the gates closed. The Labour Party's initial response to the 1962 Act was principled and opposed, but the defeat of Labour's Patrick Gordon Walker at Smethwick in 1964 by a racist Conservative soon persuaded the leaders of the Party of the need to moderate their stand. That retreat was further quickened by the Labour government's decision to refuse entry to Kenyan Asians caught up in East African discrimination in 1968, and by Enoch Powell's 'rivers of blood' speech in the same year.

'The period between the 1968 and 1971 Immigration Acts marks a low-water mark in race relations in Britain; and though the main focus in this period fell on the threat posed by those immigrants already here and the possibility of repatriating them, the danger of a possible fresh influx from abroad of Asians from East Africa who held British passports only added fuel to the fire.'[75] The 1971 Act nipped that 'danger' in the bud, taking away the Commonwealth citizen's right to permanent settlement here, reducing that right to the lesser one already experienced by non-Commonwealth people, of having to apply to the Home Secretary for citizenship, and having to prove four years of 'good behaviour' to get it. At a stroke by this Act, the whole status of Commonwealth immigrants changed: those who came before 1971 were 'not immigrants, they (were) settlers, black settlers'. Those 'who came after the Act (were) simply migrant workers, black migrant workers'.[76] Like 'guestworkers' elsewhere, these new migrants had to cope with extensive harassment by the agencies of the state that soured still further the already strained relations between the entire ethnic communities and the police. For 'the really tough "hassling" of the immigrant communities, the police "fishing expeditions" for illegal immigrants, the inspection of passports and documents, the routine "moving on" of groups of black youths, the heavy surveillance of ghetto areas, the raids on black social centres – dates from this period'.[77] Thereafter, and through the 1970s, the rising popularity and street activity of the National Front (it turned itself into the fourth most popular political party in the elections of 1974) pulled the Tory Party after it, to the point at which the Tory leader could openly worry in public about immigration creating a situation in which 'this country might be swamped by people with a different culture'[78] (Margaret Thatcher in 1978). Four years later her government passed a new Nationality Act that restricted automatic right of entry to Britain to people one of whose parents was British, or one of whose grandparents was born here. It should be no surprise to find that very few black Commonwealth citizens meet those requirements, but that most white ones do!

The political response by members of the ethnic minorities to this mixture of state racism, social discrimination, racial attacks and heavy unemployment has taken a number of forms. One current has attempted to deal with, and benefit from, the agencies and powers created by the laws banning discrimination. Another has concentrated on trade union action. The 1970s saw a number of industrial disputes initiated by immigrant workers, including the particularly heavily oppressed Asian women – strikes such as those at Imperial Typewriters in 1974 and at Grunwicks in 1976–7 – the first of which precipitated white racism in the local labour force, the second of which inspired the greatest show of working-class industrial solidarity since the Saltley Gates clash of 1971. Yet another current of ethnic minority politics runs into the Labour Party, there to join forces with the white Labour Left in the pursuit of effective measures against discrimination. The revolutionary Left also has its comrade organizations among the ethnic minorities, equally committed to the creation of a common black–white struggle for a non-racist socialism, but disagreeing dramatically with the Labour Party on the means of achieving it. It was that coalition that effectively countered the National Front and mobilized large numbers of young black and white kids, in the Anti-Nazi League of the mid 1970s.

The predominant response, especially among young blacks, has been neither so formal nor so charitable to the white Left. Indeed there is considerable anger against the white Left among many young blacks. Roger Ballard has argued that the predominant response to racial discrimination has been one of autonomous *ethnic* organization: the *construction* of 'ethnic colonies' in 'places such as Brixton, Brick Lane, Gerrard St., Southall, St Paul's, Foleshill, Handsworth, Moss Side, Manningham and so forth'.[79] This 'ethnicity' has been a conscious construct, a way of resisting white hostility, by the creation of self-contained and self-sustaining worlds. Within these worlds recently, and particularly within the West Indian ones of late, we have seen 'the beginning of another resistance – of black youths condemned by racism to the margins of existence and then put upon by the police. . . . By the middle of the 1970s the youth had begun to emerge as the vanguard of black struggle'.[80] Stuart Hall and his colleagues explained it in the following way:

Black youth has had to survive and make a life by choosing among the range of strategies pioneered by the first immigrant wave. But they encounter their subordination at a different stage in the historical evolution of their class. The economic and cultural responses which they have developed collectively thus differ significantly from those originally open to their parents. The first wave constructed the 'colony'; the second generation was born into the 'colony'. They are its first true progeny. They have no other home. Their parents are the bearers of that double consciousness common to all migrant classes in the period of transition; the second generation is the bearer of the exclusive consciousness of the black 'colony'. Their earliest experience is of a black enclave in an embattled position at the heart of a white society. They have grown up with racial segregation as a fact of life. . . . Black youth has also had an experience of which their parents were deprived: cultural expropriation through the school system. Better equipped in terms of educational skills to take their place beside the white peers of their own class in the ranks of skilled and semi-skilled labour, they feel the closure of the occupational and opportunity structure to them – on grounds not of competence but of race – all the more acutely. English racism, both as a material structure and as an ideological presence, cannot be explained away to them as a temporary aberration, the result of a fit of white absent-mindedness. It is how the system works. In their experience, English society *is* 'racist' – it *works through race*. They cannot avail themselves of the first-generation immigrants' principal source of optimism: that everything improves with time. In fact, things have palpably become much worse. To casual discrimination and the loss of job opportunities must now be added the political mobilisation of white hostility, new legal disabilities governing the movement of their relatives – above all, the constant pressure of police harassment on the streets. Nothing makes one aware of living in a 'colony' so much as the permanent presence of an 'occupying force'. They have no greener memories of home to turn back to: 'home' is Willesden Junction, Handsworth, Paddington, Moss Side, St Annes. These people are permanent internal exiles.[81]

As exiles in their own land, many young blacks have turned to separatist cultures (to Rastafarianism for example) and to styles of living which have brought them into conflict with a racist police force. In addition, black separatist organizations and community defence groups have emerged in response to fascist attacks, and when police harassment has proved too great, black militants have

rioted. They did so on such a scale in 1981 that they shook the liberal establishment and brought much talk of expenditure on urban renewal from a temporarily embarrassed state. The riots of April 1980 in St Pauls in Bristol were followed in April 1981 by the explosion in Brixton, and in July 1981 by riots in Southall, 'Liverpool, Manchester, Coventry, Huddersfield, Bradford, Halifax, Blackburn, Preston, Birkenhead, Ellesmere Port, Chester, Stoke, Shrewsbury, Wolverhampton, Southampton, Newcastle, High Wycombe, Knaresborough, Leeds, Hull, Derby, Sheffield, Stockport, Nottingham, Leicester, Luton, Maidstone, Aldershot and Portsmouth'.[82] This scale of urban unrest – unknown in post-war Britain – brought white and black youngsters together in a common attack on police power in the inner city. The state responded by quietly developing police preparations for riots to come. For as the police know only too well, their harassment of the black community met a changing tempo and character of resistance as the 1970s progressed. By the end of the decade 'the response had become sharper, quicker, tougher – above all, more organised, collective and *politicised*'. By the late 1970s the police faced a young black population radicalized by racism and recession, and found themselves 'responsible for controlling and containing this widespread dissatisfaction among the black population, attempting to confine it to the black areas'.[83] As the recession deepens, the scene is now set for a greater and more regular sequence of urban unrest and police repression in the years to come.

Religion and class in the politics of Northern Ireland

Finally we must consider politics in Northern Ireland. Northern Ireland remains the 'great exception' to virtually everything we have established so far about class and politics. Politics in the six counties are qualitatively different from those elsewhere in the United Kingdom in a number of crucial ways. To begin with, in the northern part of Ireland at least, religion rather than class shapes the political self-identification and social interests of large swathes of the population. On the mainland, the fact that you are either black or white, male or female, will affect your life and your political interests in a whole range of ways; but the fact that you are either Protestant or Catholic will hardly affect life or politics at all. In the six counties of Northern Ireland, on the other hand, very little else seems to matter except that people are Catholic or Protestant. 62 per cent of all Catholics and at least 46 per cent of all Protestants go to church regularly in Northern Ireland, and nowhere else in the United Kingdom is church attendance anywhere near so high.[84] Certainly nowhere else in the United Kingdom is religion so dominant a force in education (schooling is broadly segregated), housing or patterns of socializing (all of which in Northern Ireland tend to run on religious lines). Religious identity also fixes political loyalties within definite spectrums (Protestant–Unionist, Catholic–Nationalist) and those who operate outside these politico-religious boundaries are the exception, not the rule.

Furthermore, religious politics have been extremely violent again of late. In Northern Ireland, people are shot because of their religion; elsewhere in the United Kingdom that practice largely stopped around 1700. Even now, death and destruction are a regular feature of the Northern Irish political scene. So too are British soldiers. The army patrols the streets of this province as it does no other in the United Kingdom, and both police and army are now locked in a war of attrition with para-military forces dedicated to the destruction of the link with Britain. For the legitimacy of the state itself is in question in Northern Ireland, in a community internally divided and economically depressed. The recent toll of political violence in Northern Ireland con-

tinues at a level and in a manner that has no parallel elsewhere in the United Kingdom. In the seven years between 1968 and 1975, 1 per cent of all Ulstermen were either wounded or killed; at least 10 per cent of all Belfast families were forced to move to safer accommodation; there were 22,000 shooting incidents, 4500 bombs went off and house searches averaged 75,000 a year. Since then, things have eased a little, as is shown in Table 32, but the rhythm of violence continues to ebb and flow, and to persist at an unusually high level.

Presumably we are all familiar with the violence of politics in Northern Ireland, but probably not with the history from which that violence comes. That ignorance also divides the population of mainland Britain from the people of Northern Ireland, for they know particular versions of their own history, and know them extremely well. Their schools and churches see to that. As Eamomn McCann said of his own schooling, he was taught that Jesus Christ died for the Christian faith and Patrick Pearce for the Irish section of it (Pearce was shot by the British after the abortive Easter rising of 1916).[85] Protestant schools tell a different story, one that is equally partial; and this merely demonstrates that history is a crucial part of contemporary politics in the province, consciously kept alive there, not least by the ritualistic observation of the anniversaries of key events by the different sections of a divided community. This is not to say that the Irish have broken free of the politics of social class, and of the inequalities of gender and ethnic background that we have charted for the rest of the United Kingdom; nor to imply that the development of politics in Belfast and Londonderry has less to do with the logic of capitalist expansion than have politics in London or Manchester. It is to stress instead that the Irish have had a particular experience of that process of capital accumulation which continues to shape their politics in powerful and unique ways.

To understand the contemporary politics of

Northern Ireland we have to go far back in time, and recognize that political loyalties now are the legacy of a complex past of colonial rule, uneven economic development and liberation struggle. Ireland was the first, and Northern Ireland seems set fair to be the last, of England's colonies. English rule was consolidated there by the Tudors, and by Cromwell, because Ireland constituted a dangerous outpost of Catholicism (and hence a possible base for the invasion of England) in the English battle for national survival against the Catholic powers of France and Spain in the Counter-Reformation years. English rule was consolidated by different methods in the North and South. In each, after William of Orange's convincing military defeat of the Stuarts and their Irish allies at the Battle of the Boyne in 1690, Catholicism was made a bar to long-term land ownership and to entry to the professions and the state. Class and religion were locked together to guarantee English power, at the cost of destroying the Catholic gentry and allowing political leadership to move away into the hands of the Catholic clergy. Indeed, 'the tremendous political influence wielded by the Catholic church in modern Ireland has its roots in the historic elimination of alternative avenues for Catholic political participation in Irish politics'.[86] In the South, the English state made do with absentee landlordism, creating an agricultural system in which tenant farmers rack-rented an oppressed peasantry to maintain an Anglo-Irish landed ruling class. But in Ulster, the scene of the fiercest resistance to English rule, a deliberate policy of Presbyterian colonization was followed from Tudor times. Catholic land was taken over by Presbyterian farmers imported in the main from the lowlands of Scotland, and so English power was consolidated by the creation of an embattled community of peasant farmers, united by their religion and their dependence on the English state, threatened by the parallel existence of a dispossessed Irish peasantry.

Yet it was in that northern section of Ireland that the eighteenth century saw the emergence of a Presbyterian middle class who came to find the English yoke unacceptable. Like their American counterparts, they rebelled (in Ireland in 1798) against English navigation laws and religious restrictions designed to protect English and Anglican interests. But unlike their American counterparts, the United Irishmen were defeated, and the one moment in Belfast's history when Protestant politicians championed Catholic emancipation was broken by the force of English arms and by the exploitation, within the surrounding countryside, of Protestant and Catholic rivalry. It was in 1795 that the Orange Order first made its appearance, initially among Protestant artisans, then to be cautiously adopted and encouraged by their Protestant rulers because of its use to them as an instrument which could guarantee Protestant supremacy by fermenting virulent anti-Catholicism. The Orange Order must now stand as one of the oldest institutions faced by the British state, and certainly as the only one with so consistent a record of, and preoccupation with, the uniting of Protestants against Catholics of all classes.

Politics in Ireland today reflect the shape of Irish economic development in the century that followed the defeat of the United Irishmen. The Act of Union passed immediately after the abortive rebellion exposed fledgling southern Irish industry to English competition, destroyed it, and turned southern Ireland into the granary (until 1846) and later the main supplier of dairy produce to feed the English industrial revolution. In the north, Belfast industrialized – as an integral part of that English industrial revolution. Heavy industry established itself in the triangle that linked Belfast to Liverpool and the Clyde. Like those cities, Belfast drew its workers from the surrounding countryside, and like them witnessed a wave of industrial unrest against the appalling conditions of early capitalist

Table 32   *Violence in Northern Ireland*

	1971	1972	1973	1974	1975	1976	1977	1978	Jan.–March 1979	1981	1982
Shooting incidents	1,756	10,628	5,018	3,206	1,803	1,908	1,081	755	189	815	382
Explosions	1,022	1,382	978	685	399	766	366	455	90	398	219
Bombs neutralized	493	471	542	428	236	426	169	178	35	131	113
Weight of explosives (in lbs)[1]											
In explosions	10,972	47,462	47,472	46,435	13,753	17,596	2,839	5,443	2,015·5	9,621	11,198.61
Neutralized	3,001	19,978	32,450	27,094	11,159	16,252	2,188	5,860·5	559·5	9,168	7,300.23
Armed robberies	437	1,931	1,215	1,231	1,201	813	591	439	132	587	580
Amount stolen (in £s)	303,787	790,687	612,015	572,951	572,105	545,497	446,988	231,250	64,354	54,929	1,392,202
Malicious fires[2]			587	636	248	453	432	269	58	536	499
Deaths: civilians[2] (sectarian, interfactional and intra-factional assassinations shown in brackets)	115	322 (122)	171 (87)	166 (95)	216 (144)	245 (121)	69 (42)	50 (14)	7 (1)	57	57
Deaths: army/UDR	48	129	66	35	20	29	29	21	3	23	28
Deaths: RUC/RUC'R'	11	17	13	15	11	23	14	10	–	21	12
Injuries: civilians	1,838	3,813	1,812	1,680	2,044	2,162	1,027	548	113	878	328
Injuries: Army/UDR	390	578	548	483	167	264	188	117	22	140	98
Injuries: RUC/RUC'R'	315	485	291	235	263	303	183	274	51	332	99
Houses searched[3]	17,262	36,617	74,556	71,914	30,092	34,939	20,724	15,462	1,285	4,104	4,045
Finds: firearms	717	1,264	1,595	1,260	825	837	590	400	95	398	321
Finds: ammunition (in rounds)	157,944	183,410	187,399	147,202	73,604	70,306	52,091	43,511	8,419	47,070	41,453
Finds: explosives (in lbs)	2,748	41,488	38,418	26,120	11,565	21,714	3,809	2,108	744.25	7,536	5,066

Apart from the figures for deaths and explosives, a breakdown of violence over the period gives an idea of the scale of the upheaval, of the enormous outpouring in energy and resources involved. Either the shooting incidents for 1972 (over 10,000) or the house searches for 1973 (over 7000) tell a story of disruption and danger that was all the more acute by virtue of so much of it being compressed into a small area that made up many of the Catholic districts of West Belfast and the working-class ghetto areas of the Catholic towns throughout the North. Then if one thinks of all the security and legal personnel involved in the apprehension, prosecution and ultimate detention of those involved in the figures below, the scale of the war really emerges. And those figures are of course not financial. One has also to think of the figures for compensation, for injury, death or destruction.

Persons charged with serious security-type offences[2]

	31 July–31 Dec. 1972	1973	1974	1975	1976	1977	1978	Jan.– March 1979	1981	1982
Murder	32	71	75	138	120	131	60	11	48	50
Attempted murder	16	85	75	88	121	135	79	13	72	96
Firearms offences	242	631	544	460	353	301	225	49	155	173
Explosives offences	86	236	161	100	215	146	79	9	39	41
Theft act	111	186	232	314	188	203	151	42	158	130
Other	63	205	275	97	279	392	249	63	446	196
Total	531	1,414	1,362	1,197	1,276	1,308	843	187	918	686

Notes [1] Estimated weight only.
[2] Consolidated figures not available for earlier years.
[3] Includes occupied and unoccupied houses searched.

Source: T. P. Coogan *The IRA* (Fontana 1980), pp. 478–9; 'Keesings', Contemporary, Archives, vol. xxix, p. 32194.

industrialization. Local employers re-activated the Orange Order to divide that working-class response, and set Protestant against Catholic in a series of sectarian riots from the 1850s. Catholics flowed into Belfast from rural Ulster after the famine, so that by 1881 more than 30 per cent of the city's population were Catholic. 'But these Catholics were generally the lowest strata of the working population, they were mostly segregated into certain parts of the city (notably the Falls area) and they tended to be pitted against Protestant workers in fierce competition for jobs. The sectarian conflict that had precipitated the Orange movement in rural Armagh in 1795 was reproduced in a concentrated form in a mushrooming industrial city'[87] as the material base for an alliance between Protestant employers and workers was laid by the granting of differential privileges by Protestant employers to a proletarianizing Protestant peasantry.

The rising call for Home Rule from southern Ireland later in the century, and its associated promises of industrial tariffs to protect Irish industry from English competition, consolidated that alliance still further, by threatening the short-term interests of Belfast workers and employers alike. From the 1880s it turned Belfast into the key centre of resistance to Irish independence. In the process the Orange Order was transformed and revitalized, as its leadership passed from landlords and ranting clerics to major Belfast capitalists threatened with extinction by the economic consequences of the first Home Rule Bill of 1886. The class alliance between Protestant landlords and Protestant peasants that had dominated the Orange Order in its first phase was now replaced by an alliance between landowners, employers and workers. In that change, the Orange Order was 'completely and rapidly transformed, and instead of being a somewhat disreputable and obsolete survival, it became a highly respectable as well as an exceedingly powerful political organisation'.[88]

This realignment of 1886 does not figure large in contemporary Protestant mythology, which likes to trace its ancestry back to the Battle of the Boyne. But that 'ancestry' forgets the United Irishmen of 1798 and the liberal sympathies of Belfast employers before 1886. It underestimates the degree to which contemporary Orangism is a consequence of a deliberate decision to hold Protestant working class unity behind local capital by conflating opposition to Home Rule with traditional anti-Catholicism. For it was 'the introduction of the Home Rule Bill by a Nationalist-supported Liberal cabinet in London (that) caused a virtual instantaneous and universal swing of Irish Liberals to Unionism, fusing the landed aristocracy, the big bourgeoisie and the Orange lodges into a compact bloc'.[89] That compact bloc was extremely successful at the time, and remained so until the late 1960s. Although there were moments when Irish labour seemed on the edge of unification against a common class enemy (not least in the Belfast dock strike of 1907), in the end class solidarity was drowned in the divisions of religion and material interest precipitated by the call for Irish independence and orchestrated by Organism. In this way, the uneven economic development of nineteenth-century Ireland, the heavy involvement of Northern Unionists in the British Conservative Party, and the ability of those Unionists to mobilize a cross-class coalition in rebellion against Home Rule, in the end forced the partition of Ireland in 1922, and left the British state responsible for a gerrymandered Northern province in which Protestant interests were maintained only by the systematic subordination of a Catholic minority.

From the unfinished struggle for Irish independence have come the main formal patterns of contemporary Northern Irish political support. Catholic voting in the main has gone to Nationalist parties, and Protestant voting to parties committed to maintaining the separate Northern Ireland state. If that state was threatened, then history had already bequeathed the standard Protestant response: in para-military mobilization as Ulster Volunteers. Likewise the Catholic community also has its military tradition, in an IRA that dates back to the 1916 rising. In fact the UVF went into decline after 1922, because the Northern Ireland state was strong enough (and partisan enough – a Protestant state for a Protestant people) to render its existence unnecessary. Protestant supremacy in Northern Ireland was maintained through the gerrymandering of electoral districts, the persistence of religious discrimination in jobs and housing, and Protestant dominance of the local police force (the RUC) and its auxiliary B specials. Even the Catholic community shed its active support for the IRA in the face of the apparent permanence of the Northern Ireland statelet; and the IRA border campaign of 1956–62 was so unsuccessful that it precipitated a move away from armed struggle towards quasi-Marxist popular politics. Indeed, even the traditional Catholic nationalist vote was slipping away towards the newly-formed SDLP by 1970. So if this book had been written two decades ago, the history of Ireland would have seemed irrelevant to explain anything other than the rituals of Northern Irish political life and the apparently anachronistic demagoguery of a young Ian Paisley.

However, things have changed and that history has reasserted itself. At the base of those changes lie the declining fortunes of the Northern Ireland economy. The industries on which that economy was built – particularly shipbuilding and textiles – were those which led the first long wave of capitalist industrialization in the nineteenth century, and are now in terminal decline, incapable of sustaining employment even for the Protestant sections of the Northern Irish working class. So even at the height of the post-war boom, unemployment in the province was capable of touching 10 per cent and by then was threatening the capacity of the Unionist coalition to

hold on to its working-class base. As a result, Northern Irish politics in the 1960s was dominated by the tentative reforms introduced by the liberal wing of Ulster Unionism under Terence O'Neil, reforms that sought new economic outlets through greater connections with a reviving South and with multinational companies not so sensitive to local employment practices. By the 1960s too, the 1940s expansion of welfare (particularly the provision of higher education) that Northern Ireland had inherited from the Attlee Government, had produced a generation of Catholic middle-class youth – no longer willing to bear in silence the discrimination tolerated reluctantly by the generation before. Seeing an opportunity for reform at the hands of O'Neil, the Catholic students of the *People's Democracy* marched to demand it; and seeing the seeds of betrayal at the hands of reformist Unionism, the Paisleyite wing of the Protestant ascendancy moved to block it. Caught between the two in the demonstrations of 1968, the local B specials reacted with their usual partisan sectarianism, attacking civil rights demonstrators under the watchful eye of the world's television cameras, and raising Catholic fears again of Protestant pogroms to come. To forestall those, a Labour government that had hitherto neglected Northern Irish politics almost entirely responded by sending in the army to hold the two communities apart, and by insisting on civil rights reforms to remove the worst abuses of Protestant control.

From that moment, the British state has been directly involved in the politics of Northern Ireland. Debate rages on the Left about how best to characterize that intervention:[90] whether to see it as directly *imperialist*, seeking to maintain the hold of British capital on Northern Ireland by reconstituting Protestant power, or as merely *neo-colonialist*, content to produce any settlement that will restore social order and facilitate the revival of capital accumulation. There is just too great a distance between the British state and the Protestant power structure in Ulster to permit any easy characterization of the situation as conventionally imperialist. Power-sharing between the two communities, not the re-establishment of untrammelled Protestant control, has been the persistent goal of state policy since 1968; and successive British governments have pushed funds into Northern Ireland in an attempt to raise employment and output there. But the 'autonomy' of state policy here has been relative, not absolute. It has been the Catholic community, not the Protestant one, which has borne the brunt of army harassment, and it is with the militant wing of Catholic nationalism – the Provos and the INLA – that the army has been primarily concerned. Indeed after a brief flirtation with IRA negotiations in 1972, 1974 and 1975, the British state has steadfastly refused to treat IRA activity as political rather than criminal, and has set as its goal the re-establishment of a local political structure to be tied to the United Kingdom for as long as the majority Protestant community requires it.

In pursuit of that goal, the British state has come into increasing conflict with a revitalized IRA. When the B specials charged into Catholic ghettos in 1968, the IRA was not there to defend Catholic housing and people because it had effectively disarmed itself in its retreat from militarism after 1962. But the helplessness of the Catholic communities in the face of the B specials reactivated community support for an IRA that now split between a moderate Official and a more traditionally militaristic Provisional wing. The growing subordination to Stormont influence of the British army brought those Provos into increasingly violent conflict with the security forces; and the parallel nervousness of Protestant extremists manifested itself in the creation and growth of the para-military UDA. The British government sought a military solution to the IRA (through the re-

introduction of internment in August 1981) that only strengthened Catholic opposition further; and its attempts to force power-sharing on the Protestant community were defeated by Protestant working-class action in the general strike of May 1974. Since then, politics in the province has been totally stalemated. The Catholic military struggle for independence has been met by army repression and UDA counter-violence. Protestant intransigence has split the Unionist coalition, as the moderates willing to share power have been disowned by the die-hard Unionist core. That division has eroded the credibility of centre and moderate Catholic forces calling for dialogue with the Protestant community, strengthening instead Catholic support for IRA intransigence and military struggle.

In Northern Ireland more than anywhere else, the British state faces an impasse of incompatible social and military forces. Voting patterns in the province are remarkably stable and divided. At the first Stormont election in 1921, Unionism took 66.9 per cent of the votes. At the final Stormont election in 1969, it took 67.4 per cent. Unionist votes (though now divided between a number of Unionist parties) still totalled 54.8 per cent of the entire vote for the Northern Ireland convention in 1975, and 52.73 per cent of the vote for James Prior's Assembly in October 1982. The Catholic vote for the SDLP was steady at 23.7 per cent in the 1975 poll, and although it slipped away in 1982 (to 18.79 per cent), the main beneficiaries of its decline were not the parties of the Centre (the Alliance took its usual 9 per cent) but Provisional Sinn Fein. They took 10.15 per cent of the poll and won five seats.

In the face of that stalemate, the British state has oscillated between political and military initiatives. It has launched a series of so far abortive attempts to create a new executive power within Northern Ireland acceptable to moderate opinion within both communities, while refusing to contemplate

Irish unity without majority Northern Irish support. Yet even this contemplation has blocked Protestant participation in those political initiatives, just as the promise of what is effectively a Protestant veto on Irish unity has prevented full Catholic involvement. In that impasse, the British state has dropped back increasingly to a military solution. It has steadily 'Ulsterfied' its security presence – incrementally shifting back military power to local Protestant police control – and it has developed and refined its own methods of community control, forging for itself an expertise in social repression that it might one day use elsewhere.

'Since 1969 repression has been developed considerably. The military and para-military agencies of the state have rapidly grown in size and become much more sophisticated', such that 'if ancillary security agencies and personnel are included, this means that someone is employed in policing "the troubles" for every 38 persons in Northern Ireland'.[91] In the course of those 'troubles' too, the state has taken to itself emergency powers (in the 1974 Prevention of Terrorism Act which passed through Parliament in just twenty-four hours after the Birmingham bombings of that year), created special courts in Northern Ireland (the Diplock courts) where conventional rights of jury trial do not apply, and regularly engaged in the use of interrogation techniques which the European Court of Human Rights denounced in 1978 as 'inhuman and degrading' – as, in effect, *torture* in the old-fashioned meaning of the term. As the military wing of the IRA struggles for Irish independence, it has posed serious questions of political support for the rest of the British Left. It has also encouraged the British state to develop habits to which the Left as a whole may yet one day be exposed. These too are themes – this rise of a strong and potentially repressive state and the unfinished question of Irish independence – to which we shall return in the last chapter.

9 Social stability and hegemonic politics

We have covered a great deal of ground so far, and it may be that our initial purpose of explaining the character of modern politics and the role of the contemporary state is in danger of being lost in the sheer complexity of the universe within which that state operates. Yet as we have seen, that complexity is itself a vital feature of contemporary political life, making the job of governments difficult because of the multiplicity of pressures to which it gives rise; but also, as we shall see, making government vital (and giving the state a central role) as *the* institution within society which is able to co-ordinate and consolidate coalitions of such pressures, as it acts to mould the balance of class forces and to allay popular-democratic struggles to which the contradictions within its complex social universe give rise. Yet before we look at the state in detail, to see it doing that, there remains one constellation of features of its economic and social context that we have not yet addressed directly: namely *the extent to which that context governs itself*, through the reproduction there of patterns of human action and social practices which are sustained by broadly distributed and largely shared clusters of attitude and belief. In other words, we have yet to look at the area of *social stability*, at the way in which the key social relationships of a complex capitalist society are *reproduced*, and at the extent to which central to that reproduction stand institutions and practices that are *hegemonic* in their character and role.

This may seem complicated, but in essence it is very simple. We have charted already a complex array of economic processes and institutions, social positions and experiences. It should now be clear that those generate (and are themselves shaped by) particular sets of *social interests* and *political demands*. It should be clear too that, because those positions and experiences are different, so too are the interests and demands to which they give rise. Moreover, because the positions and experiences dominant in this society are also unequal in quality and range, the interests and demands that result from them may be expected not simply to differ in general, but to do so in particular in the degree of conservatism or radicalism which they contain. And they do. Governments face groups demanding an increase in privilege or committed to the defence of existing patterns. They also face (normally more intermittently and with less leverage) groups seeking a quite fundamental equalization of the social distribution of resources. Yet for all that diversity and disagreement, governments also find a broad consensus across groups on a whole range of social practices and political activities. Governments find that, for all the inequality and instability experienced by the most deprived sections of the community, any radicalism which results is relatively muted, and the legitimacy of the entire social order (and of their role as governors within it) is only very occasionally challenged. When that challenge comes – as now in the occupied counties in the north of Ireland, as elsewhere in the empire in earlier times – government becomes very difficult indeed; but if we are to understand why the state elsewhere in the

United Kingdom is more gently treated by its subjects, we need to explore more generally the sources of social stability in contemporary capitalism, locate the content of whatever degree of social consensus exists, and probe the mechanisms which hold together that consensus.

This is only a problem, of course, if you expect a society such as ours to show more internal dissension than in fact is the case; and is not a problem at all for those who, schooled in liberal-pluralist traditions of scholarship, expect societies to hang together naturally around a set of commonly-held central values and mutually-respected institutions. Indeed, such a view of how a society naturally functions is, and has been, dominant in English Conservative thought from at least the time of Edmund Burke, and was the unexamined assumption of the vast majority of academic political sociology produced here in the 1950s and early 1960s, when the writings of Talcott Parsons in particular moulded the literature of an entire generation of scholarship in the social sciences. But that Parsonian dominance has now totally gone, a casualty in part of the re-emergence of the very contradictions of economic process and social structure in late capitalism discussed in the previous eight chapters, a casualty too of a revival within the faculties of social science of a commitment to Marxist explanations of just those contradictions. But if Marxism's impact on a new generation of scholarship has grown precisely because it is so good at explaining why governments now are so beset with problems, Marxism too has its weaknesses. For it has to explain why, if the social order of late capitalism is so riddled with contradictions, the social forces committed to its replacement by a democratic socialism are so weak. If the problem for liberal scholarship of late has been the re-emergence of generalized social conflict and economic instability, the problem for Marxism has been the persistence of generalized stability and the weakness of

the revolutionary current in contemporary political life.

There are, of course, Marxist explanations as to why the Left is weak, and why the dominant political groups within the Left tend to be situated towards the conservative end of the socialist spectrum. At their least elegant, those explanations focus on the weakness of political leadership on the Left – and in Britain on the failure of the Labour Party in particular to clarify correctly the nature of the socialist task. This type of explanation has its place, and will be met again in Chapter 11, when we look at ways forward for the Left in the remaining years of the century. What we need to recognize now, however, is that there are more sophisticated explanations, ones that stress the absence within the working class as a whole of any generalized interest in more radical political projects. Those explanations, as we shall see, will stress material, social and political factors – questions of prosperity, cross-cutting patterns of social division, commitments to parliamentary institutions created by working-class struggle. They will stress too how capitalism (like all class societies) fulfils certain *general* needs (not least material existence and physical security) through its exploitative structures; and so attracts to itself general support (even from its exploited classes) precisely because its claim to be concerned with the carrying out of essential social functions is not totally fraudulent. Industrial investment, for example, is not just investment for capital and profits. It has a social function also.[1] Indeed on this argument, the distinctive feature of class societies is that common interests can be pursued *only* through structures that are exploitative. The material needs of society as a whole can be met only through a system of production which depends upon private initiative and control. Physical security for the majority can be attained only by structures which reinforce the wealth of the minority, and so on. It is in this way that the interests of the majority are 'inevitably drawn into support of class institutions as well as in to opposition to them', with the result that the legitimacy of an unequal society gathers a genuinely 'popular' base without any direct or conscious ideological penetration and manipulation.

Yet what we must also recognize is that the capacity of class institutions to meet such general needs is always accidental and limited, and that as a result popular support is inherently brittle and restricted. Investment decisions in a capitalist society, for example, are geared primarily to profits and capital accumulation, and serve a social function adequately (if they do so at all) only secondarily and within the constraints imposed by the competitive struggle between capitalist units. In such a society, the generalized support of the majority of the population for processes so intimately connected with the maintenance of privilege can therefore never be automatic and total, but will turn in the end on the balance and content of ideas, attitudes and values in a society divided by basic contradictions between classes. For that reason many Marxist explanations of capitalist stability have in the end come to stress, as I want to stress here, the distinct impact of *ideas* themselves. They say that the stability of capitalism in Britain in the last quarter of the twentieth century rests eventually on the ability of conservative patterns of thought to 'drown out' in the minds of the disadvantaged the otherwise radicalizing impact of their daily experience of relative deprivation. Capitalism is still stable, and the Left weak, because and to the extent that the capitalist class persuades workers of all sorts that the existing social order is natural, inevitable, reformable and just; and that responsibility for the inequality and instabilities within it rest with those most exposed to them, having nothing to do with the existence of privilege as such. Capitalism is stable, that is, because the bourgeoisie are a *hegemonic* class; and the task of the Left is to replace that hegemony with a socialist one of its own.

Class position and prevailing patterns of thought

For politicians face more than inanimate economic and social processes, or well organized institutions and groups. They face people – people who do more than simply act as 'bearers' in their own lifetime of the experience and interests associated with the class position they occupy, the institutions in which they serve, and the role given to them in the spheres of consumption and social reproduction. People are 'bearers' of those things of course, but they also carry sets of ideas, beliefs and values – whole ideologies, conceptions of life and even coherent world views – which are not simply to be read off as the ideational equivalent of the social experiences, class positions and political interests they are used to define and comprehend. People have a certain range of factual information about the economic and social structures surrounding them, and about their character and history. They have a particular vocabulary within which to conceptualize themselves, their position, their needs and those of others. They have a particular moral code – a sense of what does and does not constitute legitimate and illegimate modes of behaviour, both in society as a whole and in the political sphere in particular. People possess too a whole apparatus of inherited notions, languages, symbols and codes, within which to render intelligible themselves and their universe.

This is not to say that all this is necessarily consciously held, or that the entire content of such systems of thought is always, or even often, intellectually coherent and consistent. In fact, neither of these things is likely to be true. It is not uncommon for analysts to differentiate belief systems by their range, centrality, persistence, internal coherence and degree of conscious articulation. There are clearly opinions, attitudes and beliefs that differ in their persistence and centrality for those who hold them. It seems worthwhile too to differentiate *common sense* (a set of relatively unquestioned and invariably 'eclectic and disjointed'[2] ideas *and* practices) from more consciously constructed *ideologies* and philosophies, and to distinguish them both from the *hegemony* of an entire set of social views and practices associated with the dominance of a particular class.

Armed with these distinctions it is possible to recognize that each age will have both its 'common sense', its set of unquestioned axioms and associated social practices, and its own range of more consciously constructed and internally coherent ideologies – ideologies that are used by intellectuals (in the service of particular political parties and their associated social classes) to legitimate or change those common sets of thought and practice. It is also possible to recognize that the precise content of that 'common sense', and the degree of exposure to different and more coherent ideologies, is likely to vary across the society between classes, and between gender, racial and generational groups. This may be recognized while stressing also that this 'ideational' dimension of social reality has its own autonomy – its own history, content, mechanisms of reproduction and political significance – which mean that it cannot be reduced to, and subsumed under, some more 'material' specification of social position and interests. As we shall see, the ideas people hold have definite material consequences, and at times can be consciously manipulated for class reasons; such that the class interests of the privileged are best served by the generalized dominance of one kind of 'common sense' as distinct from another. But class position does not dictate in any automatic way the patterns of thought that prevail among those who occupy any one class position. Indeed, as Stuart Hall has observed:

ideologies are linked to interest and position, but not in a simple relation of correspondence. Workers can define their 'interests' within *different* ideologies (and) since groups can be attached to and detached from different ideologies, it matters greatly *which* ideologies they identify with; for that will help to determine how they see their relation to society – and thus what they do.[3]

Were it not so, and were class positions totally defining of ideas and practices, then the consciousness of the dispossessed would long ago have swept away capitalism. That profoundly unequal social order only persists here because, and to the degree that, people in subordinate strata are open to patterns of belief that *both* service their own immediate situation and help to reproduce the structures of their own subordination. For it is not enough, if capitalism is to survive, 'to reproduce the places secured for agents in the process of production . . . it is also necessary to confer upon those agents not only knowledge and ability but also a subjectivity which they will need to fulfil, without questioning, the roles assigned to them'.[4] It is for this reason that processes of general and political socialization – the training of individuals to accept and play out a particular set of roles – are crucial to social stability; and that ideologies are vital, in 'constituting concrete individuals as subjects'[5] in ways that are functional to the reproduction of capitalist relations of production and their associated civil society.

British political culture

There is plenty of contemporary evidence to support the claim that the vast majority of people in Britain, regardless of their class, gender, race or geographical location, agree on many important things. They certainly demonstrate a quite remarkable and consistent unanimity whenever they are questioned in the street about whatever set of issues is currently preoccupying the privileged and the powerful in this society. We are all too familiar, no doubt, with the repeated capacity of even trade union members to assert their belief that the unions have too much power; of the poor to put law and order (or inflation) higher than unemployment on their list of political priorities, or of vast sections of public opinion to see in the slaughter of Argentinians in the Malvinas clear proof of the strength of Britain and the importance of its world role and contribution to freedom and civilized living.

The degree of unanimity on such questions is never total – and that is important as we shall see – but it is high, and sits alongside a similarly marked propensity for a general consensus on the desirability and legitimacy of existing political institutions and conventions as a whole (on the viability of the monarchy, the democratic nature of the parliamentary state, the illegitimacy of the use of industrial power for political ends, and so on). Here too there is dissent to a degree. It is possible to find an occasional republican in mainland England, or a socialist as offended by the political power of the City as are his contemporaries by that of the unions. The voting system has lately lost much public credibility because of its systematic under-representation of the Liberals and SDP. Acceptance of parliamentarianism seems quite compatible with a general sense of how difficult it is for individuals, as citizens and voters, to shape the detail of national policy. But there is no widespread constituency for radical constitutional change: and politics is for most people a marginal aspect of their existence, about which they think little and talk less. This is not an actively politicized (in the sense of a participatory) society. Indeed, and instead, it is possible to find at least a resigned acceptance of, and quite often an enthusiastic commitment to, the existing social order and its central economic and social processes.

'The free play of market forces' is invariably taken as inherently superior to and more desirable than the planning of economic life; and private property inherently more legitimate than collective ownership. The possibility of achieving 'a fair days wage for a fair days work' in a capitalist society goes largely unquestioned, and indeed the vocabulary of an alternative perspective is largely unknown to the vast majority of those who are denied precisely that fairness. People talk not of 'accumulation' but of 'investment', not of 'capital' but of 'profit', and not of 'capitalism' but 'the economy'. Instead of drawing on the rich reservoir of radical terminology, politics is unashamedly discussed by the vast majority of English people, if it is discussed at all, in terms of a 'national interest' which governments are generally granted the unique capacity to specify. It is a national interest which is generally understood (with critical exceptions in Ireland as we have seen) as centring on the strength of the British military and economic presence abroad, and on the preservation of existing institutions (and hence inequalities) at home. The vast majority of people think of themselves as British in a quite distinct way: that to be British is to be white, powerful internationally, tolerant, moderate and reasonable at home; and that to be British establishes a point of contact and identification that transcends the division of class, gender and religion, in a common unity against the inadequate foreigner and in a common heritage of national pride and imperial glory. The cement of conservatism in the British political culture lies in this particular sense of nationalism – a potent sense of national identification coloured by a particular reading of Britain's immediate past as an imperialist power now in decline.

This is not to deny that, going down the social hierarchy, there is a growing sense of class division. People use the language of 'class' with more or less facility to locate themselves and their interests. But that sense of class is again very distinctive. It clearly coexists with well-established sets of sexist and racist ideas and practices in large sections of the population as a whole. It is clearly compatible with the acceptance of the broad shape of inequalities as at least inevitable and possibly desirable; and it coexists with the absence of any strong sense of class interests as revolutionary. On the contrary, it is precisely that dimension of class radicalism which is broadly missing from the thinking and aspirations of the vast majority of the British working class. What there is instead is a highly instrumental and calculative sense of class, and of class institutions, and a highly privatized set of individual and family ambitions.

Such attitudes can at times sustain considerable industrial militancy, but in my lifetime have yet to be translated into political radicalism of any significant and sustained kind. So when Goldthorpe and Lockwood went to probe these issues in Luton twenty years ago, the picture they drew of a 'new', 'instrumental' and 'privatized' working class dedicated to earning more money, to enhancing family health and happiness, and to using trade unions and even the Labour Party merely as means to such private ends – was roundly condemned as too industrially quiescent and politically moderate in its thrust, and too romantic in its implied heroic age (now gone) when a truly traditional proletarian class-conscious labour force stalked the land. Yet although those strictures were sound, it is true that two decades later, in a year in which more skilled workers voted Tory than Labour in a general election fought on a radical Labour programme, the central if partial truth of the Luton findings remains: that this is a society in which the visible sense of class division is not easily productive of any generalized challenges (even industrially and certainly not politically) to the pattern of inequality to which we are all subject, and from which, without that radicalism, there will be no escape.

Given all that, it is tempting to write off the political project of the Left as hopeless, to characterize the British political culture as inherently and irredeemably conservative, and even – if your politics are equally moderate – to welcome the existence in Britain of a 'civic culture',[6] a particular kind of orientation to politics in the mass of the population as a whole that leaves them committed to democratic institutions without wishing to participate overmuch within those institutions. Yet such a conservative complacency would be misplaced for at least three reasons: first because it ignores the changing material base of conservative culture, and the degree to which such survey findings, though real enough in their day, were gathered in the main in the years of the long boom, before the return of generalized recession eroded the confidence that those attitudes articulated in the bounty of a market economy; second because that 'civic culture' was never total in its coverage and support, and is less so now than it was then. The 'nationalism' at its core was never acceptable to at least sections of the Catholic community in Northern Ireland, and was challenged too by counter-nationalisms in Scotland and in Wales in the mid 1970s. If the civic culture ever existed, it was a distinctly English phenomenon. Even here – as a third ground for left-wing optimism – it was never based, for the vast majority of the working class at least, on anything more than a *pragmatic acquiescence* of the status quo – a conservatism rooted that is, not in conviction but in the absence of a coherent alternative.[7]

For against the reports of a consensual society created by the reports on a 'civic culture' has to be set the considerable evidence, some of which was discussed in Chapter 7, of the existence of more radical views of a relatively underdeveloped and incoherent kind. 'The continued imperviousness of Western capitalism to radical social change does not imply that workers have become normatively integrated into the system. There is a fair amount of consensus among the rulers', in Michael Mann's words, but it 'does not extend very far down the stratification system'.[8] In fact, Mann's general findings are worth citing, namely that:

1   value consensus does not exist to any significant degree

2   there is a greater degree of consensus among the middle class than among the working class
3   the working class is more likely to support deviant values if those values relate either to concrete everyday life or to vague populist concepts than if they relate to an abstract political philosophy
4   working class individuals also exhibit less internal consistency in their values than middle class people.[9]

What is striking about the political consciousness of the English people, moving down the social hierarchy, is the extent to which they demonstrate a fractured or dual consciousness of their situation. Alongside a formal articulation of conventional orthodoxies sit beliefs in the excessive power of business and the special leverage enjoyed by the rich. Alongside intensely racist and sexist attitudes and practices sit commitments to human dignity and equality of rights and opportunities. Alongside the commitment to parliamentary democracy and its codes lies the belief that ordinary people have no political power, politicians no special status, and the legal system no capacity to treat rich and poor alike. The status quo is tolerated because it is there, and because no obvious alternative exists with which to replace it. But survey after survey shows that the *normative* commitment to prevailing institutions is something which middle and upper class people show in large numbers. Among the dispossessed the orientation is that of resignation and cynicism far more than of positive identification. This is coupled there with 'an extremely accurate subjective perception of the objective reality of the class system in Britian' that 'in British society now, as ever, money is a divider of persons, money *gives* power, money *is* power'.[10] Indeed, the predominant pattern of action and belief across the working class as a whole is of 'a failure to question the dominant generalised philosophies of society, conjoined with a cynical attitude towards those in positions of power and a readiness to engage in actions (going on strike, for example) deprecated by other sections of society'.[11]

This is of course still an immense source of political stability, but it suggests that its existence is as much a product of the failure of the Left to harness that cynicism and sporadic resistance behind a new alternative as it is of some inexorable process of social cohesion. It suggests too that Frank Parkin is correct in arguing that what politicians face in Britain is actually a dominant value system – one identified with and articulated by people in middle and upper class positions – which is then orchestrated downwards as the dominant framework of belief made available to subordinate classes. 'Parkin sees the situation as one in which dominant values are negotiated to fit the realities of working class life so producing accommodative responses, meaning that inequalities and deprivations may be accepted, but fatalistically rather than enthusiastically.'[12] The impact of such dominant values at lower levels is enhanced by the material prosperity of the society they legitimate. Their impact there is enhanced too by the absence of any convincing alternative, by the power and penetration of the channels and élites that orchestrate them, and by the existence within sections of the working class of traditions of deference and loyalty which have not been replaced there, as they have in other sections of the class, by the self-confidence created by industrial concentration, communal unity, trade union organization and industrial militancy.

But the impact of such a dominant value system is never total. Its credibility is continually eroded by the gap between its claims and the harshness and insecurity of the daily reality it would legitimate. Its penetration is restricted too by the degree of working class industrial organization and class struggle in which subordinate strata participate, and can thus be expected to vary over time, between areas, and in relation to the kind of left-wing political leadership made available to the class. Even in the absence of such countervailing forces, its penetration will be mediated by differences of language, life-style, and ambitions induced by the very class structure that the dominant value system would have us ignore. As Bob Jessop observed:

it is in the nature of socialisation and communication in class stratified societies that belief systems are not successfully transmitted as unchanging, unbroken packages. Inequalities in linguistic and communicative competence, in the social distribution of knowledge, in locations within communication networks, and in the primacy of different needs and interests (derived in turn from inequalities in the distribution of power and rewards) all combine to inhibit successful transmission of meaning systems and to encourage the re-interpretation and innovation of elements within them.[13]

What happens to dominant value systems, as they percolate down the social structure, is that they are 'not so much rejected or opposed as modified by the subordinate classes as a result of their social circumstances and restricted opportunities'.[14] Social stability persists as a result only so long as that 're-negotiation' continually and successfully takes place – just so long, that is, as it is not blocked by the insertion between the dominant and subordinate classes of a radical and coherent alternative. The task of the Left is first to recognize that this is in fact so, that the political universe it faces is less one of normative consensus than of an articulation of dominant and subordinate value systems in need of 'disarticulation' by a radical insertion of a socialist kind. Then the Left must see too how that conservative and stabilizing articulation emerges, how it is sustained, and how it can be broken.

The pattern of hegemonic politics in Britain

That a particular set of values and beliefs should have such a powerful influence on the thinking of vast numbers of people in Britain is a product of a particular pattern of hegemonic politics. The term 'hegemony' derives in its modern usage on the Left from the work of Antonio Gramsci, and has been the subject of considerable recent controversy. Gramsci used the term in a number of slightly different ways, as part of his explanation of why the Russian Revolution failed to spread across Western Europe after 1917. He drew the attention of the Left to the ability of a complex capitalist society to stabilize itself not simply through a reliance on force, but through the voluntary compliance of exploited classes. Capitalist society was 'hegemonic' in this sense because, and to the degree that, its central practices and social relationships were treated as natural and inevitable by those subject to them.[15] It was stable too to the degree that its ruling class was also a hegemonic force, able to project its class interests as the 'neutral' interests of the society as a whole, able to absorb and partially accommodate (through the granting of genuine concessions) the conflicting interests of subordinate classes, and able to mobilize institutions in the state and civil society which could articulate and reproduce the consensual patterns that its dominance required. Such a ruling class, precisely because it was able 'through ideological struggle to articulate to its hegemonic principle the majority of the important ideological elements of a given society' created stability through its capacity to 'create a determinate conception of the world and to establish a certain "definition of reality" which (was) accepted by those over whom hegemony (was) exercised'.[16] Finally, stability turned also on the absence of a counter-hegemonic force among the dispossessed, and the consolidation instead within the proletariat of politial leaderships and cultural patterns that induced that class voluntarily to subordinate its demands and practices to the axioms and interests of the dominant order. In sum then, hegemony in a Gramscian sense refers to the 'predominance obtained by consent rather than force of one class/group over other classes; and it is obtained through the myriad ways in which the institutions of civil society operate to shape, directly or indirectly, the cognitive and affective structures whereby men (sic) perceive and evaluate problematic social reality'.[17] Capitalism in Britain has been stable this long because its social system has been hegemonic in that complex and three-sided sense.

Capitalism in Britain is certainly hegemonic in the first sense. The formal equality that we each enjoy as consumers helps to obscure the profound inequalities of income, job experience and power that alone facilitate the accumulation of capital in the process of production that precedes consumption. The 'noisy sphere'[18] of individual exchange – what Marx called the exclusive realm of Freedom, Equality, Property and Bentham – precisely because it is a sphere of human existence under capitalism in which people are encouraged to act in terms of private self-interest, provides a powerful set of material experiences with which to underpin commitments to liberal and market perspectives in the consciousness even of the proletariat. 'In short, to adopt a phrase from Althusser himself, this "noisy sphere" provides the basis in which men are forced to "live an imaginery relation" of equivalence and individualism that actually stands in stark contrast with their real (non-equivalent, collective) conditions of existence';[19] and as such, disguises the 'hidden abode' of capitalist production, and works against the creation of a collective consciousness of proletarian solidarity.

Moreover, this fetishism of commodities – not only in the sphere of consumption but also in that of technology in the labour process itself – the extent to which we feel subject to the dictates of machines and wage goods as 'things' rather than to the privileged élites whose rule they enshrine – all that acts too as a powerful barrier to the full recognition of how

capitalist inequality has to be reconstituted on a daily basis through the playing out of social relationships that are inherently exploitative. Indeed, it is possible to trace 'the development of two ideologies of abstract individualism, one arising within the process of exchange and one within the labour process. Each has fetishism as its necessary correlate, so to speak, for each directly identifies social relations with things, precisely by conceiving of people as individuals in abstraction from their social connection'.[20] This is capitalism's real strength: that 'the general conditions of production, applicable equally to all, and expressed through an impersonal mechanism, do not present themselves to the producers as something which they by their actions are continually reproducing, but as general conditions which are mysteriously independent of them, a social nexus which is imposed upon them from outside',[21] by 'technology', 'the market' or 'the facts of economic life'. Capitalism is so stable, that is, because its own structures and practices obscure its true class character, inducing people to believe that to be free is to be subject to the accident of things – things which, perceived by their victims in fetishized form (see, that is, as 'things') are not recognized for the class relationships which in fact they are.

The dull logic of market forces – the 'coercion of the workplace (and) the routine of everyday life'[22] – in a society dominated by capitalist exchange and production relations, helps to induce a fatalism in those who suffer most from them. 'The constraints of the market are matters of cognition rather than evaluation, taken for granted as part of (workers') conceptualisation of society or learnt from experience.'[23] Faced with a painful and unpredictable reality that is difficult to control, the tendency of many is not to radicalize but to acquiesce. Indeed, Michael Mann has argued convincingly that the longer depriving work goes on, the more likely we are to see the individual worker 'come to terms with his life in a pragmatic, adjustive way'. As Mann says, 'this non-normative acceptance seems to be generalised to his attitudes as a whole. The most frequent defence mechanism is fatalism. The most deprived workers develop fatalistic views about life in general: they feel their work life cannot be changed because they lack the necessary abilities, or because the bosses have always exploited the workers, or even because of the inherent selfishness of man'.[24]

Even where that fatalism is disturbed by class resistance and struggle, the accommodation of such resistance in the limited degree of trade union bargaining space allowed by capital helps to reinforce that defensive fatalism, encouraging workers to feel satisfied with (or at least relieved to get) marginal shifts in income that impersonal market forces can then quietly erode. For the very scale of the task involved in qualitative social change is itself a key element in the persistence of social inequality. 'The massive constraining quality of everyday life resists change or challenge.'[25] The act of challenge is so time consuming and so arduous that even the most committed challengers are under heavy and persistent pressure to lower their sights and to exaggerate their victories – in a process of social accommodation made easier by the manner in which the 'hidden nature' of capitalist exploitation is enshrined in a wage contract whose procedural fairness obscures the substantive inequalities which it in fact embodies. Indeed the main effect of these seemingly 'natural' economic processes is less to fill the minds of workers with particular ideas than to block the formulation of coherent alternative visions and to erode working-class self-confidence. A universe lived and understood in fetishized terms is difficult to see as a whole. A reality experienced as overwhelming in its immediate pressure and beyond immediate control is a reality which eats away at radical self-confidence. In both senses, and long before any ruling class began to articulate its

own vision and to suppress its own critics, the task of socialist transformation had already been made much harder than socialists had initially expected, by the sheer tenacity and particular character of capitalism's daily routines.

Yet of course the 'impersonal' processes within capitalism are inherently contradictory. They do not merely induce confusion, apathy and resignation, but also generate the material and social base for their own transcendence. The capacity of the wage form to obscure exploitation is challenged by the daily rigours of the capitalist labour process. The power of consumerism to anaesthetize class tension is eroded even in late capitalism by instabilities of employment and the steady pressure on working-class living standards. As an anaesthetic it was in any case much weaker at earlier stages of capitalist development, when levels of real deprivation were necessarily much higher for the mass of the working class as a whole. Even the formal equality of individuals as consumers and citizens is visibly eroded by the inequalities of power and wealth consolidated by the accumulation process. Because that is so, ruling classes have felt the need to do more than to rely on the dull logic of the market to protect their position. They have acted, quite consciously, to establish and protect a hegemony that might otherwise so easily evaporate.

The content of ruling-class hegemony has changed down the years. The nineteenth-century struggle for middle-class political power left the early English proletariat exposed to a self-confident bourgeoisie articulating the axioms of *laissez-faire* liberalism, with the assertiveness and self-righteousness which only that class's temporary world monopoly could sustain. Mid Victorian England was, after all, the period of 'the pervasive power of bourgeois ideas about economic life and the absence of theoretically-articulated alternatives', and in which 'the terrain of the state and of public discussion and policy making was

. . . reshaped by the intellectuals of the industrial bourgeoisie'.[26] Of course, the power bloc dominant in mid Victorian England was riven (as power blocs invariably are) by divisions of strategy and tactics: broadly between 'a conservative . . . bloc of big urban and rural property . . . (and) a radical-liberal bloc of urban classes and strata, finding its ideological cohesion in hostility to the "aristocracy"'.[27] As a result, the hegemonic ideas and practices to which the working class were subject 'had differentiated versions and interpretations, and (were) constantly argued out and reformulated within the ruling class'.[28] In their detail and application they were a perennial cause of contention between conservative and radical elements within the dominant coalition of classes and fractions. For all their differences of detail, however, both conservatives and radicals were committed to the extension of industrial capital, and each presided in turn over that crucial mid century watershed by the end of which an entire generation of workers had been habituated to the labour processes and wage relationships of industrial capital. The fight *against* capitalism was lost with the defeat of Chartism; and the incorporating logic of 'dull market forces' (of the kind we have just discussed) then came fully into play, and did so in a mid century period that was in addition characterized by the 'immersion' of Victorian wage labour in an 'ideological gale' of self-help, *laissez-faire* liberalism and religious evangelism.

It was in this period that the Conservative Party too came to terms with industrial capital, beginning to build bridges between its land-owning base and the emerging class of industrial owners who would later be weaned away from liberalism as the Liberal Party's coalition of capital and skilled labour disintegrated under the impact of working class militancy and war. Toryism prior to 1844 had contained a strong paternalistic and anti-capitalist strain; but from the 1850s even the Tory sense of 'two nations' was subordinated to a common Victorian liberalism – one with its own quite distinct political theory and social practices. The social codes of the Victorian bourgeoisie were generalized downwards, stressing particularly 'external conformity to norms of domestic life and sexual morality'[29] within a patriarchial family unit, and their underpinning commitment to regular church going, to 'respectability and moderation' in public activity, and to the orchestration of 'charity' as the only appropriate social response to the existence of mass poverty.

For the intellectual certainties of the mid Victorian bourgeoisie were very hard on the poor that they had created. Poverty was the fault of idleness and excess; and social unrest a consequence of ignorance, indiscipline or immorality – such that, in each case, neither poverty nor protest could be allowed to throw into question the 'natural justness' of the social order into which they came. On the contrary, 'the dominant cultural perspective, persistently inculcated by the various agencies of social indoctrination, (was) that high material advantages (were) the rewards for personal ability, effort or initiative, a prize potentially open to all'.[30] This refusal to face the basic structural causes of inequality remains a powerful component of ruling-class thought today, one whose intellectual trajectory can be traced back directly to the 1850s and beyond. For the legacy of mid Victorian England to the hegemonic culture of twentieth-century Britain lies in just this potent liberal mixture – with its stress on individualistic modes of explanation and conduct, its glorification of privatized and patriarchial personal relationships, and its central belief in the class neutrality and social efficacy of market processes undisturbed by trade unions or state controls.

In its purest form, this liberalism was the world view of an industrial ruling class in the heyday of its power. It was quickly checked, at its edge, both by the growth of industrial competition abroad and the rise of working-class industrial and political power at home. To the first challenge, the English ruling class responded by a move into empire. To the second, they reacted with a limited degree of political and social reform. In neither case did they break decisively with liberalism. They just added new strands to their vocabulary and thought. The 'imperialist card' proved vital as a means of reconstituting a sense of 'national unity' that could transcend the increasingly bitter class divisions of a now declining capitalist economic power.[31] The justification of imperial expansion as a civilizing mission by white races, and the accompanying material degradation of non-white societies, inserted a powerful racist current into popular consciousness, as we have seen. The struggle between 'white' capitalist powers for empire and markets between 1914 and 1945 then reconstituted and generalized a sense of national identification even against other whites – an identification, after all, which the nation-state had continually striven to create since its inception, and which easily consolidated itself around a common language, history and territory. The more recent struggle for world domination between capitalist and socialist blocs then completed that process of national identification and gave it its modern content, as ruling classes in Western Europe, threatened by the post-war industrial strength of their own working classes, played the 'Russian card' to build a new cold-war consensus of 'social unity made vital by the existence of an external enemy'.

The economic and military struggle between industrial capitalisms in the twentieth century gave a powerful boost to the 'jingoism' latent in the mid Victorian sense of national unity. That boost came first from war, then from economic competition, as people experienced massive military slaughter in the name of national defence, and then, in easier times, the impact of foreign competition on the security and prosperity of their daily exist-

ence. The new national consensus created by twentieth-century war and social unrest gave a place to labour in the new governing coalition. The strength of working-class pressure had nearly swept away the existing order between 1912 and 1926; and had been accommodated (in a classic example of what Gramsci called a 'passive revolution')[32] only by giving labour a voice at the highest levels of the state. This democratization and 'corporatization' of the British state will be one topic of the next chapter. What we must grasp now is how that democratization and incorporation helped to win working-class identification with the still dominant imperialist and capitalist preoccupations of the British ruling class. We must remind ourselves too that the rhetoric of the cold war (as we saw in Chapter 2) was vital to the hegemony of that ruling class in the post-war years: justifying the repression of radicals; splitting labour movements; legitimating military expenditure and foreign wars, and providing the base from which once again a ruling class could persuade the vast majority of workers to accept its project as their own.

That the Labour Party played such a central role in creating the military alliances of the cold war takes us to hegemony in Gramsci's third sense. For capitalism is stable in Britain not simply because of the 'dull logic of market forces' and the sophistication of ruling-class ideas. It is stable too because down the years the working class has given its political support to non-revolutionary forms of socialist politics. In the critical years between 1880 and 1926 the battle for political leadership between revolutionary and reformist currents in the British labour movement was won decisively by the reformist wing. That in its turn helped to incorporate the working class as a whole into a subordinate position within a capitalist social order whose basic structure was neither effectively challenged nor transformed. The reasons for that pattern of working-class politics are complex and controversial, and will be the subject of a later volume.[33] Certainly they have something to do with the fact that Britain industrialized first and relatively slowly, and that its industrial capitalism was sufficiently successful to provide the material base on which reformist institutions and practices could consolidate themselves, and on which a ruling class threatened by rising working-class strength could manoeuvre, accommodate and buy off. But for our purposes now, the legacies of that Labourist domination are more important than its causes. For the exposure of three whole generations of workers to Labour Party leadership has had a number of crucial consequences for social stability and political attitudes.

The dominance of Labour has drained from the collective consciousness of the class any familiarity with the language, strategy and tactics of revolutionary socialism. Instead it has placed at the disposal of industrial militants and political radicals a different and more moderate vocabulary and imagery. For Labourism, of course, has its radical face – seeing unemployment and poverty as the result of capitalist excess, and arguing for a socialism understood as a mixture of welfare provision, full employment and limited state direction of a still predominantly capitalist (in Labour terminology, 'private') economy. Instead of the language of class struggle, capitalist transcendence and proletarian dictatorship, the Labour Party has offered a scenario of 'democratic progress', the 'public control of private industry', and the generation of a new, more socially-just consensus and collaboration between managers, workers and consumers. Yet it is the very paucity of that Labourist perspective in the face of the realities of capitalist power (and the Labour Party's own retreat between 1947 and 1970 from even its limited brand of socialism) that has helped both to lock the working class into a position of social subordination and to leave the existing structures of privilege and command securely intact. In that sense, capitalism

is still here in Britain because the Labour Party, for all its rhetoric, does not 'touch the essentials'. It is not genuinely counter-hegemonic – and has acted instead, as Leo Panitch correctly noted, 'as one of the chief mechanisms for inculcating the organised working class with national values and symbols and of restraining and re-interpreting working class demands in this light'.[34]

The success of Labourism as an electoral force has served to reinforce the identification of politics with parliamentarianism across society as a whole. The Labour Party's willingness to play the parliamentary game according to the rules established for it by its Tory and Liberal opponents has similarly consolidated in the public mind as a whole the 'rightness' of certain practices and beliefs that are in fact far from inevitable even in parliamentary regimes – not least the 'neutrality' or judges and civil servants, and the illegitimacy of using working-class industrial power as a political lever. The Labour Party's own belief in the possibility of gradual reform, and in the potential of collaboration between classes in national projects of economic and social reconstruction, has helped to consolidate that sense of national unity for which the ruling class has striven. It has also discouraged the Labour Party from building arguments, programmes, institutions and practices of a counter-hegemonic kind which might be able to push back the official orthodoxies and government policies by openly stressing the *class* character of the interests that lie behind them. Instead the commitment of the Labour Party to electoral politics has 'depoliticized' its mass base in subtle and important ways, marginalizing politics from their lives, discouraging participation in other than electoral terms, discrediting the socialist alternative by associating it in the public mind with bureaucratic nationalization and half-cock state planning, and inviting the electorate to judge the Labour Party as just one party among many – not qualitatively different in its practices and aims from the pro-capitalist parties it faces. Invited to judge in that way, the electorate has done just that, and has retreated from the Labour Party as its own governmental performance has declined with the reappearance of crisis in late capitalism.[35] In that sense, the Labour Party has been a crucial mechanism in drawing the working class into a position of subordination to existing political and social élites. It has also been the first casualty of that subordination, as the hegemonic impact of those élites has moved its electorate to the Right, stealing ever greater numbers of Labour voters as it has done so. In the final pages of this book (Chapter 11) we shall return to the question of how to stop that process.

The reproduction of hegemony

This weakness of the Labour Party as a counter-hegemonic force serves to remind us of another feature of hegemonic domination – namely that it can be challenged, and that it is inherently unstable. The hegemony of a ruling class is never so much a structure as a process, one that is necessarily characterized by struggle. Subordinate classes have to be contained. Hegemonies have to be sustained in cultural systems littered with 'traces' of 'previous ideological systems and sedimentations',[36] from which residual pockets of old resistance, and emergent possibilities of new ones, can never be totally eradicated. Moreover, what constitutes the hegemonic requirements of the dominant bloc will be a matter of controversy between the fractions that compose it, so that hegemonies have to be organized as well as disseminated. Submission to the existing order, that is, has to be perpetually *reproduced*. That reproduction occurs through the workings of crucial social institutions that extend beyond the state, and are linked only tangentially to the system of production as such. These institutions are, in an Althusserian sense, 'ideological state apparatuses'.[37]

Analysts on the Left vary in the extent to which they see them as part of the state, and in the relative rankings that they are prepared to give to each. Althusser placed great stress on what he called the 'School-Family' couple; but his list extended to take in the churches, the media, the state itself, and those institutions created by the working class (like trade unions) which, in their corporate subordination, are available for use by the dominant order to police and reproduce their own subordinate incorporation. Stuart Hall has mapped this universe in the following way: 'the reproduction of labour power through the wage requires *the family*: the reproduction of advanced skills and techniques requires the *education system*: (and) the reproduction of the submission to the ruling ideology requires the *cultural institutions*, the *church* and the *mass media*, the *political apparatuses* and the overall management of the state'.[38] Since this is so, and because space is short, we will choose from the list just two, to illuminate the general truth. We shall look in turn at the media and the state.

The media

It is impossible to discuss the transmission of values and practices of a hegemonic kind without examining the role of the media. Clearly in a capitalist society such as this, 'political and economic power is shadowed by what we may call the unequal distribution of cultural power' – by a differentially distributed 'command over certain crucial processes', not least 'the power to define *which issues* will enter into the circuit of public communications, . . . the power to define the *terms* on which the issue will be debated . . . the power to define *who will speak* to the issues and the terms, (and) the power to manage the debate itself'.[39] Politics operates in a cultural space presided over by a network of mass media, whose resources, technologies, penetration and range are of a scale that is qualitatively greater than any set of cultural institutions dominant hitherto. If, in 1984, we are not quite in the Orwellian nightmare of 'newspeak', the very existence of that dreadful and pessimistic vision is itself testimony to the potential impact on popular consciousness possessed by modern modes of communication, and the possible political consequences of so great a concentration of power in the hands of the relatively small number of people who own and work in the media. It is also testimony to the extent to which the media have become 'key institutions in the operation of cultural hegemony'.[40]

Modern forms of communication are many and various: books, films, videos, radio, newspapers and television, to name but the major ones. For our purposes it seems sensible to focus on the last two. For those have attracted a considerable degree of social analysis and political controversy, and have done so regularly down the years. The 'existence of a free press' and a 'neutral' broadcasting system has been the proudest boast of the Western democracies in the rhetorical clashes of the cold war; and has entered popular consciousness as one defining feature of the liberal state. But critics of that liberalism have been less certain. Labour movements have bewailed their lack of a popular press, or the paucity of their media resources against those of capital. They have regularly decried the bias against them which they have perceived in much of that capitalist press. Others have seen in that 'freedom' of the press a crucial source of capitalist stability – a 'relative autonomy' of media activity and output which has served to obscure the real concentrations of social power and enabled the media to act as an ideological extension of the state – formally free but in practice locked into relationships of subordination to capitalist economic and political power which media products serve only to reproduce. An earlier body of critical theory on the Left regularly went still further, seeing in the *output* of the media (understood as a 'culture industry') the creation of a new, one-dimensional culture, an impoverished and anaesthetizing commodity which, in its banality, standardization, repetitiveness and ubiquity, has systematically drained popular consciousness of any capacity to forge a radical and more humanistic alternative to the dull logic of capitalism. To someone like Adorno, the output of the culture industry impedes 'the development of autonomous, independent individuals who judge and decide consciously for themselves', developing and reinforcing instead 'a state of dependence, anxiety and ego weakness'.[41] The whole thrust of the media's output now serves to reinforce privatization and consumerism, to manipulate sexuality and to undermine indigenous working class culture. As Adorno put it, even 'music today is largely a social cement'.[42]

So the media must be looked at with our usual sense of theoretical controversy, and their precise role in the consolidation of a capitalist society must be charted with what care and sophistication we can manage. To do that, we must first recognize that the media as we know it does itself have a history. It has grown as capitalism has grown. Of course, 'ever since the invention and development of the printing press by Gutenburg in 1457 mass media technology has played an increasingly important role in the development, form and struggle over ideas'.[43] But mass modes of communication are much more recent than that. Artistic products first became a generalized commodity with the rise of the novel and the periodical/newspaper in the first phase of capitalist development in the eighteenth century, and developed apace only with the spread of industrialization and the associated development of transport networks and urban markets in the nineteenth century. As a commodity generated in capitalist processes, the output of the culture industry proved vulnerable to exactly the same logics as capitalist industry as a whole: monopolization, bureaucratization, and commodification of a conventional capitalist sort. In the sphere of cultural commodities, as elsewhere, twentieth-century capitalism came to be dominated by a limited number of private (and in the case of the media, occasionally public) monopolies, whose size and bureaucratic strength enabled them to 'install themselves as the principle means and channels for the production and distribution of culture, and absorb more and more of the sphere of public communication into their orbit'.[44] This is not the place to tell the detailed story of that development. That has been done elsewhere.[45] What we need to recognize is its consequences: the way in which the media 'have established a decisive and fundamental leadership in the cultural sphere' and 'the manner in which the whole gigantic complex of public information, intercommunications and exchange – the production and consumption of "social knowledge" in societies of this type'[46] has come to depend upon them.

Because we are concerned to explain the stability of the social structure in total, something will be said about that 'social knowledge' and its relationship to the content of media output as a whole. But because our more localized focus is on politics and the state, we might begin by looking at how the media handle issues generated in the political sphere. Here we find that the popular consciousness is exposed to a particular form of media output that reflects the triple impact of bureaucracy, capitalism and the state. It is simply not the case that the 'news' which the media regularly present is self-defining. On the contrary, it is manufactured and produced, as journalists select from a mass of possible stories those to be *identified* as newsworthy, and as they then tell that story in a particular way, contextualizing it within a 'frame of meanings familiar to the audience'.[47] In late capitalism, 'news' is itself a commodity produced and sold at the end of a labour process that shows all the hallmarks of the state-regulated, hierarchially-organized and pre-

dominantly capitalist-controlled institutions from which it emerges.

As Stuart Hall and his colleagues have observed, 'the social identification, classification and contextualisation of news events in terms of these background frames of reference is the fundamental process by which the media make the world they report on intelligible to readers and viewers. This process of "making an event intelligible" is a social process – constituted by a number of specific journalistic practices, which embody (often only implicitly) crucial assumptions about what society is and how it works'.[48] We can say first that what constitutes news is that which is thought of as 'newsworthy' by the journalists who produce it. Clearly their decision on this in part reflects the particular logic of their work situation and their by now well-established journalistic practices. So many news stories have the same features. They concentrate on the dramatic, the unusual and the sensational. They report the famous and the powerful more regularly than the rest. They have a tendency to report immediate events, and to downplay underlying processes and previous histories. They show a marked preoccupation with happenings in the West, and a distinct propensity to seize on the 'British' aspect of any foreign event. When asked why this is so, journalists often cite quite technical reasons. Stories have to be produced to deadlines; they lack time for research. They come locally in the main because foreign correspondents are now too expensive for most papers to maintain. Much foreign news relies on agency sources as a result. If certain local institutions get disproportionate coverage (not least Parliament itself) this too reflects in some measure the distribution of journalists and the expertise of the lobby correspondent. Parliament can always be relied upon to produce a 'newsworthy' story, and is thus one crucial prop on which heavily-pressed editors are happy to depend. Stories have to fit into restricted spaces – of words (press) or time (television) –

and to be intelligible in that format to the audience at which they are directed, they must play to, and be constituted around, categories and stereotypes that are already well and generally known. Those stereotypes play to the whims of the powerful and the well-placed because journalists need regular, accessible, reliable and legitimate sources to give their stories credibility and some status in the battle for the sub-editor's eye. Sources, of course, if they are to be available regularly, need to be protected and sustained.

In fact these 'technical' reasons exist only in very definite institutional and social contexts. It would be just as easy to run a headline, 'Royal Family squares up for massive wage claim' or 'Traffic to be disrupted by Queen's procession'[49] as to run the usual sycophantic trash on royal events. That does not happen in the vast majority of cases, partly because of internal controls on the journalistic function, partly because of processes of occupational socialization that constrain the journalistic mind. Radical journalists do not survive long on capitalist newspapers, nor do they find it easy to gain resources in television journalism. They try, of course, and win space at times, but at considerable cost to their own careers and effectiveness as journalists if they persist. Most journalists are not very radical anyway. They learn their trade on provincial newspapers, come to see what a 'good story' is, live under the watchful eye of sub-editorial control, learn 'empirically by seeing what is permitted and what is not and, more indirectly, by absorbing the traditional wisdom of the organisation, (learning) from the conversation, comments, anecdotes and reactions of . . . fellow workers'.[50] If they make it to the BBC, they experience a new and powerful socializing pressure to 'neutrality' and the 'middle ground'.

Journalists find too that the papers for which they work are not simply institutions, but capitalist ones – and monopolies at that. Ownership in the newspaper industry in particular is highly restricted. Just three companies (Reed, Trafalgar House and News International) were responsible for 82 per cent of total Sunday, and 71 per cent of national daily output, in 1980. In fact, given the internal organization of those companies, 'for 6 of the 9 national newspapers, ultimate control rests with a single individual or with a family or their trusts. Only in the case of Reed International owning the *Daily Mirror, Sunday Mirror* and *The People* are the shares widely held. The net result is that a handful of extremely rich men . . . between them now control most of the newspapers sold to the British people' (Table 33).[51] This is a degree of ownership-concentration matched in other sectors of the culture and leisure industries, and is in fact an even higher degree of monopolization than that prevalent elsewhere in the monopoly sector.

Far from enjoying a 'free press', by the 1980s the logic of market forces under capitalism had well and truly established 'the press as an instrument of social control'.[52] For as an industry, that monopolization came at the cost of the destruction of the labour press. Neither the *Daily Herald* nor the *News Chronicle* survived to sustain the *Mirror*'s residual commitment to right-wing Labourism, as the labour movement in the boom years allowed the press to drift into an almost wholly conservative mould. That happened because newspapers lose money; and labour (unlike capital) felt no compulsion to sustain bankrupt institutions. For that is what national newspapers are in Britain – companies which reproduce the general characteristics of the ailing economy as a whole: earning low/ negative profits, facing the possibility of new technology, and blocked in its introduction by the defensive strength of trade union power. The principle result of this has been 'the break up of the old press empire, the formation of news conglomerates, with the leading sectors in the electronics-based communications systems and their leisure ancillaries, with the

Table 33 *Concentration of ownership of daily and Sunday newspapers, 1948–76*

The three leading corporations' share of . . .

	Total daily and Sunday circulation (%)	Total daily circulation (%)	Total Sunday circulation (%)	National daily circulation (%)	National Sunday circulation (%)
1948	46	45	61	62	60
1961	65	67	84	89	84
1976	64	49	80	72	86

Proportion of the total market accounted for by leading five companies in selected mass media sectors (%)

Commercial television programmes (transmitted)	50
National dailies (circulation)	95
National Sundays (circulation)	96
Regional evening (circulation)	58
Regional morning (circulation)	69
Women's magazines (circulation)	87
Paperback books (sales)	74
Cinema admissions	52
Single records (sales)	70
Record albums and tapes (sales)	61

Source: James Curran and Jean Seaton, *Power without Responsibility* (Fontana 1981), pp. 106, 108.

press as a relatively backward and unprofitable sector'.[53] In that context, advertising revenue and circulation figures alone keep the newspapers afloat, and together increasingly shape their content. Advertising can be attracted only by large (or in the case of the 'quality press', wealthy) readerships, and can be alienated by anti-capitalist reporting. Circulation is to be won only by turning newspapers from fact sheets into semi-pornographic entertainment brochures, reducing political coverage, trivializing and sensationalizing news items, and, when the opportunity arises (as in the Argentinian recapture of the Malvinas), pandering to and reinforcing nationalist strands in the popular consciousness that the weakness of the radical press only helps to reinforce. Radical and honest journalism survives in spite of all that, but in a 'space' systematically eroded by the capacity of a monopoly capitalist press to create, and then

feed off, an audience increasingly trained to prefer the pithy to the profound, and the erotic to the educative.

These practices feed themselves into television journalism too, although there the situation is slightly different. The journalists who work the television networks are creamed from the world of the press, and simply reproduce its patterns to a large extent. In the commercial networks, advertising revenue and profit-seeking are part of the journalists' daily reality. The BBC too is under a similar 'ratings' pressure, and dependent ultimately on the government for its revenue. Entry into the BBC is carefully controlled, with radicals heavily constrained by the widespread use of very short contracts ('it is known that the BBC refers the files of candidates for production jobs to the Special Branch for vetting');[54] and once in, too much radicalism can so easily mean that 'your promotion may well be held up, perhaps indefinitely, and your job may be made so frustrating that you decide to leave of your own accord'.[55] Senior executive positions in the BBC are dominated by the 'great and the good', who invariably use their internal position in order to protect the BBC as an institution from direct government control, by making journalists operate only within the political space thought legitimate by leading politicians. At times they clash with these politicians, of course, and individual programmes cause temporary dissention. But in general Lord Reith's 1926 assertion still holds: that 'they want to be able to say that they did not commandeer us, but they know that they can trust us not to be really impartial'.[56] As E. P. Thompson has so correctly observed, 'these non-elected and non-vetted persons arrogate to themselves powers which would astonish our ancestors. It's supposed that they alone can determine what is the "national interest" and invoke the awesome imperative of "national security". In this sense they protract into the present the traditions of an old anti-democratic imperial élite, whose last colony is this island'.[57]

All this pulls television journalism into a similar and conservative mould. Yet that mould has its distinctive feature because of the statutory obligation imposed on the television networks to show objectivity and neutrality in their reporting of political events. As a result television journalism does not show the partisan bias of the commercial press. Its format is ostensibly more open and detached. Neutrality here is understood as the articulation of all sides of opinion within a certain range; and it is that range, and the nature of those sides, that makes television news so potent a hegemonic phenomenon for the social order of late capitalism. For as Stuart Hall has said, television reporting is 'a world at one with itself'.[58] The frameworks of debate within which it operates are those of the parliamentary state and the mixed economy. If television journalism has an ideology, it is a social

democratic one; and as such is unacceptable both to the extreme Right (who in their wilder moments see the BBC as infiltrated by Maoists) and to the far Left. It is an ideology which takes consensus as natural, operates with an unquestioned faith in the ability of institutions to handle conflict and of reasonable people to find an acceptable compromise, and sees in parliamentary institutions a natural framework within which to resolve matters of interest to the nation as a whole. It is, moreover, an ideology that is also, in its normal and unreflective moments, sexist, racist and anti-communist, happier with élites than with masses, easier with managers than with workers, more tolerant of the violence of the state than of anti-state struggle, and content with British and American imperialism, but really quite hostile to the more limited imperialism of the Soviet bloc. Indeed, in recent years one of life's more bizarre moments has been watching the television news balance its anti-unionism and its anti-communism in its coverage of events in Poland, and to hear the change of tone and vocabulary as news items slide from Polish strikes to strikes nearer home!

To show their neutrality, television journalists take opinions from both sides. To justify their stories, both sides are understood as 'official' (accredited) in their origins and status; and to show a due sense of national responsibility, this view of balance is not systematically extended to those who challenge the prevailing power structures. The result is partly to give élite figures disproportionate exposure, and their preoccupations disproportionate coverage. Accompanying this is a propensity to 'encode' and 'contextualize' the news in terms of the language and perspectives of the powerful. 'In this way television does not favour one point of view, but it *does* favour, and reproduce, one definition of politics: by definition it excludes, represses or neutralises other definitions.'[59] This is very clear in the language of news reporting on television. What is a 'terrorist' to the BBC or to ITN is someone else's 'freedom fighter'. The general drift of news reporting tends to give legitimacy to governments simply because they are there, and to moderate forms of political pressure because they are constitutionally sanctioned. Even when the BBC comes out to examine areas of conflict in detail, still the anchorage of their news teams in the universe of the powerful shows through time and time again. Trade union coverage is so often biased and hostile. Labour Party politics is so often trivialized and anchored in the perspectives of the Labour Right. Peace movement politics, though reported, is quickly balanced by official ministerial statements; and the struggle in Ireland is wholly reported from a standpoint close to the British government. Indeed in the Irish case more than any other lately, with the possible exception of the Malvinas invasion, the 'needs of national defence' have produced direct censorship and the actual banning of programmes on an unprecedented scale. This use of 'D' notices, government directives and ministerial pressure is a very clear indication of the limits to which those who rule us will allow television journalists to go.

This is not to say that social forces hostile to, or in conflict with, aspects of state policy cannot 'carve' their way into news coverage if they are big and persistent enough. They can. The trade unions have done it, the peace movement also. But once there they will not get neutrality of treatment, nor will their perspectives be allowed to define the issues that they raise; and if those issues are thought to constitute a radical challenge to existing patterns of power and policy, they will not be given regular coverage at all. The 'world at one with itself' has no understanding of, or sympathy for, the need for structural change, and will treat those who advocate it not as newsworthy, but as deviants – to be deprecated, dismissed, ridiculed or even criminalized. The consensus on which television

journalism operates will tinker with detailed disagreements within the mainstream of political life, and play the neutral arbiter well; but when classes clash, imperialist interests diverge and the under-privileged rebel, the consensus disintegrates and the television has to choose. It is at those moments that the conservatism of its anchorage is plain for all to see.

There is a mass of evidence now to sustain this view, and to cite it all would take the rest of this volume. In all the areas we have covered here – economy and class struggle, gender division, racial oppression and Irish independence – systematic bias and the under-representation of radical opinion is the order of the day. The bias in the news here is complex and subtle. At times, there is quite straightforward distortion – sins of both commission and omission. The trade union studies show that very well: distortion through the choice of story, headlines, words and image, tone of interview and contextualization, and the maintenance of 'certain strategic areas of silence'.[60] But the reaction of television journalists to the criticisms levelled at them by the Glasgow team is well founded: that their own statutory obligation to show 'balance' does build in a mechanism to correct the Glasgow findings. What that defence fails to see, however, is how the interpretation of 'balance' ends up reinforcing the pattern of inequality about which it claims to be neutral, allowing governments and managers a predominant role as 'primary definers' of issues, and excluding groups and demands which those who rule us deem to be 'beyond the pale'. At times, individual journalists step beyond that limit. This is not yet a dictatorship. But their existence also helps to sustain the myth of a 'free press' that is denied by the daily reality of subtle pressure and control; and the speed of their condemnation by the 'great and the good', whom they have dared to criticize, soon pulls back the managers of the central media institutions into their conservative moderation once again. It is in this sense that the media help to reproduce the status quo not simply by their 'bias', but by their 'objectivity'. For that objectivity operates within a framework defined by the powerful – one in which the 'national interest' is supposed to emerge from a clash of opinion and opposing viewpoint. By orchestrating that clash between views that are united in their commitment to the basic distribution of social and economic power, the media both help to generate that common interest vital to social stability, and to provide a limited and controlled theatre of disagreement and democracy that obscures – in its strategic silences – the actual concentrations of private power that democracy has not yet touched.

This would not matter so much if the media were not so important as a force shaping popular consciousness, but they are. It is, of course, impossible to show that programme 'X' shaped opinion 'Y' to the degree 'Z'. The impact of the media does not work that way. Instead, the media map problematic events 'within the conventional understandings of the society'; and this is 'crucial in two ways. The media define for the majority of the population *what* significant events are taking place, but also they offer powerful interpretations of *how* to understand these events'.[61] It is not that the media simply 'transmit the ideology of the ruling class in a conspiratorial fashion'.[62] It is rather that the practical pressures of journalism and the professional need for impartiality and balance turn television journalists into 'camp followers of the establishment',[63] in that their 'structured relationship to power has the effect of making them play a crucial but secondary role in *reproducing* the definitions of those who have privileged access, as of right, to the media as "accredited sources". From this point of view, in the moment of news production, the media stand in a position of structured subordination to the primary definers'.[64]

In this way the media act as a bridge between the privileged and the masses, articulating into the popular consciousness the preoccupations and perspectives of the powerful in a process of transmission which recasts ruling ideas in the popular idioms of the day, and reinforces consensual notions already established there. In societies like this one, 'where the bulk of the population have neither direct access to nor power over the central decisions which affect their lives, where official policy and opinion is concentrated and popular opinion is dispersed, the media play a crucial mediating and connecting role in the formation of public opinion, and in orchestrating that opinion together with the action and views of the powerful'.[65] In societies like this one, the press on a daily basis encourage certain sets of self-definitions and, in their silences, exclude others: they actively 'do not produce representations which allow class members to recognise themselves as working people, as the producers of wealth, as an exploited class, as the producers of surplus value'[66] and so on. Instead they fill our heads with the clichés of the privileged, so that we all come to 'know' that 'what is wrong with British Leyland is its work force', that '*we* have a racial population problem', and that the Labour Party has been infiltrated by 'extremists'. Connecting the centres of power with 'the dispersed publics', and mediating 'the public discourse between élites and the governed', the media are 'pivotally, the site and terrain on which the making and shaping of consent is exercised, and to some degree, contested. They are key institutions in the operation of cultural hegemony'.[67]

The state

Finally, a brief note on the state itself as a source of hegemony. Brief not because the role of the state here is slight but because, and on the contrary, it is so central that it will occupy us in its various facets in the two chapters that remain. The aim here is to link what has gone before to that full and later discussion of the state. We shall do that by making three separate but related points. First we must establish the state in its Gramscian sense – not just as a set of administrative institutions but as 'hegemony fortified by coercion'. For the stability of capitalism, in Britain as elsewhere, depends ultimately on the existence of what Gramsci called an 'integral state', one capable of establishing its moral and intellectual leadership through the society as a whole. That is not an easy thing for the state to do. We have seen already how the nature of the wage relationship and the commodity form do enable the economic relationships of capitalism to be fetishized (that is to have their true class character obscured) in a relatively automatic way. But political power under capitalism is much more difficult to present in a similarly neutral and non-partisan fashion. Yet that presentation has to occur if stability is to persist, and if the state is to be able to act as a capitalist state. Indeed the 'structural problem of the capitalist state' lies precisely here, in that it must at the same time practice its class character and keep it concealed, because it 'can only function as a capitalist state by appealing to symbols and sources of support that conceal its nature as a capitalist state'.[68]

In the pursuit of that hegemonic impact, the state in late capitalism generally, and the British state no less than the rest, does two things of considerable importance. First, it articulates a quite distinctive juridico-political ideology which parallels the fetishism of commodities with a similar fetishization of political relationships and legal processes. It talks the language not of classes, but of citizens. It repeatedly asserts the neutrality of law, the freedom of the press, the rights of free speech and association. In this way, a particular liberal political ideology, and its associated way of telling the 'story' of British political development (as the incremental and peaceful extension of citizenship)[69] both *separates and*

unites the members of subordinate social strata. Classes are separated into individual political–legal subjects; and are then rebound 'as members of a nation . . . within the imaginery coherence of the state, the nation, and the "national interest"'.[70] In this way, 'not only does the constitution of all members of society as political subjects endowed with equal rights regardless of their class affiliation complement their formal equality as economic agents, it also encourages their atomisation and individuation, and disguises the substantive inequalities in political rule'. 'By defining the contradictions of capital as a national problem, and voters as abstract citizens in relation to those national problems, liberal democratic elections enable capital to appear as identified with the national interest';[71] and create a situation in which 'citizens believe that they exercise self-determination. This does not serve to legitimate a ruling class but [rather] denies its existence'.[72] It is in this crucial way that a particular state-induced and state-disseminated liberal political ideology stabilizes a capitalist order by paralleling the commodity fetishism of capitalist exchange relations with a political and legal fetishization of enormous power.

Yet as ever with fetishized relationships, the gap between the reality and the claim always leaves open the possibility of radicalization. Accordingly, these fetishized perspectives have to be sustained by ideological struggle in its widest sense. Here too the state plays a crucial role. It is not just that a particular political perspective has to be repeated and re-emphasized. It is also that the class interests sustained by it (and those frustrated by it) have to be orchestrated and accommodated by distinct ranges of state policy. The power bloc, as we shall see in the next chapter, has to be organized. Subordinate classes have to be accommodated. A collective interest for the capitalist class as a whole has to be specified. Liberal democratic parliamentary regimes are splendid institutions for doing that, opening the state to the pressures it must experience if the job of orchestration, accommodation and specification is to be performed effectively. 'For not only does parliament provide a forum for different interests to hammer out a common policy in conditions where failure to do so will immobilise effective government in the interests of capital, it also permits modifications in the balance of power without serious threat to the stability of the state apparatuses. The imperatives of electoral competition also require that the power bloc articulate and aggregate the interests of the dominated classes as well as its own interests.'[73] But even in liberal-democratic regimes, stability can be assured only if the state is itself active in specifying and pursuing a *national project* around which ruling-class interests can cohere, and within which the potentially threatening working-class interests and popular democratic struggles of the dispossessed can be accommodated and shaped. Capitalism has been stable in Britain ultimately only because of the effectiveness of state initiatives in this area – only because (and to the extent that) successive governments have been able to 'integrate popular-democratic values and demands into an ideology and programme that secures the representation of bourgeois interests'.[74]

Social consensus has been built around different 'national projects' at different times.[75] We have already noted the hegemonic impact of mid nineteenth-century *laissez-faire* liberalism. The *social imperialism* of Edwardian Britain replaced it, and was in its turn superseded by the *Keynesian corporatism* of the welfare state. Each project represented a particular balancing of class forces under the hegemony of the state. Each involved 'the sacrifice of certain short-term interests of the hegemonic class (fraction) and a flow of material concessions to other class and fractional forces'.[76] Indeed at times, not least in 1945, the scale of such concessions was enough to constitute – in Gramscian terms – a

veritable 'passive revolution' – the buying of social peace at the price of extensive reforms and the toleration of enhanced social equality. While each lasted, political life turned on incremental adjustments of policy within an overriding consensus, underpinned by a relatively fixed distribution of class power. Each declined only as the consensus was eroded by the changing balance of power and situation within and between classes, as capitalism as a world system moved through its various stages.

So *laissez-faire* liberalism was destroyed, in the end, by the growth of foreign competition and its impact on the local power bloc, with its shifting focus from industrial to financial capital. Social imperialism fell victim to the generalized recession of the 1930s, the quickening anti-colonial struggle, and the rise of working-class power through wartime mobilization and full employment. Keynesianism succeeded as a hegemonic project through the years of the long boom, because the balance of class forces that it consolidated did not impede too severely the accumulation of capital in easy market conditions. For that very reason Keynesianism has been the prime political casualty of the return of recession and the intensification of foreign competition. Politics in Britain now is a politics of transition, as both the Conservative Right and the Labour Left struggle to formulate and consolidate a new national project in the wake of the demise of the old. Indeed, in late capitalism the state generally was so extended in its Keynesian phase that the crisis of Keynesianism has been interpreted by some as a *crisis of legitimacy* for the state as a whole. But whether or not that is true – and it is a question to which we will return – it is clear that the basis on which the British state orchestrated the hegemonic domination of the capitalist class in the post-war years is now having to change. This, after all, is the significance of *Thatcherism*, that it constitutes a *new national project* for an entire ruling class which can no longer rely on

Keynesian corporatism to maintain its hegemony. It is for this reason too that, when we have examined the role of the state in detail, we will have to look once more at the emergence of Thatcherism as a hegemonic project, in order to locate the immediate political context in which to set the tasks facing the Left in our generation.

Part Three: Political Options for the Contemporary State

10 Function, form and crisis in the contemporary British state

So at last we arrive at the state itself. In our intellectual journey through the economic and social context of British politics we have already met the state in a number of different places. We have seen the role of state spending in the long boom, and its contradictory contribution to the recession. We have explored its relationship to various fractions of capital, and to the ruling class as a whole; and discussed the contribution of state policy down the years to the growing weakness of the economy's manufacturing base. We have explored the relationship of the state to labour, and its role as an employer; and seen how state policy helps to reproduce patterns of discrimination by gender, race and religion. What we have not done is to pull together those various facets of state policy, by examining the state as a whole. Nor have we yet looked in detail at the political forces acting directly on the state, forces seeking to use state power to reconstitute its economic and social context. That is the task before us in the final part of this volume.

Four features of the contemporary British state call out for special attention. The first is its *growth*. The modern state is much bigger than its predecessors. More of the national product passes through its hands now than before the war. Total state expenditure as a percentage of GNP at factor cost in 1975 was 57.9 per cent. In 1937 it had been 25.7 per cent.[1] The state directly consumes 30 per cent of that national product, and 35 per cent if the nationalized industries are included. It is directly responsible for the production of a smaller, though still sizeable element, of total output as a whole. For example, almost 43 per cent 'of the money for gross domestic capital formation came from public funds in 1971, and the figure had been as high as 48% in 1967'.[2] Moreover the state employs vast numbers of people: 6.8 million in 1974 as against 5.3 million in 1967. It employs them in units far larger than any constituted by even the biggest of the private monopolies. The largest of those in Britain in 1975 was General Electric; it employed 202,000 people. Yet in the same year the Post Office employed 434,000; the health service employed 914,000, the education service contained 595,000 teachers, and even defence employed 336,000 people. State employment has grown much more quickly of late than has employment in the private sector. 'The number of public service employees working directly for government agencies increased by nearly two-thirds between 1961 and 1976.'[3] As the labour force as a whole grew by 6 per cent between 1958 and 1974, public sector employment rose by 15 per cent with virtually the entire increase concentrated in the area of local government. So whereas 'central and local government between them employed about 2% of the civilian labour force in 1891; some 5% in the years shortly before World War I; around 8% during the inter-war period; and over 11% in 1950'[4] that figure had risen to 17 per cent by 1971 – and if the nationalized industries were included, was anywhere between a quarter and a third of all employees. The trends in employment and resource consumption by the state are consolidated in Table 34. Later we shall explain the rhythms they capture.

The second feature of the contemporary British state that is in need of explanation is the concomitant of that pattern of employment and resource use – namely the *changing range and character of the things that the state does*. The notion of the nineteenth-century state as a *laissez faire* state, responsible only for law, order and defence, has always been a myth; but there is no mistaking the sea-change

which has occurred in the scale and scope of government activity this century. The modern state regulates everything: from economic activity to the family, from cultural pursuits to war. It does so not just in general but in detail; and commands vast resources of a material, administrative and coercive kind to ensure that its detail is obeyed.

State activities have expanded in a number of crucial areas in the post-war period. The most striking is the whole area of economic

Table 34   *The growth of social expenditure in the United Kingdom, 1921–75*

	1921	1931	1937	1951	1961	1971	1975
Total state expenditure as % of GNP	29.4	28.8	25.9	44.9	42.1	50.3	57.9
resource spending	16.2	14.2	16.0	25.1	22.5	26.8	29.6
transfer spending	13.2	14.6	10.0	19.8	19.6	23.5	28.3

		Percentage of GNP at factor cost					
	1910	1921	1931	1937	1951	1961	1971	1975
All social services	4.2	10.1	12.7	10.9	16.1	17.6	23.8	28.8
Social security		4.7	6.7	5.2	5.3	6.7	8.9	9.5
Welfare	}	1.1	1.8	1.8	4.5	0.3	0.7	1.1
Health						4.1	5.1	6.0
Education		2.2	2.8	2.6	3.2	4.2	6.5	7.6
Housing		2.1	1.3	1.4	3.1	2.3	2.6	4.6
Infrastructure	0.7	0.6	1.0	1.0	3.6	4.8	6.3	6.8
Industry	1.8	4.5	3.2	2.8	6.9	4.9	6.5	8.3
Justice and law	0.6	0.8	0.8	0.7	0.6	0.8	1.3	1.5
Military	3.5	5.6	2.8	5.0	10.8	7.6	6.6	6.2
Debt interest and other	1.9	7.7	8.2	5.2	6.9	6.3	5.9	6.3
Total state expenditure	12.7	29.4	28.8	25.7	44.9	42.1	50.3	57.9
Total state revenue	11.0	24.4	25.0	23.8	42.7	38.5	48.6	46.6
Borrowing requirement	1.7	5.0	3.8	1.9	2.2	3.6	1.7	11.3

No. of state employees (000s)	1923	1931	1951	1961	1971	1975
Central government	160	110	1136	1302	1561	1910
Local government	227	292	1415	1782	2651	2993
Nationalized industries	—	—	2789	2196	2001	2003
Armed forces	250	189	827	474	368	336
Total	637	591	6167	5754	6581	7242

Sources: I. Gough, *The Political Economy of the Welfare State* (Macmillan 1979), p. 77; *British Labour Statistics Year Book* (1969 and 1975); *British Labour Statistics: Historical Abstract, 1886–1968.*

management: in shaping (and occasionally attempting to plan) aggregate levels of activity in the economy as a whole, while also intervening at the level of industries and firms with the proliferation of state aid, state purchasing, state controls and at times state ownership; plus state involvement in industrial training and retraining, in manpower servicing and (more recently) in the twin encouragement and cushioning of mass unemployment (through redundancy pay and the like). State provision of infrastructural services to industry and to civil society has also grown significantly in the post-war years, in the fields of transport, post and communications, energy and other urban facilities. Throughout the post-war period the state has played an important role internationally in the economic sphere: negotiating an entire post-war framework and participating in the resulting international agencies; taking its economy into and out of different free trade areas (EFTA, EEC, etc.), underpinning export drives by its leading private companies, and perpetually negotiating with other governments on terms of trade for individual commodities. Welfare provision has also expanded dramatically in range and volume since 1945: in the areas of education, social services, health care and housing – an expansion that peaked first in the late 1940s and then again twenty years later. Less visibly, and more recently, as welfare provision has been cut back, state expenditure has grown, and qualitatively changed, in the area of social control and surveillance, with new budgets for, and increasingly centralized control of, both the police and the army as guarantors of state-specified 'law and order'.

This last point throws into relief a third feature of the contemporary British state that also needs documentation and explanation – namely its changing composition and form. 'Composition' refers to the set of institutions that make it up, and the bureaucratic structures that operate within each. The modern state is bigger and more internally specialized than its predecessor states. Those who run the modern state have at their disposal a larger set of 'arms' with which to penetrate into the detailed fabric of the whole social order than did state chiefs even a generation ago. For the boundary between the public and the private has shifted dramatically this century in favour of the state, as a whole set of hitherto 'private' practices have moved not simply into the sphere of state control, but into that of state organization and provision. As that has happened, the formal institutions linking the private and the public spheres have also changed. The basis of representation has altered, new representative channels have been created, and old ones allowed to fall into disrepair. This too needs to be documented and explained.

Finally, we must also note and explain the crisis of the contemporary state. For changes are being made to the size, role and form of the modern state that stand in stark contrast to, and indeed consciously attempt to reverse, certain of the dominant patterns of state development that have operated this century. These are altering once more the position of, and relationship across the boundary of, the public and the private. The state is currently under challenge from outside: from groups denying the legitimacy of its rule at all (as in Ireland), through groups seeking radical shifts in state policy (from monetarists to radical feminists and peace campaigners), down to groups engaged in the daily negotiation of detailed policy changes. The state faces internal challenge, most effectively now from the Conservative Right, but also from the Labour Left, each of which is seeking, in its different ways, to alter the content of state policy and to recast its general relationship with the economic and social groups and processes that surround it. That relationship involves at any one time a particular balance of control and domination, of representation and responsibility, of involvement and reproduction. It is that balance which is now shifting in the contemporary crisis of the state.

Theoretical frameworks around the state

To explain all that properly requires more than the accumulation of historical detail. It also requires that the detail be set in, and illuminated by, a particular theoretical framework. Here, as in all other aspects of contemporary British society that we have explored, a veritable plethora of alternative frameworks are available to us. One widely canvassed in the literature is broadly of a *pluralist* kind: that the form, functions and size of the contemporary British state are to be understood in terms of the political pressures that operate upon it. Businesses lobby for this policy, then that. Trade unions press for one reform and then another. Specialist interest groups colonize this ministry and that department, and mould the policy of the state by steady and persistent attrition. Electorates grow used to measuring politicians against social and economic performance, and their expectations feed into and sustain the ambitions of the state. The state itself, in the face of all these pressures, experiences a 'space' in which to play off one pressure against another, avoiding the total domination of any, and is more or less successful at this balancing act depending on the quality of its own political leadership. Indeed, even the crisis of the contemporary state can be so explained – as a problem of 'overload' – of governments pressed to do more than they can, and encouraged to bid up their own ambitions in the electoral auction room, to the point at which the state is over-stretched, its capacity to deliver diminished, and the legitimacy of the whole system as a result seriously impaired.[5]

As always, the main intellectual challenge to that view comes from the traditions of Marxist scholarship. The dispute here has been partly an empirical one, a challenge to

the pluralism of power. Marxist critics have stressed the close connections of state personnel to privileged élites, have documented the disproportionate political resources enjoyed by capital as against labour, and have mapped out the range of activity pursued by the state in the interest of capital as a whole. But the dispute has also been theoretical, probing beneath the surface pluralism of democratic politics to locate the imperatives that oblige the state to service capital. At its most vulgar, Marxism has canvassed a crude *conspiracy* theory – of a tiny capitalist élite manipulating the state behind the scenes. According to this argument, capital's dominance arises from 'the existence of a social group which has a disproportionate share of national resources, and which ensures the subordination of the state and ideology to its interests'. In this view, 'the dominance of capitalist relations of production is reduced to the dominance of capitalists within the sphere of interacting social groups in civil society',[6] and the state emerges quite simply as the instrument of the all-powerful capitalist interests. Less vulgarly, other Marxists have listed the *functions* which the state must play if capitalist relations of production are to be reproduced, functions which stretch from the reproduction of labour power to the legitimation of capitalist social relations as a whole. At its most sophisticated, Marxism has matched pluralism with a *pluralism* of its own – a recognition of the way in which contradictory class relationships both within capital and between capital and labour produce a multiplicity of antagonistic political pressures within which the state enjoys a significant degree of autonomy.

In picking one's way through that minefield of theory it is as well to go in stages. In essence the initial choice to be made goes in one of four directions, depending on the answer to two quite basic and interconnected questions: of whether the society that surrounds the state in Britain is capitalist or not; and whether the state enjoys autonomy from other élites or is merely their puppet. That choice is represented in Figure 17. Those are big questions. The answer here, as we have tried to show in Parts One and Two, is that the society is still capitalist in a Marxist sense of that term; and that accordingly our choice of theoretical framework has to be between 'C' and 'D'. What I want to show now is the superiority of 'D' over 'C' as a guide to contemporary developments in the British state.

It is easy enough to accumulate evidence that superficially supports a conspiratorial ruling-class model. The social background of key state personnel is very similar to that of private capitalist élites, as will be documented later. The political resources of capital, as was seen in Chapter 4, are enormous, and are extremely difficult for governments to redress or to ignore. Indeed, and on the contrary, as we shall see later (pp. 229–31), a large amount of state policy is quite directly geared to successful capital accumulation, and therefore to the reinforcing and enhancing of capital's political power. Macro-economic policy, state aid to industry, labour training, not to mention general legal codes on property and market transactions – all facilitate that accumulation

process. Many studies show too that governments which attempt to reduce the power of capitalist interests (in the British context, invariably Labour governments) are quickly pulled into line by a set of market forces, business pressures and co-ordinated (even conspiratorial) activity by state personnel, foreign governments, bankers and the like.[7]

Yet there are distinct dangers in that formulation. To begin with it suggests that social background is a key element linking the state with capital, such that the replacement of one set of state personnel by another might free the state to do other and more radical things. That in its turn might imply that the rise of a 'service class' would weaken state–capital relations whereas, in fact, as we have already seen, such people have been incorporated fully and neatly into extended capitalist hierarchies and do identify closely with capital. History has shown too that Labour governments, no less than Conservative ones, seem subservient to capital in spite of their more proletarian origins and connections with the labour movement. Indeed in some hands the argument can well be reversed: that it is Conservative governments, precisely because of the more elevated social background and élite connections of their leaders, who have greater autonomy here. The CBI experience since 1979 might be a case in point. What the experience of Conservative government under Margaret Thatcher serves to remind us is both that the state has a degree of *autonomy* – it can decide to pursue one strategy for capital rather than another – and that its freedom here derives in part from divisions within capital itself. Different sections of capital, as we have already seen, have different immediate interests, although they share similar concerns about capital in general and class privileges in particular. The rise and fall of different fractions of capital then alter the balance of political resources which can be mobilized on capital's behalf, and shift the demands emerging from capital on the state.

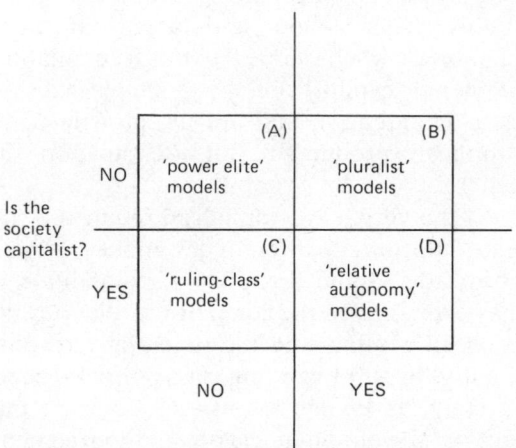

Figure 17   *Is the state autonomous of private élites?*

Nor should we forget that capital exists only through a relationship of exploitation and expropriation of wage labour, and through the consolidation of exploitative relationships with other oppressed strata outside wage relationships as such, particularly with women locked into domestic production. We have seen that even the class structure directly surrounding the accumulation process (that of global capital and the collective worker) is an immensely complex one, generative of a whole range of potentially conflicting political demands. The state is subject to those too; and even if we still hold to the view that its 'function' is to service capital, this gives it another source of autonomy. For in addition to its role as the articulator of the interests of 'capital in general' in the face of fractional divisions within capital itself, the state also needs to mediate and absorb political demands from below, lest their frustration precipitate movements against capital itself.

Indeed, to my mind that formulation is still too functionalist. It is presumably self-evident that capital does require the existence of a state power, and always needs state policies of a distinctly autonomous type, because of at least two weaknesses in capitalism: 'first the economic weakness of being unable to produce the necessary inputs of accumulation through accumulation itself; and second, the weakness that the ruling class, being made up of essentially competitive accumulating units, is unable to develop a class consciousness containing assented and workable directives as to how the state should operate'.[8] This in its turn means that capital always requires certain things of its state – that certain structures are 'indispensable for the functioning of the capitalist economy: the circuit of capital, the production, realisation and appropriation of surplus value; generalised commodity production and exchange; the reproduction and restructuring of capital and labour power, the conditions that allow the circuit of capital to exist'.[9] That imposes certain imperatives on the state, as the one agency available in the capitalist mode of production capable of providing these things.

In particular, the persistence of capitalism requires from its state 'the provision of an appropriate legal framework for generalised commodity production, the creation of the general material conditions for production (infrastructure), the regulation of the conflict between wage labour and capital, and the protection and expansion of the total national capital on the world market'.[10] Precisely because capitalism accumulates through production and exchange, and not through force or coercion of an overtly political kind, what it 'needs' its state to do is less to expropriate the surplus directly (as, say, in feudalism) than *to protect the commodity form*, and to 'remove all barriers which prevent the unimpeded circulation of commodities . . . on the principal of equal exchange'.[11] That in its turn makes it vital for the state to play a role in both the production of surplus value (by facilitating the reproduction of labour power) and in its realization (not least by its control of money as the universal commodity-equivalent). Indeed, as de Brunhoff has correctly observed, 'state management of the particular commodity labour power (inseparable from a regular supply of cheap labour) and state management of money (which is linked to the accumulation of money capital) are the principle axes of state intervention and are inseparable from capitalist production and circulation in general'.[12]

At the very least, capitalism requires of its state 'appropriate forms of law, money, labour power and labour discipline'.[13] In addition it may even – given the competitive relationship between capitals and the potentially revolutionary thrust of working class politics – need its state, as Poulantzas has it, to secure the unity of the dominant classes and to fragment and atomize its subordinate classes; thus providing 'those general conditions of production which cannot be assured by the private activities of the members of the dominant class', while at the same time repressing 'any threat to the prevailing mode of production' and integrating the ruling groups into a stable power bloc.[14]

But the specification of a 'need' is no guarantee of its performance. What capitalism generates around the state is not a set of unavoidable imperatives so much as a set of conflicting demands, a particular balance of class and popular forces, which determines whether, to what degree and in what form those 'functions' are performed. As a result neither 'instrumentalist' nor 'essentialist' treatments of the capitalist state are adequate here. Where 'essentialist' theories fail – theories, that is, which derive the activities of the state from some functional imperatives essential to the logic of accumulation itself – is in their inability to cope adequately with the way in which those functional demands are *filtered* into the political arena through the complex groups and interests called into existence by the civil society that capitalism also creates. By confusing 'mode of production' with 'social formation', such theories leave us unable to situate properly the impact of class and popular struggles, and the pressures of non-capitalist classes, on the trajectory of state policy. Where 'instrumentalist' theories fail on the other hand – theories, that is, which treat the state simply as an instrument of the capitalist class, normally guaranteed by the shared social background of senior state and business personnel – is in their inability both to explain working-class political successes and to cope adequately with the way in which state policy changes over time, even though the élite structure remains firmly intact and largely unaltered. Instrumentalist views of politics in capitalism have difficulty in dealing with the *autonomy* of the state, and with the distance between the political demands of capital and the policy which the state pursues in the interests of capital as a whole. Yet it is just this autonomy that we need to

understand if we are to grasp the true character of the state's role in contemporary Britain.

What the state enjoys in contemporary Britain is an important degree of relative autonomy. It enjoys autonomy – it is not the passive tool of any private élite – and yet that autonomy is relative, operating only within definite constraints. Both the autonomy and the constraints should be traced back to the complex character of the capitalist mode of production and its associated civil society. The sources of autonomy are in essence *fivefold*. First, the state enjoys autonomy because in capitalism the process of surplus creation and expropriation takes place in a distinct economic sphere. The state has a role to play in facilitating that process, but is not organically locked into it. On the contrary, its autonomy is vital here to the accumulation process from which it is excluded, precisely because, as we have just seen, successful private accumulation requires 'an institution that is not immediately subordinate to market forces . . . to provide those general preconditions of capital accumulation as a whole that are inappropriate or impossible for any particular competing capital to secure'.[15]

Autonomy arises too because that economic sphere achieves its successful accumulation only through competition between capitalist units, each of which is thus incapable of specifying the long-term interests of capital as a whole. The very 'anarchy of competition-geared capitalist production' makes it extremely unlikely that any 'standardised concept of capitalist class-interest would emerge'[16] automatically. Different sectors of capital are too locked in competition with one another for that, and too pressed to take the short-term view for their own survival, to allow any longer-term perspective to evolve. As a result, the state finds that its autonomy here is more *creative* than *additive*. It finds itself obliged not just to sum and to coordinate a set of immediate political demands articulated at it by private firms, banks and peak organizations of business. It finds rather that it is obliged to specify independently what the long-term interests of capital actually are, in processes of consultation of course, but in the end in processes of considerable autonomy also. 'For it is only when', and to the degree that, 'the state is removed from a direct relationship with particular fractions (of capital) that it can provide the necessary conditions for general capitalist production.'[17]

Moreover, in the pursuit of those longer-term interests, the state also finds that an accumulation process subordinated to capitalist imperatives necessarily generates class and popular forces opposed to the resulting market-specified allocation of power and rewards. The accommodation of these forces is also a vital long-term concern of capital as a whole – one which the state is called upon to achieve (not least through the *electoral* pressures to which it is regularly subject). In fact, the universe of the state becomes immensely complex at just this point, as we have seen. Precisely because capitalism is a system of generalized commodity production – one with a sphere of circulation and exchange as well as of production – the state faces a universe structured not simply by the social relationships of capitalist production but also by its associated patterns of distribution, exchange and consumption. It is into that civil society that the state finds itself drawn, both to meet the demands of disadvantaged and privileged consumer groups struggling with one another, and to structure the reproduction of labour power vital to the underlying production process. All this too is a source of autonomy of the state from any direct and unmediated control by any section of capital.

Finally, the autonomy of the state derives too from the concentration of resources, the proliferation of bureaucratic structures, and the immediate political interests that accrue to the state sector as it seeks to facilitate private capital accumulation, working-class accommodation, and the stability of civil society as a whole. That is, autonomy derives for the state from divisions within capital, from the force of popular and class dissent, and from the bureaucratic and electoral interests of state personnel and processes themselves.

This autonomy, however, is relative; one beset by constraints that in practice pull state policy towards the pursuit of the interests of capital as a whole. In fact, in capitalist societies, given 'the "surrogateship" of business and the heavy dependence of government on business for the realisation of its own objectives, the "natural" situation is for the policies of the government to be heavily constrained by the goals and interests of business'.[18] Again, the constraints can be listed, this time as *four*. First, the very separation of politics and economics in the capitalist mode of production leaves the state dependent – for its revenue and resources – on a private system of capital accumulation. Regardless of any pressures directed at it from that process, therefore, the state has an independent interest in, and commitment to, successful accumulation as such. 'Thus every interest the state (or the personnel of the state apparatus, its various branches and agencies) may have in their own stability and development can only be pursued if it is in accordance with the imperative of maintaining accumulation',[19] and so in this way the 'health' of the economy becomes a preoccupation colouring every aspect of state policy to some degree. It is a preoccupation, moreover, which results, not from outside control by capital, but 'from an institutional self-interest of the state which is conditioned by the fact that the state is *denied* the power to control the flow of those resources which are indispensible for the *use* of state power'. The state then necessarily becomes interested, 'for the sake of its own power – in guaranteeing and safeguarding a "healthy" accumulation process upon which it depends'.[20]

Moreover, the class-controlled nature of that accumulation process, and the centrality of the state to its success, has encouraged down the years the consolidation of very intimate connections between senior state personnel and the wider capitalist class, as we will see in detail later. The personnel of the state, its hierarchies and its practices, are locked into an intimate relationship with private capital. Yet the closeness of that relationship between capital and the state does not enable the state to escape from the crisis-ridden and contradictory nature of the accumulation process under capitalism. On the contrary, as the state is drawn in more and more to service that accumulation process, and to offset the worst social consequences of recession and industrial decline, it finds that it cannot remove permanently those features of capitalism from its own agenda. For it remains ultimately subordinate to the laws of motion of capitalist economies; and finds its autonomy restricted too by the degree of political mobilization and social power sustained by those adversely affected by crises. In sum, the state has to operate in the 'space' left to it by capitalist pressures on the one side and popular resistance on the other. In times of rapid capital accumulation and/or working-class passivity, that space can be quite wide; but the inherently unstable nature of the accumulation process means that the boundaries of that space are perpetually in flux and inherently prone to close in times of recession.

To understand this and to direct our thinking on the development of state policy in Britain since the war, a diagram will be useful. A simple 'ruling class' model, of the kind in Figure 18, is too static and too crude for our purposes. For 'the state is not to be derived either from the dominant class(es) whose supposed instrument it is, nor from the nature and movements of capital. It is rather to be seen as resulting from the interdependent relations between the economy and civil society: the former sets its demands, the latter provides the context within which it struggles to resolve them'.[21] Accordingly it seems more

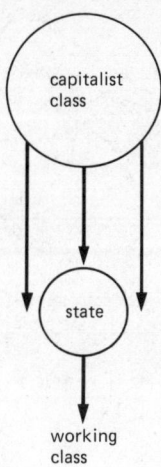

Figure 18 *'Ruling-class' model*

sensible to think of the relationship between the state, capital and labour as it is shown in Figure 19.

In Figure 19, 'A' and 'B' represent the range of common interests articulated at the state by capital, and 'C' the set of pressures emerging from oppressed classes. What is not obvious from this figure, but was discussed in Chapter 9, is the extent to which one job of the state is to actively shape the content of 'C'. For the moment what we must recognize is 'C''s material base – in a set of interests deriving from the same accumulation process as 'A' and 'B', but fundamentally in contradiction with them. For although capital and labour share a similar dependence on successful accumulation, they differ in their interests within that accumulation process. If 'A' and 'B' seek higher profits, 'C''s concern might be for higher wages. If 'A' and 'B' need greater productivity, 'C''s need is for greater job control, and so on. Putting it this way may help to suggest, among other things, that in periods of capitalist prosperity the constraints posed by 'A' and 'B' will be fairly mild and wide, and the pressure from 'C' muted by full employment and local bargaining power; but that as capitalism weakens, 'C' may be expected to

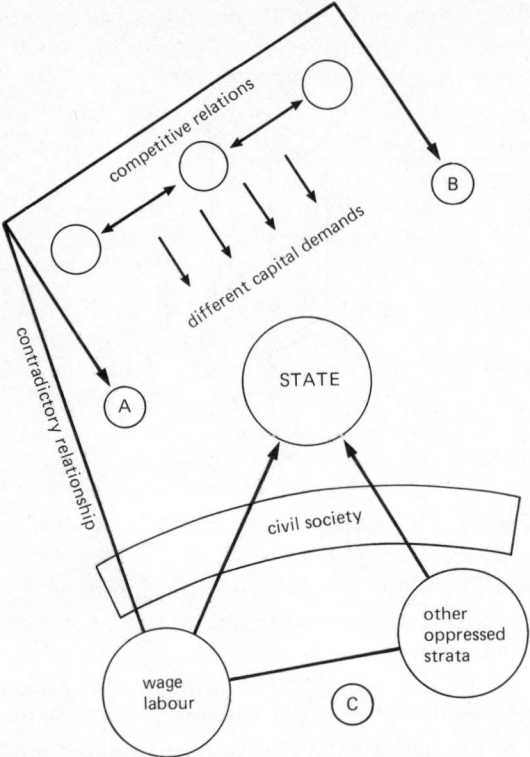

Figure 19 *'Relative autonomy' model*

radicalize at just the moment that 'A' and 'B' narrow and intensify. That certainly has been an important element in the story of British politics since the war, as we shall see (Chapter 11).

State involvement in the development of capitalism

The state has been involved in the development of capitalism in Britain from the outset. Down the years the interests of successive governments in economic strength and social peace have been reflected in different balances of intervention, aimed at encouraging the development of productive forces, ensuring that private wealth and capital could accumulate in that process, weakening by well-timed

reforms any radical and revolutionary forces that might develop, and meeting genuine commitments to a fairer and juster society characteristic of sections of each generation's political élite. That last impulse has generally been the weakest of the four, most evident in early capitalist industrialization among sections of the ruling class opposed to the process as such, and evident later in the 'one nation' strand of the Conservative Party and in the Radical Liberalism from which the early generations of Labour Party leaders and thinkers were predominantly recruited. More normally, the state has had to be pulled into reforms by popular mobilizations, which paradoxically (on issues such as Factory Acts) might help to enhance the long-term stability of the capitalist system against whose immediate practices they were directed, but which in the short-run were always ferociously resisted by the political spokesmen of capital.[22]

As we have seen already, and will discuss again, it may well be that the recent political (and industrial) strength of the post-war labour movement has gone beyond this, to constitute in its own right an important if subsidiary barrier to capital accumulation in Britain in an epoch in which capital is internationally mobile, and as such to constitute one element in the contemporary crisis of the British state. But what is clear from the history of British capitalism overall is that this working-class power is new in political terms, and that prior to 1945 the rhythm and scope of state intervention in economic activity was fixed predominantly by the political demands articulated by capital, and by the independent perceptions of appropriate policy by leading figures in the state. Except for those brief periods of working-class mobilization around the two world wars, economic and social policy took its shape from the way in which the needs of the local accumulation process were perceived in government, a perception greatly influenced over the years by the interests of finance capital (as we have seen, pp. 60–7), and by the changing character of industrial capital (as we must now establish).

In characterizing this changing relationship between capital and the state over the years, we might draw on the work of O'Connor, Habermas and Offe. Habermas suggests we distinguish three historical forms of state intervention: 'market constituting forms', 'market complementing' and 'market replacing'.[23] That is, in the *constitutive* years of capitalism, the state assisted its growth, to the extent that it did, by 'securing the system of civil law, based on property and contract, protect[ing] the market from . . . internal self-destructive side effects (e.g. currency reform) . . . [and] external military and trade threats, and . . . helped promote domestic and international competition and crushed internal class enemies'.[24] Then, as liberal capitalism began to be replaced by a system dominated by monopolies, the state's role expanded to *complement* market activity with new forms of business finance, laws and so on. Only in the monopoly stage proper, particularly from 1945, has the state been drawn further, into directly *replacing* certain market activities by economic activity of its own. We have lived for a generation in that period, in which the state has moved beyond a purely 'allocative' and 'enabling' relationship with private capital, into one which is directly 'productive' in its own right.[25]

We must be careful here, however, not to fall back on a simple functionalism, into the assertion that the state does whatever the capitalist mode of production requires of it. In fact, the changing functions of the state are themselves a result of struggles and pressures released by forces and processes at different stages of capitalist development. In early capitalism, where surplus value was expropriated 'absolutely' – by working the emerging proletariat for long hours with little machinery – state policy grew out of the interplay of at least three processes of struggle: from nascent capitalist interests demanding an appropriate

legal and monetary framework, and a basic infrastructure of roads and communications; from popular forces seeking the right of labour to limit its hours, to establish minimum conditions of work, and to enjoy minimum rights of union organization; and from the campaign to extend the formal equality of the capitalist market-place into the political equality embodied in universal franchise. Indeed, in the early years of capitalist take-off, the state's main job was often to guarantee that labour power itself was available – to 'constrain' the bearers of labour power to sell their labour, by destroying their capacity to avoid the wage-relationship through self-sufficient agricultural work or through statute/guild protected artisanal modes of petty commodity production.

That 'need' to reproduce labour power in a form suitable for successful capital accumulation remained as one central imperative on the state thereafter. Indeed, 'the need to maintain the continuous presence of the three elements – work discipline, insecurity of employment and a permanent supply of proletarian labour power costing as little as possible – implies state intervention which is immanent in the process of capital accumulation at the same time as it is fundamentally external to it'.[26] But in the early competitive stage of industrial capitalism, the reproduction of labour power with these characteristics did not require major state activity of a detailed and interventionist kind. All the state had to ensure was that labour was available and looking for work. If the state's job in this field now is to 'manage . . . a certain level of global employment' its job then was different and more brutal: to force 'a mass of independent workers into the capitalist wage system'.[27] With labour power available, and production organized on simple lines in small and competitive units, all that early industrial capital required of its state was a *quick return*, and the state therefore found itself heavily pressed to lubricate the sphere of circulation – to facilitate transport development, to open markets, to guarantee currencies, to penalize debt. This was the liberal moment of the state, one that was eroded quickly by the arrival of machinery and the rise of monopolies.

That move into capitalism's later stage happened more or less quickly, depending on the outcomes of struggles around the state in capitalism's liberal stage. If the rate of accumulation was blocked – by a heavy peasant presence in national politics, as in France, for example – the transition was inevitably delayed. If the local state was dominated by class fractions only loosely involved in industrial production – as with finance capital in pre-1914 Britain – then again state policy would be slow to pick up the new imperatives. But eventually, as competition between capitals brought a centralization and concentration of capital and allowed the consolidation of an industrially-strong set of trade unions, the political demands of industrial capital and of labour began to alter. The scale of capital investment dominant in the industrial sector made the realization of profits problematic, and built in a tendency to 'permanent over-accumulation' (leaving, that is, always the possibility that levels of demand would be inadequate to sustain the profitability of the existing amount of capital investment). In its first manifestation, this fuelled the drive for colonies and the building up of military machines by the states of capitalism's metropolitan centres. In the post-war years it lent corporate support to state policies which inflated domestic demand and extended the base of private credit. The reproduction of labour power of a particular kind – better educated, healthier and more disciplined – also became increasingly vital to sections of industrial capital; and here these needs often merged with the concerns of organized labour for better social provision, guaranteed employment and rising standards of living. For with basic political rights won in the period of liberal capitalism, labour movements then turned to wider social and industrial rights, and added their voice to that of corporate capital in the pursuit of greater state regulation of the market economy.

Over time, that is, the state has been drawn into increasing the scale of, and altering the balance between, expenditure of three types. Two of these were, and remain, indirectly productive of surplus value for capital: social investment (projects and services that increase the productivity of labour) and social consumption (projects and services that lower the reproduction costs of labour power). One was, and is, not even indirectly productive of surplus value: namely social expenses (projects and services which are required to maintain social harmony, to fulfil the state's legitimation function). Down the years, of course, any particular expenditure has normally involved a mixture of all three, but precisely because the reproduction of favourable conditions for accumulation has come to depend more and more upon the active intervention of the state, certain features of the accumulation process in late capitalism have required the state to increase the scale of provision of them all.

We noted certain of these features in Chapter 2, not least 'the increasing socialisation of the forces of production, the growing capital-intensity of production and the growing importance of technological innovation in improving labour productivity, the lengthening turn-over time of certain key branches of production, and the emergence of cyclical crises associated with dislocations in the private credit system'.[28] The sheer scale and concentration of capital in big monopolistic units drew the state into the provision of inputs vital to accumulation but too costly for any individual private capital concern to provide alone. State provision of certain inputs arose because private capital could no longer run them viably at all. The nationalization of basic energy sources is a case in point. The extension of transport systems is another. State provision of other inputs merely socialized costs, and underwrote expenditure, too risky for even large monopolies to carry with any enthusiasm. State funding of research and development, and state subsidies to firms located in under-developed areas, may also be explained largely in these terms.

The state found that the *realization* of profits in the monopoly sector required guaranteed and rising levels of aggregate demand, the systematic extension of private credit under government direction, and large direct government purchases from state-organized military institutions, welfare organizations and infrastructural services. It found too that the protection of accumulation domestically, in an increasingly competitive world market, required extensive state initiatives both internally – to strengthen productivity and enhance returns on capital – and externally, through the negotiation of trade deals, the guaranteeing of export-credits and the manipulation, after 1971, of exchange rates.

The actual pattern of state intervention here has taken its shape from the experience of the monopoly sector as a whole, with the state finding it enough merely to guarantee aggregate demand and nationalize basic utilities in the early years of the long boom, but finding itself drawn more and more into detailed interventions as competition intensified and the recession deepened. The driving force in all this was not, however, merely capital alone. For the state – in doing all these things for capital – was obliged also to mediate other pressures, particularly those emanating from the labour movement. The pressure to nationalize basic industries, to construct a broadly-based set of welfare services, and to guarantee full employment through the manipulation of aggregate demand, was placed on the agenda of national politics not by capital but by labour – as the price that labour insisted capital must pay for inter-war depression and world conflict. In fact there were moments when it looked as though that price would be

greater still: until the flood-tide of radicalism was stemmed by the victory of moderate forces within the Labour Party under Attlee after 1935, and by the rearguard action of private capital and its foreign allies, not least the United States government, in the years of immediate post-war reconstruction.

The 'space' for that accommodation between capital and labour was provided by the rapid capital accumulation of the long post-war boom, which enabled the adverse long-term consequences for capital of entrenched working-class power to be obscured for a generation by the rapid increase in world trade and output as a whole. The shift in class forces produced by full employment was reflected in the late 1960s in two things which we have already mentioned: in the low productivity of capital in British industry, and in the steadily increasing share of GNP being directed, through the state, into welfare provision of various kinds – education, health, social services and recreation – both of which were then to contribute to the deepening crisis of the British economy and its state, to which we shall refer again in a moment. It is important to understand now the way in which the changing character of monopoly capitalism in Britain, and the attendant strength of organized labour, have combined to expand the range of activities pursued by the post-war British state, to move it far beyond the merely 'formal' and 'substantive' facilitation of private accumulation into the sphere of active 'direction' of economic activities,[29] and to integrate it fully into the 'valorisation, realisation and expanded reproduction of the total social capital'.[30]

To argue this, of course, is not to say that the state necessarily does any of these things very well. On the contrary, 'there is no guarantee that the state will discover the correct forms of . . . intervention nor even that it will avoid making catastrophic mistakes'. It is simply to point out the degree to which successful capital accumulation in Britain has come to depend upon the 'increasingly direct involvement'[31] of the state. This is manifest in so many developments of the post-war British state. Government after government after 1945 took as its prime responsibility the management of the domestic economy, and until the late 1960s at least, struggled to maintain full employment there. Indeed state agencies became major employers in their own right, buying machinery, hiring labour, struggling over wages and profits; and at the same time governments made it their responsibility to shape output, investment, productivity and pay in the private sector as a whole. Successive governments created, and then expanded, a whole battery of welfare services. Basic utilities were nationalized between 1945 and 1950 (coal, gas, electricity, railways and steel); and later governments took into public ownership large private concerns deemed too valuable to lose, including Rolls Royce in 1971 and British Leyland in 1974.

In each case, although at different times and under different immediate imperatives, state ownership was followed by extensive re-organization – by the scrapping of old capital, the writing off of old debts, the shedding of labour, and the imposition of new and tighter working methods. The kinds of 'restructuring' that the private sector could not manage in these industries, the state eventually performed, constrained only by the degree of worker resistance and by any absence of market competition and political pressure for greater efficiency. It took until the 1960s for those pressures to build up in the coal industry, for example; but when they did, successive governments shut pits at the rate of one a week, and reduced the mining labour force by half a million. Similar stories can be told for steel, machine tools and cars,[32] where competitive pressures led to massive re-organization in the 1970s, as the 'heat' came off the coal industry, at least temporarily, because of rising oil prices and rekindled industrial militancy among the remaining

miners. Throughout, these nationalized industries acted in the market, treated their workers, and chose their managers, as though they were private capitalist concerns, departing from that model, if they did so at all, only in pricing policies which effectively subsidized the costs of production in the private sector proper.[33] As such they constituted an important area of socialized production in the United Kingdom economy, contributing 11 per cent of GDP in 1975, employing 8 per cent of the total labour force, and providing 19 per cent of all total fixed investment.

Moreover, a vast apparatus of state controls on, directions for, and aids to industrial production proliferated in the post-war period, as the state moved in to promote new combinations of capital, take control of particular companies, and reorganize relations between firms and between employers and labour. As a result, any standard economic textbook on post-war industrial policy is now obliged to move through a growing list of economic and fiscal controls, legal regulations, mechanisms of encouragement and exhortation, financial inducements, and state-provided advice and services. Governments have acted too to manage industrial conflict and to socialize certain of the immediate costs of reproducing labour power, by introducing new labour laws, maintaining minimum factory conditions, providing redundancy payments and funding industrial retraining. Governments in the 1960s repeatedly initiated incomes controls (to cheapen labour power), experimented with new planning mechanisms for the economy as a whole, and set up specialist institutions (the IRC in the 1960s, the NEB in the 1970s) to organize industrial mergers and provide 'risk capital' for new enterprises. It is striking that across this whole list of extended activities, government involvement was broadly consistent, regardless of party colour. There was some unevenness, of course. It was Labour governments who showed the greater propensity to nationalize, to plan, to extend welfare provision and to fund mergers; but time and again, until 1979 at least, incoming Conservative governments quickly shed their anti-socialist rhetoric and pursued equally supportive and interventionist industrial and welfare policies within the same commitments to the mixed economy and full employment. In all these ways successive governments in the post-war years expanded their expenditure on 'social investment' and 'social consumption' as they balanced capital and labour in the pursuit of successful accumulation and their own electoral survival.

What is striking about state policy in these areas is the contradictory elements that appear among them. State policies to facilitate capital restructuring and enhance productivity sit alongside policies which give rights against compulsory redundancy, rights to organize in unions and rights to enjoy minimum standards of health and safety at work. That contradiction is itself a reflection of the way the state is obliged to react to both capital and labour, with its policies shaped by the balance of class forces mobilized around it. For although the growth of state intervention 'primarily reflects the interests of capital and the tendencies inherent in the capital accumulation process, the continuing class struggle ensures that the requirements of capital are not the only determinants of state policy'.[34] It is with this in mind that we can locate the whole question of welfare provision by the state in late capitalism.

It is customary in certain political circles these days to see the spending which the state provided on welfare as running against its growing involvement in the process of accumulation – to see it, that is, as a 'burden' to be borne by capital as the price of post-war social peace. It is certainly the case that the creation of the welfare state was greeted in these terms by spokesmen for capital in the 1940s. This is not surprising, since a significant percentage of welfare provision makes no direct contribu-tion to the reproduction of labour power, and in that sense is a 'social expense', tolerated by capital because of working-class power, and 'rollable back' in times of working-class weakness and capitalist crisis. But not all welfare provision should be seen in that light. The construction of a broadly-based welfare state after 1945 is a testimony to the way in which, at crucial moments of class conflict, even a capitalist state has to respond to working-class pressure, has to play, that is, the card of 'passive revolution' to which we have already referred. The subsequent growth of the welfare system is also testimony to the entrenched power that the welfare bureaucracies themselves come to constitute, with their own private sets of interests in greater social spending by the state. Growth here too has reflected quite distinct campaigns by the TUC and other labour organizations for better health care, more schools, proper state pensions and more generous financial assistance to the sick and disabled – the very success of which reinforces the commitment of the organized working class to parliamentary democracy in particular and the existing social order in general. Indeed it is clear that the legitimacy of the existing social order is enhanced, in the eyes of those least privileged

Table 35 *Growth of welfare state expenditure in the United Kingdom, as a percentage of GNP, 1921–75*

	1921	*1961*	*1975*
Welfare state expenditure	10.1	17.6	28.8
social security	4.7	6.7	9.5
health and welfare	3.3	4.4	7.1
education		2.2	7.6
housing	2.1	2.3	4.6
Other state expenditure	19.2	24.4	29.1
Total state expenditure	29.4	42.1	57.9

Source: M. Campbell, *Capitalism in the UK* (Croom Helm 1981), p. 183.

by it, by the existence of a 'safety net' of welfare provision, and by the apparent 'reformability' of the capitalist state to which its creation seems to stand witness. This too makes welfare provision highly functional for capital.

Indeed, the fact that the post-war state built a National Health Service, and expanded education and welfare provision, at the behest initially of the labour movement and of radical middle-class opinion, is also evidence of the way in which working-class pressures actually help to reproduce capitalism and to enhance its long-term stability: in this case by generating higher levels of demand for capitalist products as a whole, by getting the state to socialize the costs of the reproduction of a healthier and more educated labour force vital to late capitalism, and by providing a new basis of legitimacy for the entire social order. If working-class mobilization has often been a catalyst for such social reform, capital itself has proved immensely adept at shaping its subsequent administration, adapting to its contours, and modifying its provision to the benefit of the accumulation process. It is in this sense that welfare provision under capitalism should be seen as at one and the same time a victory for working-class pressure (an area free from the direct dictates of the law of value) and a mechanism of social integration (helping to reproduce capitalist social relations and consolidate their legitimacy in working-class eyes).

For state expenditure on 'collective commodities such as education and infrastructure can become forms of "social investment" which increase the productivity of labour, or "social consumption" which lower the reproduction cost of labour power'.[35] If not all welfare provision is of this kind, much of the rest still constitutes 'social expenses' vital to the reproduction of capitalism as a whole. The very fact that capitalism, as it develops, leaves more and more people wholly dependent on their wage for survival, also means that, unless

the state acts, few social mechanisms are left to sustain those without wages; and the volatility of capitalist competitive relationships means that at times the scale of that unemployment can be expected to grow very rapidly indeed. In these cases, the welfare 'safety net' may be a burden on the employed, but the cost to capital of the social upheavals of a less caring society would no doubt be considerably greater. Indeed, even in times of rapid accumulation, capitalism needs some external agency to reproduce its labour power; and this is particularly so in late capitalism, where 'the increasing use of machinery, and the ever finer division of labour, require new and changing skills in the labour force and hence changes in the education and training fields'.[36] There are therefore plenty of good 'capitalist reasons' why state activity here should expand: providing health care, maintaining the unemployed and the sick, training and retraining workers, and even providing the services of social workers to help smooth the family problems, mental illness and delinquency that the daily reality of capitalist pressures can build up in deeply oppressed sections of capitalism's poor. At least one important commentator on welfare provision has argued strongly that these 'needs' lie behind the bulk of recent welfare growth: that 'rising costs, changing population structure and the emergence of new needs probably account for almost all of the growth of social expenditure since the Second World War. Very little, or conceivably none at all, represents a real improvement in the satisfaction of needs'.[37]

Moreover, the internal organization, working and finance of the whole welfare system can be quite functional to the private accumulation process. The way in which the NHS was organized – in vast bureaucratic structures which reproduced social inequalities inherited from the capitalist labour process, meant that the welfare state as it expanded also reproduced the divisions of the capitalist class structure, locked its 'consumers' into relationships of subordination to its own official specifications of their needs and illnesses, and continued to train individuals for their 'place' within a highly unequal social order. Massive barriers of bureaucratic complexity continue to divide ordinary workers from the full enjoyment of, let alone control over, their existing welfare rights; so that for many, the state's welfare provision is experienced as yet another control agency of capital, obliging them to sell their labour power cheaply and to restrict their consumption to the minimum. It is here, more than anywhere else, that 'state service shades into class control'.[38]

In addition, and as we have already seen in an earlier context, the assumptions on which the social security system was built helped to reproduce inequalities of gender, locked women into domestic production, and enhanced their status as a cheap source of industrial labour. Nothing in the whole area of social provision, least of all the level of unemployment pay, is allowed to erode the wage relationship of capitalism, or to hinder the availability of a supply of cheap and co-operative labour power. Although the maintenance of the non-working population – the aged, sick, disabled and those unable to work – by welfare provision is a 'cost' which takes away part of the total surplus from capital, the whole system of taxation works to restrict the main burden to the employed working class, and away from the income and privileges of the capitalist class itself.[39] 'A limited amount of redistribution between classes apart, the state in effect acts as an agent for the collective self-security of earners and their dependents . . . reallocating resources from one stage of individual life cycles to others and . . . giving some assurance of bed-rock provision for the old, the sick, the unemployed and some of the lowest paid.'[40] That of course is a vital gain for a working class hitherto denied even that, but it hardly constitutes a major penetration of the privileges of capital.

In total then, the welfare state can be seen to 'operate to secure the necessary conditions for reproducing capitalist social relations: that is, reproducing labour power, maintaining the non-working population and ensuring social stability'.[41] So its existence may be said to be quite compatible with general state policy aimed at strengthening accumulation. Indeed, as we shall see (pp. 250–2), it was only when that accumulation process met serious difficulties in the recession of the 1970s that the scale of welfare provision hitherto deemed vital to capitalist reproduction came under serious challenge from capital and the state.

The composition and form of the state

Before commenting in detail on the growing difficulties surrounding the pursuit of its functions by the contemporary British state, a comment is necessary on the composition and form of that state. This topic is more properly a subject for specialists in the fields of public administration and comparative institutional analysis, but the context within which the state acts has a bearing on their concerns that we need to note, and state forms play an important role in shaping the functions and wider impact of state activity, and so are of concern to us.

The first thing to observe here is perhaps the most obvious: that the internal composition and administrative practices of the state are not neutral between classes, in at least two senses. State personnel are not neutral. Nor is the general drift of the state's administrative behaviour. It is true that 'the correlation which can be established in class terms between the state élite and the economically dominant class'[42] is not sufficiently strong and unambiguous a piece of evidence to demonstrate that the state is a class state. On the contrary, since Kautsky's remark is broadly accurate, that 'the capitalist class rules but does not govern: it contents itself with ruling the government',[43] it should not surprise us that the state élite is recruited from a wider social base than that common for leadership positions in the private corporate sector. That is indeed the case. Not all senior civil servants come from privileged backgrounds;[44] and especially when a Labour government is in power, senior executive positions in the state are occupied by predominantly lower middle class and professional people, if not these days by the sons (or very occasionally the daughters) of manual workers and their wives.

Nevertheless the linkage at the level of personnel between the state and private capitalist élites is a close and significant one, and must not be overlooked.[45] It remains the case that linkages between the Conservative Party, industry and finance are extremely close, and that senior cabinet figures in Conservative governments are drawn disproportionately from the propertied class. As John Ross has observed, 'the connection between the Tory party and the ruling class is one of the closest and tightest of any capitalist party in the world'.[46] In this respect the first Thatcher Cabinet was fairly typical of its predecessors. 71 per cent of its members were company directors, 14 per cent were large landowners and 10 per cent were lawyers. The bulk of Tory MPs (74.2 per cent in 1979) were similarly company directors, lawyers or accountants. The contemporary Conservative Party, like Conservative parties before it, continues in Parliament to be 'totally dominated by company boards, professions closely tied to business such as accountancy and law, and some sections of the state apparatus such as the armed forces' (Table 36).[47]

It is still the case too that a very large percentage of senior civil servants, particularly in finance departments such as the Treasury, do have at least an Oxbridge (and to a lesser extent public school) background. Between 1945 and 1963, 84.4 per cent of all permanent secretaries had been to Oxbridge, and 74.7 per cent to public school.[48] The figures for administrative trainees were still 51.9 per cent

and 56 per cent in 1975.[49] It is also true that on retirement a very large number of senior civil servants move into senior positions in the private capitalist sector. Brian Sedgemore listed twenty-seven such retirements by permanent secretaries between 1974 and 1977, and was able to locate at least thirty-five top jobs into which nineteen of them moved.[50] There is still a significant degree of social interaction between senior civil servants and private élites, not least in the 'old boy' network of the London clubs;[51] and the selection of personnel within the state is such as to socialize them into a set of attitudes and values that legitimate private capital accumulation and the privileges of the capitalist class. As John Scott has written, 'occupants of positions within the state are selected and moulded in such a way that their personal interests in maintaining their position and their public duties in protecting the state both coincide with the objective requirements of continued capital accumulation which have been structured into the state apparatuses they run'.[52]

For as Ernest Mandel has correctly observed, the state in capitalist society is 'twice over-determined by the bourgeois class': with its senior officials 'filtered by a long promotion process' to ensure their general identification with capital, and with its own bureaucratic structures and practices designed, just as capitalist hierarchies are, to prevent the direct exercise of power by the working class.[53] The growth of bureaucracy in general and the growing concentration and centralization of state power in particular, reinforces the political subordination of the people as a whole. For it separates them from the exercise of state power and leads to their isolation as individual clients or consumers of the administration and its services. This is reinforced by the monopoly of official secrets and state control over information.

Indeed, Mandel's comment on state structures and practices reminds us of a second

Table 36   *Educational and occupational backgrounds of Conservative MPs, 1945–74*

	1945	1950	1951	1955	1959	1964	1966	1970	1974a	1974b
				Numbers of MPs at each election						
Education										
Eton	55	77	75	75	70	66	56	62	54	47
All public	169	240	216	264	274	232	199	243	222	206
Oxford	62	94	99	106	104	66	80	93	89	76
Cambridge	46	62	68	74	79	88	64	75	76	76
All universities	131	187	199	217	219	190	169	208	198	186
Total no. of Conservative MPs	213	297	320	343	365	301	253	330	297	277
Occupation										
Barrister	37	51	55	60	66	58	48	50	50	47
Solicitor	4	10	11	11	12	13	13	13	11	9
Civil service	3	2	2	1	1	0	0	0	1	1
Diplomatic service	8	11	12	14	14	17	14	12	11	8
Military	30	30	31	36	30	20	11	12	4	4
Director	67	100	109	113	122	85	74	94	83	81
Banking and finance	1	4	2	2	3	3	4	7	13	13
Commerce and insurance	7	8	10	14	17	13	9	13	11	9
Farmer, landowner	25	28	32	30	36	36	34	35	28	22
Other	31	53	56	62	64	56	46	94	85	83
Total	213	297	320	343	365	301	253	330	297	277

Note: the two entries for 1974 relate to the two elections of that year.
Source: J. Scott, *The Upper Classes* (Macmillan 1982), pp. 163, 175.

sense in which the modern state is locked into an organic relationship with capital: through administrative procedures which guarantee that under normal circumstances (that is, when not formally controlled by anti-capitalist, left-wing forces) the state will operate as a capitalist one. It is here that the work of Claus Offe has been particularly important, exploring the extent to which 'selective mechanisms' operate *within* the state's own routines and formal structures to keep its policy broadly in line with the needs of the accumulation process. Offe differentiates between *negative* selection mechanisms, 'exclusion rules' operating at the four levels of 'structure, ideology, power and repression' as a 'system of filters'[54] to exclude anti-capitalist interests, and *posi-*

tive ones which predispose the state towards capital in general. Offe is in fact pessimistic about the state's capacity to service capital properly, but is in no doubt that the modern state is organized to filter out (through its bureaucratic procedures, and its constitutional and ideological predisposition towards private property) any radical anti-capitalist forces that might seek to use it.

Given the repeated failure of the British state to reconstitute the competitiveness of British industrial capital, it may be that Offe's pessimism here is well grounded, although more prosaic and parochial factors could well be more important in this instance. For it is clear too that the distribution of power between different sections of the state bureaucracy is itself a crucial mechanism for establishing the dominance of one fraction of capital over another; and that in this respect the hegemony of the Treasury within the state is one important reason for the disproportionate influence of banking capital in the power bloc as a whole. Rather than any inexorable and invariable conflict between bureaucratic rationality within the state and the needs of accumulation outside it, it may be that the failure of the state to 'modernize' British industry can be best explained in part by noting Treasury strength, and in part by observing the way in which – as Offe has seen – the state's necessarily 'reactive' relationship to crises gives it a propensity to 'muddle through' rather than to plan and to execute coherent policy designs.

Be that as it may, it remains the case that the close 'partnership' between the modern state and private capital means quite simply that 'any civil servants concerned with economic decision-making, intervention and regulation can ill-afford to ignore the fact that attitudes and actions which are capable of being construed as "anti-business" are bound to antagonise powerful and influential people, and are not likely to be particularly popular with political office-holders either'.[55] Ever more immersed into the 'management' of the accumulation process by the Keynesian policies of the late capitalist state, such bureaucrats can be neither neutral between classes nor radical between social systems. Their very function, job experience, social background, training and bureaucratic practices necessarily make them 'conservative', with a small if not a large 'C'.

This is not to say, however, that the relationship between the state and capital has to be understood only at the level of personnel and administrative practices. There are deeper, structural processes at work too. There is some relationship, however loose, between the stages of capitalist development and the characteristic form of the state. That

fit is not a total one. At any stage of capitalist development various state forms seem possible – from liberal regimes to authoritarian ones – depending on the pattern of incorporation of the particular national capitalism in the uneven but combined development of world capitalism as a whole, and the associated character and balance of class forces dominant in each. Nevertheless, the kind of class relationships, and accumulation processes, peculiar to different stages of capitalist development seem to invite certain state forms.[56]

The process of primitive accumulation associated with the emergence of industrial capitalism required primarily coercion and protection from its state, and seemed to fit most easily with authoritarian political regimes. Early capitalist industrialization occurred best with a state that respected private property and yet was unresponsive to the protests of the poor, taking either the form of a liberal representative (but not yet full democratic) regime or some kind of authoritarian state underpinned by limited forms of political representation for the middle class. In the age of monopolies and rising working-class militancy, the stability of the state came to require an extension of the franchise, the beginning of welfare provision and the first tentative construction of linking institutions between the state and private capital. Now in late capitalism those pressures have developed apace, as working-class power has consolidated substantial welfare institutions and as the greater pressure for state involvement in the economy has imposed the necessity for new ways of linking and co-ordinating state activity there. Bob Jessop's summary and Dominic Strinati's suggested schematization (Table 37) capture this well. To quote Jessop first:

the form of political representation and the apparatuses and techniques of economic intervention change with the historical development of capital accumulation: absolutism plus mercantilism in the transition from feudalism to capitalism; bourgeois

Table 37   *The development of capitalism and modes of state intervention*

Economy	State–economy relation				Polity and state	
Structure and problems	General form of state intervention	Method of state intervention	State strategies (goals)	Functions of state re: economy	Political representation	Forms of state control of industrial relations
Primitive Accumulation	'Military'	Force	Inception of capitalism	Creative	Exclusionist	Coercion
Competitive Capitalism (absolute surplus value extraction, business cycle, unemployment)	Laissez-faire	Allocation (politics)	Inaction	Facilitative	Liberalism or paternalism	
Monopoly Capitalism (relative surplus value extraction, profitability crises, lack of accumulation, inflation)	Interventionist	Production (policies)	Protective-welfare / Administrative re-commodification	Supportive / Directive	Pluralism or corporatism	

Capital accumulation class struggle

Class struggles restructuring state apparatus

Source: D. Strinati, 'Capitalism, the state and industrial relations', in C. Crouch (ed.), *State and Economy in Contemporary Capitalism* (Croom Helm 1979), p. 198.

parliamentary democracy and an essentially laisser-faire state in the period of liberal accumulation; a growth of executive strength and interventionist policies as the tendency of the rate of profit to fall becomes dominant, and the development of supra-national political organisation as the internation-alisation of production becomes dominant in the world economy.[57]

It is in this general context that certain key features of recent institutional changes in the area of British government need to be situated. The move of power away from Parliament to the executive is one such. Parliamentary pressure has been contained by pulling contentious issues back into executive control as working-class attempts to gain parliamentary power created disciplined party structures no longer free to exercise untrammelled parliamentary autonomy, and as Parliament was left – because of its wider social composition – no longer able to play its nineteenth-century role of co-ordinating the common interests of the propertied class alone. Instead, the sheer scale of government intervention in every sphere of social life has left 'professional politicians . . . in practice unable to understand the full significance and effect of much new legislation, let alone (able) to formulate it'; and 'in this situation the private lobbies of the capitalist class have a greatly enhanced importance'[58] as a source of government policy and administrative efficiency. In this way 'the state apparatus, rather than parliament, now serves as the principle medium for maintaining the rule of capital';[59] and the permanent bureaucracy of the state has come to be an important source of policy in its own right.

Moreover, the executive arm of the state has become a powerful force calling into existence *corporatist* institutions. Governments have actually encouraged cartelization and the creation of spokesmen bodies in order to facilitate their own better penetration of civil society and its underpinning economy;

and as the state has loomed ever larger in private life, groups and organizations have coalesced more or less spontaneously, recognizing that they too need size to enjoy political control. The result has been the creation of a whole new network of institutions linking the private and the public, a new system of representation parallel to, and to a degree in tension with, Parliament itself. Initially that network was one of pressure groups lobbying an autonomous state. It has slowly transmuted itself into a network of quangos, in which specified areas of executive power have been delegated to, and hence shared explicitly with, private organizations representative of (because generated from and sustained by) organized sections of civil society. These private networks reproduce, without significantly democratizing, patterns of inequality dominant in civil society. Those who organize do so more or less easily depending on the resources they enjoy, the status they control, and the contacts they possess. These grow as we move from the poor to the rich, from the dispossessed to the privileged, and from those far removed from the propertied class to those close to its centre. The modern state has surrounded itself with a whole structure of advisory committees and semi-executive administrative bodies; and these in their turn are peopled by the privileged, by 'the good and the great'.[60] Even in the nationalized industries, very senior personnel are drawn heavily from the propertied class. In 1972–3, of 145 full-time board members on fourteen nationalized boards, only fifteen came from the labour movement, against thirty-eight from management, company ownership and banking, and fifty from the managerial structure of the industries themselves.[61] Indeed, because this pattern of privilege is general throughout the system, and only moderated at the margin by a token representation of trade union bureaucrats, it is possible to move in at random and pick one illustration to underline a general truth. Figures 20 and 21 do that.

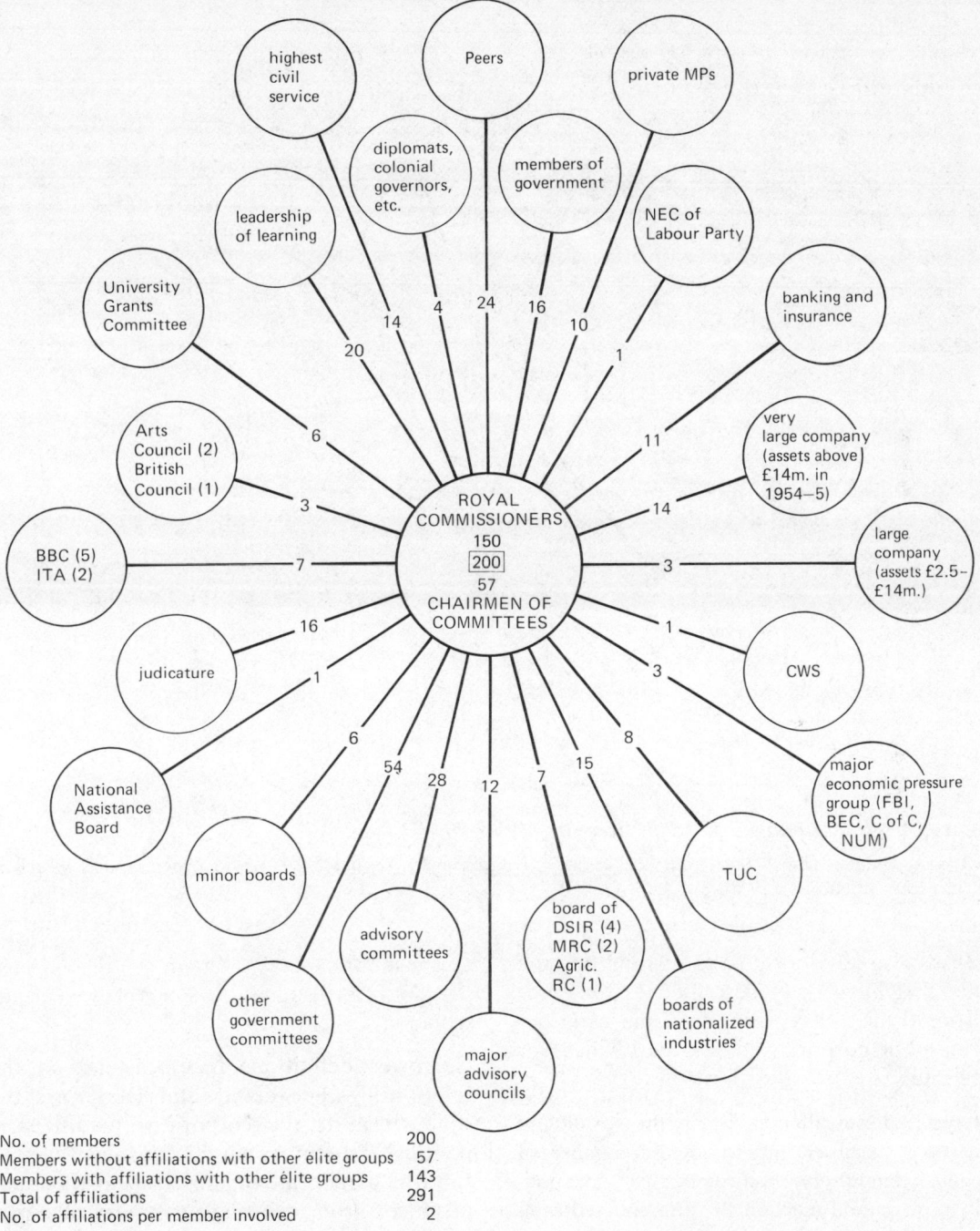

Figure 20 *Affiliations of Royal Commissioners and chairmen of committees with other élite groups.*   *Source:* W. L. Guttsman, *The British Political Elite* (MacGibbon and Kee 1968), p. 367.

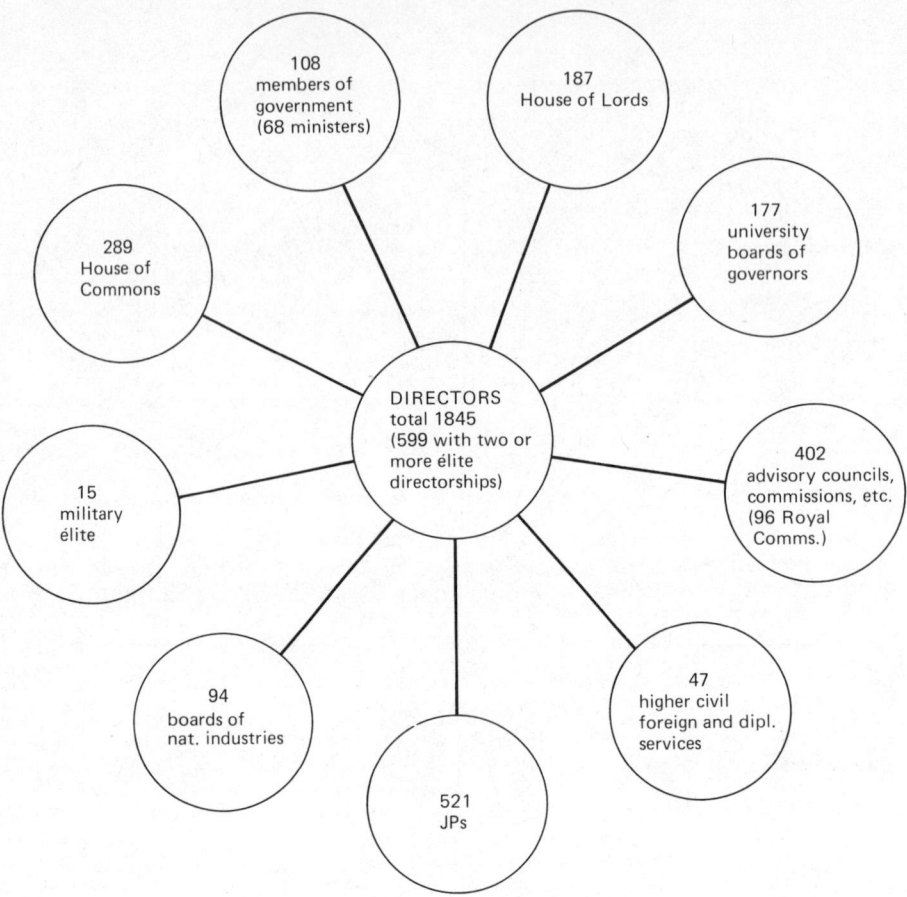

Figure 21   *Élite linkages of 1845 directors, 1906–70*

Source: A. Giddens and P. Stanworth, 'Elites and privilege', in P. Abrams (ed.), *Work, Urbanism and Inequality* (Weidenfeld and Nicolson 1978), p. 232.

It is these advisory groups surrounding the state that have been described as the 'new corporatism'.[62] According to some wide definitions of corporatism, it occurs wherever you find:

interest representation in which the constituent units are organised into a limited number of singular compulsory, non-competitive, hierarchially ordered and functionally differentiated categories, recognised or licensed (if not created) by the state and granted a deliberate representational monopoly within their respective categories in exchange for observing certain controls on their selection of leaders and articulation of demands and supports.[63]

Narrower definitions focus instead on the relationships between capital, labour and the state, locating the corporatist paradigm in political structures 'within advanced capitalism which integrate organised socio-economic producer groups through a system of representation and co-operative mutual interaction at the leadership level of mobilisation and social control at mass level'.[64] The debate at this point then turns on whether corporatism in this narrow sense constitutes a wholly new mode of production or simply a common strategy for incorporating and subordinating well-organized labour movements in late capitalism.[65]

These wider and narrower senses of corporatism are not necessarily in tension, for clearly the state has encouraged, and will continue to encourage, the consolidation of corporatist structures and relationships with a whole series of consumer groups in civil society: with health care 'clients', with owner-occupiers, and with specialist interests in fields of welfare provision, animal protection and the like. The state is inspired to do that, as Beer showed long ago, by its 'need for the expert advice in the formation of policy, for their acquiescence or voluntary agreement to administer state policies (from pressure groups and other functional organisations), and for their approval or legitimation of state policy in the eyes of their members'.[66] The result of that, by the late 1970s, was the existence of at least 600 quagos/quangos, and the existence of well-established consultative procedures between government departments and a wide array of organized pressure groups. In this wider sense corporatism is alive, well and no doubt thriving – constituting as it does 'a massive extension of bureaucratic domination over economy and civil society . . . and a significant increase in *ad hoc* discriminatory intervention oriented to specific goals at the expense of general rational-legal administration'.[67] What is more contentious, however, is the status and future of corporatism in its narrow sense in the sphere of production. We shall now concentrate on that.

The most dramatic expansion of corporatist structures in post-war Britain has occurred in the area of accumulation itself, as the state has established tripartite decision-making bodies on which labour, capital and the state sit in formal equality, to discuss – even to settle – basic questions of economic activity (and by implication, of class relationships in the production process). The arrival of these institutions has not qualitatively altered the social structure into some post-capitalist 'thing'. John Westergaard's rejection of Pahl and Winkler's 'new corporatism' is unanswerable on this.[68] Indeed, what came in Britain was hardly full-blown corporatism in its European sense. It was 'more a relatively ineffective system of tri-partite discussions among incompletely incorporated and fragmented peak organisations and representatives'.[69] In fact the state was slow to move into the direction of industry or even to give it much aid and protection; and the handling of the 'labour question' was always the dominant theme here. Keith Middlemas has argued that this *corporate bias* is quite old in British politics, stretching back to 1918 at least, when it arose initially as a classic 'passive revolution', a way of containing working-class pressure by drawing trade union leaders into subordinate relationships with the state. In his view, 'what had been merely interest groups around the political threshold became part of the extended state', so that what we have at the centre of British politics now is a 'political cartel' in which the peak organizations of capital and labour have become 'governing institutions, existing thereafter as estates of the realm, committed to co-operation with the state, even if they retained the customary habit of opposition to specific party governments'.[70]

Critics have suggested that, put in this way, the case is too strong. In particular, it mistakes the formal equality of power between the parties for the actual inequality of resources experienced still by labour. Yet there is no doubt that the post-war British state has faced a strong labour movement, demanding direct representation at the highest levels of the state, and pressing for greater welfare provision and trade union rights once there. It is also the case that the post-war British state faced a capitalist economy in increasing competitive difficulties from the mid 1950s, and that its characteristic first response was a corporatist one, drawing both sides of industry together in a search for a joint solution to economic decline. The NEDC, the NBPI, the IRC, and more recently the NEB, sectoral working parties, ACAS, the MSC, and the Health and Safety Executive, all stand as evidence of that drift in state policy, and the associated changes in state form. It is in this sense that Bob Jessop is right to build an argument about stages: to say, that is, that 'if the post-war Keynesian political economy and welfare state represents the first stage of social democracy as a form of state, corporatism represents its second and highest stage'.[71]

The incentive here has invariably been economic decline, and the perception by senior state personnel that any solution to that decline required wage control. This was as true of the Conservative government's 'corporatist initiatives' in indicative planning between 1961 and 1964 as it was of the Labour government's much more ambitious trading of political representation for trade union 'good behaviour' in the social contract between 1974 and 1979. The resulting pattern of union involvement in tripartite structures is given in Table 38.

Such corporatist structures are not unique to Britain. On the contrary, they are general across late capitalism wherever labour movements are strong. They are 'best regarded as a strategy pursued by capitalism when it cannot adequately subordinate labour by preventing its combination and allowing market processes to work'.[72] They arise there, as here, because as a structure they coincide closely with changing state functions and the balance of class forces within late capitalism. They are consolidated because they seem capable of doing the two things vital for the state at this stage of capitalist development: namely integrating strong working-class industrial power within existing class relationships and political structures; and exposing the state to dialogues that are essential if it is to play effectively not simply its older, more passive, role in relation to the accumulation process, but a more direct and interventionist one. Indeed, to the degree that the importance of corporatist structures has been recognized by senior state personnel, they in their turn have thrown state support behind the private élites of capital and labour with whom they dialogue. Governments have been willing to preserve the peak organizations' monopoly of representation against interlopers. The Conservative government's refusal to give representation to a white-collar challenger to the TUC is the major case in point, to stand comparison with the Labour government's role in the creation of the CBI.[73] In return, governments have periodically urged the peak organizations to exercise greater control of their own rank-and-file. The Conservative government of Edward Heath, for example, used the CBI to run a prices freeze, just as Labour governments have regularly used the TUC to police the price of its members' labour.

Yet corporatist structures are not only common. They are also extraordinarily brittle. This is due in part to the limitation of their own form. They are just too narrow and frozen in their mode of representation to act as a total replacement for parliamentary modes more sensitive in electoral terms to new social forces and new sets of attitudes and opinions. Indeed the two modes of representation (corporatism and Parliament) are inherently incompatible, with corporatism 'requiring the large scale hierarchial organisational and political incorporation of socio-economic groups authoritatively sanctioned by the state, rather than the more fragmented diversity of interest groups and political parties autonomous from state control'[74] characteristic of parliamentarianism. As the newcomer, corporatist structures lack the generalized legitimacy accorded to parliamentary practices, stand fair to lose popular support quickly if the short-term claims made for them fail to materialize (on

Table 38   *Union involvement in tripartite structures*

Modes of influence	Microlevel institutions (plant, company, locality)	Intermediate level institutions (industry, region)	Macrolevel institutions (economy, society)
Economic			
Collective bargaining	Rapid extension of steward-based bargaining in 1960s, followed by some shift to company bargaining in 1970s	Industrywide agreements from post WWI in decline by 1960s	NBPI (1965–71) and Pay Board (1973–4) as incomes policy agencies
	Legislation in 1970s to impose recognition, information disclosure, etc.	Standing Commission on Pay Compatability (1979)	Social Contract (1974) as a negotiated incomes policy
			Unilateral TUC incomes policy in 1975
Planning	Planning agreements (1975)	Economic Development Committees (1963)	National Economic Development Council (1962)
		Sectoral Working Parties (1976)	Industrial Reorganization Commission (1966–70)
			National Enterprise Board (1975)
			Scottish and Welsh Development Agencies (1975)
			Industrial Investment Agency (19?)
			Tripartite Assessment of Economic Prospects (1979)
Policy determination and administration	Company consultative bodies	Industrial Training Boards (1964)	CIR (1969–74) industrial relations policy
	Health and Safety committees (1977)		ACAS (1974) industrial relations policy
	Board level representation (19?)		Price Commission (1971)
	Pension fund representation (19?)		MSC (1973) manpower policy
	Company 'strategy discussions' (19?)		CRE (1976) race policy
Political	Influence in Labour Party constituency parties	Regional TUCs (mainly 1970s)	Influence through Labour Party Conference. National Executive, and Parliamentary Party

Table 38   *(Cont)*

Modes of influence	Microlevel institutions (plant, company, locality)	Intermediate level institutions (industry, region)	Macrolevel institutions (economy, society)
Political	Trades councils		Labour Party – TUC Liaison Committee (1972)
	Industrial democracy in local government (19?)		
Judicial–arbitral	Industrial Tribunals (1964, extended 1971, 1975)		Industrial Court (1919–71)
			Industrial Disputes Tribunal (1940–59) and Industrial Arbitration Board (1971 – 5) tripartite arbitral bodies succeeded by Central Arbitration Committee (1976)
			NIRC. (1971–4) tripartite judicial body succeeded by Employment Appeals Tribunal (1975)
			TUC Independent Review Committee (1976)
			Monopolies Commission (TUC representation from 1975)

Note: The dates given represent the year of inception and demise, where necessary, of a particular institution. Institutions dated by a question mark have only reached the proposal stage, but only important proposals that have had a high probability of implementation are included.

Key to Initials

ACAS = Advisory Conciliation and Arbitration Service
CIR   = Commission on Industrial Relations
CRE   = Commission for Racial Equality
EOC   = Equal Opportunities Commission

HSC   = Health and Safety Commission
MSC   = Manpower Services Commission
NBPI = National Board for Prices and Income
NIRC = National Industrial Relations Court

(*Source:* A. W. Thomson, 'Trade Unions and the corporate state in Britain', *Industrial and Labour Relations Review*, vol 33, no. 1, October 1979, pp. 39–40.)

prosperity and growth, for example), and can expect resistance to their mandate from groups in civil society excluded from their deliberations, and from parliamentary representatives rendered ever more redundant and impotent by corporatist developments.

Corporatist 'brittleness' arises too because of opposition from sections of both capital and labour. Sections of capital resent the constraints on their freedom of action imposed by tripartite negotiation, and flee from corporatist structures with alacrity unless powerful working-class pressure holds them there. Trade union leaders for their part find that corporatist structures pressure them not 'to cut their ties with their base but . . . (to) use those ties to legitimate state policy and to elaborate their control over their members'.[75] In the end that just erodes their freedom of action too. Capital always resists their more radical demands; and the state's concern with squeezing economic growth out of a private economy always works to block radicalism too. The result is invariably the creation of a gap between rank-and-file protest and leadership acquiescence, which trade union leaders eventually are obliged to bridge by a tardy retreat from corporatism itself.

Corporatist structures have been relatively easy to construct in Britain because of the strength of social democratic labourism in the working-class movement, but have proved brittle as the hegemony of labourism has declined. For the maintenance of that hegemony, as we discussed earlier, always relied on the 'provision of certain concessions of symbolic and material kinds to workers and other dominated categories and classes';[76] and began to erode precisely as the dwindling competitiveness of British capitalism made that provision more and more difficult. Corporatist structures have proved brittle here of late because the 'project' on which they were based – of class collaboration for national economic reconstruction – fell foul of the contradictions between wage labour and capital. Governments just failed to deliver their side of the 'social contract'. Such contracts quickly declined into simple wage controls; and the pursuit of conditions for greater profitability drowned any move to enhance welfare provision, let alone to share industrial and social power more equally. Used as a mechanism to organize and legitimate working-class sacrifice, on the basis of a promise of better times soon in return for restraint now, corporatist structures inevitably began to fall apart as key sections of the working class perceived that the sacrifice required was permanent rather than temporary, and that

co-operation in the first stage only invited requests for further sacrifice in the second or the third.

Eventually these contradictions emerged everywhere in late capitalism, thrown into relief by generalized recession. They emerged as visibly as anywhere in Britain, precisely because the balance of class forces to which corporatism gave institutional expression was itself a central cause of the economic weakness that the institutions were created to overcome. As that was realized – or at least as its consequences manifested themselves in inflation, stagnation and periodic 'winters of discontent', corporatism went into retreat: unpopular among trade union members because of the fear of wage control, and rejected by a New Right conservatism bent on pruning back the state, taking down its corporatist structures, and shifting class power decisively away from labour. Corporatism in this narrow sense of tripartism in the economic sphere, has been a casualty in the 1980s of that generalized crisis of the state to which we must now turn.

The crisis of the state

The rise and fall of corporatism in the contemporary British state is but one local theme in a much more general crisis of state forms and functions characteristic of states in all advanced capitalist countries of late. Here in Britain that crisis was understood for two decades as a crisis of *governments* – as one party after another was elected to office promising full employment, economic growth, rising living standards and better social provision, only to fall at the end of its first full five-year term of office, rejected by the electorate that had chosen it precisely because unemployment was higher, the recession deeper, and both the private and social wage less than they had been when that government had been elected. The fact that Mrs Thatcher's Conservative government did not pay the same price as the Conservatives in 1964 and

1974, and Labour in 1970 and 1979, marked the first break in that twenty-year pattern; and cannot be written off merely as 'the exception that proved the rule', the fortunate beneficiary of the Falklands War and the Labour Party's internal wrangles. Rather, the fact that the Labour Party was so deeply divided by the experience of government between 1974 and 1979 that it could not unite to win again in 1983, should be understood as yet another indication of the depth of crisis of the contemporary state. For it is a crisis not just of governments, but of a whole national project, common to both parties before 1976, and central to Labourism in particular for at least two generations – a project in which the state, pursuing Keynesian demand management techniques within the context of an expanding welfare provision, built a coalition of classes behind a state-encouraged programme of private capital accumulation. It is this project of social democracy which no longer works, and with which Thatcherism has been the first successful political force to break decisively.

The most obvious level at which social democracy and its Keynesianism failed was in the dilemmas it created for economic management in the changed circumstances of the recession. Classical Keynesianism had offered Treasury ministers a basic option: of inflating an economy with unemployment, or of deflating an overheated one vulnerable to price inflation. But it had no answer to a 1970s crisis in which unemployment and inflation occurred together. When Jim Callaghan told the 1976 conference that 'we could no longer spend our way out of recession' he was merely articulating the demise of Keynesianism, and its abandonment by a Labour government beset by self-defeating paradoxes. His was a government unable to solve its immediate economic problems by borrowing from abroad without finding that the resulting burden of interest and debt obliged it to make the very cuts in social expenditure that it had borrowed to avoid. It was a government unable even to

sustain a weak pound by selling foreign reserves without encouraging foreign holders of sterling to sell sterling ever more quickly in the belief of the inexorable depreciation that their selling guaranteed. It was also a government unable to solve the competitive weakness of an economy starved of private investment because private investment was wary of immersion in an economy whose weakness its absence served only to reproduce. So when North Sea oil arrived, temporarily to restore the value of sterling and to remove the immediate threat to domestic expansion from any balance of payments difficulties, it was less the signal for the prosperity expected through the 1970s than yet another nail in the coffin of British industrial capital. For British industry was pricing its products yet further out of export markets, and cheapening the imports of foreign-made manufactured goods that were already eroding local control of even home markets. Far from giving British governments the 'space' in which to successfully 'modernize' British industrial capital back into competitive strength, North Sea oil simply reinforced the cumulative pattern of decline from which no post-war government has yet been able to escape, and turned Britain into a net importer of manufactured goods for the first time since the Industrial Revolution.

These 'surface' paradoxes of British politics in the late 1970s reflected underlying weaknesses of two related but distinct kinds. First the failure of corporatist politics, and of the strategy of class alliances on which that politics rests. Keynesianism, as a 'national project' for capital, was one in which working-class support for private capital accumulation was guaranteed by full employment, welfare provision and rising living standards. It worked for a generation only because the rapid leap in labour productivity associated with the third technological revolution of the long boom created the material conditions on which the mass of profits could grow, and wages rise, simultaneously – and on which the tendency of the rate of profit to fall could be held at bay by a quickening of the rate of exploitation. The conditions favourable to successful Keynesianism vanished everywhere in late capitalism by the mid 1970s, as the boom ended, and in many of the chancellories of Europe, Keynesianism bowed out to a new monetarism of the Right. In Figure 19 (see p. 228) the space for the accommodation of 'C' allowed by the width of 'A' and 'B' was seriously reduced everywhere by the twin impact of the recession, squeezing capital ('A' and 'B'), and initially at least radicalizing workers (inflating 'C'), to the immense discomfiture of governments caught in the middle.

This 'squeeze' occurred earlier here because, even in the long boom, the particular balance of class forces established in post-war Britain eroded the competitive position (and hence the rate of profits) of industrial capital more quickly than in stronger competitors elsewhere. The defensive industrial strength of the British working class kept rates of exploitation low by international standards, as we have seen. The political strength of that class obliged governments to maintain high welfare expenditure, and persuaded them to keep unemployment lower than they might otherwise have done. In the context of a weakening industrial base, these factors were both inflationary. Most of all, and as we have just observed, the strength of the labour movement encouraged governments to seek 'corporatist' solutions to economic weakness, pulling both sides of industry into joint negotiations in the pursuit of more rapid capital accumulation. But by then the weakness of industrial capital was already a barrier in its own right, predisposing private investment to move abroad, or into non-industrial sources; and to do all this not least because industrial returns were undermined by trade union strength. The Labour Left came eventually to realize part of this, and sought to radicalize corporatism into a new policy in which state direction of investment played a

greater part (that is, to push back 'A' and 'B'). Thatcherism represents the same recognition, but the other class response: that only massive unemployment and trade union legislative restrictions would so weaken working-class industrial strength that private accumulation could begin again profitably here (that is, by significantly reducing 'C'). Each of these strategies has its difficulties, as we shall see in the next chapter, but each had at least the virtue of recognizing that the crisis of the British state derived centrally from the stalemate of class forces that surrounded it, such that a return to generalized prosperity in Britain would require major changes of a structural kind, beyond the scope of the incremental adjustments characteristic of corporatist politics.[77]

The failure of Keynesianism was also reflective of the immobilism of the corporatist state in late capitalism, both here and abroad. The class compact underpinning corporatism called into existence powerful internal pressure groups committed to the maintenance of the status quo and free of any direct market control on their ambitions. Its welfare networks created vast arrays of consumers, winnable in elections by the promise of greater returns. Its state bureaucracies provided employment and established unions, whose survival and prosperity depended on political (and hence lobbyable) decision-making processes, rather than on the market as such. Moreover, those institutions (mainly private companies) and workforces involved in the market came to see the state as a source of aid and protection when competition proved too tough, and sought shelter in the form of public ownership or state funding of a quite massive kind – funding which politicians were under heavy electoral pressure to provide. This is not to say that constraints did not operate here, but is rather to stress that the mechanism that orchestrated them was not the capitalist market so much as 'fiscal crises and dramatic cuts in public expenditure'.[78]

Non-Marxist analyses have seen in all this the 'politics of overload', and have suggested cut-backs in government expenditure and promises as their solution to the crisis of the British state: a sort of political monetarism.[79] But it seems more sensible to see the 'notion of "overload" as a Marxist "contradiction"',[80] to recognize, that is, the capitalist logic that has pulled the state into its expanded role – a logic deriving from the needs of the accumulation process in late capitalism and from the strength of the working class consolidated in the long boom; and to see instead that the crisis of the state is better understood as the reappearance in the political arena of contradictions between capital and labour that state expenditure has not removed so much as shifted, has not transcended but only politicized.

We will return to that point in a moment. First we must recognize that the immobility of the corporatist state has not been simply the product of internal class balances. It has arisen too because of the increasingly *international* character of the accumulation process itself. The nation state continues to be called upon to 'manage' its own national economy, to protect and encourage accumulation there, to facilitate the reproduction of labour power, and to guarantee social harmony. Accumulation always goes on in a particular national site, and can occur only if the local state is strong enough to facilitate the reproduction of these vital inputs. But capital is also increasingly multinational in its scale of operation, and as such is destructive of that very state power on which it depends. Simply stated, the contradiction is that, while multinational

corporations cannot renounce the traditional state functions that are necessary to create favourable conditions for the viable functioning of a capitalist economy and for their privileged position within it (i.e. fostering consensus and social peace) at the same time those very corporations, through their operations, hinder the performance of state econo-mic policies, such as monetary, fiscal and employ-ment policies, which are instrumental in achieving those broader social goals.[81]

The result locally is the 'over determination' of national politics by international forces: world recession, increased international com-petition, big multinational companies, and international financial agencies like the IMF. National politics here has to operate in the tiny 'space' left to it by those international move-ments. This constraint, just as much as the shortfall in performance caused by internal 'overload', eats away at the local credibility of particular governments and potentially jeopardizes the legitimacy of the whole system.

Politics in Britain now is beset with the consequences of all this. Politics here, as elsewhere in advanced capitalism, is caught between the *contradictions of accumulation and legitimation*. Called upon to facilitate private capital accumulation and to help to stabilize and legitimate the associated social order, governments find it increasingly dif-ficult to finance the resulting range of their responsibilities. The reappearance of econo-mic crisis in late capitalism has pulled the state into permanent 'crisis management', only to find that the intractability of crises generates problems of legitimacy for the state itself. 'The socialisation of costs and the private appro-priation of profits creates a *fiscal crisis*, a "structural gap" between state expenditures and state revenues. The result is a tendency for state expenditures to increase more rapidly than the means of financing them',[82] in a fiscal crisis which manifests itself in the first instance as a problem of funding. Chancellors find themselves faced with a choice of revenue sources: taxation (on wages, on wage goods or on corporate profits), or borrowing. Taxation on profits hits accumulation directly: that on wages and wage goods does so to the extent that strong unions compensate by greater wage demands. But borrowing has its problems too, hitting accumulation via higher interest rates (if the money supply is held constant) or inflation (if the money supply is allowed to grow). The contradictions are manageable so long as the social productivity of labour continues to increase rapidly; but when it does not, an enormous gap quickly opens between revenues and expenditure – a gap created by an industrial recession that erodes the tax base and simultaneously increases government social expenditure. 'In the United Kingdom', for example, between 1971 and 1975, 'the gap between expenditure and revenue widened to 11% of GNP, requiring state borrowing to the tune of £11 billion in 1975.'[83]

The paradox of greater state activity here is that its non-inflationary provision requires a greater rate of exploitation of labour power in the private sector it exists to service and in its own manufacturing sector – so that while state spending is vital in late capitalism to facilitate the private accumulation that alone can sustain large numbers of state employees without inflation, it is at the same time an incentive to cartelization and capital investment in the private sector. These are processes which eventually erode profit rates there and turn state spending from a prerequisite to a burden.

This paradox will emerge most starkly and earliest in national capitalisms in which the social productivity of labour is relatively low, not least because the defensive strength of their working classes is well established. It will be most evident there because the State had a greater role to play in order to compensate for deficient private capital accumulation and to meet working-class demands for social reform; and because the resulting growth in the money supply will face a lower than average social productivity of labour, and hence have earlier and greater inflationary consequences. That economy will then find itself doubly bound: inflation-ridden because of relatively low capital accumulation in the past, and with low capital accumulation in the present and future because its higher-than-average rate of inflation acts as a barrier to

successful competition, sales and profit realisation, and (through the weakening of its currency) erodes still further its internal levels of cost competitiveness. Britain in the 1970s found herself in just such a situation.[84]

State expenditure, once vital to fuel the accumulation process, has now become a burden upon it. This is partly because the rate of accumulation has slowed down, in spite of government support. Government spending in the boom years had a twin relationship with that accumulation. Some of it was indirectly productive of surplus value for capital – reproducing labour power more cheaply or increasing its productivity, and so facilitating accumulation. But as we saw, much welfare provision was not productive for individual capitals at all. Its spending facilitated the realization of profits (via increased demand) and brought social peace, but was in itself a direct burden on capital. Characteristically, such welfare provision is also labour intensive and of low productivity, not least because it is free of the social relationships of capitalist production, being geared to the generation of use values rather than exchange values, with its employers under no direct market pressure to reduce labour time by mechanization and restructuring. Yet those who perform it are well organized and free of the direct market pressures experienced by workers in the private sector. As a result, in the 1970s many state employees managed to negotiate wage settlements parallel to (and derivative on) those achieved in the higher productivity monopoly sector, in spite of state productivity levels more akin to the low wage competitive area of the capitalist economy. The result was that, as output slackened even in the monopoly sector in the mid 1970s, the wage bill in the state sector did not, and an inflationary gap opened (too much money chasing too few goods) which impeded an already damaged accumulation process still further.

Since the resulting inflation also temporarily

redistributed income 'to the disadvantage of unorganised workers and other marginal groups'[85] it left Conservative demands to 'roll back the state' popular in a much wider area of even the working class than Socialists anticipated. It struck a cord with taxed (and now insecure) workers in a threatened monopoly sector, with state 'clients' squeezed out by high state wage bills, and with workers in the less unionized competitive sector, as well as with capital and its middle classes as a whole. In this way, the inflationary consequences of welfare provision in capitalist recession weakened political support for the whole welfare system. For this reason, Ian Gough is correct in observing that: 'if the long boom of post-war capitalism and the golden age of the welfare state share a common origin, so they may share a common fate'.[86]

State expenditure is now contradictory in another way too. Even in the long boom, as the state acted to facilitate private capital accumulation, it took whole areas of production out of the sphere of private capital altogether. It strengthened commodity production only by decommodifying whole areas of education, welfare provision, infrastructural services and research and development. It did so not by choice, but of necessity. For 'capitalism is a system founded upon private accumulation of capital which however increasingly depends upon the provision of socialised services', and 'the state finds itself chronically trapped between the contradictory pressures these generate'.[87] Particularly in the welfare field, successive governments created universal provision (and hence social peace) at the cost of reducing the terrain for profitable private investment. In this way they created an area 'foreign to capital' – an area of 'state organised non-exchange value goods and services',[88] one in which, moreover, 'the labour process is partly conditioned by the professional and ethical considerations of

workers who refuse to treat health, education and social work as productive processes'.[89] This again was 'functional' to late capitalism for as long as alternative areas of profitable private investment continued to open up. But as that ceased to apply in the generalized recession of the 1970s, the 'boundary' of the state became contentious again, as capital looked to 'reprivatize' areas of state provision, and to return to commodity relations in spheres of social activity decommodified for a generation, in order to enlarge the sphere of private accumulation.

The first response of those most directly threatened by this – welfare employees and workers in state manufacturing now to be reprivatized – characteristically has been to call again for a return to Keynesian corporatism, rather than to see in the Keynesian failure any incentive to go on to a more socialist recasting of the state–economy–welfare triad. Instead, even workers here have been susceptible to the appeals of monetarism, offered as a new 'national project' in the interests of capital as a whole. Yet the costs of monetarism to those exposed to its darker side are enormous: unemployment, cuts in welfare provision, real poverty again. So by breaking so decisively with the consensus of a generation, re-establishing large-scale deprivation and challenging head-on the job security and wages of its own employees, the state under Margaret Thatcher has put its own legitimacy and that of the whole political system on the line, and raised again the possibility of social unrest and political radicalization. As Keynesianism failed in the crisis of the state in late capitalism, the tempo of political debate rose significantly, and the range of alternatives canvassed widened for the first time in a generation. It is time, finally, to take stock of that new debate, and to consider the possibility of a revitalized socialist alternative to the growing 'barbarism' of capitalism in crisis.

11 The repressive state and the construction of the progressive alternative

The growing involvement of the state – Keynesian style – in managing the crises of late capitalism carried with it enormous dangers for the stability of democratic politics. For as the contradictions of that state involvement became clear, and as governments found that it was becoming progressively more difficult to maintain employment and prosperity for all, the failures of economic policy ate away at their electoral support and threatened to erode the legitimacy of the political order as a whole. Indeed, one influential school of analysis on the Left argued persuasively in the 1970s that we faced at least the possibility of a 'legitimation crisis' in Western politics. On that argument, the pressure on the state to act as a collective capitalist – to initiate coherent and consistent policies for capital as a whole – was likely to fall foul of the conflicting and anarchic pressures released upon it by particular capitals, so opening up what was termed a 'rationality deficit'. At the same time the state had to maintain mass loyalty, and the more it intervened to do that the more likely it was that the contradiction between social classes at the base of the capitalist mode of production would not be overcome so much as *displaced* into the political arena, there to emerge as policy failures, and as failure to meet the expectations created by its own intervention. To the degree to which that happened, crises of legitimation were likely to ensue.[1]

However, it is hard to sustain the claim that events have yet moved so far in British politics at least. It is true, of course, that the legitimacy of the state is under challenge in Northern Ireland, and that nationalist movements came briefly to prominence in Scotland and Wales in the middle 1970s. But Catholic resistance to British rule in the occupied north of Ireland derives from a much earlier period of colonization, as we saw, and Scottish and Welsh nationalism had more to do with the uneven development of capitalism territorially than with contradictions associated with state spending as such. We have evidence that much working-class support for existing political institutions is pragmatic and passive rather than principled and committed, but that is likely always to have been the case, and is not the result of recent state policy alone. What we have seen instead, as the boom has petered out, are alterations in patterns of political support, and in the general drift of social opinion, of a less fundamental yet vital kind. We have seen both main political parties lose electoral support from election to election: from 1959 for the Conservatives, and from 1951 (or technically 1966 if you do not care for exceptions that prove the rule) for the Labour Party (Table 39). We have seen the growing propensity of public opinion as a whole to respond positively to a new set of political themes of the neo-Right which challenged the Keynesian orthodoxy of mainstream politics as practised by both those parties between 1948 and 1976.

As we have seen, post-war British politics before 1970 (and with Labour in power until 1976) was built around an interventionist state, one charged (and charged by itself) with responsibility for ensuring economic growth

Table 39 *Percentage electoral support for the two main parties at General Elections since 1945*

	Conservative Party %	Labour Party %
1945	39.8	47.8
1950	43.5	46.1
1951	48.0	48.8
1955	49.7	46.4
1959	49.4	43.8
1964	43.4	44.1
1966	41.9	47.9
1970	46.4	43.0
1974 (February)	37.9	37.1
1974 (October)	35.8	39.2
1979	43.9	36.9
1983	43.5	28.3

and rising affluence through its own management of the domestic economy. In the 1950s, when that management was easy, the rhetoric of political debate focused on the emergence of a classless affluence, and on the pleasant problems (of leisure time, consumerism and bountiful welfare) that affluence necessarily would bring. In the 1960s, as the relative economic decline of British industrial capital came into view, that easy optimism slipped away, and governments moved to correct the decline by more purposive intervention themselves, by bringing labour and capital into a closer relationship with the state, and by expanding public spending on industrial restructuring and welfare provision. In the process, new social phenomena grew to prominence: large and all-embracing welfare bureaucracies willing and keen to plan, organize and dispense; affluent young people set on spending, playing, and breaking with older, more restrained codes of individual conduct; immigrants settling into urban ghettos, there to consolidate their culture amid an indigenous English one; students and workers willing to sit in and strike in defence of what

they saw as their interests; and in Ireland, a Catholic middle class youth marching the streets in demand of their civil rights. Older, more conservative and less permissive social strata remained in abundance, but their political voice and impact was momentarily stilled by the success of Keynesianism and the overarching confidence of the interventionist state. As late as 1966 – in the Labour landslide of that year – the politics of an older conservatism seemed to have gone for ever. But they were to come back in the wake of the unrest of 1968, in response to the industrial militancy of the 1969–73 period, and in reaction to the visible failure of Keynesianism to stop the economic rot.

For particularly with the recession of the 1970s and the emergence of stagflation, older economic and social themes found their moment again. The silent majority were silent no more. As Keynesianism disintegrated, and inflation soared, themes of anti-collectivism, anti-permissiveness and anti-radicalism returned to the centre of public debate. They did so with such effectiveness because they were taken up by a rising force within the Conservative Party. The Thatcherite wing of that Party set themselves the task both of winning power and of winning public opinion: by calling again for a return to the virtues of the market, a reassertion of older family values and practices, the strengthening of the agencies of law and order against criminals and political radicals alike, and a rolling back of those social phenomena that were novel to the affluence of the 1960s: welfare spending, trade union power, black immigration and sexual permissiveness. In the process the Tory Right turned again, for the first time since Butskellism (a term used to describe the consensus on economic policy between the last Chancellor of the Exchequer in the Labour Government of 1951 [Hugh Gaitskell] and the first Chancellor of the incoming Conservatives [R. A. Butler]), to an 'open frontal attack on the whole idea of equality, a shameless advocacy of élitism, and a complete refurbishing of the competitive ethic'.[2] In this way, a new ortho-doxy began to be expressed: that Britain had gone 'soft' through too much welfare 'cushion-ing', through too much state bureaucracy, and through the loss of respect for the proper centres of power by workers, students and immigrants who no longer possessed that discipline vital to social order and economic competitiveness.

The Tory Right argued for the importance of self-discipline, the attractiveness of thrift, the vital role of small business, the centrality of the middle class, and the need to defeat 'the bully boys of the Left' if Britain was ever to be great again. Jingoism of an old imperial and racist kind was never far from the surface of this new Right revival, and of course it moved centre-stage during the Falklands/Malvinas campaign. But long before that, the rising tide of right-wing Conservatism had created a new orthodoxy both authoritarian in its thrust and populist in its appeal that shifted the centre of political debate to the right from the mid 1970s, creating a new 'common sense' that cut across social classes – 'free market, strong state, iron times: an authoritarian populism'[3] – before which a Labour government already in retreat could only tack and run. For 'one of the most important features of the radical Right in the period between 1975 and 1979 was the degree to which its protagonists grasped the argument that there was no point taking political power with a radical-reactionary programme unless they had already won the ideological terrain. And they set about doing just that . . . between 1975 and 1979 an effective ideological campaign was waged by the radical Right',[4] deploying the language of 'nation' and 'people' against 'class' and 'unions', and parading the myth that 'the country [had] fallen victim to the stealthy advance of socialist collectivism'. Margaret Thatcher made her electoral appeal to '"the little man", the private citizen' in need of pro-tection 'against the anonymous corporate

tentacles of the state',[5] and rode this authori-tarian populism to power in 1979.

Thatcherism is a novel phenomenon in recent British politics because it constitutes a serious attempt to create a new hegemony in British society, a new national project behind which to reconstitute the space for successful capital accumulation here. Its project has been nothing less than 'to reverse the whole postwar drift of British society, to roll back the historic gains of the labour movement and other progressive movements, and to force-march the society, vigorously into the past. These aims give some indication of the *radicalism* of its project. It opened a struggle on all fronts, the like of which has not been seen – from left or right – since the War'.[6]

On the economic front, Thatcherism consti-tuted itself as one solution to a declining competitiveness caused by the particular ba-lance of class forces consolidated in the years of the long boom. It deliberately set out to reduce working-class power and to roll back the state, in order to expose capital and labour to the invigorating force of competition, so to inspire new technologies and the acceptance of new working conditions. At the political level, Thatcherism was an attempt to forge a new conservative coalition linking the in-terests of monopoly capital with that of small business, and to bring into the Conservative camp significant sections of the white-collar salariat and skilled manual workers, in a common opposition to heavy personal taxa-tion (and hence heavy welfare provision) and common resistance to radicalism and permis-siveness. To do that required innovations in programme and ideology; and at the level of ideology and political discourse, Thatcherism must be understood as constituting a *princi-pled* challenge to the working assumptions of social democracy; a challenge that aimed to forge a new set of political distinctions in the popular mind: between 'productive' private capital and 'unproductive' welfare bureau-cracies; the industrious employed and the idle welfare scrounger; the English and the foreigner in our midst; and the law-abiding and the lawless.

In that new discourse, the 'public' became synonymous with the 'parasitical', 'inequality' with 'freedom', and 'bureaucratic' with 'totalitarian'. Indeed, preoccupied with isolating (and rendering impotent) the enemy without (communism) and within (radicals of any shade), Thatcherism has made a virtue out of strengthening the repressive arm of the state at just that moment that it has also launched a major ideological campaign to preach the virtues of liberal capitalism and individual self-reliance. In truth, of course, the Thatcherite defence of the 'little man' has been directed against welfare bureaucracies rather than bureaucracies as such (the bureaucratic structures of multinational monopoly capital, or of the armed forces or police, are not poised to be broken up by Thatcherism in practice). But that cannot obscure the extent to which Thatcherism has successfully reconstructed the 'market' as an ideological force, and put the onus of proof in popular discussion on those who would use the state to moderate its inequitable impact.

All this makes Thatcherism a different kind of Conservative government from any which we have seen since the Second World War, Edward Heath's included. Its strategic sense has kept it on course, compromising at the edges under pressure, but never 'U turning' back towards the Keynesian corporatist centre. At the heart of economic policy has been deflation, engineered by restrictions in the money supply through high interest rates and curbs on government spending. Those spending cuts have been highly selective. Aid to industry has been curtailed, but not abandoned. Spending on the armed forces and on the institutions of law and order has grown. It is welfare provision that has been cut, and cut heavily, to lessen the pressure on capital of public spending. Trade union rights have also been steadily eroded, in a series of trade union

bills. Union leaders have been excluded from the corridors of power, and unemployment allowed to soar. In the quite deliberate pursuit of a low wage and docile labour force, a whole set of policy initiatives on incomes, education, employment and training have eaten away at existing trade union practices, apprenticeship schemes, job control and working habits.[7] Capital for its part has been given its head. Exchange controls have been removed, and parts of the public sector 'privatized' to widen the area of private capital accumulation. The burden of taxation has been shifted downwards, to leave the richer sections of the community with greater freedom to retain and deploy their wealth to their own advantage. Tax laws, welfare provision and nationality legislation have all been recast to intensify the restrictions under which the poor (particularly women and immigrants among them) are obliged to operate. Cuts in provision have been one aspect of this recasting of the whole welfare system; qualitative shifts in welfare criteria have been the second, 'designed to reassert individualism, self-reliance, and family responsibility, and to reverse the collective social provision of the post-war era'.[8] Thatcherism, that is, has gone for a 'two nation' national project – of the favoured and the excluded – while maintaining an ideological stance worthy of Victorian liberalism (that to be excluded here is to demonstrate personal failing, and not simply to be the victim of the inequalities of social structure and government policy).

The costs have been at least threefold. Large sections of British industry have totally gone to the wall, as small and outmoded firms collapsed in the recession. The general scale of that collapse was documented at the start of Chapter 3, and all we need to note now is the fact that, under the Thatcher government and in spite of the social base of the Conservative Party in the country, bankruptcies in the small business sector have reached new and record heights. So too has poverty, and the intensification of the exploitation of women and ethnic minorities. That is the second cost. The third is the cost to individual liberties, for the darker side of this authoritarian populism has been its strengthening of the coercive arm of the state. There have been legislative changes, removing trade union rights, restricting citizenship, and enhancing police powers to stop, search and detain without trial. There has been a steady increase in spending on the police and the army. There has also been (and this predates Thatcher) a steady change in police training and practices, and in the public visibility of the police function. Computerization has increased the quality of police surveillance, and the wider use of guns by the police has increased its lethal impact. Riot training, the setting up of special police units (SPGs and PSUs in particular), and the expansion of the Special Branch have enhanced police control of civil disorders. Police chiefs and the Police Federation have openly entered public political debate, as advocates of a new moralistic authoritarianism which seeks to criminalize political dissent and to increase police and court powers. In Britain, as elsewhere, the rise of the new Right has pushed the capitalist state in an authoritarian direction, a process most visible in Northern Ireland, but one that is by no means confined to that province. On the contrary, and as Stuart Hall and his colleagues have said, 'liberalism, that last back-stop against arbitrary power, is in retreat. It is suspended. The times are exceptional. The crisis is real. We are inside the "law and order" state'.[9]

This growth in police powers, resources and public standing is no accident, for the social dislocation of a Thatcherite strategy is already massive, and is likely to become larger still. There can be no guarantee that Tory ideologues alone – no matter how eloquent and publicized – can persuade those dislodged to accept their 'medicine' in silence and in peace. This is particularly so because the geographical and social distribution of that medicine is so uneven. Economically, Thatcherism exposes British industrial capital to the full force of international competition, and as we saw in Chapter 3, seems set fair to deindustrialize large areas of the North and the Midlands. Certainly it has already completed the deindustrialization of many older urban centres, hitting the ethnic minority young in particular, and they rioted extensively in 1981. The level of unemployment is such that an entire generation of the working-class young are shut off from regular employment altogether, and are now an alienated and disaffected force open to political recruitment and prone to vandalism, crime and the occasional riot. The cutbacks in welfare employment also threaten well-organized public sector workers, and hit women in particular, to add two further potential constituencies to the anti-Thatcher camp. Indeed, if Thatcherism does manage to produce economic growth, even the moderating impact of mass unemployment on working-class militancy may abate, to add trade union strength to a potential coalition of protest. If, as is more likely, it does nothing of the kind, then the persistent danger of redundancy is also there to spark proletarian dissent too. The very fact that the Thatcherite retreat from the concerns of social democracy is accompanied by a strengthening of the police and the army makes it clear that the Conservatives at least recognize the possibilities of resistance; and it is in that resistance that lies scope for a revival of the Left.

The problems and tasks facing the Left

There is no way in which in a book of this size I can even begin to specify in detail the form which such a revival might take, or the programme and strategy most able to bring it about. Other people are better placed to do that, and in any case the task is too important, too complicated and too difficult to be squeezed into the final pages of this volume. But of course the arguments developed here do have very serious implications for the direction which that specification ought to take; because if what I have said is broadly accurate, then the general nature of the problems and tasks faced by left-wing activists should now be clear. Those problems are in essence, as always for socialists, those of capitalist power. The need is to find ways of controlling multinational industrial and financial capital, of rolling back the orthodoxies and institutions of bourgeois hegemony, and of removing the power of the capitalist state. The tasks which grow from those problems are equally daunting: of how to transcend divisions within (and how to widen the range of support for) the left-wing constituency, and of how to build an alliance of class and popular democratic forces willing to move against all those manifestations of capitalist power. It is the putting together of that alliance which is so extraordinarily difficult, and to which all the energies of contemporary socialism need to be directed. I would like to finish by merely commenting on certain features of our contemporary situation which ought to be remembered as that alliance is sought.

The first is this: that any revival of the Left will need to be built on an honest recognition of why Thatcherism's appeal has been so wide, and on why the Labour Party has been so incapable of turning around that appeal. Thatcherism's anti-collectivist populism has gathered strength from its capacity to tap real contradictions in Labour's social democracy. The world the Labour Party built when in power after 1945 and 1964 was one of massive state bureaucracies servicing a mixed economy still predominantly in capitalist hands. What the Labour Party offered as 'socialism' was more properly understood as a mild form of *corporatism*, the sharing of political power with bureaucratized trade union leadership and corporate capital. Yet as we have seen, that power sharing (and the balance of class forces it embodied) was itself a major barrier to capital accumulation, and so proved des-

tructive of the very economic growth that Labour governments sought to extract from the mixed economy. It was experienced by even Labour Party voters as productive of falling living standards, job insecurity and state-initiated wage controls. Moreover, the welfare provision offered by a Labour government as a *quid pro quo* for wage restraint was invariably experienced by its recipients as yet another coercive and external control, as an alien state power directing their lives through a myriad of complicated bureaucratic procedures and finely-tuned administrative decisions over which they could exercise no direction.

In addition, to workers struggling to survive in the harsh competitive world of declining private capitalism, those employed in welfare bureaucracies could so easily be seen as a privileged and cossetted section of the labour force, whose existence added to private capital's difficulties and to their own tax burdens. Labour in opposition always talked the language of the dispossessed, offering social democracy as the key mechanism by which working-class power could find political expression in a social contract with a reforming state. But in power, Labour government after Labour government found that working-class power blocked the short-term economic growth they sought from private capital, and were impelled to discipline the working class by dissolving the class-to-party linkage of the Opposition period, replacing it with 'an alternative articulation: government to people (and) the rhetoric of the national interest'.[10] This too prepared the ground for a party of the Right able to exploit the failure of social democracy in practice and to capitalize on its shifts in terminology. For we must not forget that the crisis of the state in late capitalism to which we have referred at length has been the crisis of the *social democratic* state. Thatcherism's appeal has been so strong because it exploited the real crisis in social democracy which the contradictions of state spending in late capitalism brought into full relief. For this reason, as the Left seeks to rekindle popular support for its project, it will not do so if it merely reasserts the viability of a Keynesian corporatism which is now so generally discredited.

Thatcherism too has its problems, and these must also be remembered. It too is experiencing a gap between its promises and its performance, and the social suffering produced by that gap is, and will continue to be, very heavy indeed. Thatcherism is not about to reconstruct small-scale Victorian capitalism. Instead, the lifting of all restrictions on capital movements will (and indeed already has) quickened the export of capital and exposed weak and uncompetitive British industry to ferocious international competition. On the world scale, capital is being redeployed away from Britain towards new growth centres in the richer markets of the USA, West Germany and Japan, and in the easier labour conditions of Taiwan, South Korea and even Brazil. Try as it will, the Conservative government will not attract back vast quantities of that capital, even if it restricts trade union rights still further, allows the depression to strengthen managerial control still more, and cuts welfare spending yet again. Large sections of British industry are now too under-capitalized to catch up through market forces alone, and the defensive tradition of British trade unionism is too well entrenched to be easily destroyed or quickly forgotten. City interests may benefit from Thatcherite policies, and multinational industrial capital may feel more comfortable with her lack of controls than with a Labour government's talk of planning agreements. But even they may come to feel that untrammelled industrial decline is too risky politically, given the social deprivation and potential unrest to which it will necessarily give rise. For the only sustained growth that Thatcherism seems set fair to generate is the growth in the list of its casualties: the rising tide of white male unemployed; women thrown back into the home and burdened with extra private care of the sick and the old; ethnic minority communities systematically discriminated against and locked in urban poverty; public sector employees thrown on to the dole queue, and small businesses sent into liquidation. The job of the Left is to harness those casualties to its cause, and to offer them a safer and more prosperous future under a revitalized democratic and socialist government.

To do that will take time, and requires action on a number of fronts. Thatcherism's credibility turns as much as anything on the disunity and lack of credibility of its opponents; and powerful pressures remain within the labour movement to peddle again tired and outmoded Labourist alternatives that will not bring back that credibility. Indeed, those pressures are made more acute by the penetration of Thatcherite orthodoxies into the popular consciousness. The very conservatism of the electorate, and the dwindling support for the Labour Party at general elections, combine to persuade many leading Labour politicians that a retreat from radicalism is vital if Thatcherism is to be defeated. Their personal investment in, and commitment to, Keynesian corporatism pulls those same Labour politicians in a similar direction. Yet even a conservative electorate cannot be fooled. As they showed in June 1983, they know that old-style Labourism does not work; and if nothing else is on offer, they will drift to Thatcherism with more or less enthusiasm because at least its rhetoric taps their own sense of the inadequacies of social democracy in practice.

So now is the time for courage on the Left. Socialists must challenge the hegemony of the Tory Right long before seeking power at a general election. The immediate task confronting us is of ideological struggle, in the Gramscian sense, fighting Thatcherism in the spheres of both ideas and class practices. That in its turn requires of socialists unambiguous support for, and involvement in, the struggles of the exploited and the oppressed. It makes each resistance to wage cuts, job losses, erosions of public provision and build-up of nuclear weapons, part of our common concerns and the responsibility of all of us (not just of those most directly affected). For socialists need to be active in these manifestations of popular resistance, helping to link them together, and to demonstrate their wider political significance.

Yet the credibility of socialist alternatives will not be established here by acts of solidarity alone, vital as those are. The *case* has also to be built and argued for, on every available public platform and in every struggle that occurs. That case can best be made, in the first instance, by challenging directly Thatcherite explanations of the origins and nature of the present crisis, offering socialist arguments to refute Tory claims on inflation, trade union power, social inequality, racism and the like.[11] We have to capture again the 'common sense' of the age, 'in order to educate and inform it, to make common sense, the ordinary everyday thoughts of the majority of the population, move in a socialist rather than a reactionary direction'.[12] In addition, we must offer and widely publicize a quite different and sophisticated analysis of the distribution of power in contemporary Britain, and of the major economic and social processes at work here. We must also draw the correct conclusions from that analysis about the degree of radicalism necessary by any future left-wing government that genuinely wants to create for itself the space within which to transform property relationships and their associated pattern of social privilege and disadvantage.

If the argument put forward here is accurate, that will mean taking on the private power of finance capital, the multinationals and the press, in a dramatic extension of public ownership and workers' control that alone can create the conditions in which trade can be planned, and output and employment demo-cratically controlled. It also means taking on the legacies of British imperialism in Ireland, and the deeply engrained practices of racism and sexism in Britain. Yet just to propose that will bring the Tories back shouting about individual freedom and the danger of totalitarianism, so we are going to have to argue the stronger about how private capital destroys freedom and how public ownership of the means of production need not. Before we can make that case with any conviction, however, we must decide what would be an appropriate balance in a socialist society between planning and the market, central and local control, large-scale public ownership and small-scale private capital. We might well look to the experience of Eastern Europe as at least a negative guide. We need too to be open about the difficulties of radically recasting social relations here in the context of a world capitalist system and American military power. But what we do not need to do is to pretend that capitalism can be transformed incrementally, or a mixed economy run any longer with full employment. And we do not need to be apologetic for our radicalism. With over four million unemployed and the growing threat of nuclear war, now is the time to stress again the bankruptcy of private ownership and the need for democratic socialism.

Of course we must not underestimate the scale of the task confronting the Left today. The sources of conservative stability in capitalist societies are enormous. The sheer complexity and invisibility of its central economic and social processes, the great concentrations of power and resources which it generates, and the severity of its many crises, are themselves major moderating forces on the individuals they affect. The market has its own 'dull logic' that invites respect and demands subordination. Because people fear unemployment, they tolerate declines in living standards and job conditions which in happier times they would have resisted. The very fact that firms which cannot compete do go bankrupt means that workers are aware that their militancy can cost them jobs. Once unemployed, the problems are different but equally real. Cut off from the solidarity of the workplace, or in the case of the young unemployed, never exposed to it, organization is difficult, militancy is blocked by the absence of an obvious focus, and self-confidence is eroded by the daily experience of poverty and 'uselessness'. The potential coalition which the Left would harness is in any case a divided and already polluted one. Divisions of class, skill, race, age and gender are all long established, and the ideologies to sustain them are well entrenched. The growth of state employment of late, and of welfare provision on a large scale, has merely added to that fragmentation, creating the situation in which it is hard for many people to believe that the material well-being of any one section of the labour force is not bought at the cost of that of another, or that the status of one group is not threatened whenever another advances its claims.

In fact, life for the Left is difficult precisely because, under the social relationships of a patriarchial and racist capitalism, the Left's potential constituencies *do* exploit one another. There is a hierarchy of exploitation (men of women, whites of blacks) against which the Left has to struggle, within the general framework of the exploitation of all colours and genders of labour by capital itself. The enemy is not just 'capital'. If it were, mobilizing a coalition against it would be relatively easy. Instead the Left has to say to men in struggle against capital that a free society can never be built on exploitation of any kind, and that the socialist project must not be contaminated by the differential privileges that capitalism distributes to its oppressed. That, of course, is an extraordinarily difficult argument to sell; but ease of persuasion is no criterion here. Without that persuasion, any socialism that results will not be worth having. 'White male workers of the world unite' is no slogan for socialists.

Instead, the Left must move towards an explicitly socialist, feminist, anti-racist platform, with all the theoretical and strategic problems which that involves. It will not be sufficient for 'women' and 'blacks' to be viewed as sectional interests, sporadically generating struggles, with demands that need to be 'tacked on' to existing left-wing programmes hitherto blind to their needs. Instead, a socialism that was traditionally reducible to 'white male workerism' needs to be recast fundamentally, to place patriarchy and imperialism at the heart of its analysis of the social inequalities created by capitalism; so that the alliance between white male workers, white women and ethnic minorities can then be forged on the basis of a full understanding of the complex interconnections between exploitation and oppression under capitalism.[13]

Moreover, while we are discussing the difficulties faced by the Left, we must also recognize that people do not live just as workers. Their differential involvement in complex processes of consumption and social reproduction also creates new divisions of experience and interests to set group against group. Much time and effort are put into sustaining those divisions through processes of ideological domination and hegemonic politics that create new problems for the Left. So even if that majority coalition can be harnessed by the Left, its commitment to radical goals will be hard to consolidate. For radicalism implies a wager, a commitment to the unknown. It involves a possibly dangerous conflict with the well-armed forces of reaction. It is always easier to see the difficulties of radical change than to perceive its future possibilities; and so many radical initiatives have gone wrong in the past that common sense seems to invite at best scepticism and at worst rejection of radicalism now. In any case, the Left is so divided, and its major party (the Labour Party) so discredited by its own record, as to raise serious doubts about its future viability and credibility as an alternative to Thatcherism.

Since those divisions between us reflect genuine problems of strategy that have long bedevilled the radical cause, they are not likely to go away easily. Can change come peacefully, or must it be violent? Can capitalism be transformed by stages, or only in a swift movement of enormous dislocation? How can existing freedoms be protected in that transition, and the dangers of a degeneration into a new and awful tyranny be kept at bay? If the risks are so great, is not the present, however awful, to be tolerated in preference? Moreover, the task we set ourselves is so difficult, and runs so directly against the grain of a dominant capitalist order, that many working-class institutions have already given up the project, and now in their turn constitute an obstacle to socialism, with their own vested interest in a moderate politics of accommodation and subordination. That in its turn means that the struggle against capitalism has also to be a struggle within the labour movement against the impact of capital's lieutenants there. Little wonder then that many ask whether, facing such a task with such divisions, with a constituency so subject to counter-ideologies and internal sectional divisions, is not the socialist project now long gone, too difficult to recapture, and beyond the capacities of us all?

The answer to that last desperate question has to be a resounding 'No'. We have to stress again that there are no easy solutions, and certainly no acceptable capitalist ones. So no matter how difficult and long the struggle for socialism turns out to be, it remains humanity's only civilized hope. We have to be realistic enough, and pessimistic enough, to say that 'Britain . . . is a country for whose crisis there are no viable capitalist solutions left, and where, as yet, there is no political base for an alternative socialist strategy. It is a nation locked in a deadly stalemate: a state of unstoppable capitalist decline'.[14] We have to

say too that until and unless the centre of political activity is shifted dramatically towards socialism the danger of nuclear war will not go away. The pursuit of peace, as well as the pursuit of prosperity and freedom, requires a new democratic and socialist initiative. The constituencies to sustain that initiative are there in abundance, if we have sufficient courage in our own convictions to go out and win them on our own terms, and if we are sufficiently sensitive to the complexities of life in late capitalism to make that approach constituency by constituency, recognizing the quite particular needs of each.

To move ourselves into that position, we must find the intellectual honesty to do our homework properly, as Thatcherism did in its period of opposition, and have the courage to draw the correct political lessons from that homework, however awesome those may be. Socialism is not advanced by the quick dash to power on any terms characteristic of Labour politicians. For only by the enthusiastic espousal of a strongly-grounded case can we hope to create our own socialist counter-hegemony to set against the orthodoxies of Thatcherism. Only by breaking decisively with the legacies of that conservative orthodoxy in the minds of our own supporters, only by confronting and rejecting jingoism, sexism and racism, will we be able to build strong connections that will stand the test of time with the various constituencies whose support we must harness.

The tragedy of our generation is that so much of this work and learning on the Left has yet to be done. The 'forward march of labour' has indeed been halted;[15] and will not begin again without purposive intervention from the Left itself. The failures of Labourism, and the degeneration of the Russian Revolution into Stalinist terror, has discredited the whole socialist project, and has so weakened the link between the working class and socialist parties as to give Thatcherism a greater vote among skilled workers in 1983 than even the Labour

Party achieved. These are bad times for socialists. The Left is weak now and on the defensive, internally divided and in a minority position in the country as a whole. Yet for that very reason this is a good time for stock-taking, and for the reconsideration of basic positions. Since we face the politics of the long haul, debate and dialogue on the Left, an openness to new ideas and a willingness to shift from entrenched positions, are going to be vital ingredients in our politics. 'Pessimism of the intellect, optimism of the will' is needed now on the Left as never before. The credibility of the socialist alternative, and of a strategy for its attainment, have to be reconstructed, and that is a massive task. I should like to end by saying that one, although only one, of the preconditions for its successful reconstruction is a greater clarity about the nature of the terrain on which we now operate. If capitalism is to be replaced, it must first be understood, in all its complexity. I can only hope that, in its small way, this book has helped to enhance that understanding.

Notes and references

Chapter 1   Introduction

1   There are, of course, important exceptions. The work of Professor Beer is a case in point.

2   For a recent discussion of this, see the debate between Ralph Miliband and Nicos Poulantzas, reprinted in J. Urry and J. Wakeford (eds.), *Power in Britain* (Heinemann 1973).

3   For two wide definitions of the state from very different theoretical perspectives, see L. Althusser, 'Ideology and ideological state apparatuses', in his collection, *Lenin and Philosophy and Other Essays* (New Left Books 1971) and K. Middlemass, *Politics in Industrial Society* (André Deutsch 1979).

4   As documented in R. H. S. Crossman, *The Crossman Diaries* (3 vols) (Hamish Hamilton and Jonathan Cape 1975–7); or M. Williams, *Inside Number 10* (Weidenfeld and Nicolson 1972).

5   It is important to be clear at the outset about the relationship to be understood throughout this text between 'élites' and 'classes'. Since the two categories are often said to derive from two quite different theoretical traditions (the first liberal, the second Marxist), there are schools of thought that suggest they should not be mixed, and that – within the Marxist tradition – it is better to use terms such as 'strata' and 'fractions' to locate distinctions *within* classes. But the term 'élite' sits easier on the English ear than 'class fraction' will ever do, and so will be used here in preference. Private élites are to be understood as component elements of the dominant class, the full character of which is discussed in Chapter 7.

6   K. Marx, 'The Eighteenth Brumaire of Louis Bonaparte', in K. Marx and F. Engels, *Selected Works* (Lawrence and Wishart 1968), p. 97.

7   For a similar analysis of the power relationships surrounding the Department of Education and Science, see R. D. Coates, *Teachers' Unions and Interest Group Politics* (Cambridge University Press 1972), pp. 34–47.

Chapter 2   The character of the world order

1   Precision is important here. It is worth distinguishing between 'capitalism' as a term used to describe a whole society and 'capitalism' as a term applying only to a particular mode of production – to one way of organizing the economic process within that society. Capitalism is really only properly applicable as a noun in this second sense. In the first sense, the term ought really to be used just as an adjective – a capitalist society being one in which the capitalist mode of production is dominant – one, that is, in which the economy is organized predominantly on capitalist lines. 'Predominantly' is an important qualification here, for the capitalist mode of production can exist alongside earlier, non-capitalist sectors of the economy. (Indeed it invariably does, as will be seen in Part 2.) To talk of capitalist society is then to imply that the centre of gravity of the economy as a whole has shifted in favour of its capitalist sector, *and* that the character of the economic process gives the ultimate shape to the society in total. It is for these two reasons that the verbal slippage occurs and 'capitalism' is used as a noun to describe the society. But as I say, more accurate usage would

restrict the noun to the mode of production and would use the adjectival form when talking of the society (or 'social formation' as it is often described).

2　On this, see R. Brenner, 'The origins of capitalist development', *New Left Review* **104** (July–August 1977), pp. 25–73; A. Brewer, *Marxist Theories of Imperialism* (Routledge and Kegan Paul 1980); R. Hilton (ed.), *The Transition from Feudalism to Capitalism* (New Left Books 1976); and E. Mandel, *An Introduction to Marxist Economic Theory* (Merlin 1962), ch. 4.

3　On this, see Barrington Moore Jr., *Social Origins of Dictatorship and Democracy* (Penguin 1969); T. Kemp, *Industrialisation in Nineteenth Century Europe* (Longman 1969); I. Wallerstein, *The Modern World System* (New York, Academic Press 1974); and P. Anderson, *Lineages of the Absolutist State* (New Left Books 1974).

4　For a seminal statement on this, see E. Mandel, *Late Capitalism* (New Left Books 1975) and the critique by Bob Rowthorn 'Mandel's Late Capitalism', *New Left Review*, **98** (July–August 1976), pp. 56–73.

5　On this, see the articles by Therborn and Jessop in D. Held *et. al.*, (eds.), *States and Societies* (Martin Robertson 1983), pp. 261–89.

6　A. Gamble, *Britain in Decline* (Macmillan 1981), p. 8.

7　ibid., p. 8.

8　Whether or not the Soviet Union is still entirely 'out' of the capitalist world system is a matter of controversy. The Socialist Workers' Party, for example, treat the Soviet Union as 'state capitalist', and today even those who do not are obliged to recognize the impact on Eastern Europe's economic development of the growing financial and trading links with the West.

9　The references cited in notes 2–4 are important here.

10　As Mandel has put it:

The history of capitalism on the international plane thus appears not only as a succession of cyclical movements every 7 or 10 years, but also as a succession of longer periods, of approximately 50 years, of which we have experienced four up till now:

– the long period from the end of the 18th century up to the crisis of 1847, characterized basically by the gradual spread of the *handicraft-made or manufacture-made steam engine* to all the most important branches of industry and industrial countries; this was the long wave of the industrial revolution itself.

– the long period, lasting from the crisis of 1847 until the beginning of the 1890s, characterized by the generalization of the *machine-made steam engine* as the principal motive machine. This was the long wave of the first technological revolution.

– the long period, lasting from the 1890s to the Second World War, characterized by the generalized application of electric and combustion engines in all branches of industry. This was the long wave of the second technological revolution.

– the long period, beginning in North America in 1940 and in the other imperialist countries in 1945–48, characterized by the generalized control of machines by means of *electronic apparatuses* (as well as by the gradual introduction of nuclear energy). This is the long wave of the third technological revolution. (*Late Capitalism* (New Left Books 1975), pp. 120–1.)

11　By this, I mean policies of demand management by governments using techniques advocated by J. M. Keynes.

12　The Organization for Economic Co-operation and Development is made up of the twenty-four major industrial countries in the capitalist bloc, with the exception of Israel and South Africa. For a glossary of initials used in the text, see p. 9.

13　See Mandel, *Late Capitalism*, pp. 120–1.

14　See also E. Mandel, *The Second Slump* (New Left Books 1978), p. 15.

15　T. Kawakami, 'The crisis of the capitalist world: a Marxist view', *Cambridge Journal of Economics*, **3** (1979), p. 191.

16　Between 1946 and 1952, for example, US aid to Western Europe and Japan was US $35.9 billion, and between 1952 and 1960 was US $41.5. US direct investment abroad was worth US $11 billion in 1950 but US $70 billion by 1970.

17　Note that this was not a trade deficit. US

exports exceeded imports until the early 1970s, but that excess was not enough to match the export of capital, government aid and military spending abroad.

18 E. P. Thompson, 'The logic of exterminism', *New Left Review*, **121** (May–June 1980), pp. 3–32.

19 ibid., p. 17.

20 ibid., p. 17.

21 ibid., p. 16.

22 ibid., pp. 6–7.

23 ibid., p. 7, p. 17.

24 S. Aaronovitch *et al.*, *The Political Economy of British Capitalism* (McGraw Hill 1981), p. 156.

25 ibid., p. 157.

26 See, for example, IMF supervision of the UK devaluation of sterling in 1967, and of the cuts in public expenditure in 1976.

27 V. Pillay, 'The international economic crisis', in D. Currie and R. Smith (eds.) *Socialist Economic Review* 1981 (Merlin 1981), p. 18.

28 Mandel, *Late Capitalism*, p. 171.

29 ibid., p. 181.

30 R. Cohen, 'The end to the migrant labour boom', *Newsletter of International Labour Studies* (April 1981), p. 2.

31 The proportion of employment in manufacturing fell earliest in Britain because of the existence here of only a tiny agricultural sector. Elsewhere, it was agricultural employment which fell to create the space for service employment, although in the 1970s manufacturing employment as a percentage of total employment fell slightly also in West Germany and the US. On this, see A. Singh, 'UK industry and the world economy: a case of deindustrialisation', *Cambridge Journal of Economics*, **1** (1977), p. 126.

32 I. Gough, 'State expenditure in advanced capitalism', *New Left Review*, **92** (July–August 1975), p. 63.

33 A. Gamble and P. Walton, *Capitalism in Crisis: Inflation and the State* (Macmillan 1976), pp. 168–9.

34 See M. Kidron, *Western Capitalism Since the War* (Penguin 1968).

35 Gough, p. 58.

36 Mandel, *The Second Slump*, p. 29.

37 ibid., p. 12.

38 ibid., p. 19.

39 Aaronovitch *et al.*, p. 19.

40 Pillay, p. 21.

41 D. Cameron, 'Order and disorder in the world economy: international finance in evolution', *Studies in Political Economy*, **11** (1982), p. 108.

42 Pillay, p. 22.

43 The hidden unemployed in the UK certainly exceeded 1 million in the early 1980s.

44 Mandel, *Late Capitalism*, p. 180.

45 For details, see M. Barrett Brown, *From Labourism to Socialism* (Spokesman 1972), p. 119.

46 Mandel, *The Second Slump*, p. 11.

47 ibid., p. 10.

48 ibid., p. 11.

49 'In 1974, primary products were on average 65% more expensive relative to manufactures than they had been two years earlier . . . in the late 1960s the industrial countries ceased to benefit from improving terms of trade, and then in 1972–4 there was a high transfer of resources from them to the primary producing countries.' (Rowthorn, p. 74.)

50 Pillay, p. 24.

51 ibid., p. 25.

52 Aaronovitch *et al.*, p. 177.

53 See E. Mandel, *The Decline of the Dollar* (New York, Monad Press 1973), p. 83.

54 R. Parboni, *The Dollar and its Rivals* (Verso 1981), p. 7.

55 D. Innes, 'Capitalism and Gold', *Capital and Class*, **14** (summer 1981), p. 24.

56 M. Itoh, 'The inflational crisis of capitalism', *Capital and Class*, **4** (spring 1978), p. 5.

57 Between 1965 and 1975 the US government spent US $139 billion funding the Vietnam War, and the export of private capital from the US amounted to a further US $76 billion in the 1960s and US $225.5 billion in the 1970s. (Pillay, p. 35.)

58 ibid., p. 35.

59 ibid., p. 37. 'According to figures published by the Bank for International Settlements, . . . the total of outstanding Eurodollar deposits in June 1980 amounted to something of the order of US $1,200,000,000,000 which is three to four times the entire money stock of the whole of the USA.' (W. P. Hogan

and I. F. Pearce, *The Incredible Eurodollar* (Counterpoint 1982), p. 3.)

60 Rowthorn, p. 68.

61 Pillay, p. 22.

62 'Organic composition of capital' refers to the balance of capital and labour in the production process. As the organic composition rises, this balance shifts from labour to machinery (from 'living labour' to 'dead labour'), so reducing the source of surplus value, labour power itself.

63 Aaronovitch *et al.*, p. 181.

64 Mandel, *The Second Slump*, p. 12.

65 ibid., pp. 17–18.

66 Parboni, p. 107.

67 ibid., p. 102.

68 A. Glyn and J. Harrison, *The British Economic Disaster* (Pluto 1980) p. 21.

69 No less than 800 complaints were presented to the 1977 conference on GATT, the final report of which complained of a 'disturbing resurgence of protectionist pressure which in recent months has reached a level not experienced for more than a generation' (quoted by Glyn and Harrison, p. 31).

70 Parboni, p. 23.

71 Mandel, *The Second Slump*, pp. 63–4.

72 ibid., p. 76.

73 ibid., p. 115.

74 Glyn and Harrison, p. 32.

75 Pillay, p. 40.

76 ibid., p. 30.

Chapter 3   The weakness of the British economy

1 B. Rowthorn, 'The past strikes back', *Marxism Today* (January 1982), p. 11. As the UK's GNP fell by 3.3 per cent in real terms between 1979 and 1981, Japan's rose by 7.7 per cent, Italy's by 3.2 per cent, the USA's by 2.6 per cent and that of West Germany by 0.3 per cent (*The Times* 22 July 1981), p. 12.

2 G. B. Stafford, 'The class struggle, the multiplier and the Alternative Economic Strategy', in M. Sawyer and K. Schott (eds.), *Socialist Economic Review 1983* (Merlin 1983), p. 4.

3 F. Cripps *et al.*, *Manifesto* (Pan 1981), p. 13.

4 T. Nairn, 'The future of Britain's crisis', *New Left Review*, **113–14** (January–April 1979), p. 44.

5 See A. Gamble, *Britain in Decline* (Macmillan 1981), for a discussion of these earlier debates.

6 A. Glyn and J. Harrison, *The British Economic Disaster* (Pluto 1980), p. 36.

7 S. Aaronovitch *et al.*, *The Political Economy of British Capitalism* (McGraw Hill), p. 57.

8 Gamble, p. 21.

9 E. Hobsbawn, *Industry and Empire* (Weidenfeld and Nicolson 1968), p. 161.

10 Stafford, p. 14.

11 R. Caves and L. B. Krause, *Britain's Economic Performance* (Washington DC, Brookings Institution), p. 19.

12 Gamble, p. xiv.

13 D. Purdy, 'British capitalism since the war', *Marxism Today* (October 1976), p. 312.

14 S. Aaronovitch, *The Road from Thatcherism* (Lawrence and Wishart 1981), p. 6.

15 G. Ingham, 'Divisions within the dominant class and British "exceptionalism" ', in A. Giddens and G. MacKenzie (eds.), *Social Class and the Division of Labour* (Cambridge University Press 1982), p. 216.

16 See A. Francis, 'Families, firms and finance capital', *Sociology*, **14** no. 1 (February 1980), p. 24.

17 Ingham, p. 214.

18 ibid., p. 220.

19 J. Ross, *Thatcher and friends* (Pluto 1983), p. 54.

20 Gamble, p. 85.

21 G. Hodgson, *Labour at the Crossroads* (Martin Robertson 1981), p. 164.

22 Nairn, p. 53.

23 This point is Stuart Hall's, in his main unit for the Open University course D209 on 'The State'.

24 Nairn, p. 55.

25 Glyn and Harrison, pp. 49–50.

26 A. Kilpatrick and T. Lawson, 'On the nature of industrial decline in the UK', *Cambridge Journal of Economics*, **4** (1980), p. 96.

27 On this, see A. Glyn and J. Harrison, *British Capitalism Workers and the Profits Squeeze* (Penguin 1972), passim.

28 A. Freeman, 'The AES: a critique', *International*, **3** no. 2 (spring 1980), p. 24.

29   Nairn, p. 53.
30   S. Blank, 'Britain: the politics of foreign economic policy, the domestic economy and the problem of pluralistic stagnation', *International Organisation,* **31** no. 4 (autumn 1977), p. 680.
31   ibid., p. 680.
32   ibid., p. 716.
33   On this, see D. Coates, 'The character and origin of Britain's economic decline', in D. Coates and G. Johnston (eds.), *Socialist Strategies* (Martin Robertson 1983).
34   Blank, pp. 675, 686–7.
35   D. Currie and R. Smith, 'Economic trends and crisis in the UK economy', in D. Currie and R. Smith (eds.), *Socialist Economic Review 1981* (Merlin 1981) p. 12. See also an important article by T. Brett *et al.*, 'Planned trade, Labour Party policy and US intervention: the successes and failures of post-war reconstruction', *History Workshop,* issue 13 (spring 1982), pp. 130–42.
36   Purdy, p. 275.
37   Gamble, p. 115.
38   Nairn, p. 52.
39   Gamble, p. 113.
40   ibid., pp. 113–14.
41   ibid., p. 114.

Chapter 4   The political power of capital

1   G. Thompson, 'The relationship between the financial and industrial sector in the UK economy', *Economy and Society,* **6** no. 3 (August 1977), p. 236.
2   ibid., p. 247.
3   See the debate between H. Overbeek, 'Finance capital and the crisis in Britain', *Capital and Class,* no. 11 (summer 1980), pp. 98–110, and R. Minns, 'A comment . . .', *Capital and Class,* no. 14 (summer 1981), pp. 98–109.
4   H. McCrae and F. Cairncross, *Capital City* (Eyre and Methuen 1973) p. 131.
5   ibid., p. xiii.
6   Minns, p. 107.
7   M. Moran, 'Finance capital and pressure group politics in Britain', *British Journal of Political Science,* **11** (1981), p. 403.
8   On this, see M. Moran, 'Power, policy and the City of London', in R. King (ed.), *Capital and Politics* (Routledge and Kegan Paul 1982).
9   J. Coakley and L. Harris, *The City of Capital* (Blackwell 1983), p. 222.
10   J. Coakley and L. Harris, 'Evaluating the role of the financial system', in D. Currie and M. Sawyer (eds.), *Socialist Economic Review 1982* (Merlin 1982), p. 218.
11   G. Ingham, 'Divisions within the dominant class and British "exceptionalism" ', in A. Giddens and G. MacKenzie (eds.), *Social Class and the Division of Labour* (Cambridge University Press 1982), p. 226.
12   F. Longstreth, 'The City, industry and the state', in C. Crouch (ed.), *State and Economy in Contemporary Capitalism* (Croom Helm 1979), pp. 160–1.
13   M. Moran, 'Finance capital and pressure group politics' (unpublished paper 1981), p. 31.
14   Thompson, p. 275.
15   S. Aaronovitch *et al.*, *The Political Economy of British Capitalism* (McGraw Hill 1981), p. 214.
16   Longstreth, p. 161.
17   Coakley and Harris, *The City of Capital,* p. 219.
18   Coakley and Harris, *Socialist Economic Review 1982,* p. 217.
19   ibid., pp. 217–18.
20   Moran, p. 18.
21   S. Aaronovitch, cited in J. Urry and J. Wakeford, *Power in Britain,* (Heinemann 1973), p. 129.
22   W. Grant, 'Business interests and the British Conservative Party', *Government and Opposition* (May 1980), p. 156.
23   J. Ross, *Thatcher and friends* (Pluto 1983), p. 38.
24   Longstreth, p. 185.
25   On this, see D. Coates, *The Labour Party and the Struggle for Socialism* (Cambridge University Press 1975), p. 106.
26   ibid., *passim.* See also R. Miliband, *Parliamentary Socialism* (Merlin 1973), and D. Coates, *Labour in Power?* (Longman 1980).
27   By 1976 the Labour Left was again demanding the public ownership of key financial institutions.

28 Particularly on the question of interest rates, the C B I can be very ineffective at times.

29 Longstreth, p. 161.

30 S. Blank, 'Britain: the politics of foreign economic policy, the domestic economy, and the problem of pluralistic stagnation', *International Organisation*, **31** no. 4 (autumn 1977), pp. 704–5.

31 Longstreth, pp. 186–7.

32 All figures here are from Coakley and Harris, *The City of Capital*, p. 5 *passim*.

33 R. Minns, *Pension Funds in British Capitalism* (Heinemann 1980), p. 22.

34 *New Statesman* (31 July 1981), p. 2.

35 A. Francis, 'Families, firms and finance capital', *Sociology*, **14** no. 1 (February 1980), p. 24.

36 J. Scott, *Corporations, Classes and Capitalism* (Hutchinson 1979), p. 90.

37 J. Scott, *The Upper Class* (Macmillan 1982), pp. 143–4.

38 Scott, *Corporations, Classes and Capitalism*, pp. 97–8, 103.

39 Thompson, pp. 270–1.

40 Minns, *Capital and Class*, p. 102.

41 Overbeek found two great coalitions within the City, linking financial institutions and multinational industrial capital. For details, see H. Overbeek, 'Finance capital and the crisis in Britain' *Capital and Class* **11** (summer 1980), p. 117.

42 T. Nairn, *The Break up of Britain* (New Left Books 1977) pp. 382, 388.

43 D. Marsh and G. Locksley, 'Capital: the neglected face of power', in D. Marsh (ed.), *Pressure Politics* (Junction Books 1983), p. 35.

44 A. Martinelli, 'Multinational corporations, national economic policies and labour unions', in L. Lindberg *et al.* (eds.), *Stress and Contradiction in Modern Capitalism* (Lexington Books 1975), p. 425.

45 R. Murray, *International companies and nation states* (Spokesman 1971), p. 42.

46 M. Hodges, *Multinational Corporations and National Governments* (Saxon House 1974), p. 30.

47 ibid., p. 30.

48 ibid., p. 34.

49 ibid., p. 22.

50 Historically, apart from American based companies, it has been British companies that have contributed most to the rise of foreign direct investment. Even between 1962 and 1968, years of persistent pressure on the British balance of payments and the pound sterling, the book value of British foreign investment rose . . . 64%. The value of British direct manufacturing investment overseas (that is, not counting the figures for the oil industry, or financial activities like banking and insurance) rose by nearly a third between 1965 and 1968. The whole weight of this expansion was in industrial countries. . . . Indeed the value of assets owned by British companies abroad grew in this period by more than the sum total of foreign investments owned by Japanese, French, German and Swedish companies put together. British overseas investment is in fact worth fully a quarter of American foreign based investment. In relation to the disproportionate size of the U S economy, this is a measure of the international character of British-based industry. (H. Stephenson, *The Coming Clash* (Weidenfeld and Nicolson 1972), p. 24.)

51 Hodges, pp. 21–2.

52 V. Droucopoulos, 'The non-American challenge: a report on the size and growth of the world's largest firms', *Capital and Class*, **14** (summer 1981), p. 38.

53 Aaronovitch *et al.,* p. 268.

54 ibid., p. 210.

55 J. Hughes, *Britain in Crisis: deindustrialisation and how to fight it* (Spokesman 1981), p. 30.

56 ibid., p. 31.

57 Hodges, p. 61.

58 See S. Young and A. V. Lowe, *Intervention in the Mixed Economy* (Croom Helm 1974), pp. 18–28.

59 See D. Coates, *Labour in Power?* (Longman 1980), chs. 3 and 4.

60 S. Holland, *Socialist Challenge* (Quarto 1975), pp. 75–6.

61 S. Holland, *Strategy for Socialism* (Spokesman 1975), p. 27.

62 Martinelli, p. 429.

63 See Coates, pp. 102–6, 116–28.

64 ibid., pp. 106–7.

65 Young and Lowe, p. 189.

66 Grant, p. 152.

67 For the balance of local and company funding, see ibid., p. 155.

68   See *Big Business and Politics* (Labour Research Department pamphlet 1974) for details.

69   G. Causer, 'Private capital and the state in Western Europe', in S. Giner and M. S. Archer (eds.), *Contemporary Europe: social structure and cultural patterns* (Routledge and Kegan Paul 1978), p. 30.

70   W. Grant, 'Representing capital' (unpublished paper 1981), pp. 17–18. (This paper is now published, in amended form, in R. King (ed.), *Capital and Politics* (Routledge and Kegan Paul 1983), pp. 69–84.)

71   *The Times* (12 November 1980), p. 1.

72   Grant, *Representing Capital*, pp. 9–10.

73   For example, the CBI recently protested *outside* the County Council Headquarters in Avon against rate increases. (See the *Guardian* (21 February 1982) for details.)

74   T. Nairn, 'The future of Britain's crisis', *New Left Review*, **113–14** (November–December 1981), p. 54. See also the recent major study of this culture in M. Weiner, *English Culture and the Decline of the Industrial Spirit, 1850–1980* (Cambridge University Press 1981). Weiner (p. 158) had this to say:

The new society created by the later Victorians rested on a domestication of the wilder traits of earlier British behavior; the riotous populace, the aggressive and acquisitive capitals, and the hedonistic aristocrats of the Georgian world became endangered, if not extinct, species of Englishmen. Their descendants were more restrained, more civilized, and also more conservative, in that they now had an established and secure place in the social order, or, in the case of the aristocracy, had come to terms with social change and recemented their place in the status quo. By Victoria's death, British society had weathered the storms of change, but at the cost of surrendering a capacity for innovation and assertion that was perhaps the other face of the unruliness and harshness of that earlier Britain.

In particular, the later nineteenth century saw the consolidation of a national élite that, by virtue of its power and prestige, played a central role both in Britain's modern achievements and its failures. It administered the most extensive empire in human history with reasonable effectiveness and humanity, and it maintained a remarkable degree of political and social stability at home while presiding over a redistribution of power and an expansion of equality and security. It also presided over the steady and continued erosion of the nation's economic position in the world. The standards of value of this new elite of civil servants, professionals, financiers, and landed proprietors, inculcated by a common education in public schools and ancient universities and reflected in the literary culture it patronized, permeated by their prestige much of British society beyond the elite itself. These standards did little to support, and much to discourage, economic dynamism. They threw earlier enthusiasms for technology into disrepute, emphasized the social evils brought by the industrial revolution, directed attention to issues of the 'quality of life' in preference to the quantitative concerns of production and expansion, and disparaged the restlessness and acquisitiveness of industrial capitalism. Hand in hand with this disparagement went the growth of an alternative set of social values, embodied in a new vision of the nation.

75   S. Blank, *Government and Industry in Britain* (Saxon House 1973), p. 203.

76   See P. Nettl, 'Consensus or élite domination: the case of business', in F. Castles *et al.*, *Decisions, Organisations and Society* (Penguin 1971), pp. 232–52.

77   Blank, p. 198.

78   So, for example, in the reaction to Beckett's 'bare knuckles' speech, 5 big companies withdrew from the CBI. They all had staunch Conservative Party supporters as chairmen (*Guardian* (13 November 1980), p. 19).

79   Westergaard and Resler, quoted in Grant, 'Representing Capital', p. 4.

80   ibid., p. 13 (the CBI had 74 per cent of all manufacturing firms as members in 1974).

81   ' . . . most City institutions are content to use their traditional links with government through the Bank of England and to devote their energies to their own growing trade associations'. (ibid., pp. 13, 15).

82   J. Westergaard and H. Resler, *Class in a Capitalist Society* (Heinemann 1975), p. 142.

83   ibid., pp. 143–4.

84   See Coates, chs 3 and 4, for details.

Chapter 5 The political power of organized labour

1 See Marx, *Capital* (vol. 1), or E. Mandel, *An Introduction to Marxist Economic Theory* (Merlin 1962).

2 On the general role of trade unions in capitalism, see the essays by Anderson and Hyman reproduced in L. Clarke and L. Clements (eds.), *Trade Unions Under Capitalism* (Fontana 1977).

3 R. Miliband, 'The power of labour and the capitalist enterprise', in J. Urry and J. Wakeford (eds.), *Power in Britain* (Heinemann 1973), p. 145.

4 On syndicalism, see B. Holton, *British Syndicalism 1900–14* (Pluto 1967), and W. Kendall, *The Revolutionary Movement in Britain 1900–21* (Weidenfeld and Nicolson 1969).

5 Labourism has been defined as 'a theory and practice which accepted the possibility of social change within the existing framework of society; which rejected the revolutionary violence and action implicit in Chartist ideas of physical force; and which increasingly recognised the working of political democracy of the parliamentary variety as the practical means of achieving its own aims and objectives. Labourism was the theory and practice of class collaboration'. (J. Saville, 'The ideology of Labourism', in R. Benewick *et al.* (eds.), *Knowledge and Belief in Politics* (Allen and Unwin 1973), p. 215.)

6 For figures on union growth, see R. Price and G. S. Bain, 'Union growth revisited: 1948–74 in perspective', *British Journal of Industrial Relations*, **14** no. 3 (1979), pp. 339–55.

7 See D. Coates, *Teachers Unions and Interest Group Politics* (Cambridge University Press 1972), pp. 95–100.

8 Restricting the closed shop, insisting on secret ballots, outlawing secondary picketing, and restricting the number of pickets allowed even in official strikes.

9 W. Keegan and R. Pennock Rea, *Who runs Britain?* (Temple Smith 1979), p. 124.

10 See D. Coates, *Labour in Power?* (Longman 1980), chs. 1–3 for details.

11 It is more likely over 5 million in practice, as official figures understate the actual level of unemployment.

12 See the *Guardian* (23 November 1982).

13 On this, see L. Minkin, 'The Labour Party has not been hijacked', *New Society* (6 October 1977), pp. 6–8; *The Labour Party Conference* (Manchester University Press 1982).

14 The 'Alternative Economic Strategy' is explained in S. Aaronovitch, *The Road from Thatcherism* (Lawrence and Wishart 1981), and discussed in D. Coates, 'The Labour Left and the transition to socialism', *New Left Review*, **129** (September–October 1981), pp. 15–30.

15 For a fuller discussion of this, see D. Coates, 'The question of trade union power', in D. Coates and G. Johnston (eds.), *Socialist Arguments* (Martin Robertson 1983), pp. 74–8.

16 Miliband, p. 136.

17 ibid., pp. 136–7.

18 ibid., p. 136.

19 ibid., p. 136.

20 R. Hyman, *Marxism and the Sociology of Trade Unionism* (Pluto 1971), pp. 38–9.

21 For a general discussion of the trade union bureaucracy as a factor in union conservatism, see D. Coates, *Labour in Power?* (Longman 1980), ch. 5. On the incorporation of shop stewards, see R. Hyman, 'British trade unionism in the 1970s', *Studies in Political Economy*, **1** no. 1 (1979), pp. 93–112.

22 T. Lane, 'The unions: caught on the ebb tide', *Marxism Today* (September 1982), p. 7.

23 ibid., p. 8.

Chapter 6 Class and politics in contemporary Britain

1 J. Urry, *The Anatomy of Capitalist Societies* (Macmillan 1981), p. 6.

2 P. Calvert, *The Concept of Class* (Hutchinson 1982), p. 209.

3 For this, see A. Giddens, *The Class Structure of the Advanced Societies* (Hutchinson 1973), pp. 105–12, 127–39.

4 E. O. Wright has described the defining features of a Marxist theory of class as follows:

First, classes are defined in *relational* rather than in *gradiational* terms. Classes are not understood as being 'above' or 'below' other classes; rather, classes are always defined in terms of their social relations to other classes. As a result, the names for classes are not 'upper', 'middle', or 'lower' but such terms as 'capitalists', 'workers', 'feudal lords' and 'serfs'. Second, the social relations that define classes are analysed primarily in terms of the *social organisation* of economic relations, rather than in the *technical organisation* of economic relations. Class relations are not simply based on the forms of technology, the level of industrialisation, or the technical division of labour. Class relations are irreducibly social, and thus the analysis of those relations requires a systematic analysis of the forms of social organisation of economic relations. The Marxist concept of 'mode of production' provides the basic conceptual framework for this task. Third, within the social organisation of economic relations, class relations are primarily defined by the social relations of *production* rather than by the social relations of exchange. This third element sharply distinguishes Marxist conceptions of class from various Weberian notions. Within Weberian conceptions, classes are above all defined by their 'market capacity', by the resources they bring into exchange relations. Marxists however see class relations as above all structured by the social relations within the production process itself. This is not to suggest that exchange relations are irrelevant but rather that their theoretical relevance is itself determined by the social relations of production. ('Varieties of Marxist conceptions of class structure', *Politics and Society*, **9** no. 3 (1980), pp. 334–6.)

5   See also D. Coates, 'Politicians and the sorcerer', in A. King (ed.), *Why is Britain becoming harder to govern?* (BBC 1976), pp. 34–9; and D. Coates, *Labour in Power?* (Longman 1980), pp. 265–70.

6   The best guide to this remains J. Westergaard and H. Resler, *Class in a Capitalist Society* (Heinemann 1975).

7   K. Roberts *et al.*, *The Fragmentary Class Structure* (Heinemann 1977), p. 29.

8   Miliband, quoted in R. Hyman, *Strikes* (Fontana 1972), p. 87.

9   *The Times* (7 February 1979), p. 3.

10   P. Townsend, *Poverty in the United Kingdom* (Penguin 1979).

11   The *Guardian* (2 June 1981), p. 3.

12   L. Burgher, 'The old order', in F. Field (ed.), *The Wealth Report* (Routledge and Kegan Paul 1979), p. 29.

13   Westergaard and Resler, p. 346.

14   Coates, *Labour in Power?*, p. 268.

Chapter 7   The position and interests of white males in the class structure

1   J. Scott, 'Property and control: some remarks on the British propertied class', in A. Giddens and G. MacKenzie (eds.), *Social Class and the Division of Labour* (Cambridge University Press 1982), p. 229.

2   P. Stanworth, 'Property, class and the corporate élite', in I. Crewe (ed.), *Élites in Western Democracy* (Croom Helm 1974), p. 252.

3   See J. Galbraith, *The New Industrial State* (Penguin 1969).

4   Crewe, p. 24.

5   For a general discussion, see the introduction to the collection edited by Ivor Crewe; and the chapter by R. Pahl and J. Winkler in P. Stanworth and A. Giddens (eds.), *Elites and Power in British Society* (Cambridge University Press 1974).

6   J. Wakeford *et al.*, 'Some social and educational characteristics of selected elite groups in contemporary Britain', in Crewe, p. 173.

7   A. Giddens, *The Class Structure of the Advanced Societies* (Hutchinson 1973), p. 172.

8   A. Giddens and P. Stanworth, 'Elites and privilege', in P. Abrams (ed.), *Work, Urbanism and Inequality* (Weidenfeld and Nicolson 1978), p. 239.

9   Scott, p. 229.

10   Giddens and Stanworth, 'Elites and privilege', p. 239.

11   R. Blackburn, 'The new capitalism', in his *Ideology in Social Science* (Fontana 1972), p. 180.

12   R. Crompton and J. Gubbay, *Economy and Class Structure* (Macmillan 1977), p. 68.

13   Giddens, pp. 170–1.

14   Blackburn, p. 166.

15   Pahl and Winkler, p. 104.

16   ibid., p. 111.

17   On this, see the debate between Pahl and

Winkler, and Scott, in the references cited above.

18 Scott, p. 238.

19 ibid., p. 225.

20 Pahl and Winkler, pp. 121–2.

21 R. D. Whitley, 'The City and Industry: the directors of large companies, their characteristics and connections', in Stanworth and Giddens (eds.), *Elites and Power*, pp. 67, 70.

22 Giddens and Stanworth, 'Elites and privilege', p. 220.

23 Stanworth and Giddens (eds.), *Elites and Power*, p. 83.

24 ibid., p. 89.

25 A. B. Thomas, 'The British business élite: the case of the retail sector', *Sociological Review* **28** no. 2 (1978), p. 316.

26 Whitley, p. 80.

27 R. Martin, *The Sociology of Power* (Routledge and Kegan Paul 1977), p. 145.

28 C. B. Otley, 'The social origins of British army officers', *Sociological Review*, **18** no. 3 (1970), p. 219.

29 C. B. Otley, 'Public school and army', *New Society* **8** (1966), p. 756.

30 J. Griffith, *The Politics of the Judiciary* (Fontana 1977), p. 31.

32 K. Thompson, 'Church of England bishops as an élite', in Stanworth and Giddens (eds.), *Elites and Power,* p. 201.

32 Crewe, p. 24.

33 J. Scott, *The Upper Class* (Macmillan 1982), p. 162.

34 J. Rex, 'Capitalism, élites and the ruling class', in Stanworth and Giddens (eds.), p. 215.

35 For details, see W. L. Guttsman, *The British Political Élite* (MacGibbon and Kee 1968).

36 J. H. Goldthorpe *et al.*, *Social Mobility and Class Structure* (Oxford University Press 1980).

37 G. Salaman and K. Thompson, 'Class structure and the persistence of an élite: the case of army officer selection', *Sociological Review* **28** no. 2 (May 1978), p. 283.

38 Quoted in Wakeford *et al.*, pp. 172–3.

39 Scott, *The Upper Class*, p. 158.

40 ibid., p. 124.

41 *New Statesman* (15 February 1980), p. 239.

42 See Stanworth, pp. 254–5.

43 C. Thomas, 'Family and Kinship in Eaton Square', in F. Field (ed.), *The Wealth Report* (Routledge and Kegan Paul 1979), p. 144.

44 See Scott, *The Upper Class*, pp. 158–79.

45 N. Poulantzas, 'Marxist Political Theory in Great Britain', *New Left Review* **43** (May–June 1967), p. 70.

46 Stanworth and Giddens (eds.), *Elites and Power*, p. 101.

47 Stuart Hall, in his main unit for the Open University course D209 on *The State*, p. 22.

48 K. Burgess, *The Challenge of Labour* (Croom Helm 1980) pp. 46–7.

49 T. Nairn, 'The future of Britain's crisis', *New Left Review*, **113–14** (January–April 1979), p. 53.

50 W. D. Rubenstein, 'Wealth, élites and the class structure of modern Britain', *Past and Present* no. 76 (1977), pp. 77, 124.

51 H. Overbeek, 'Finance capital and the crisis in Britain', *Capital and Class,* **11** (summer 1980), p. 100.

52 Thomas, p. 158.

53 Stanworth and Giddens (eds.), *Elites and Power*, p. xi.

54 Scott, 'Property and Control . . .', p. 228.

55 ibid., p. 228; and Giddens, p. 176.

56 W. L. Guttsman, *The British Political Élite* (MacGibbon and Kee, 1968), p. 357.

57 See J. Westergaard and H. Resler, *Class in a Capitalist Society* (Heinemann 1975), pp. 147, 275–6.

58 R. Miliband, *The State in Capitalist Society* (Weidenfeld and Nicolson 1969), 48.

59 N. Poulantzas, *Classes in Contemporary Capitalism* (New Left Books 1975), pp. 285–6.

60 G. D. H. Cole, *Studies in Class Structure* (Routledge and Kegan Paul 1955), p. 73.

61 The term is used by J. Goldthorpe in his chapter in A. Giddens and G. Mackenzie (eds.), *Social Class and the Division of Labour* (Cambridge University Press 1982), pp. 162–86.

62 R. King and J. Raynor, *The Middle Class* (Longman 1981), p. 118.

63 ibid., p. 119.

64 Scott, *The Upper Class*, p. 130.

65 I. Bradley, *The English Middle Classes are Alive and Kicking* (Collins 1982), p. 197.

66   By, for example, A. Maude and R. Lewis, *The English Middle Class*, (Phoenix House 1949).

67   See J. Burnham, *The Managerial Revolution* (Penguin 1962); A. Gouldner, *The Future of Intellectuals and the Rise of the New Class* (Macmillan 1979); Bradley.

68   K. Marx, *Theories of Surplus Value* (Lawrence and Wishart n.d.), part 2, p. 573.

69   F. Parkin, *Marxism and Class Theory: a bourgeois critique* (Tavistock 1979), p. 17.

70   See A. Cutler *et al., Marx's Capital and Capitalism Today* (Routledge and Kegan Paul 1978).

71   For details, see G. Ross, 'Marxism and the new middle classes: French critiques', *Theory and Society*, **5** no. 3 (1978), pp. 163–90.

72   N. Poulantzas, 'The new petty bourgeoisie', in A. Hunt (ed.), *Class and Class Structure* (Lawrence and Wishart 1977), p. 123.

73   ibid., p. 124.

74   See P. Walker (ed.), *Between Capital and Labour* (Harvester 1979).

75   See S. Mallet, *The New Working Class* (Spokesman 1973); and A. Tourraine, *The Post-Industrial Society* (Wildwood House 1974).

76   F. Bechhofer (ed.), *The petite bourgeoisie* (New York, St Martin's Press 1981), p. 194.

77   G. Carchedi, 'On the economic identification of the new middle class', *Economy and Society*, **4** no. 1 (1975), p. 31.

78   H. Braverman, quoted by R. Crompton, in 'Trade unionism and the clerk', *Sociology*, **13** no. 3 (1979), p. 406.

79   R. Crompton and J. Gubbay, *Economy and Class Structure* (Macmillan 1977), p. 154.

80   T. Johnson, 'What is to be known? The structural determination of social class', *Economy and Society*, **6** no. 2 (1977), p. 217.

81   E. O. Wright, 'Class boundaries in advanced capitalist societies', *New Left Review*, **98** (July–August 1976), p. 28.

82   H. Braverman, quoted by D. Held and A. Giddens in their collection, *Classes, Power and Conflict* (Macmillan 1982), p. 96.

83   Wright, p. 39.

84   ibid., p. 31.

85   ibid., p. 26.

86   R. Crompton, 'Approaches to the study of white collar unionism', *Sociology*, **10** no. 3 (1976), p. 416.

87   Wright, p. 32.

89   E. O. Wright, 'Varieties of Marxist conceptions of class structure', *Politics and Society*, **9** no. 3 (1980), p. 330.

90   Wright, 'Class boundaries . . .', p. 35.

91   See Crompton and Gubbay, pp. 120–3, for a discussion of this.

92   Poulantzas, *Classes in Contemporary Capitalism*, pp. 142–5.

93   R. Scase, 'The petty bourgeoisie in modern capitalism: a consideration of recent theories', in Giddens and MacKenzie, p. 157.

94   Bechhofer, p. 195.

95   King and Raynor, p. 117.

96   Bechhofer, p. 184.

97   F. Bechhofer and B. Elliott, 'The voice of small business and the politics of survival', *Sociological Review*, **26** (1978), p. 62.

98   ibid., p.73.

99   R. King and N. Nugent (eds.), *Respectable Rebels* (Hodder and Stoughton 1979), pp. 5, 6.

100 K. Roberts *et al., The Fragmentary Class Structure* (Heinemann 1977), p. 114.

101 Bechhofer, p. 190

102 ibid., pp. 190–1.

103 F. Bechhofer *et al.*, 'Structure, consciousness and action: a sociological profile of the British middle class', *British Journal of Sociology*, **29** no. 4 (December 1978), p. 420.

104 For details, see King and Nugent *passim*.

105 ibid., p. 140.

106 B. Elliott and S. Black, 'Mobilisation and the political process: a study of the middle class movement' (unpublished paper 1979), p. 26.

107 Poulantzas, *Classes in Contemporary Capitalism*, part 3.

108 Wright, 'Class boundaries . . .', p. 24.

109 Crompton, 'Approaches to . . .', p. 414.

110 King and Raynor, p. 98.

111 Goldthorpe, in Giddens and MacKenzie (eds.), p. 169.

112 Crompton and Gubbay, p. 197.

113 Wright, 'Varieties . . .', p. 350.

114 Goldthorpe, in Giddens and MacKenzie (eds.), p. 170.

115 G. Carchedi, *On the Economic Identification*

of Social classes (Routledge and Kegan Paul 1977), p. 85.

116 ibid., p. 89.

117 J. Goldthorpe *et al.*, *Social Mobility and Class Structure*, p. 264.

118 J. Goldthorpe, in Giddens and MacKenzie (eds.), p. 180.

119 A. Gould, 'The salaried middle class in the corporatist welfare state', *Policy and Politics*, **9** no. 4 (1981), p. 414.

120 ibid., p. 413.

121 In the Braverman sense, of 'conception' split from 'execution', and work reduced to a series of fragmented and repetitive operations. See H. Braverman, *Labour in Monopoly Capitalism* (Monthly Review Press 1974).

122 See Roberts *et al.*, pp. 28–34; and P. Townsend, 'Inequality at the work place: how white collar always wins', *New Society* (18 October 1979), pp. 120–3.

123 Wright, 'Class boundaries . . .', pp. 36–7.

124 King and Raynor, p. 133.

125 J. Westergaard and H. Resler, *Class in a Capitalist Society* (Heinemann 1975), p. 349.

126 See D. Volker, 'NALGO's affiliation to the TUC', *British Journal of Industrial Relations*, **4** (1966), pp. 59–76; and D. Coates, *Teachers' Unions and Interest Group Politics* (Cambridge University Press 1972), ch. 8.

127 See the chapter by T. May in King and Nugent.

128 See G. S. Bain, D. Coates and V. Ellis, *Social Stratification and Trade Unionism* (Heinemann 1972).

129 King and Raynor, p. 142.

130 The title of a book by B. C. Roberts, published by Heinemann in 1972.

131 ibid., p. 26.

132 Roberts, p. 140.

133 Poulantzas, 'The new petty bourgeoisie', p. 124.

134 Poulantzas, *Classes in Contemporary Capitalism*, p. 330.

135 See E. P. Thompson, *The Making of the English Working Class* (Penguin 1962).

136 Quoted by R. Taylor, 'George Orwell and the politics of decency', in Bradford Centre Occasional Papers No. 3, George Orwell (1981), p. 27.

137 For evidence on this, see S. Cotsgrove and A. Duff, 'Environmentalism, middle class radicalism and politics', *Sociological Review*, **28** no. 2 (1980), pp. 333–51.

138 ibid., p. 337.

139 ibid., p. 340.

140 ibid., pp. 343–4.

141 D. Jary, 'A new significance for the MCL', in J. Garrard, (ed.), *The Middle Class in Politics* (Saxon House 1978), p. 165.

142 J. O'Connor, *The Fiscal Crisis of the State* (New York, St Martin's Press 1973), p. 241.

143 On this, for an earlier generation of peace campaigners, see F. Parkin, *Middle Class Radicalism* (Manchester University Press 1968).

144 Cotsgrove and Duff, p. 340.

145 King and Rayner, p. 209.

146 Bechhofer, Elliott, and McCrone, p. 419.

147 Roberts *et al.*, p. 165.

148 Ross, p. 175.

149 H. Braverman, *Labour in Monopoly Capitalism* (Monthly Review Press 1974) pp. 24–5.

150 J. Clarke *et al.*, *Working Class Culture* (Hutchinson 1979), p. 239.

151 P. Townsend, 'Inequality at the workplace: how white collar always wins', *New Society* (18 October 1978), p. 120.

152 See the book by Braverman, and the references cited in the suggested reading.

153 Brighton Group, 'Labour Process', *Capital and Class*, **1** (spring 1977), p. 12.

154 Unit 6 of the Open University course D102 has an excellent summary of this, pp. 20–1.

155 S. Aaronovitch *et al.*, *The Political Economy of British Capitalism* (McGraw Hill 1981), p. 307.

156 Cited on the jacket cover of R. M., Blackburn and M. Mann, *The Working Class and the Labour Market* (Macmillan 1979).

157 Braverman, p. 231.

158 ibid., p. 206.

159 G. Salaman, 'Managing the frontiers of control', in A. Giddens and G. MacKenzie, *Social Class and the Division of Labour* (Cambridge University Press 1982), p. 60.

160 D. J. Lee, 'Skill, craft and class', *Sociology*, **15** no. 1 (February 1981), p. 72.

161 A. Giddens, 'Power, the dialectic of control and class structuration', in Giddens and MacKenzie, p. 41.

162   T. Elgar, 'Braverman, capital accumulation and deskilling', *Capital and Class*, **7** (1979), p. 70.

163   '. . . the post-war valorisation and accumulation strategies of capital' in the car industry 'have not created a totally homogeneous unskilled stratum of workers but a mass of semi-skilled workers embodying a limited heterogeneity of forms of training and experience. This mass of semi-skilled work tasks has constituted a terrain on which major struggles have developed between capital and labour, both around attempts at the intensification of labour and around the structuring and advancement of wages'. (ibid., p. 87.)

164   ibid., p. 88.

165   On the general character of the labour process under capitalism, see the references cited in the suggested reading.

166   E. O. Wright, *Class, Crisis and the State* (New Left Books 1978), pp. 65–6.

167   Brighton Group, 'Labour Process', *Capital and Class*, **1** (spring 1977), p. 16.

168   A. Giddens, *The Class Structure of the Advanced Societies* (Hutchinson 1973), pp. 203–4.

169   H. Beynon and T. Nichols, *Living with Capitalism* (Routledge and Kegan Paul 1977), p. 68.

170   ibid., p. 12.

171   ibid., p. 170.

172   H. Beynon, *Working for Ford* (Penguin 1973), p. 102.

173   ibid., p. 119.

174   Beynon and Nichols, p. 200.

175   See A. Friedman, *Industry and Labour: class struggle at work and Monopoly Capitalism* (Macmillan 1977), pp. 44–76, for documentation of this.

176   M. Mann, 'The working class', *New Society* (4 November 1976), p. 242.

177   Clarke, p. 248.

178   S. Hall, 'The long haul', *Marxism Today* (November 1982), p. 19.

179   ibid., p. 19.

180   ibid., p. 19.

181   D. Stark, 'Class struggle and the transformation of the labour process', *Theory and Society*, **9** (1980), p. 115.

182   P. Dunleavy, 'The political implications of sectoral cleavages and the growth of state employment', *Political Studies*, **23** (1980), p. 548.

183   D. Held and A. Giddens, *Classes, Power and Conflict* (Macmillan 1982), p. 284.

184   Blackburn and Mann, p. 302.

185   ibid., p. 299.

186   See Braverman, pp. 29–30 for a critique of this kind of sociology.

187   Beynon and Nichols, pp. 161–2.

188   J. Westergaard and H. Resler, *Class in a Capitalist Society* (Heinemann 1975), pp. 367, 368.

189   K. Roberts *et al.*, *The Fragmentary Class Structure* (Heinemann 1977), pp. 42–3.

190   J. Saville, 'Reflections on recent labour historiography', in R. Miliband and J. Saville (eds.), *The Socialist Register 1982* (Merlin 1982), p. 312.

191   Raymond Williams, in E. Hobsbawn, *The Forward March of Labour Halted* (New Left Books 1981), p. 145.

192   For this, see R. M. Blackburn and A. Cockburn (eds.), *The Incompatibles: Trade Unions and the Consensus* (Penguin 1967), pp. 48–51.

193   M. Mann, 'The social cohesion of liberal democracy', in Held and Giddens, p. 356.

194   R. Hyman, 'Industrial conflict and the political economy', in R. Miliband and J. Saville (eds.), *The Socialist Register 1973* (Merlin 1973), p. 126.

195   Roberts, p. 51.

196   ibid., p. 56.

197   ibid., p. 103.

198   Beynon, p. 319.

199   Braverman, p. 30.

200   Westergaard and Resler, pp. 397–8, 403–5.

201   Hyman, p. 126.

202   Roberts, p. 55

203   Beynon, p. 319.

Chapter 8   Gender, race and religion in the British social formation

1   S. Delamont, *The Sociology of Women: an Introduction* (Allen and Unwin 1980), p. 6.

2   S. Rowbotham, *Woman's Consciousness, Man's World* (Penguin 1973), p. 68.

3   A. Showstack-Sassoon, 'Dual role: women

and Britain's crisis', *Marxism Today* (December 1982) p. 7.

4   H. Wainwright, 'Women and the Division of Labour', in P. Abrams (ed.), *Work, Urbanism and Inequality* (Weidenfeld and Nicolson 1978), p. 168.

5   J. Garner and S. Smith, 'Feminism and the Alternative Economic Strategy', in D. Currie and M. Sawyer (eds.), *Socialist Economic Review 1982* (Merlin 1982), p. 32.

6   V. Beechey, 'Discussion', in Currie and Sawyer, p. 101.

7   See J. West, 'Women, sex and class', in A. Kuhn and A.-M. Wolpe (eds.), *Feminism and Materialism* (Routledge and Kegan Paul 1978); N. Britten and A. Heath, 'Women, men and class', in E. Gamarnikow *et al.* (eds.), *Gender, Class and Work* (Heinemann 1983); J. Gardner, 'Women in the labour process and class structure', in A. Hunt (ed.), *Class and Class Structure* (Lawrence and Wishart 1977); and A. Oakley, *Subject Women* (Fontana 1981) pp. 281–96.

8   M. Barrat, *Women's Oppression Today* (New Left Books 1980), pp. 135, 139.

9   J. Westergaard and H. Resler, *Class in a Capitalist Society* (Heinemann 1975), p. 105.

10 Wainwright, p. 163.

11 A. Oakley, *Subject Women* (Fontana 1981), pp. 292–3.

12 Cited in Barratt, p. 135.

13 Wainwright, p. 163.

14 ibid., p. 165.

15 Barratt, p. 156.

16 M. Currell, *Political Women* (Croom Helm 1974), p. 150.

17 Oakley, p. 150.

18 A. Coote and B. Campbell, *Sweet Freedom* (Picador 1982), p. 52.

19 CIS Report, *Women in the 80s*, p. 8.

20 Wainwright, p. 171.

21 E. Garnsey, 'Women's work and theories of class and stratification', in D. Held and A. Giddens (eds.), *Classes, power and conflict* (Macmillan 1982), p. 440.

22 Coote and Campbell, p. 66.

23 H. Hartmann, 'The unhappy marriage of Marxism and feminism: towards a more progressive union', *Capital and Class*, **8** (summer 1979), p. 11.

24 See the debate between Sheila Rowbotham, Sally Alexander and Barbara Taylor, in R. Samuels (ed.), *People's History and Socialist Theory* (Routledge and Kegan Paul 1981).

25 D. Morgan and D. Taylorson, 'Class and work; bringing women back in', in E. Gamernikow *et al.* (eds.), *Gender, Class and Work* (Heinemann 1983), p. 9.

26 Barrett, p. 76.

27 C. Middleton, 'Patriarchial exploitation and the rise of English capitalism', in Gamernikow.

28 For a survey of the literature on this, see E. Fox-Genovese, 'Placing women in history', *New Left Review*, **133** (May–June 1982), pp. 5–29.

29 Wainwright, p. 197.

30 P. Hunt, *Gender and Class Consciousness* (Macmillan 1980), p. 1.

31 Barratt, p. 182.

32 For details, see Oakley, p. 238; and Wainwright, p. 197.

33 H. Hartmann, 'Capitalism, patriarchy and job segregation by sex', in Held and Giddens, pp. 459–60.

34 See F. Anthias, 'Women and the reserve army of labour: a critique of Veronica Beechey', *Capital and Class*, **10** (spring 1980), pp. 50–63.

35 Barrett, p. 158.

36 Wainwright, p. 177.

37 See the article by Hilary Wainwright for this.

38 M. MacIntosh, 'The state and the oppression of women', in A. Kuhn and A. M. Wolpe, *Feminism and Materialism* (Routledge and Kegan Paul 1978), p. 264.

39 Wainwright, p. 179.

40 This is a difficult and controversial area; see S. Delamont, pp. 170–7; J. Evans, 'Women in politics: a reappraisal', *Political Studies*, **28** (June 1980), pp. 210–21; and part 2 of J. Siltanen and M. Stanworth (eds.), *Women and the Public Sphere* (Hutchinson 1984).

41 Delamont, pp. 166–7.

42 L. Middleton (ed.), *Women in the Labour Movement* (Croom Helm 1977), p. 167.

43 Coote and Campbell, p. 147.

44 Delamont, p. 157.

45 Oakley, pp. 301–2.

46 Delamont, p. 163.

47   ibid., p. 164.
48   ibid., p. 174.
49   Wainwright, p. 203.
50   T. Rees, 'Immigration policies in the United Kingdom', in C. Husband (ed.), *Race in Britain* (Hutchinson 1982), p. 75.
51   S. Castles and G. Kosack, *Immigrant Workers and Class Structure in Britain* (Oxford University Press 1973), p. 29.
52   D. J. Smith, *Radial Discrimination in Britain: the PEP report* (Penguin 1977), p. 21.
53   ibid., pp. 28–9.
54   Runnymede Trust, *Britain's Black Population* (Heinemann 1980), p. 10.
55   A. Sivanandan, *A Different Hunger* (Pluto 1982), p. 102.
56   Smith, p. 72.
57   J. Allen, 'Race and Class' (unit 11 of Open University course D102), p. 102.
58   A. Phizacklea and R. Miles, *Labour and Racism* (Routledge and Kegan Paul 1980), p. 18.
59   S. Hall *et al.*, *Policing the Crisis* (Macmillan 1978), pp. 341–2.
60   E. Cashmore and B. Troyna, *Black Youth in Crisis* (Allen and Unwin 1982), p. 5.
61   Runnymede Trust, p. 67.
62   M. Kettle and L. Hodges, *Uprising* (Pan 1982), pp. 141–2.
63   R. Miles, *Racism and Migrant Labour* (Routledge and Kegan Paul 1982), p. 180.
64   J. Rex and R. Moore, *Race, Community and conflict* (Oxford University Press 1969), p. 289.
65   Miles, p. 182.
66   See ibid, pp. 1–43; and J. Bourne, 'Cheerleaders and Ombudsmen: the sociology of race relations in Britain', *Race and Class*, **21** no. 4 (1980), pp. 331–52.
67   For an extended discussion, see Hall *et al.*, pp. 362–89.
68   B. Munslow, 'Immigrants, racism and British workers', in D. Coates and G. Johnston (eds.) *Socialist Arguments* (Martin Robertson 1983), p. 198.
69   Hall *et al.*, p. 381.
70   P. Gilroy, 'You can't fool the youth . . . race and class formation in the 1980s', *Race and Class*, **23** (1982), p. 208.
71   Smith, p. 192.
72   Phizacklea and Miles, p. 27.
73   L. Kushnik, 'Parameters of British and American racism', *Race and Class*, **23** (1982), p. 190.
74   Hall *et al.*, pp. 349–50.
75   ibid., p. 298.
76   Sivanandan, quoted by Hall *et al.*, p. 344.
77   ibid., p. 299.
78   Quoted in A. Sivanandan, 'From resistance to rebellion', *Race and Class*, **23** (autumn 1981), p. 145.
79   Roger Ballard, 'Racial inequality, ethnic diversity and social policy' (ASA conference paper 1983), p. 17.
80   Sivanandan, p. 137.
81   Hall *et al.*, pp. 353–4.
82   Sivanandan, p. 149.
83   Hall *et al.*, p. 331.
84   A. H. Birch, *Political Integration and Disintegration in the British Isles* (Allen and Unwin 1977), p. 85.
85   E. McCann, *War and an Irish Town* (Penguin 1974), p. 1.
86   B. Probert, *Beyond Orange and Green* (Zed Books 1978), p. 21.
87   K. Moody, *The Ulster Question 1603–1973*.
88   A. Boserup, 'Contradictions and struggles in Northern Ireland', in R. Miliband and J. Saville (eds.), *The Socialist Register 1972* (Merlin 1972), p. 160.
89   ibid., p. 162.
90   For different positions, see A. Boserup, 'Contradictions and struggles in Northern Ireland', in Miliband and Saville, *The Socialist Register 1972*; M. Farrell, *Northern Ireland: the Orange State* (Pluto 1976); T. Nairn, *The Break up of Britain* (New Left Books 1977); and Probert.
91   M. Tomlinson, 'Reforming repression', in L. O'Dowd *et al.*, *Northern Ireland: between civil rights and civil war* (CSE Books 1980) p. 179.

Chapter 9   Social stability and hegemonic politics

1   The points in this paragraph are drawn from private correspondence with David Beetham.
2   Centre for Contemporary Cultural Studies, *On Ideology* (Hutchinson 1978), p. 49.

3   In Unit 21 of the Open University course D102 (p. 25).

4   C. Mouffe, 'Hegemony and the integral state in Gramsci: towards a new concept of politics', in G. Bridges and R. Brunt (eds.), *Silver Linings* (Lawrence and Wishart 1980), p. 169.

5   L. Althusser, 'Ideology and ideological state apparatuses', in his *Lenin and Philosophy and other essays* (New Left Books 1971), p. 160.

6   The title of an influential book by G. Almond and S. Verba, published by Princeton University Press in 1963.

7   On this, see H. F. Moorhouse, 'Attitudes to class and class relationships in Britain', *Sociology*, **10** no. 4 (1976), pp. 38–53; and M. Mann, 'The social cohesion of liberal democracy', in D. Held and A. Giddens (eds.), *Classes, Power and Conflict* (Macmillan 1982).

8   Mann, p. 356.

9   ibid., p. 388.

10 Moorhouse, 'Attitudes to class . . .', pp. 484, 490.

11 R. Hyman and I. Brough, *Social Values and Industrial Relations* (Blackwells 1975), p. 208.

12 K. Roberts *et al.*, *The Fragmentary Class Structure* (Heinemann 1977), p. 94.

13 R. Jessop, *Traditionalism, Conservatism and British Political Culture* (Macmillan 1974), pp. 82–3.

14 F. Parkin, *Class Inequality and Political Order* (MacGibbon and Kee 1971), p. 92.

15 Hegemony in this sense turned on the existence of 'an order in which a certain way of life and thought is dominant, in which one concept of reality is diffused throughout society, in all its institutional and private manifestations, informing with its spirit all tastes, moralities, customs, religions, political principals, and all social relations, particularly in their intellectual and moral connotations'. Gwyn Williams, 'Gramsci's concept of hegemonia', *Journal of the History of Ideas*, **21** (1960), p. 587.

16 Mouffe, p. 173.

17 J. Femia, 'Hegemony and consciousness in the thought of Antonio Gramsci', *Political Studies*, **23** (March 1975), p. 31.

18 J. Urry, *The Anatomy of Capitalist Societies* (Macmillan 1981), p. 34.

19 Centre for Contemporary Cultural Studies, pp. 60–1.

20 D. Wells, *Marxism and the Modern State* (Harvester 1981), p. 37.

21 ibid., p. 11.

22 N. Abercrombie and B. Turner, 'The dominant ideology thesis', *British Journal of Sociology*, **29** no. 2 (June 1978), p. 161.

23 R. M. Blackburn and M. Mann, *The Working Class and the Labour Market* (Macmillan 1979), p. 303.

24 M. Mann, *Consciousness and Action among the Western Working Class* (Macmillan 1973), p. 29.

24 N. Abercrombie, S. Hill and B. Turner, *The Dominant Ideology Thesis* (Allen and Unwin 1980), p. 166.

26 J. Gray, 'Bourgeois hegemony in Victorian Britain', in J. Bloomfield (ed.), *Class, Hegemony and Party* (Lawrence and Wishart 1976), p. 78.

27 ibid., p. 83.

28 ibid., p. 81.

29 ibid., p. 79.

30 Hyman and Brough, p. 201.

31 See M. Blanch, 'Imperialism, nationalism and organised youth', in J. Clarke *et al.* (eds.), *Working Class Culture* (Hutchinson 1979), pp. 103–20.

32 For this, see A. Showstack-Sassoon, *Gramsci's Politics* (Croom Helm 1980), p. 3.

33 In R. J. Looker and D. Coates, *Class Conflict and Industrial Capitalism* (Wheatsheaf, forthcoming).

34 L. Panitch, *Social Democracy and Industrial Militancy* (Cambridge University Press 1975), pp. 235–6.

35 On this, see D. Coates, *The Labour Party and the Struggle for Socialism* (Cambridge University Press 1975); D. Coates, *Labour in Power?* (Longman 1980); R. Miliband, *Parliamentary Socialism* (Merlin 1973); and Panitch.

36 S. Hall, 'Culture, the media and the "ideology effect" ', in J. Curran *et al.*, *Mass Communications and Society* (Arnold 1977), p. 333.

37 See Althusser, 'Ideology and ideological state apparatuses'.

38 Hall, p. 335.

39 S. Hall, 'The structured communication of events', C C C S Media series no. 5, p. 32.
40 ibid., p. 32.
41 D. Held, *Introduction to Critical Theory* (Hutchinson 1980), p. 106.
42 ibid., p. 108.
43 P. Beharrell and G. Philo (eds.), *Trade Unions and the Media* (Macmillan 1977), p. 118.
44 Hall, 'Culture, the media . . .', p. 340.
45 See J. Curran and J. Seaton, *Power without responsibility: the press and broadcasting in Britain* (Fontana 1981); and G. Murdock and P. Golding, 'For a political economy of mass communications', in R. Miliband and J. Saville (eds.), *The Socialist Register 1973* (Merlin 1973).
46 Hall, p. 340.
47 Hall *et al.*, *Policing the Crisis* (Macmillan 1978), p. 54.
48 ibid., pp. 54–5.
49 Beharrell and Philo, p. 1.
50 S. Hood, 'The politics of television', in D. McQuail (ed.), *Sociology of Mass Communications* (Penguin 1972), p. 417.
51 Campaign for Press Freedom, *Towards Press Freedom* (n.d.), p. 3.
52 J. Curran and J. Seaton, *Power without responsibility: the press and broadcasting in Britain* (Fontana 1981), p. 17.
53 S. Hall, 'Newspapers, parties and classes', in J. Curran (ed.), *The British Press: a manifesto* (Macmillan 1978), p. 30.
54 Beharrell and Philo, p. 75.
55 ibid., p. 76.
56 Quoted in S. Hood, *Stuart Hood on Television* (Pluto 1980), p. 1.
57 E. P. Thompson, 'The heavy dancers of the air', *New Society* (11 November 1982), p. 244.
58 The title of an essay by Stuart Hall reprinted in S. Cohen and J. Young, *The Manufacture of News* (Constable 1978), pp. 85–94.
59 S. Hall, 'External influences on broadcasting', C C C S media series no. 4 (1972), p. 13.
60 Hall *et al.*, p. 65.
61 ibid., p. 57.
62 ibid., p. 58.
63 P. Elliott, 'All the world's a stage: or what's wrong with the national press', in Curran, (ed.), p. 158.
64 Hall *et al.*, p. 59.
65 ibid., pp. 63–4
66 Hall, 'Newspapers, classes . . .', p. 51.
67 Hall, 'The structured communication of events', p. 32.
68 C. Offe, 'The theory of the capitalist state and the problem of policy formation', in L. Lindberg (ed.), *Stress and Contradiction in Modern Capitalism* (Lexington 1975), p. 127.
69 Hall, 'Newspapers, classes . . .', p. 38.
70 Hall, 'Culture, the media . . .', p. 337.
71 B. Jessop, 'Recent theories of the capitalist state', *Cambridge Journal of Economics*, **1** (1977), p. 368.
72 Urry, p. 15.
73 B. Jessop, 'Capitalism and democracy: the best possible political shell', in G. Littlejohn *et al.* (eds.), *Power and the State* (Croom Helm 1978), p. 32.
74 ibid., p. 38 (quoting Laclau).
75 On this, see B. Jessop, 'The democratic state and the national interest', in D. Coates and G. Johnston (eds.), *Socialist Arguments* (Martin Robertson 1983), p. 97.
76 B. Jessop, *The Capitalist State* (Martin Robertson 1982), p. 243.

Chapter 10   Function, form and crisis in the contemporary British state

1 I. Gough, *The Political Economy of the Welfare State* (Macmillan 1980), p. 77.
2 J. Westergaard and H. Resler, *Class in a Capitalist Society* (Heinemann 1975), p. 172.
3 P. Dunleavy, 'The political implications of sectoral cleavages and the growth of state employment', *Political Studies*, **23** (1980), p. 366.
4 Gough, p. 62.
5 For this, see the essays by King and Britten in A. King (ed.), *Why is Britain becoming harder to govern?* (B B C 1976).
6 J. Urry, *The Anatomy of Capitalist Societies* (Macmillan 1981), p. 19.
7 For a detailed recent example, see D. Coates, *Labour in Power?* (Longman 1980), especially pp. 156–61.
8 C. Offe, 'The theory of the capitalist state and the problem of policy formation', in L. Lindberg (ed.), *Stress and Contradiction in Modern Capitalism* (Lexington 1975), p. 134.

9 D. Strinati, 'Capitalism, the state and industrial relations', in C. Crouch (ed.), *State and Economy in Contemporary Capitalism* (Croom Helm 1982), p. 193.

10 B. Jessop, 'Capitalism and Democracy: the best possible political shell', in G. Littlejohn *et al.*, *Power and the State* (Croom Helm 1978), p. 17.

11 Urry, p. 95.

12 S. de Brunhoff, *The State, Capital and Economic Policy* (Pluto 1980), p. 7.

13 B. Jessop, 'Recent theories of the capitalist state', *Cambridge Journal of Economics*, **1** (1977), p. 362.

14 E. Mandel, *Late Capitalism* (New Left Books 1975), p. 475.

15 Jessop, 'Recent theories . . .', p. 362.

16 C. Offe, 'Structural problems of the capitalist state', in K. von Beyme, *German Political Studies*, vol. 1 (Sage 1974), p. 33.

17 R. Scase, *The State in Western Capitalism* (Croom Helm 1977), p. 23

18 G. Causer, 'Private capital and the state in Western Europe', in S. Giner and M. S. Archer (eds.), *Contemporary Europe: social structure and cultural patterns* (Routledge and Kegan Paul 1978), p. 39.

19 C. Offe, 'The theory of . . .', p. 126.

20 C. Offe and V. Rouge, 'Theses on the theory of the state', in D. Held and A. Giddens (eds.), *Classes, Power and Conflict* (Macmillan 1982), p. 250.

21 Urry, p. 123.

22 On this, see J. Holloway and S. Picciotto, (eds.), *State and Capital: a German debate* (Arnold 1980), p. 20.

23 B. Frankel, 'On the theory of the state: Marxist theories of the state after Leninism', *Theory and Society*, **7** (1979), p. 40.

24 ibid., p. 40.

25 C. Offe, 'The theory of . . .', p. 128.

26 de Brunhoff, pp. 10–11.

27 ibid., p. 73.

28 B. Jessop, *The Capitalist State* (Martin Robertson 1982), p. 237.

29 ibid., pp. 233–4.

30 ibid., p. 49.

31 D. Gold *et al.*, 'Recent developments in Marxist theories of the capitalist state', *Monthly Review* (November 1975), pp. 48–9.

32 See Coates, ch. 3.

33 See R. Crompton and J. Gubbay, *Economy and Class Structure* (Macmillan 1977), pp. 107–14; and S. Aaronovitch *et al.*, *The Political Economy of British Capitalism* (McGraw Hill 1981), pp. 126–9.

34 M. Campbell, *Capitalism in the United Kingdom* (Croom Helm 1981), p. 176.

35 J. Scott, *Corporations, Classes and Capitalism* (Hutchinson 1979), p. 151.

36 Campbell, p. 186.

37 Gough, p. 94.

38 Westergaard and Resler, p. 191.

39 ibid., p. 175.

40 ibid., p. 177.

41 Campbell, p. 186.

42 R. Miliband, *Marxism and Politics* (Oxford University Press 1977), p. 69.

43 Quoted in R. Miliband, *The State in Capitalist Society* (Weidenfeld and Nicolson 1969), p. 55.

44 For details, see the article by Kelsall in P. Stanworth and A. Giddens (eds.), *Elites and Power in British Society* (Cambridge University Press); and J. Urry and J. Wakeford (eds.), *Power in Britain* (Heinemann 1973), p. 127.

45 See Miliband, *The State in Capitalist Society*, pp. 55–67.

46 J. Ross, *Thatcher and Friends* (Pluto 1983), p. 23.

47 ibid., pp. 18–19.

48 A. Giddens and P. Stanworth, 'Elites and privilege', in P. Abrams (ed.), *Work, Urbanism and Inequality* (Weidenfeld and Nicolson 1978), p. 215.

49 B. Sedgemore, *The Secret Constitution* (Hodder and Stoughton 1980), pp. 149–50.

50 ibid., pp. 157–8.

51 Giddens and Stanworth, p. 226.

52 Scott, p. 153.

53 Mandel, p. 493.

54 Offe, 'Structural . . .', p. 39.

55 Miliband, *The State in Capitalist Society*, p. 128.

56 On this, see Jessop, *The Capitalist State*, pp. 235–41.

57 B. Jessop, 'Capital accumulation, class struggle and the nation state' (unpublished paper n.d.), pp. 5–6.

58 Mandel, p. 490.

59 Mandel, quoted by Frankel, p. 22.

60   W. L. Guttsman, *The British Political Elite* (MacGibbon and Kee 1968), p. 338.
61   Westergaard and Resler, p. 213.
62   On this, see M. Harrison (ed.), *Corporatism and the Welfare State* (Gower 1984).
63   P. Schmitter and G. Lehmbruch, *Trends towards Corporatist Intermediation* (Sage 1980), pp. 73–4.
64   L. Panitch, 'The development of corporatism in liberal democracies', *Comparative Political Studies* **10** no. 1 (1977), p. 66.
65   See R. Pahl and J. Winkler, 'The coming corporatism', *New Society* (10 October 1974), pp. 72–6; J. Westergaard, 'Class inequality and corporatism', in A. Hunt (ed.), *Class and Class Structure* (Lawrence and Wishart 1977), and L. Panitch, 'Recent theorisations of corporatism', *British Journal of Sociology*, **3** no. 2 (1980).
66   Panitch, p. 80.
67   B. Jessop, 'The transformation of the state in post-war Britain', in R. Scase, p. 61.
68   J. Westergaard, 'Class Inequality and corporatism', in A. Hunt (ed.), *Class and Class Structure* (Lawrence and Wishart 1977).
69   Jessop, 'The transformation . . .', p. 54.
70   K. Middlemass, *Politics in Industrial Society* (André Deutsch 1979), pp. 372, 373, 382.
71   Jessop, 'Capitalism and . . .', p. 46.
72   Crouch, p. 19.
73   See D. Coates, *Teachers' Unions and Interest Group Politics* (Cambridge University Press 1972), pp. 95–100.
74   Strinati, p. 202.
75   L. Panitch, 'The limits of corporatism: trade unions and the state', *New Left Review*, **125** (January–February 1981), p. 42.
76   Jessop, 'Capital accumulation . . .', p. 11.
77   See D. Coates, 'Britain in the 1970s: economic crisis and the resurgence of radicalism', in A. Cox (ed.), *Politics, Policy and the European Recession* (Macmillan 1982).
78   Urry, p. 130.
79   See the references to note 5 to this chapter.
80   Crouch, p. 24.
81   A. Martinelli, 'Multinational corporations, national economic policies and labour unions', in Lindberg, p. 428.
82   J. O'Connor, *The Fiscal Crisis of the State* (New York, St Martin's Press 1973), p. 9).
83   Gough, p. 95
84   Coates, *Labour in Power?*, pp. 189–90.
85   J. Habermas, quoted by Frankel, p. 214.
86   Gough, p. 151.
87   Held and Giddens, p. 193.
88   Offe, quoted by Frankel, pp. 48–9.
89   Aaronovitch *et al.*, p. 135.

Chapter 11   The repressive state and the construction of the progressive alternative

1   For details, see D. Held, *Introduction to Critical Theory* (Hutchinson 1980), pp. 287–92.
2   S. Hall *et al.*, *Policing the Crisis* (Macmillan 1978), p. 314.
3   S. Hall and M. Jacques (eds.), *The Politics of Thatcherism* (Lawrence and Wishart 1983), p. 10.
4   S. Hall, 'The battle for socialist ideas in the 1980s', in M. Eve and D. Musson, *The Socialist Register 1982* (Merlin 1982), pp. 13, 14.
5   Hall *et al.*, p. 314.
6   Hall and Jacques, p. 11.
7   For details, see P. Scofield, E. Preston and E. Jacques, *Youth Training: The Tories' Poisoned Apple* (ILP 1983).
8   I. Gough, 'Thatcherism and the welfare state', *Marxism Today* (July 1980), p. 8.
9   S. Hall *et al.*, p. 323.
10   S. Hall, 'The great moving right show', *Marxism Today* (January 1979), p. 17.
11   For one attempt to do this, see D. Coates and G. Johnston (eds.), *Socialist Arguments* (Martin Robertson 1983).
12   Hall, 'The battle . . .', p. 18.
13   I am grateful for guidance from Tessa ten Tusscher on this.
14   Hall *et al.*, p. 309.
15   See E. Hobsbawn, *The Forward March of Labour Halted* (New Left Books 1982) for one discussion of this.

Suggested reading

A work of this kind relies quite literally on hundreds of secondary sources. To list them all would take many pages, and unless it was annotated, would not necessarily be of very great value as a guide to further study. So instead of printing such a list here, I shall instead indicate those books and articles to which you might turn most productively in the first instance if you want to read more about a particular area of social or economic life. Then if you would like to see the full list of sources, all you need to do is to write to me at the Department of Politics, The University of Leeds, Leeds LS2 9JT and I will happily send that list to you.

The most exciting literature in this whole field is often that which enables you to situate Britain in a much bigger context, by locating some of the crucial processes shaping the world order as a whole. Outstanding among these of late has been Nigel Harris's *Of Bread and Guns* (Penguin 1983); and you might look too at D. Held (ed.), *States and Societies* (Martin Robertson 1983). Then read E. Mandel, *Late Capitalism* (New Left Books 1975) and his *The Second Slump* (New Left Books 1978) for a view of the economic processes underpinning the pattern of expansion and recession in the world capitalist economy. Supplement that with R. Parboni, *The Dollar and its Rivals* (New Left Books 1981) and E. P. Thompson's collection *Zero Option* (Merlin Books 1982).

The relative weakness of British industrial capital within that world order is dicussed more fully in my chapter in D. Coates and G. Johnston (eds.), *Socialist Strategies* (Martin Robertson 1983) and by S. Aaronovitch, R. Smith *et al.*, *The Political Economy of British Capitalism* (New York, McGraw Hill 1981). You should look too at A. Gamble, *Britain in Decline* (Macmillan 1981); T. Nairn, *The Break up of Britain* (New Left Books 1977); S. Pollard, *The Wasting of the British Economy* (Croom Helm 1981); M. Weiner *English Culture and the Decline of the Industrial Spirit* (Cambridge University Press 1981), and, if you can get hold of it through your library, the article by S. Blank, 'Britain: the politics of foreign economic policy, the domestic economy and the problem of pluralistic stagnation', in *International Organisation*, **31** no. 4 (autumn 1977), pp. 673–722.

The power of financial interests in British politics

is best approached through F. Longstreth, 'The City, Industry and the State', in C. Crouch (ed.), *State and Economy in Contemporary Capitalism* (Croom Helm 1979) and J. Coakley and L. Harris, *The City of Capital* (Blackwell 1983). Multinational industrial capital is discussed by J. Goldstein in R. Miliband and J. Saville (eds.), *The Socialist Register 1972* (Merlin 1972); and by A. Martinelli in L. Lindberg *et al.*, *Stress and Contradiction in Modern Capitalism* (Lexington Books 1985). The standard work on the CBI remains the book of that title by W. Grant and D. Marsh published by Hodder and Stoughton in 1977. That may be supplemented usefully by D. Marsh (ed.), *Pressure Politics* (Junction Books 1983), and by the articles by W. Grant and M. Moran in R. King (ed.), *Capital and Politics* (Routledge and Kegan Paul 1982). The best general guide to British trade unionism remains R. Taylor, *The Fifth Estate* (Pan 1982); and that may be supplemented by R. Hyman, *Industrial Relations: a Marxist introduction* (Macmillan 1975); R. Hyman, *Strikes* (Fontana 1972); T. Lane, *The Union Makes Us Strong* (Fontana 1974); T. Clarke and L. Clements (eds.), *Trade Unions under Capitalism* (Fontana 1977), and articles in D. Coates and G. Johnston (eds.), *Socialist Arguments* (Martin Robertson 1983) and D. Coates, *Labour in Power?* (Longman 1980).

The best general guide to the British class structure remains J. Westergaard and H. Resler, *Class in a Capitalist Society* (Heinemann 1975). That now needs to be read in conjunction with P. Abrams (ed.), *Work, Urbanism and Inequality* (Weidenfeld and Nicolson 1978), R. Crompton and J. Gubbay, *Economy and Class Structure* (Macmillan 1977), and A. Giddens and G. Mackenzie (eds.), *Social Class and the Division of Labour* (Cambridge University Press 1982). D. Held and A. Giddens (eds.), *Classes, Power and Conflict* (Macmillan 1982) is also essential reading here. The ruling class is best approached through J. Scott, *The Upper Class* (Macmillan 1982) and his earlier work, *Corporations, Classes and Capitalism* (Hutchinson 1979). It is still worth consulting too W. Guttsman, *The British Political Elite* (MacGibbon and Kee 1968); P. Stanworth and A. Giddens (eds.), *Elites and Power in British Society* (Cambridge University Press 1974); J. Urry and J. Wakeford (eds.), *Power in Britain* (Heinemann 1973) and I. Crewe (ed.), *Elites in Western Democracy* (Croom Helm 1974). The middle class is well documented by R. King and J. Raynor in *The Middle Class* (Longman 1981); and the theoretical debate around the class has been surveyed comprehensively lately in N. Abercrombie and J. Urry, *Capital, Labour and the Middle Classes* (Allen and Unwin 1983). The seminal contributions to that debate remain N. Poulantzas, *Classes in Contemporary Capitalism* (New Left Books 1975) and the critique by E. O. Wright in *New Left Review*, **98** (reprinted in his *Class, Crisis and the State* (New Left Books 1978)). Working-class industrial experience is best approached through H. Beynon, *Working for Ford* (Penguin 1973), and H. Beynon and T. Nichols, *Living with Capitalism* (Allen and Unwin 1977). Both may be compared usefully with working-class industrial experience in the early 1960s recorded in J. Goldthorpe *et al.*, *The Affluent Worker* (3 volumes, Cambridge University Press 1968–9). Why that experience should have taken such a form is best understood through H. Braverman, *Labour in Monopoly Capitalism* (Monthly Review Press 1974) and its critics, including S. Wood (ed.), *The Degradation of Work? Skill, Deskilling and the Labour Process* (Hutchinson 1982); T. Nicols (ed.), *Capital and Labour* (Fontana 1980) and A. L. Friedman, *Industry and Labour: Class Struggle at Work and Monopoly Capitalism* (Macmillan 1977).

On gender and class, start with A. Coote and B. Campbell, *Sweet Freedom* (Picador 1982), E. Wilson, *Half-way to Paradise* (Tavistock 1980), and the essay by Hilary Wainwright in the collection edited by P. Abrams and cited earlier. Then turn to A. Oakley, *Subject Women* (Fontana 1981); S. Delamont, *The Sociology of Women: an introduction* (Allen and Unwin 1980); M. Barrett, *Women's Oppression Today* (New Left Books 1980) and J. Siltanen and M. Stanworth (eds.), *Women and the Public Sphere* (Hutchinson 1984).

On black politics, see both A. Sivanandan, *A Different Hunger* (Pluto 1982) and S. Hall *et al.*, *Policing the Crisis* (Macmillan 1978). The Centre for Contemporary Cultural Studies' collection, *The Empire Strikes Back: Race and Racism in 70's Britain* (Hutchinson 1982), is an important additional source, as is the journal *Race and Class*. Ireland is best approached through B. Probert *Beyond Orange and Green: The Political Economy of the Northern Ireland Crisis* (Zed Books 1978),

and P. Bew, P. Gibbon and H. Patterson, *The State in Northern Ireland, 1921–72* (Manchester University Press 1979).

On cultural politics, see the essay by Stuart Hall in J. Curran *et al.*, *Mass Communications and Society* (Arnold 1977), and read again the quite remarkable *Policing the Crisis*. See also J. Bloomfield (ed.), *Class, Hegemony and Party* (Lawrence and Wishart 1976); and the essay on Gramsci by Chantal Mouffe in G. Bridges and R. Brunt (eds.), *Silver Linings* (Lawrence and Wishart 1980). On the modern state, the outstanding guide to the theoretical literature is B. Jessop, *The Capitalist State* (Martin Robertson 1982). The best guide to its welfare provision is I. Gough's *The Political Economy of the Welfare State* (Macmillan 1980). The debate between Ian Gough, Lawrence Harris and Ben Fine on state expenditure is also important, and can be found in *New Left Review*, **92** (July–August 1975) and **98** (July–August 1976). A full understanding of the contemporary British state would not be possible without a careful examination of the work of Ralph Miliband, and in particular his *The State in Capitalist Society* (Weidenfeld and Nicolson 1969), *Capitalist Democracy in Britain* (Oxford University Press 1982), and *Class Power and State Power* (New Left Books 1984).

On contemporary Conservatism and the options of the Left, begin with S. Hall and M. Jacques (eds.), *The Politics of Thatcherism* (Lawrence and Wishart 1983), and E. Hobsbawn, *The Forward March of Labour Halted* (New Left Books 1981). Then read the essay by D. Strinati in A. Stewart (ed.), *Contemporary Britain* (Routledge and Kegan Paul 1983), J. Ross *Thatcher and Friends* (Pluto 1983), and A. Gamble's essay in R. Miliband and J. Saville (eds.), *The Socialist Register 1979* (Merlin 1979). The strategic choices facing the Left are fully discussed in D. Coates and G. Johnston (eds.), *Socialist Strategies* (Martin Robertson), and in the debate in *New Left Review* nos. 129, 132, 133 and 135. A similar debate has continued in recent editions of the magazines *New Socialist* and *Marxism Today*, both of which remain essential reading for socialists. So too, I hope, will be the third volume of the *Socialist Primer* series published by Martin Robertson, this one to be edited by D. Coates, G. Johnston and R. Bush as *A Socialist Anatomy of Britain*, which will come out at much the same time as this volume.

Index